America's
TEST KITCHEN

Light &
Healthy

2012

THE YEAR'S BEST RECIPES LIGHTENED UP

BY THE EDITORS AT
AMERICA'S TEST KITCHEN

PHOTOGRAPHY BY
CARL TREMBLAY, KELLER + KELLER, AND DANIEL J. VAN ACKERE

AMERICA'S TEST KITCHEN
17 Station Street, Brookline, MA 02445

AMERICA'S TEST KITCHEN LIGHT & HEALTHY 2012
The Year's Best Recipes Lightened Up

1st Edition

Hardcover: $35 US
ISBN-13: 978-1-933615-91-2   ISBN-10: 1-933615-91-5
ISSN: 2162-6758

Manufactured in the United States of America

10 9 8 7 6 5 4 3 2 1

Distributed by America's Test Kitchen
17 Station Street, Brookline, MA 02445

EDITORIAL DIRECTOR: Jack Bishop
EXECUTIVE EDITOR: Elizabeth Carduff
EXECUTIVE FOOD EDITOR: Julia Collin Davison
SENIOR EDITORS: Louise Emerick, Suzannah McFerran
ASSOCIATE EDITORS: Chris O'Connor, Dan Zuccarello
TEST COOKS: Rebecca Morris, Christie Morrison
ASSISTANT TEST COOK: Kate Williams
PHOTOSHOOT KITCHEN TEAM:
    ASSOCIATE EDITORS: Yvonne Ruperti
    ASSISTANT TEST COOKS: Daniel Cellucci, Danielle DeSiato-Hallman, Kate Williams
EDITORIAL ASSISTANT: Alyssa King
DESIGN DIRECTOR: Amy Klee
ART DIRECTOR: Greg Galvan
ASSOCIATE ART DIRECTORS: Erica Lee, Matthew Warnick
FRONT COVER PHOTOGRAPH: Carl Tremblay
STAFF PHOTOGRAPHER: Daniel J. van Ackere
ADDITIONAL PHOTOGRAPHY: Keller + Keller
FOOD STYLING: Marie Piraino and Mary Jane Sawyer
PRODUCTION DIRECTOR: Guy Rochford
SENIOR PRODUCTION MANAGER: Jessica Quirk
SENIOR PROJECT MANAGER: Alice Carpenter
PRODUCTION AND TRAFFIC COORDINATOR: Kate Hux
ASSET AND WORKFLOW MANAGER: Andrew Mannone
PRODUCTION AND IMAGING SPECIALISTS: Judy Blomquist, Heather Dube, Lauren Pettapiece
COPYEDITOR: Barbara Wood
PROOFREADER: Leslie Evans
INDEXER: Elizabeth Parson

PICTURED ON THE FRONT COVER: Herb-Crusted Pork Tenderloin with Fennel, Tomatoes, and Artichokes (page 91)
PICTURED OPPOSITE TITLE PAGE: Spaghetti al Limone (page 130)
PICTURED ON BACK OF JACKET: Shrimp Burgers (page 118), Weeknight Turkey Bolognese with Linguine (page 139), Chicken Pot Pie (page 72), Rich and Creamy Banana Pudding (page 283)

Contents

STEAMED CHINESE DUMPLINGS

APPETIZERS & SNACKS

M   = TEST KITCHEN MAKEOVER

MARINATED ARTICHOKE HEARTS WITH LEMON AND BASIL

THE ANTIPASTO SECTION IN THE SUPERMARKET IS usually filled with a colorful array of marinated snacks: juicy olives, rich cheeses, and glistening vegetables. We love adding one or two of these to a spread for an easy and elegant appetizer. However, not only do most antipasto marinades consist almost entirely of oil, if you opt for the olives or cheeses, then even the starring ingredient is full of fat. We wanted to create a recipe for a marinated antipasto that upheld the spirit of the original without the caloric sacrifice.

First, we knew that since we couldn't entirely give up an oil-based marinade, we'd have to choose our main component carefully. Olives and cheeses were out, and vegetables of some type were in. We also knew that the process of marinating vegetables takes time, so we wanted to include only easily prepped ingredients to keep the hands-on cooking time as short as possible. Artichoke hearts, which are fat-free, are full of potassium and vitamin C, and come frozen and preprepped in the supermarket, seemed like the perfect solution.

For our first test, we mixed thawed hearts into a light, lemony dressing with basil, shallots, lemon juice, and garlic and dropped the oil from the ¾ cup we found in a standard recipe to 3 tablespoons. Then we let the mixture meld for a few hours in the refrigerator. When it came time to taste, however, our bright dressing had become watery, and all the flavors had seemingly disappeared. The artichokes looked naked and tasted, well, like diet food. We needed to find a way to make a dressing that coated the artichokes and didn't become waterlogged.

To concentrate flavor and ensure that our marinade coated the artichokes properly, we turned to a technique we had discovered a few years ago in the test kitchen when making healthy vinaigrettes. We had found that we could substitute reduced fruit juice for most of the oil in these dressings. Fruity syrups not only add another flavorful dimension, but their viscosity mimics that of olive oil. Since high-quality fresh orange juice is readily available, we decided to see how it would fare in our recipe. We swapped out two-thirds of the oil for the juice, then reduced the juice on the stovetop for a few minutes until it was thick and glazy before combining it with our remaining dressing ingredients. This new dressing showed promise at first—our artichokes were generously coated and glistened like their oil-slicked cousins. Unfortunately, the flavor was totally off. The orange juice reduction was simply too sweet and overpowered the mild artichokes.

We took out the orange juice and returned to our basic dressing. We tried bulking up the dressing with extra shallot, basil, and lemon juice, but the watery artichokes still overwhelmed any additional flavors, and the dressing just wouldn't cling to the vegetables without the additional oil. It was hard to resist the temptation to stir in an extra couple of tablespoons of olive oil. We were stumped until one tester suggested adding a little mayonnaise.

While it seems counterintuitive from a lightening perspective, a small amount of light mayonnaise would help to emulsify the marinade and thus ensure that it would better coat the artichokes, and it would also allow us to reduce the amount of oil needed.

This new marinade worked like a charm, and adding mustard, another emulsifier, further boosted its flavor. The mayonnaise disappeared into the dressing, but it added just the right amount of cling. Even after a day of sitting in the refrigerator, our artichokes were well coated, the dressing finally tasted balanced, and the emulsifiers kept it from becoming watery. Our healthy marinated artichokes could now hold their own on any antipasti platter.

NOTES FROM THE TEST KITCHEN

USING FROZEN ARTICHOKE HEARTS
Preparing fresh artichokes is a labor-intensive and time-consuming task. So what are the alternatives when you want to add artichokes to a dish? Canned artichokes are packed in brine, which makes them waterlogged and salty. In most cases, we recommend frozen artichoke hearts, which are convenient, offer the purest artichoke flavor, and will brown nicely when roasted or sautéed. To thaw frozen artichokes, place them in a bowl and microwave, covered, for five to six minutes, stirring halfway through. Or, if you have time, thaw them overnight in the refrigerator.

MARINATED ARTICHOKE HEARTS WITH LEMON AND BASIL

Marinated Artichoke Hearts with Lemon and Basil

SERVES 8

Make sure to dry the artichokes thoroughly before tossing with the marinade or they will be watery.

1	shallot, minced
1	garlic clove, minced
1	teaspoon light mayonnaise
¾	teaspoon grated lemon zest plus 2 tablespoons juice
½	teaspoon Dijon mustard
¼	teaspoon red pepper flakes
	Salt and pepper
3	tablespoons extra-virgin olive oil
18	ounces frozen artichoke hearts, thawed, patted dry, and quartered if whole
¼	cup chopped fresh basil

Whisk shallot, garlic, mayonnaise, lemon zest, lemon juice, mustard, pepper flakes, ½ teaspoon salt, and pinch pepper together in bowl. Whisking constantly, drizzle in oil. Gently fold artichokes and basil into dressing, cover, and refrigerate until flavors meld, at least 3 hours or up to 1 day. Transfer artichokes to serving bowl and season with salt and pepper to taste. Bring to room temperature before serving.

PER ⅓-CUP SERVING: Cal 80; Fat 6g; Sat fat 1g; Chol 0mg; Carb 7g; Protein 2g; Fiber 4g; Sodium 200mg

CREAMY DIPS

MANY OF US IN THE TEST KITCHEN HAVE EATEN OUR fair share of creamy dips, running the gamut from rich and delicious to sweet and gloppy. But these dips, whether good or bad, share the same basic characteristic: an overload of fat and calories. They are chock-full of sour cream, mayonnaise, and often sodium-laden soup mixes. Recently in the test kitchen, we came up with a variety of dips, swapping bland dried herbs and soup mixes for fresh herbs and intensely flavored pantry staples like Parmesan cheese and sun-dried tomatoes. Even these dips, however, clock in at around 19 grams of fat (4.5 grams saturated) and 180 calories per 3-tablespoon serving. Could we revamp these recipes and come up with a few creamy dips that were both healthy and tasty?

TEST KITCHEN MAKEOVER

First we tackled the base. Our biggest challenge would be the fat. While most creamy dip recipes rely on a combination of sour cream and mayonnaise, our previous tests had turned up an interesting substitute for the sour cream: Greek yogurt. Greek yogurt shares the tangy creaminess of sour cream, and luckily, its low-fat and nonfat varieties are actually good in their own right. And as far as the mayonnaise goes, we've learned that there is a striking difference between light and low-fat mayonnaise that goes beyond the fat content. Tasted on its own, light mayonnaise is a world better than low fat in both flavor and texture, which isn't surprising given that light has more fat and calories than low fat (see page 8 for more information). Still, we wondered if, given all of the other mix-ins, low-fat mayonnaise could work.

We started by testing combinations of 2 percent fat or nonfat Greek yogurt and light or low-fat mayonnaise and were surprised to learn that we liked the lowest-fat dips—nonfat Greek yogurt and low-fat mayonnaise—the most. Light mayonnaise gave us dips that tasted more like a mayonnaise-y spread than a dip, and the 2 percent yogurt was simply too thick. We also found that, with our changes to lighten the recipe, we'd need to tweak our proportion of mayonnaise to yogurt. Our original recipe called for equal parts mayonnaise and yogurt, but we found that this amount of low-fat mayonnaise made our dip taste like, well, mayonnaise. We scaled it back to ½ cup and scaled up the Greek yogurt to ¾ cup. At this point, we were pretty happy with the flavor and fat content (only 1.5 grams per serving) of our dip base, but it was still a little bit too thick.

Since we had cut so much fat, we wondered if we could introduce a small amount of flavorful olive oil to thin out our base and give our dips a little more depth at once. One tablespoon of extra-virgin olive oil added great richness and only 1.5 grams of fat to each serving, bringing our base to 3 grams of fat per serving. But still, we found that we needed to loosen the base a little more, but this time without adding any more fat. Stirring in 3 tablespoons of water did the trick. With the base settled, we turned to the mix-ins.

Our fresh additions would need to pack a punch. To start, we created a tangy lemon-herb dip. We knew we wanted to layer in as much herbal flavor as possible, so we added ¼ cup each of chopped basil and minced chives. To balance the herbs and to add brightness, we added 1 tablespoon of lemon juice and ½ teaspoon of black pepper. For a boldly flavored

Indian-style variation, we employed mango chutney and curry powder, and we threw in a little cayenne for extra heat, which gave us a sweet, savory, and spicy dip all at once. For our second variation, we developed a complex Mediterranean-inspired dip with roasted red peppers and capers. A handful of basil and some garlic lent a burst of freshness.

For a uniform, smooth mixture, the food processor was the answer. We processed the mayonnaise, water, oil, and mix-ins until smooth, then stirred in the yogurt by hand since the sharp blades of the processor cause the yogurt to break down and become soupy. With only 3 grams of fat and between 40 and 80 calories per serving, each one of our creamy dips was colorful and flavor packed and tasted indulgent without the stomachache.

MAKEOVER SPOTLIGHT: CREAMY LEMON-HERB DIP

	CALORIES	FAT	SAT FAT	CHOLESTEROL
BEFORE	180	19g	4.5g	10mg
AFTER	40	3g	0g	0mg

Creamy Lemon-Herb Dip

MAKES ABOUT 1½ CUPS

Make sure to chill the dip for at least 1 hour or it will be too loose. See page 8 for more about low-fat and light mayonnaise. Serve with crudités.

- ½   **cup low-fat mayonnaise**
- 3   **tablespoons water**
- ¼   **cup minced fresh chives**
- ¼   **cup chopped fresh basil**
- 1   **tablespoon extra-virgin olive oil**
- 1   **tablespoon lemon juice**
-     **Salt and pepper**
- ¾   **cup nonfat Greek yogurt**

Process mayonnaise, water, chives, basil, oil, lemon juice, ½ teaspoon pepper, and ¼ teaspoon salt together in food processor until smooth, about 30 seconds. Transfer mixture to bowl and stir in yogurt. Season with salt and pepper to taste. Refrigerate dip until thickened, at least 1 hour or up to 2 days. Serve.

PER 3-TABLESPOON SERVING: Cal 40; Fat 3g; Sat fat 0g; Chol 0mg; Carb 3g; Protein 2g; Fiber 0g; Sodium 210mg

Creamy Curry-Chutney Dip

MAKES ABOUT 1½ CUPS

Make sure to chill the dip for at least 1 hour or it will be too loose. See page 8 for more about low-fat and light mayonnaise. Serve with crudités.

- ½   **cup low-fat mayonnaise**
- ⅓   **cup mango chutney**
- 3   **tablespoons water**
- 1   **tablespoon extra-virgin olive oil**
- 2   **teaspoons lemon juice**
- 1½ **teaspoons curry powder**
-     **Salt and pepper**
- ⅛   **teaspoon cayenne pepper**
- ¾   **cup nonfat Greek yogurt**

Process mayonnaise, chutney, water, oil, lemon juice, curry powder, ¼ teaspoon salt, and cayenne together in food processor until smooth, about 30 seconds. Transfer mixture to bowl and stir in yogurt. Season with salt and pepper to taste. Refrigerate dip until thickened, at least 1 hour or up to 2 days. Serve.

PER 3-TABLESPOON SERVING: Cal 80; Fat 3g; Sat fat 0g; Chol 0mg; Carb 13g; Protein 2g; Fiber 0g; Sodium 330mg

Creamy Mediterranean Dip

MAKES ABOUT 1½ CUPS

Make sure to chill the dip for at least 1 hour or it will be too loose. See page 8 for more about low-fat and light mayonnaise. Serve with crudités.

- ½   **cup low-fat mayonnaise**
- ¼   **cup coarsely chopped jarred roasted red peppers, rinsed and patted dry**
- 3   **tablespoons capers, rinsed and minced**
- 3   **tablespoons water**
- 2   **tablespoons chopped fresh basil**
- 1   **tablespoon extra-virgin olive oil**
- 2   **teaspoons lemon juice**
- 1   **garlic clove, minced**
-     **Salt and pepper**
- ¾   **cup nonfat Greek yogurt**

Process mayonnaise, red peppers, capers, water, basil, oil, lemon juice, garlic, and ¼ teaspoon salt together in food processor until smooth, about 30 seconds.

Transfer mixture to bowl and stir in yogurt. Season with salt and pepper to taste. Refrigerate dip until thickened, at least 1 hour or up to 2 days. Serve.

PER 3-TABLESPOON SERVING: Cal 45; Fat 3g; Sat fat 0g; Chol 0mg; Carb 4g; Protein 2g; Fiber 0g; Sodium 320mg

NOTES FROM THE TEST KITCHEN

CRUDITÉS 101

When done right, a platter of crudités can give you a lot of nutritional bang for your buck and be beautiful as well, if not downright irresistible. In order to make appealing (and edible) crudités, cut vegetables into bite-size pieces (such as broccoli and radishes) or elegant lengths (such as carrots and red peppers). Other items, such as green beans and snow peas, just need a bit of trimming. Some vegetables (asparagus, broccoli, green beans, and snow peas) must first be blanched, then shocked in ice water; others (carrots, endive, bell peppers, and radishes) can be served raw. To blanch vegetables, bring 6 quarts of water and 2 tablespoons of salt to a boil in a large pot over high heat. Cook the vegetables, one variety at a time, until slightly softened but still crunchy at the core. Transfer the blanched vegetables immediately to a bowl of ice water until completely cool, then drain and pat dry.

LIGHT VS. LOW-FAT MAYO

Because mayonnaise is fatty by definition, low-fat mayonnaise is a popular product among the diet-conscious. In the past, Hellmann's (known as Best Foods west of the Rockies) Light Mayonnaise (with 35 calories, 3.5 grams of fat, and 0 grams of saturated fat per tablespoon) has been the winner of low-fat mayonnaise taste tests here in the test kitchen. Hellmann's also makes a low-fat mayonnaise (with 15 calories, 1 gram of fat, and 0 grams of saturated fat per tablespoon). Still, we wondered if tasters would be able to detect a difference between these two light mayos in our Creamy Dips. Given all the other flavors in play, it wasn't too surprising that tasters found little difference in dips made with **Hellmann's Light Mayonnaise** (left) and **Hellmann's Low Fat Mayonnaise Dressing** (right), so we opted for the latter to save on fat and calories. However, in other applications tasters complained that the low-fat mayonnaise had an off, sweet flavor and lacked proper body. The light mayo performed almost as well as its full-fat cousin. Our conclusion: Hellmann's Low Fat Mayonnaise Dressing works in certain applications (like our dips), but in general we'll reach for the light.

CHEESE BALLS

TEST KITCHEN
MAKEOVER

A STAPLE ON MANY A PARTY PLATTER, CHEESE BALLS are traditionally loaded with cheese and mayonnaise and rolled in nuts: truly the definition of "guilty pleasure." They tower above chips and dip in more ways than one, clocking in with enough fat and calories for an entrée, not a snack. While we appreciate the classic dish in all its retro glory, we wanted to find a way to give the flavors a fresh spin and at the same time lighten the recipe without losing any of the charm.

We started with our recent test kitchen recipe for a cheddar cheese ball rolled in sliced almonds. The original recipe was made with a mixture of shredded extra-sharp cheddar, cream cheese, and mayonnaise, with garlic, Worcestershire sauce, and cayenne thrown in for flavor. It also contained 13 grams of fat (6 grams saturated) and 140 calories per 2-tablespoon serving. In our first attempt to lighten things up, we swapped in reduced-fat cheddar and light cream cheese for the full-fat versions, cut out the mayonnaise entirely, and rolled the chilled ball in chives instead of almonds. These changes brought us down to a modest 4.5 grams of fat and 70 calories a serving. Unfortunately, instead of becoming creamy and blending with the cream cheese, the low-fat cheddar turned into rubbery pellets in the food processor. Furthermore, the lack of mayonnaise made our final cheese ball clumpy instead of creamy, and the thickness of the light cream cheese prevented our cheese balls from being anywhere close to spreadable. At this point, we could have tinkered with adding low-fat mayonnaise, but we decided maybe we should take a different approach entirely.

We decided to abandon low-fat cheddar for a naturally low-fat substitute, goat cheese, which would give us lots of tangy flavor and an ultracreamy texture, with only a small amount of extra fat. For the Worcestershire, we swapped in a handful of basil, as well as lemon zest and juice for brightness, both a better match to the goat cheese.

To make the cheese mixture into a cheese ball, we wrapped it in plastic wrap, then shaped it. This technique worked until we tried to place the ball in the fridge, where it settled into a disk. The combination of goat cheese and cream cheese was simply too soft to hold its shape on its own. So we placed the wrapped ball in a small bowl (just large enough to hold the mixture) and gave the ball a full four hours of chilling time. Once it had firmed up and set, we rolled the cheese ball in minced chives instead of the more traditional nuts in order to cut fat and calories and maximize flavor.

Having conquered a basic cheese ball, we wondered if our goat cheese mixture would work with different flavorings. We first turned to an Italian antipasto plate for inspiration, adding roasted red peppers, pepperoncini, basil, and just an ounce of deli salami to the base, which added rich, meaty flavor without a lot of fat. We rolled this ball in chopped parsley. For a second variation, we went all-American by mixing bacon (just one slice, crisped, drained, and crumbled) with herbs and flavorings inspired by ranch dressing: parsley, cilantro, garlic, and onion powder. Thinly sliced scallions were the perfect finish for this tangy variation.

Creamy and rich-tasting, our cheese balls have all the charm of the classic, but with bright, fresh flavors. And with only 5 grams of fat and 70 calories per serving for any one of our dips, they have none of the guilt.

MAKEOVER SPOTLIGHT: CHEESE BALLS

	CALORIES	FAT	SAT FAT	CHOLESTEROL
BEFORE	140	13g	6g	30mg
AFTER	70	5g	3.5g	15mg

Lemon-Herb Cheese Ball

SERVES 16

Do not substitute fat-free cream cheese. Serve with whole wheat crackers or crudités.

- 8 ounces goat cheese, crumbled (2 cups)
- 8 ounces light cream cheese, softened
- 2 tablespoons chopped fresh basil
- ½ teaspoon grated lemon zest plus 2 tablespoons juice
- 1 small garlic clove, minced
- ⅛ teaspoon salt
- ½ cup minced fresh chives

1. Process goat cheese, cream cheese, basil, lemon zest, lemon juice, garlic, and salt together in food processor until smooth, about 20 seconds.

2. Transfer cheese mixture to center of large sheet of plastic wrap. Holding 4 corners of plastic in one hand, twist cheese with other hand to seal plastic and shape cheese into rough ball. Place in small bowl and refrigerate until firm, about 4 hours.

3. Once cheese ball is firm, reshape as necessary to form smooth ball. Unwrap and roll in chives to coat. Let sit at room temperature for 15 minutes before serving.

PER 2-TABLESPOON SERVING: Cal 70; Fat 5g; Sat fat 3.5g; Chol 15mg; Carb 1g; Protein 4g; Fiber 0g; Sodium 150mg

Antipasto Cheese Ball

SERVES 18

Do not substitute fat-free cream cheese. Serve with whole wheat crackers or crudités.

- 8 ounces goat cheese, crumbled (2 cups)
- 8 ounces light cream cheese, softened
- 2 tablespoons chopped jarred roasted red peppers, rinsed and patted dry
- 2 tablespoons chopped pepperoncini
- 2 tablespoons chopped fresh basil
- 1 ounce thinly sliced salami, chopped
- 1 garlic clove, minced
- ½ cup minced fresh parsley

1. Process goat cheese, cream cheese, red peppers, pepperoncini, basil, salami, and garlic together in food processor until smooth, about 20 seconds.

2. Transfer cheese mixture to center of large sheet of plastic wrap. Holding 4 corners of plastic in one hand, twist cheese with other hand to seal plastic and shape cheese into rough ball. Place in small bowl and refrigerate until firm, about 4 hours.

3. Once cheese ball is firm, reshape as necessary to form smooth ball. Unwrap and roll in parsley to coat. Let sit at room temperature for 15 minutes before serving.

PER 2-TABLESPOON SERVING: Cal 70; Fat 5g; Sat fat 3.5g; Chol 15mg; Carb 1g; Protein 4g; Fiber 0g; Sodium 170mg

Bacon-Scallion Cheese Ball

SERVES 16

Do not substitute fat-free cream cheese. Serve with whole wheat crackers or crudités.

- 8 **ounces goat cheese, crumbled (2 cups)**
- 8 **ounces light cream cheese, softened**
- 3 **tablespoons chopped fresh parsley**
- 3 **tablespoons minced fresh cilantro or dill**
- 1 **slice bacon, cooked and crumbled**
- 1 **garlic clove, minced**
- 1 **teaspoon lemon juice**
- ½ **teaspoon onion powder**
- ⅛ **teaspoon salt**
  Pinch sugar
- 4 **scallions, sliced thin**

1. Process goat cheese, cream cheese, parsley, cilantro, bacon, garlic, lemon juice, onion powder, salt, and sugar together in food processor until smooth, about 20 seconds.

2. Transfer cheese mixture to center of large sheet of plastic wrap. Holding 4 corners of plastic in one hand, twist cheese with other hand to seal plastic and shape cheese into rough ball. Place in small bowl and refrigerate until firm, about 4 hours.

3. Once cheese ball is firm, reshape as necessary to form smooth ball. Unwrap and roll in scallions to coat. Let sit at room temperature for 15 minutes before serving.

PER 2-TABLESPOON SERVING: **Cal** 70; **Fat** 5g; **Sat fat** 3.5g; **Chol** 15mg; **Carb** 2g; **Protein** 4g; **Fiber** 0g; **Sodium** 160mg

---

NOTES FROM THE TEST KITCHEN

SHAPING CHEESE BALLS

Transfer processed cheese mixture to center of large sheet of plastic wrap. Holding 4 corners of plastic in one hand, twist cheese with other hand to shape into rough ball. Transfer to bowl and place in refrigerator to firm up.

LIGHT CREAM CHEESE

The creamy texture and tangy flavor of cream cheese serves the test kitchen well in myriad recipes, but could we do without the 4.5 grams of fat and 50 calories in each tablespoon of regular cream cheese? When it comes to using its low-fat cousins, here's what we found: Fat-free cream cheese was awful across the board. Light cream cheese (2 grams of fat, 30 calories per tablespoon) worked well in complex dishes. American neufchatel cheese, marketed as reduced-fat cream cheese, has one-third less fat than regular cream cheese yet is strikingly similar in flavor. Still with 3 grams of fat (and 35 calories per tablespoon), it is a little too high in fat for everyday light cooking. Bottom line: For recipes with many ingredients, such as our goat cheese balls, use light cream cheese. For eating on its own, choose neufchatel.

LIGHT CREAM CHEESE   NEUFCHATEL CHEESE

SALSA VERDE

SALSA VERDE COMES IN TWO FORMS: THE ITALIAN parsley and olive oil–based sauce often served with grilled or roasted meats, fish, or poultry; and the Mexican tart, tangy tomatillo-based salsa that is in the same family as its red, tomato-based cousin. We thought having a fresh take on the familiar Mexican-style red salsa would be a great addition to our healthy appetizer spread. Salsa verde has a bright, bracing flavor and can be either chunky or smooth, cooked or raw, depending on individual taste. Since we knew this recipe would be naturally low in fat and calories, we focused our testing on finding balance in terms of flavor and texture.

The tomatillos from which salsa verde is made are a paper-skinned green tomato–like fruit with a (sometimes bracingly) tart flavor that hints at lemon, apple, and herbs. A few salsa verde recipes we found used raw tomatillos, but in most the tomatillos were cooked by either boiling or roasting. Cooking softens the fruit, which can be quite firm, and mellows its acidity. It seemed like the best route to take.

First we tested boiling the tomatillos until they were soft but still held their shape, about eight minutes, then we shocked them in cold water to stop the cooking. Next, we combined them with the traditional salsa verde seasonings—jalapeño, onion, garlic, cilantro, lime juice, and salt—in the bowl of a food processor. Using quick pulses, we pureed the salsa to a chunky consistency. The salsa tasted clean and fruity but, unfortunately, too tart and one-dimensional.

SALSA VERDE

We wondered if roasting would be a better approach, as it typically intensifies the flavor of the roasted food and adds a smoky depth. We tossed the tomatillos, along with the jalapeño, onion, and garlic, in just a teaspoon of oil. Then we spread everything on a baking sheet and put our veggies in a 450-degree oven. Unfortunately, the tomatillos broke down, releasing their juice, which prevented any significant char. The broken-down tomatillos also made for a loose and mushy salsa—not exactly what we were after.

So we turned to the broiler for help. After only 10 minutes under the broiler, our veggies emerged just softened and well charred. After they had cooled, we pureed them with the remaining ingredients and assembled a team of tasters. The broiling had tempered the tart tomatillos, sweetened the onion, and mellowed the jalapeño and garlic, and the char gave the salsa a subtle smokiness. We found the flavor to be still a little too bitter, but ½ teaspoon each of sugar and salt balanced it out perfectly.

In the interest of ease, for our final test, we decided to try using canned tomatillos. Unfortunately, these softer specimens turned completely to mush under the broiler and were a noncontender.

Nevertheless, our recipe with fresh tomatillos was certainly not difficult. In about 20 minutes, we had a smoky, tart, and slightly spicy (not to mention healthy) salsa that would satisfy even the biggest tomato salsa fan.

Salsa Verde

MAKES ABOUT 1½ CUPS

To make this dish spicier, add the reserved jalapeño seeds to the tomatillo mixture in step 2. If your tomatillos are especially bitter, add more sugar to taste. Serve with baked tortilla chips.

- 1 **pound tomatillos, husks and stems removed, rinsed well and dried**
- ½ **cup coarsely chopped onion**
- 1 **jalapeño chile, stemmed, halved, and seeds reserved**
- 1 **garlic clove, peeled**
- 1 **teaspoon olive oil**
- ½ **cup fresh cilantro leaves**
- 1 **tablespoon lime juice**
  Salt
  Sugar

1. Adjust oven rack 6 inches from broiler element and heat broiler. Toss tomatillos, onion, jalapeño, and garlic with oil and place on rimmed baking sheet lined with aluminum foil. Broil, shaking sheet occasionally, until vegetables are lightly charred, 10 to 12 minutes. Let cool slightly, about 5 minutes.

2. Pulse tomatillo mixture, cilantro, lime juice, ½ teaspoon salt, and ½ teaspoon sugar in food processor until coarsely ground, about 6 pulses. Season with salt and sugar to taste and serve.

PER ¼-CUP SERVING: **Cal** 40; **Fat** 1.5g; **Sat fat** 0g; **Chol** 0mg; **Carb** 6g; **Protein** 1g; **Fiber** 2g; **Sodium** 200mg

MOROCCAN CARROT DIP

WHILE HEALTHY CREAMY DIPS ARE CERTAINLY appreciated, sometimes a vegetable-based dip is a worthy alternative. But most veggie dips are nothing more than pureed overcooked vegetables, with a minimum of seasoning, offering up an unappetizing muddy appearance. Could we create a fresh, complexly seasoned vegetable-based dip that was healthy but could also compete with its creamy cousins?

We began by looking at various international cuisines for inspiration, and the Moroccan combination of sweet, earthy carrots and warm spices struck us as particularly appealing. Further research revealed dozens of carrot dip recipes, combining mashed or pureed cooked carrots with various warm spices. A local Mediterranean restaurant serves a particularly outstanding carrot puree appetizer, with a fresh, clean flavor that is distinctly carroty but also deeply earthy and spicy, with a bright, appealing color. We settled on the goal of creating a dip with similarly undiluted carrot flavor, an aromatic and balanced depth from Moroccan spices, and a brilliant, fresh orange color.

Our first step was to determine how to cook the carrots. In most recipes, they are boiled, steamed, or microwaved, so we tried all three methods. We cut the carrots into ¼-inch-thick rounds and cooked each batch until just tender enough to mash with a potato masher. Tasters unanimously agreed that the boiled carrots looked and tasted washed out, and the steamed and microwaved carrots didn't fare much better.

Looking for an alternative cooking method, several tasters suggested oven-roasting the carrots, as this would concentrate their flavor and bring out their natural sweetness. These carrots definitely had a deep, sweet flavor, but the dip had an unappealing brown hue from the carrots' caramelization. We tried sautéing the carrots, in the hope that we would get a similarly concentrated flavor without so much browning, but by the time the carrots were cooked through, they had also browned too much.

A hybrid cooking method seemed like the logical answer. However, oven-roasting just some of the carrots seemed fussy, as did oven-roasting the whole bunch for only a brief time, so we took oven-roasting off the table. We settled on first sautéing the carrots to concentrate their flavor, then simmering them in a small amount of liquid, effectively poaching or braising them. We needed enough liquid to finish cooking them through and avoid further browning, but not so much that we ended up boiling them. We started testing with the obvious choice of water. After trying varying amounts, we determined that ⅓ cup of water for 2 pounds of carrots was just right. Any less and the carrots started to brown before cooking through; any more and the flavor was too washed out.

To see if another liquid could enrich the flavor of the carrots, we experimented with chicken broth, coconut milk, and half-and-half in lieu of water. All three muted the carrot flavor rather than enhancing it. And while vegetable broth seemed like a logical match, the resulting dip was too sweet and had an ambiguous vegetable flavor. Water, after all, was the best choice.

Our attention then turned to the world of Moroccan spices. We wanted to keep things simple, so we limited ourselves to common pantry spices. We started with

coriander, cumin, ginger, chili powder, cinnamon, turmeric, and paprika and stirred the spices into the carrots after their initial sauté. We let them cook a few seconds in the skillet before adding the water (this technique, called blooming, is used often in the test kitchen to eliminate spices' raw flavor).

We quickly learned that adding even a smidge too much spice gave the dip an unappealing ruddy tinge, and the dip lost its distinct carrot flavor. After testing varying amounts of each spice, we found that paprika and turmeric, even in small amounts, had ill effects on the color and didn't offer much flavor, so we eliminated them. After some tweaking, we achieved a balance of both warmth and heat using relatively small amounts of the remaining five spices (less than 1 tablespoon total), ensuring that the carrot flavor and color stayed front and center. For depth we also stirred in two cloves of minced garlic.

Texture was the last issue. Up to this point, we had been making a rough mixture using a potato masher. Some recipes require a fork, and others suggest pureeing the mixture in a food processor or blender. After one test we crossed off the fork method—it took far too long. Meanwhile, a few seconds in either the blender or the food processor turned the carrot mixture into a very smooth puree, but tasters agreed it was too reminiscent of baby food. We decided to stick to the potato masher; we could quickly achieve a mostly smooth puree while leaving a few coarse bits throughout for textural appeal.

To finish, we added a couple of tablespoons of olive oil for smoothness and richness and a splash of white wine vinegar for brightness. A short time in the refrigerator allowed the flavors to meld, and a final sprinkling of cilantro added freshness and contrasting color. This dip had everything we'd hoped for: appealing texture, bright color, and clean flavors, not to mention it was quick to make. Served with any variation of our homemade pita chips, our carrot dip could definitely hold its own against its creamy, cheesy counterparts.

Moroccan Carrot Dip
MAKES ABOUT 2½ CUPS

For the dip to have a brilliant orange color and clean flavor, it is important to avoid browning the carrots when cooking them in step 1. Serve with Whole Wheat Pita Chips (recipes follow).

- 3 tablespoons extra-virgin olive oil
- 2 pounds carrots, peeled and sliced ¼ inch thick
  Salt and pepper
- 2 garlic cloves, minced
- ¾ teaspoon ground coriander
- ¾ teaspoon ground cumin
- ¾ teaspoon ground ginger
- ⅛ teaspoon chili powder
- ⅛ teaspoon ground cinnamon
- ⅓ cup water
- 1 tablespoon white wine vinegar
- 1 tablespoon minced fresh cilantro

1. Heat 1 tablespoon oil in large saucepan over medium-high heat until shimmering. Add carrots and ½ teaspoon salt and cook until carrots begin to soften, 5 to 7 minutes. Stir in garlic, coriander, cumin, ginger, chili powder, and cinnamon and cook until fragrant, about 30 seconds. Add water and bring to simmer. Cover, reduce heat to low, and cook, stirring occasionally, until carrots are tender, 15 to 20 minutes.

2. Off heat, mash carrots with potato masher, leaving few coarse pieces for texture. Stir in remaining 2 tablespoons oil and vinegar. Transfer to bowl, cover, and refrigerate until dip is chilled, about 30 minutes. Season with salt and pepper to taste and sprinkle with cilantro before serving.

PER ¼-CUP SERVING: Cal 80; Fat 4.5g; Sat fat 0.5g; Chol 0mg; Carb 9g; Protein 1g; Fiber 3g; Sodium 180mg

Whole Wheat Pita Chips

MAKES 48 CHIPS

An oil mister filled with olive oil works best here but you can also use olive oil spray.

- 4 (8-inch) whole wheat pita breads
  Olive oil spray
- 1 teaspoon salt

1. Adjust oven racks to upper-middle and lower-middle positions and heat oven to 350 degrees. Using kitchen shears, cut around perimeter of each pita bread to yield 2 thin rounds. Stack pita rounds and cut into 6 wedges.

2. Spread pita wedges, smooth side down, over 2 rimmed baking sheets. Spray top of each chip with oil and sprinkle with salt.

3. Bake chips until chips begin to crisp and brown lightly, 8 to 10 minutes. Flip chips over so smooth sides face up and continue to bake until chips are fully toasted, 8 to 10 minutes longer. Let cool before serving.

PER SERVING (6 CHIPS): Cal 110; Fat 1g; Sat fat 0g; Chol 0mg; Carb 22g; Protein 4g; Fiber 3g; Sodium 500mg

VARIATIONS

Garlic-Herb Whole Wheat Pita Chips

Mix 2 tablespoons minced fresh thyme, basil, or oregano and 1½ teaspoons garlic powder with salt before sprinkling it over pita chips in step 1.

PER SERVING (6 CHIPS): Cal 110; Fat 1g; Sat fat 0g; Chol 0mg; Carb 23g; Protein 4g; Fiber 3g; Sodium 500mg

Chili-Spiced Whole Wheat Pita Chips

Mix 1 tablespoon chili powder, curry powder, or smoked paprika, ½ teaspoon garlic powder, and pinch cayenne with salt before sprinkling it over pita chips in step 1.

PER SERVING (6 CHIPS): Cal 110; Fat 1g; Sat fat 0g; Chol 0mg; Carb 23g; Protein 4g; Fiber 3g; Sodium 510mg

NOTES FROM THE TEST KITCHEN

CUTTING PITA BREAD

1. Using kitchen shears, cut around perimeter of each pita bread to yield 2 thin rounds.

2. Stack pita rounds and, using chef's knife, cut into 6 wedges each.

RED LENTIL DIP

SINCE WE HAD JUST CREATED A GREAT HEALTHY, brightly spiced carrot dip that was a big hit in the test kitchen, we wondered if we could come up with another full-flavored, internationally inspired dip to add to our light cooking repertoire. We turned, this time, to India for ideas.

Red lentils are a common ingredient in Indian cooking, usually pureed in a thick, stewlike dish called *dal*. They are mild and slightly nutty-tasting and fade to a light mustard hue once cooked. Not only pretty, these legumes are a great low-fat and vegetarian source of protein. Since red lentils cook quickly and break down into a smooth puree within about 20 minutes (no soaking required), they are an ideal platform on which to build a quick, easy, and healthy dip.

We wanted our dip to be simple yet embody the complex flavors of Indian cuisine. So naturally, we started with the spices. Not wanting to make our lentil dip unbearably spicy, we sought out a basic blend of spices with heat as an afterthought. We settled on a combination that included coriander, cumin, cinnamon, turmeric, cardamom, and, finally, red pepper flakes. This offered a pleasing blend of deep and bright flavors that remained vibrant throughout the cooking process. We also tried adding garam masala—a blend of spices including coriander, cloves, cardamom, cumin, cinnamon, pepper, and nutmeg—but found that this resulted in too many competing flavors.

Many of the recipes we found in our research called for adding the aromatics raw, or skipping them altogether, relying entirely on spices and garnishes such as chutney for flavor. We felt this dish would benefit from the addition of onion, garlic, and ginger, but adding them to the dish raw overwhelmed the other flavors. Instead, we sautéed the aromatics in just a bit of olive oil to soften and meld the flavors before adding the lentils and liquid.

Traditionally, additional spices are toasted in a separate pan with oil or *ghee* (a type of clarified butter that originated in India that has a very high smoke point and nutty flavor) to make a mixture called *tarka*. The tarka is then stirred into the lentils at the end of cooking to fortify the flavor of the finished dish. However, we felt that this additional step seemed fussy, and it required adding unwanted oil to our otherwise light dish. Instead, we simply bloomed the spices in the oil before adding the onions, garlic, and tomato paste. We'd still get the benefit of more deeply flavored spices, but without the added fat, and with one less step.

With our aromatics settled, we moved on to the main ingredient: the lentils. Since we wanted a dip, not a stew, we knew that we needed to use a relatively small amount of liquid to cook our legumes. Finding the appropriate amount of cooking liquid and correct cooking time was easier said than done. It took us several tries to get the lentils to their ideal consistency while cooking off all the excess water in the pot. To do this, we gradually whittled down the amount of water while keeping the amount of lentils the same, finally settling on a 3:1 ratio (3 cups water to 1 cup lentils).

Our dip was now well spiced and the proper texture, but it was still missing something. We knew that coconut milk is a common ingredient in Indian dishes, so we decided to see if it would enrich our dip without dulling the other flavors. Coconut milk generally comes in regular and light varieties. The full-fat version was simply too high in fat and calories for us to even consider using, but the light variety (which is simply regular coconut milk thinned out with water) seemed appropriate. We replaced 1 cup of the water with coconut milk when cooking the lentils and kept the cooking time the same. As it turned out, the coconut milk was just what our dip needed. It was now lush and creamy and had a subtle coconut flavor that perfectly complemented the other spices.

To finish, we stirred in cilantro for freshness and lime juice for brightness. Served with homemade whole wheat pita chips, our red lentil dip was exotic, easy, and naturally healthy.

NOTES FROM THE TEST KITCHEN

COCONUT MILK
We often turn to coconut milk to add rich flavor and body to soups, curries, stir-fries, and even some dips. Although regular coconut milk is creamier than light, it also contains more fat. We prefer using light coconut milk as a healthier alternative. Do not confuse coconut milk with cream of coconut, which contains added sugar and is thus much sweeter.

Red Lentil Dip

MAKES 3½ CUPS

You cannot substitute brown lentils for the red lentils here; the red lentils have a very different texture. Serve with Whole Wheat Pita Chips (page 14).

½	teaspoon ground coriander
½	teaspoon ground cumin
½	teaspoon ground cinnamon
½	teaspoon ground turmeric
⅛	teaspoon ground cardamom
⅛	teaspoon red pepper flakes
1	teaspoon olive oil
1	onion, chopped fine
	Salt and pepper
3	garlic cloves, minced
1	tablespoon tomato paste
1½	teaspoons grated fresh ginger
2	cups water
1	cup light coconut milk
1	cup red lentils, picked over and rinsed
⅓	cup minced fresh cilantro
4	teaspoons lime juice

1. Combine coriander, cumin, cinnamon, turmeric, cardamom, and pepper flakes in small bowl. Heat oil in large saucepan over medium-low heat until shimmering. Add spice mixture and cook until fragrant, about 10 seconds. Stir in onion and ½ teaspoon salt, cover, and cook, stirring occasionally, until onion is softened, 8 to 10 minutes. Uncover, stir in garlic, tomato paste, and ginger, and cook until fragrant, about 30 seconds.

2. Stir in water, coconut milk, and lentils and bring to boil. Reduce heat to simmer and cook, uncovered, until lentils are tender and resemble coarse puree, 20 to 25 minutes. Transfer to serving bowl and let cool to room temperature.

3. Stir in cilantro and lime juice. Season with salt and pepper to taste and serve.

PER ¼-CUP SERVING: Cal 70; Fat 1.5g; Sat fat 0.5g; Chol 0mg; Carb 11g; Protein 4g; Fiber 3g; Sodium 95mg

BAKED MINI FALAFEL WITH YOGURT-TAHINI SAUCE

WHEN WE THINK OF CLASSIC HOT, SAVORY PARTY hors d'oeuvres, cocktail meatballs quickly come to mind. Easily skewered with a toothpick and eaten in one bite, they make for great party food. Unfortunately, not only are the typical cocktail meatballs bland and overly saucy, but they are worlds away from healthy. We wanted a similarly sized savory appetizer that was healthy and had a fresh take.

Similar in size and shape to meatballs, falafel seemed like a good direction to take. Since they are meatless, falafel have a healthy, vegetarian-friendly edge as well. However, traditional falafel are deep-fried and covered in a rich, creamy tahini sauce. These fried patties are often not even worth the calories—they can be dry, dense, greasy, and devoid of flavor. Our ideal was falafel with a moist, light interior and a well-browned, crisp crust. Could we develop not only a tasty appetizer-style falafel, but a healthy version to boot?

Off the bat, we knew that frying was out. To come up with an alternative method, we made a few batches of a basic falafel mixture and shaped it into 2-inch patties. First we tried cooking our patties in a skillet with a little oil. Unfortunately, the filling quickly soaked up the oil, became soggy, and fell apart before cooking through. We also had to cook our falafel in so many batches that our first batch became cold before we were finished; it was not ideal for a party. Could we take a cue from a test kitchen recipe for big-batch meatballs and switch to the oven? We placed our patties on a lightly sprayed baking sheet and cooked them at 375 degrees until they began to brown. When we reached in to flip them over, however, we discovered that they were completely fused to the pan. We were going to need to use more oil. We gradually increased the amount of oil on the pan until the patties browned evenly and came up cleanly. While we ended up needing to use ¼ cup of olive oil, we were baking so many falafel in each batch (around 30) that each patty stayed relatively lean.

Now that we had settled on baking our falafel, we got to work on the makeup of the patties themselves. We started by sorting through Middle Eastern and vegetarian cookbooks. We learned that Egyptian-style falafel are made entirely from dried split fava beans, Israeli-style are made with dried chickpeas, while others

BAKED MINI FALAFEL WITH YOGURT-TAHINI SAUCE

use some combination of the two. Unable to find dried split fava beans at our local markets, we chose Israeli-style falafel by process of elimination.

We started by testing several Israeli-style recipes that we had come across in our research. In initial tests, we decided to try canned chickpeas instead of dried for simplicity, but they were a disaster—they were simply too moist and made very mushy falafel. The key is that in none of the recipes we found were the dried

chickpeas cooked, but rather soaked in water overnight, ground in the food processor with the other ingredients, then shaped and fried. No wonder the canned didn't work! We decided to follow the advice in the existing recipes and stick with dried beans.

Next we turned to the seasonings. While tasters welcomed the flavor of onion, it released moisture, which turned our falafel mushy. And draining the minced onion seemed like too much of a bother. So instead, we turned to scallions, which we liked for their flavor and for the bright green color. Fresh herbs added another hit of freshness; tasters liked the complexity provided by a combination of cilantro and parsley over just a single herb. Garlic was a given, along with ground cumin, salt, and ground black pepper. Many recipes include ground cinnamon to season the falafel, and our tasters favored the warm floral notes that it imparted.

In our initial tests we realized that size matters when it comes to falafel. Larger falafel took longer to cook through, making them as dry as sawdust on the inside without enough of the contrasting outer crust. By contrast, smaller falafel (about 1 tablespoon each) had the perfect ratio of crispy crust to tender interior, and they were just the right size—two bites—for an appetizer. We formed some into balls and some into disks. Tasters unanimously preferred the disks, shaped ½ inch thick and 1 inch wide, which offered plenty of crisp exterior.

All that was left to do was whip up a sauce. Although falafel are traditionally served with a tahini-based sauce, we found the tahini (a paste made from sesame seeds) too high in fat for our recipe. Instead, we created a low-fat yogurt-based sauce with just enough tahini for flavor. We seasoned it simply with garlic, lemon juice, and salt. Our new sauce came together quickly and easily with a few flicks of a whisk. To transform the falafel from a street snack into a bite-size appetizer, we topped each patty with a slice of tomato for a touch of freshness and color, followed by a small dollop of sauce.

NOTES FROM THE TEST KITCHEN

THE BEST TAHINI
Tahini is a thick paste made from ground sesame seeds that's most often used to flavor Middle Eastern dishes. Because it is high in fat, we make sure to use it in moderation when cooking healthfully. We tasted five supermarket brands, and **Joyva Sesame Tahini** boasted the most tahini flavor. Tasters called it "very nutty," "buttery," and almost "peanut-butterish."

OUR FAVORITE GREEK YOGURT
The major difference between ordinary yogurt and Greek-style yogurt is that true Greek yogurt is strained to remove most of its liquid whey; the result is a yogurt that is thicker than the typical American stuff and is higher in protein, lower in carbohydrates, and usually less acidic. It's good eaten plain or drizzled with honey, and we have found it works well in creamy dips and a number of sauces. The fact that it is sold in low-fat and nonfat varieties also means it's a great candidate for light cooking. To find the best in every category (not just lower-fat varieties), we gathered 18 different nonfat, 2 percent low-fat, and full-fat plain Greek yogurts and called tasters to the table.

While some yogurts stood up in stiff peaks, others were loose and watery, and flavors ranged from bland to lightly tangy to strongly sour. A little digging revealed that some manufacturers are getting this thicker, creamier product by using shortcuts, such as skipping the straining process and fortifying their yogurt with thickeners. Notably, the yogurts that scored lowest were fortified, and tasters found them unpleasantly sour with unappealing textures.

The winner of both our nonfat and full-fat tastings was **Olympus Traditional Greek Yogurt**; the nonfat yogurt was described as "seriously creamy" and "pleasantly tangy," and the full-fat version (labeled "10% fat") was favored for its "satiny" texture and "buttery," "tangy" flavor. Interestingly, this was the only brand in our lineup imported from Greece. In the 2 percent category, we preferred **Fage Total 2%**.

Baked Mini Falafel with Yogurt-Tahini Sauce
MAKES ABOUT 30 FALAFEL

Be sure to use Greek yogurt in the sauce, or the sauce will be too watery. To quick salt-soak the chickpeas, combine 2 quarts water, chickpeas, and 1½ tablespoons salt in a Dutch oven and bring to a boil over high heat. Remove the pot from the heat, cover, and let stand for 1 hour. Drain and rinse well.

SAUCE

½ cup 2 percent Greek yogurt

1 tablespoon tahini

2 teaspoons lemon juice

1½ teaspoons minced fresh cilantro or parsley

½ small garlic clove, minced

Salt and pepper

FALAFEL

Salt

1 cup dried chickpeas, picked over and rinsed

6 tablespoons olive oil

5 scallions, chopped coarse

½ cup fresh parsley leaves

½ cup fresh cilantro leaves

3 garlic cloves, minced

1 teaspoon salt

½ teaspoon pepper

¼ teaspoon ground cumin

⅛ teaspoon ground cinnamon

6 ounces cherry tomatoes, sliced thin

1. FOR THE SAUCE: Whisk yogurt, tahini, lemon juice, cilantro, garlic, ⅛ teaspoon salt, and pinch pepper together in bowl until smooth. Season with salt and pepper to taste. Cover and refrigerate until chilled, at least 1 hour or up to 1 day.

2. FOR THE FALAFEL: Dissolve 1½ tablespoons salt in 2 quarts cold water in large bowl or container. Add chickpeas and soak at room temperature for at least 8 hours or up to 24 hours. Drain and rinse well.

3. Adjust oven rack to middle position and heat oven to 375 degrees. Coat large baking sheet with ¼ cup oil.

4. Process remaining 2 tablespoons oil, drained chickpeas, scallions, parsley, cilantro, garlic, salt, pepper, cumin, and cinnamon together in food processor until smooth, about 1 minute. Working with 1 tablespoon chickpea mixture at a time, shape falafel into small patties, about 1 inch wide and ½ inch thick, and spread out on prepared sheet.

5. Bake until falafel patties are lightly browned on both sides, about 25 minutes, flipping patties over halfway through baking. Transfer patties to serving platter, top each with 1 slice tomato, and dollop each with 1 teaspoon sauce. Serve.

PER SERVING (3 FALAFEL PATTIES WITH 3 TEASPOONS SAUCE): Cal 160; Fat 10g; Sat fat 1.5g; Chol 0mg; Carb 13g; Protein 5g; Fiber 4g; Sodium 270mg

STEAMED CHINESE DUMPLINGS

WE RECENTLY DEVELOPED A FANTASTIC RECIPE IN the test kitchen for *shu mai*, open-faced steamed dumplings filled with pork and shrimp that are ubiquitous in Cantonese cooking. The savory-briny combo of pork and shrimp is hard to beat. Their filling is juicy and tender with a pleasantly springy chew; their flavor is at once salty, sweet, and tangy, as well as faintly smoky from Chinese black mushrooms. Bite-size shu mai are a perfect choice for an appetizer spread, and since they're steamed rather than fried, they are already on their way to being a healthy option. However, we knew there was still some lightening to be done.

We began with the protein. Our original recipe consisted of a 2:1 ratio of pork to shrimp. In order to keep fat levels in check, we'd need our filling to consist mostly of shrimp, with a small amount of pork for flavor. We decided to flip the ratio and use 1 pound of shrimp with only ½ pound of pork for our healthier version.

In the original recipe, we learned that using preground pork resulted in dry, chewy dumplings, and therefore we had decided to grind our own meat. While it may seem fussy, we knew that not only would this extra step help us control the texture of our lightened dumplings, but it would also help us further monitor fat levels because we could trim whatever cut of meat we chose. For our original recipe we opted to use boneless country-style pork ribs. While not traditional (most restaurants typically use pork butt), these ribs come in small portions (usually about ½ pound each), so they were more convenient, and lucky for us, country-style ribs are easy to trim.

To grind the meat, we turned to the food processor. We had already discovered that grinding all of our protein into uniform chunks gave us crumbly dumplings that broke apart mid-bite. But if we divided the meat into two batches and ground one batch more finely, the smaller pieces helped hold the larger bits together and added a pleasing textural contrast. We pulsed the shrimp with the more coarsely ground batch, producing chunks large enough to be discernible but not distracting.

We had found the right texture for our filling, but it was still not as juicy and tender as we wanted. The smaller bits of meat, in particular, were noticeably rubbery. The culprit had to be the steam heat. Moist environments conduct heat very efficiently, and just 10 minutes of steaming cooked the pork to above

165 degrees—the point at which its proteins begin to expel water and shrink, turning the texture dry and grainy. To lubricate the meat and make it seem "juicy," restaurants typically incorporate liberal amounts of lard and fatback into the filling. But we had discovered a more convenient (and coincidentally more healthful) solution in our previous testing.

We looked to all-beef meatloaf recipes (another culprit for dry, spongy meat) for our answer. In the past, we've fixed dry meatloaves by adding a little powdered gelatin. Gelatin can hold up to 10 times its weight in water, and when added to meat, it suspends the juices in a meshlike,

semisolid state that prevents it from leaching out. This also translates to a luxuriant texture similar to the suppleness contributed by fat. Half a teaspoon of gelatin bloomed first in a little water proved plenty to give our dumplings just the moist, tender texture they needed. We got even better results by dissolving the gelatin in low-sodium soy sauce, which amplified the flavor. On a whim, we mixed in 2 tablespoons of cornstarch, which provides a protective sheath to proteins during cooking, staving off moisture loss and shrinkage.

It was time to think about flavorings. Typically, the filling of shu mai is flavored with a combination of

NOTES FROM THE TEST KITCHEN

ASSEMBLING STEAMED CHINESE DUMPLINGS

1. After brushing wrapper edges lightly with water, place heaping tablespoon of filling in center.

2. Pinch opposite sides of wrapper. Rotate 90 degrees and repeat 3 times (8 folds total).

3. Gather sides of dumpling and squeeze gently at top to create "waist."

4. Hold dumpling and gently but firmly pack down filling with flat side of butter knife.

WRAPPER ROUNDUP

We developed our Steamed Chinese Dumplings with egg roll wrappers, wide sheets made from flour, water, salt, and (sometimes) egg, since they are readily available. They are typically found in the refrigerator section of the supermarket near the tofu. (Nasoya is the most common brand.) We then cut these rectangles into smaller dumpling-size rounds with a biscuit cutter. However, some supermarkets and Asian grocers stock a few additional options. The best choice is square or round wonton skins if you can find them. Made from flour, water, eggs, and salt, they're about the right size for dumplings and don't require trimming. Stay away from gyoza wrappers; these egg-free rounds work well for sturdier dumplings like potstickers, but their resilient chew is out of place in our more delicate recipe.

EGG ROLL WRAPPERS   **SQUARE OR ROUND WONTON SKINS**

REHYDRATING DRIED MUSHROOMS

Our recipes often call for dried mushrooms to add an intense flavor to stews and sauces. To rehydrate dried mushrooms, place mushrooms in bowl, cover with water, and microwave, covered, until they are steaming, about 1 minute. Let mushrooms stand until softened, about 5 minutes. Drain mushrooms through fine-mesh strainer lined with coffee filter, then finely chop. Soaking liquid is typically discarded but may be reserved for use in some recipes.

toasted sesame oil and MSG. Clearly, sodium-heavy MSG was out, and we knew we'd need to go light on the sesame oil. So we opted to pair just 2 teaspoons of sesame oil with a little extra low-sodium soy sauce, rice wine, and rice vinegar. We also found that the concentrated, earthy flavor of reconstituted dried shiitake mushrooms made a fine substitute for the Chinese black variety, another traditional inclusion. Though not traditional, minced cilantro, fresh ginger, and the crunch of chopped water chestnuts rounded out the filling's overall flavor and texture.

For wrappers, we used widely available square egg roll skins, which we cut into rounds with a biscuit cutter. Though we'll never achieve the speed of a practiced Cantonese chef, crimping the wrappers around the filling proved easier than we thought. As a final touch, instead of using the traditional (and high-sodium) shrimp paste or roe, we garnished each dumpling's exposed center with finely grated carrot and steamed them for 10 minutes. Served with a light ginger-soy dipping sauce, these were the best juicy, flavorful (and healthy!) dumplings we'd tasted outside of Chinatown.

Steamed Chinese Dumplings

MAKES ABOUT 40 DUMPLINGS

Use any size shrimp except popcorn shrimp; there's no need to halve shrimp smaller than 26 to 30 per pound before processing. For information on rehydrating mushrooms, see page 20. This recipe was developed using readily available egg roll wrappers; for more wrapper options, see page 20. You will need a steamer basket for this recipe. Serve dumplings with Ginger-Soy Dipping Sauce (recipe follows), if desired.

- ½ teaspoon unflavored gelatin
- 2 tablespoons low-sodium soy sauce
- ½ pound boneless country-style pork ribs, trimmed of all visible fat and cut into 1-inch pieces
- 1 pound shrimp, peeled, deveined, and tails removed, halved lengthwise
- ¼ cup drained and chopped canned water chestnuts
- ¾ ounce dried shiitake mushroom caps, rinsed, rehydrated, and chopped fine
- 2 tablespoons cornstarch
- 2 tablespoons minced fresh cilantro
- 1 tablespoon Chinese rice wine or dry sherry

- 1 tablespoon rice vinegar
- 2 teaspoons toasted sesame oil
- 2 teaspoons sugar
- 2 teaspoons grated fresh ginger
- ½ teaspoon pepper
- 1 (1-pound) package 5½-inch square egg roll wrappers
- ¼ cup finely grated carrot (optional)

1. Line baking sheet with parchment paper and set aside. In small bowl, sprinkle gelatin over soy sauce and let stand until gelatin is softened, about 5 minutes.

2. Pulse half of pork in food processor until coarsely ground, about 10 pulses; transfer to large bowl. Add shrimp and remaining pork to food processor and pulse until coarsely chopped, about 5 pulses. Transfer to bowl with ground pork. Stir in soy sauce mixture, water chestnuts, mushrooms, cornstarch, cilantro, wine, vinegar, sesame oil, sugar, ginger, and pepper.

3. Divide egg roll wrappers into 3 stacks (6 to 7 per stack). Using 3-inch biscuit cutter, cut two 3-inch rounds from each stack (to make 36 to 42 rounds). Cover rounds with moist paper towels to prevent drying.

4. Working with 6 rounds at a time, brush edges of each round lightly with water. Place heaping tablespoon of filling in center of each round. Pinch dough on opposite sides of wrapper, rotate 90 degrees, and repeat 3 times (8 folds total), leaving top exposed. Gather sides of dumpling and squeeze gently to create "waist." Holding dumpling in your hand, gently pack down filling with flat side of butter knife. Transfer to prepared baking sheet and top center of each dumpling with pinch of grated carrot, if using. Cover with damp kitchen towel, and repeat with remaining wrappers and filling.

5. Cut piece of parchment slightly smaller than diameter of steamer basket and place in basket. Poke about 20 small holes in parchment and lightly coat with vegetable oil spray. Transfer 10 dumplings to prepared parchment liner, making sure dumplings do not touch. Set steamer over simmering water and cook, covered, until no longer pink, 8 to 10 minutes. Repeat with remaining dumplings in 3 more batches. Serve with dipping sauce.

TO MAKE AHEAD: The dumplings can be prepared through step 4 and frozen for up to 3 months; cook as directed in step 5, unthawed, for about 5 minutes longer.

PER SERVING (4 DUMPLINGS): Cal 150; Fat 3g; Sat fat 0.5g; Chol 70mg; Carb 16g; Protein 14g; Fiber 1g; Sodium 300mg

Ginger-Soy Dipping Sauce

MAKES ABOUT ½ CUP

Be sure to use low-sodium soy sauce or the dipping sauce will be overwhelmingly salty.

- ¼ cup low-sodium soy sauce
- 3 tablespoons mirin
- 1 scallion, chopped fine
- 2 teaspoons grated fresh ginger
- 1 teaspoon toasted sesame oil
- 1 teaspoon sugar
- 1 garlic clove, minced

Whisk all ingredients together in bowl.

PER 2-TEASPOON SERVING: Cal 20; Fat 0g; Sat fat 0g; Chol 0mg; Carb 3g; Protein 0g; Fiber 0g; Sodium 210mg

SAVORY RUSTIC TARTS

RUSTIC TARTS AND FLATBREADS MAY APPEAR TO BE a healthier appetizer option than, say, a platter loaded with nuts and fatty cheeses, but looks can be deceiving. Such tarts are usually made with either a rich pastry crust or oil-slicked foccacia bread, and they're topped with any number of cheeses, olives, and meat. We wanted to come up with our own rustic, free-form tart that had all of the flavor of these indulgent versions, but with a healthy edge.

Right from the start we focused our attention on developing a dough for the base that would be fairly lean but still appealing. While buttery pastry-style doughs are certainly satisfying and flavorful, we knew that they would be a caloric nightmare. We turned, instead, to a recipe for *pissaladière* for inspiration. Pissaladière is a rustic provençal free-form onion tart with a crisp crust made from a dough similar to pizza dough. Mostly flour and water, with only a smidge of olive oil, this type of dough was certainly our best bet for keeping the fat grams in check. For the sake of ease, we settled on using one of our favorite pizza dough recipes and used our food processor technique for kneading the dough: We pulsed our dry ingredients together, gradually drizzled in the water and oil, and processed until the dough came together in a ball.

The dough settled, we turned to our shaping and baking techniques. Our primary focus was to keep the tart both crisp and rustic in appearance. After testing a couple of shaping techniques, we decided on a combination of rolling with a rolling pin and stretching with our hands. A rolling pin allowed us to quickly form a uniform shape, and using our hands to finish maintained the rustic shape we were after. We also knew from experience cooking crisp-crust pizza that cooking the dough at a high temperature would get it crisp—crucial for a hand-held appetizer. After fiddling with oven rack positions, we found that baking the tart on the lowest rack at 500 degrees gave us the absolute crispest bottom.

But while our crust was certainly crisp, it was also dried out. Many similar recipes rely on an oil-coated baking sheet as well as copious amounts of oil brushed on top of the dough to keep the bread from becoming nothing more than a lean cracker. We knew that we wanted to use vegetable oil spray to coat the pan (it provides just enough oil to prevent sticking and drying out) and that we'd want to brush some oil on top of the crust itself (most recipes call for 3 tablespoons), but before we could know how much we could afford in terms of fat and calories, we needed to address our toppings.

Since we were modeling our crust on pissaladière, we decided to top our tart with a base of caramelized onions. When it comes to caramelizing onions, we found that most recipes subscribe to one of two methods—low and slow, or fast and furious—yet neither works. Low (heat) and slow dries out the onions before they have a chance to darken, but fast and furious (high heat) leaves the onions crunchy and burnt-tasting. The solution was to use a combination of low and high heat, starting the onions over medium-low heat so that they released their juice and softened and then increasing the heat to medium-high until they became caramelized. We also found that we needed to keep the amount of oil relatively high (1 tablespoon) in order for the onions to brown without burning. We'd just have to cut back on oil in the shaped tart to compensate.

We also found that a nonstick skillet works best for caramelizing onions. The low sides of the skillet allowed the steam to evaporate rather than interfere with browning, and the nonstick surface ensured that the caramelization stuck to the onions, not the pan.

RUSTIC TART WITH FIG JAM, PROSCIUTTO, AND BLUE CHEESE

We also found that by adding a little salt and brown sugar, we could jump-start the caramelization process and could therefore use just 1 tablespoon of oil for an entire pound of onions.

NOTES FROM THE TEST KITCHEN

MAKING A RUSTIC TART

1. Turn dough out onto lightly floured counter and roll and press dough into 14 by 8-inch rectangle.

2. Dimple dough with fingertips to prevent dough from puffing up too much during baking. Transfer dough to prepared baking sheet.

3. Top dimpled dough as directed in recipe, making sure to leave ½-inch border around edge.

THE BEST GOAT CHEESE

We conducted a test kitchen tasting of three domestic and four readily available imported fresh goat cheeses, and our tasters concluded that American producers have mastered the craft of making goat cheese. The clear favorite was **Vermont Chèvre** from the Vermont Butter & Cheese Company. It was creamy and tangy but not overpowering. Meanwhile, reviews of the imported cheeses were mixed. Tasters were enthusiastic about Le Biquet from Canada, but the French cheeses were, for the most part, described as gamy or muttony, with a chalky, spacklelike texture. A few adventurous tasters appreciated the assertive flavors of the imported cheeses, but the overall feeling was that the domestic cheeses were cleaner-tasting and more balanced.

To give this caramelized onion tart a little oomph, we added several small dollops of goat cheese for creamy contrast and richness (a great healthy cheese because it is naturally low in fat and full of tangy flavor) and a generous sprinkling of fresh herbs, elevating our humble tart to heights worthy of a dinner party.

With our toppings settled, we could backtrack to how much oil we needed, and could afford, for brushing on the tart. We found that 5 teaspoons was the right amount for ensuring richness and a nice crisp texture that wasn't too dried out, and we were still within a healthy range.

With our master recipe settled, we set out to develop a variation with an entirely different flavor profile. For maximum flavor, we paired prosciutto and blue cheese. While neither is low fat in its own right, the two pack such a punch that just 1 ounce of each was enough for our entire tart, again keeping us within our healthy target. We also switched to caramelized shallots instead of onions for a different punch of flavor. With these changes, however, we could no longer afford to brush our crust with extra olive oil. Instead, we turned to the classic partner to prosciutto and blue cheese, the fig, to protect our crust from drying out in the heat of the oven. We spread ¼ cup of jam over the crust and topped it with the shallots, blue cheese, and strips of prosciutto before baking it off. Our clever variation emerged just as moist as the original, and with an air of decadence that guaranteed it would be a sure win on any appetizer spread.

Rustic Caramelized Onion Tart with Goat Cheese and Herbs

SERVES 8

We prefer to use homemade pizza dough here (recipe follows); however, you can substitute store-bought pizza dough or pizza dough from your favorite local pizzeria.

- 8 teaspoons extra-virgin olive oil
- 1 pound onions, halved and sliced ¼ inch thick
- 1¼ teaspoons minced fresh thyme
- ½ teaspoon brown sugar
- ¼ teaspoon salt
  Pepper
- 8 ounces Pizza Dough (page 25)
- 2 ounces goat cheese, crumbled (½ cup)
- 2 tablespoons minced fresh parsley, scallion, basil, dill, or tarragon

1. Adjust oven rack to lowest position and heat oven to 500 degrees. Spray baking sheet with vegetable oil spray.

2. Heat 1 tablespoon oil in 12-inch nonstick skillet over medium-low heat until shimmering. Add onions, 1 teaspoon thyme, sugar, and salt, cover, and cook, stirring occasionally, until onions have softened and released their liquid, about 10 minutes. Uncover, increase heat to medium-high, and continue to cook, stirring often, until onions are deeply browned, 10 to 15 minutes.

3. Turn pizza dough out onto lightly floured counter. Roll and press dough into 14 by 8-inch oval. Transfer dough to prepared sheet, reshape as needed, and gently dimple with fingertips.

4. Brush dough with remaining 5 teaspoons oil and season with pepper. Scatter caramelized onions, goat cheese, and remaining ¼ teaspoon thyme evenly over dough, leaving ½-inch border around edge.

5. Bake until tart is deep golden brown, 10 to 12 minutes, rotating pan halfway through baking. Sprinkle with parsley, cut into 16 equal pieces, and serve warm.

PER SERVING (2 SLICES): Cal 170; Fat 8g; Sat fat 2g; Chol 5mg; Carb 23g; Protein 5g; Fiber 2g; Sodium 250mg

VARIATION

Rustic Tart with Fig Jam, Prosciutto, and Blue Cheese

SERVES 8

We prefer to use homemade pizza dough here (recipe follows); however, you can substitute store-bought pizza dough or pizza dough from your favorite local pizzeria.

- 1 tablespoon extra-virgin olive oil
- 8 ounces shallots, sliced ¼ inch thick
- ¼ teaspoon brown sugar
- ⅛ teaspoon salt
- 8 ounces Pizza Dough (recipe follows)
- ¼ cup fig jam, loosened with 1 teaspoon water
  Pepper
- 2 ounces blue cheese, crumbled (½ cup)
- 1 ounce thinly sliced prosciutto, cut into 1-inch strips
- ¼ teaspoon minced fresh thyme

1. Adjust oven rack to lowest position and heat oven to 500 degrees. Spray baking sheet with vegetable oil spray.

2. Heat oil in 12-inch nonstick skillet over medium-low heat until shimmering. Add shallots, sugar, and salt, cover, and cook, stirring occasionally, until shallots have softened and released their liquid, about 8 minutes. Uncover, increase heat to medium-high, and continue to cook, stirring often, until shallots are deeply browned, 8 to 12 minutes.

3. Turn pizza dough out onto lightly floured counter. Roll and press dough into 14 by 8-inch oval. Transfer dough to prepared sheet, reshape as needed, and gently dimple with fingertips.

4. Brush fig jam evenly over dough, leaving ½-inch border around edge, and season with pepper. Scatter caramelized shallots, blue cheese, prosciutto, and thyme evenly over fig jam.

5. Bake until tart is deep golden brown, 8 to 12 minutes, rotating pan halfway through baking. Cut into 16 equal pieces and serve warm.

PER SERVING (2 SLICES): Cal 180; Fat 4.5g; Sat fat 1g; Chol 5mg; Carb 30g; Protein 6g; Fiber 0g; Sodium 340mg

Pizza Dough

MAKES 8 OUNCES DOUGH

All-purpose flour can be substituted for the bread flour, but the resulting crust will be a little less crisp and chewy. If desired, you can slow down the dough's rising time by letting it rise in the refrigerator for 8 to 16 hours in step 2; let the refrigerated dough soften at room temperature for 30 minutes before using.

- 1–1¼ cups (5½–6¾ ounces) bread flour
- ¾ teaspoon instant or rapid-rise yeast
- ½ teaspoon salt
- 2 teaspoons olive oil
- 7 tablespoons warm tap water

1. Pulse 1 cup flour, yeast, and salt together in food processor (fitted with dough blade if possible) to combine. With processor running, pour oil, then water through feed tube and process until rough ball forms, 20 to 30 seconds. Let dough rest for 2 minutes, then process for 30 seconds longer.

2. Turn dough out onto lightly floured counter and knead by hand to form smooth, round ball, about 5 minutes, adding remaining ¼ cup flour, 1 tablespoon at a time, to prevent dough from sticking to counter. Place dough in lightly greased bowl, cover tightly with greased plastic wrap, and let rise in warm place until doubled in size, 1 to 1½ hours.

PERFECT POPCORN

WHEN THAT SALTY SNACK CRAVING HITS, ONE favorite choice is a bag of microwave popcorn. Popcorn is often great at hitting the spot, it's quick and convenient, and it's a great low-calorie snack. Right? Well, not always. While most of us know that movie theater–style popcorn doused in butter sauce is nowhere near healthy (perhaps even less healthy than a box of candy!), it may come as a surprise that the home-popped microwave versions are rarely better. These bags are filled not only with corn kernels but also with highly saturated oils and loads of sodium. Could we create a flavorful popcorn recipe with a lightened profile? We knew that the biggest problem was finding a method for cooking the popcorn without a generous coating of oil and still give it appealing flavor. We decided to take a step back to the classic stovetop method for popping popcorn (in a pot with some oil) and work forward from there, since this would give us control over the ingredients.

The back-of-the-kernel-box recipe calls for 3 tablespoons of canola oil to pop ½ cup of popcorn kernels. We started there, gradually reducing the oil to 2 tablespoons, and then to 1 tablespoon. The popcorn popped just fine until we reached below 1 tablespoon; any less and kernels stuck to the bottom of the pot and scorched. Unfortunately, our healthy popcorn, even with 2 tablespoons of oil, tasted just like that: healthy, and bland. Our first instinct was to generously add melted butter or oil and salt to the bowl, but we knew that doing so would bring us right back to our starting point. We'd need a new solution.

We knew that in order for popcorn to pop, we just needed to heat the kernels until they were hot enough. We did a little research and found that popcorn pops when the water inside the kernel is heated enough to turn to steam. The steam causes the kernel to burst, revealing the white airy center. If popcorn is just the result of built-up steam, did we really need oil in our pot? Could water work equally well? If so, we would be able to afford tossing our popcorn with some flavorful additions after popping.

For our next test, we put a tablespoon of water in the pot along with the kernels and crossed our fingers. Most of the popcorn popped as we'd hoped, but some kernels still stuck to the pot and scorched. We needed more steam. We tried adding more water to the pot, but some of the extra liquid stayed in the pot and made our popcorn soggy. We were stumped until a colleague suggested that we preheat the pot before adding the water. Logically, this should make the water evaporate more quickly and thus create more steam at the outset—just what the kernels needed, we hoped, to pop quickly before scorching. We preheated the pot for a full two minutes before adding the kernels and water together. Moments later, the corn began popping. This new batch popped up fluffy, light, and unscorched. Best of all, since we hadn't used any oil to pop the kernels, we could drizzle on a little extra-virgin olive oil at the end for a flavor boost. This oil also helped our modest shake of salt and pepper stick to the kernels.

Since our basic version was so successful, we decided to tackle a few flavorful variations. Most flavored popcorn recipes call for sprinkling dry toppings onto already popped kernels. The problem with this technique, as many of us have experienced, is that most of these toppings sink to the bottom of the bowl, leaving us with the same plain popcorn we started with. To remedy this problem, we turned to a technique we use in many savory recipes: blooming spices in oil.

Before popping the corn, we heated up our finishing oil with our warm spices (garlic powder, coriander, and cumin) until the mixture became fragrant. Then we popped our popcorn in the water just as before and drizzled on our flavor-infused oil before serving. This not only gave us a method for adding flavor to every bite of popcorn, but it also brought out depth from all of the spices. We then made a sweet-salty version with cinnamon and sugar, and another savory favorite with black pepper and Parmesan cheese. These popcorns were not only satisfying, healthy snacks, but they were the perfect easy addition to an appetizer spread.

Popcorn with Olive Oil
MAKES ABOUT 14 CUPS

When cooking the popcorn, be sure to keep the lid on tight and shake the pot vigorously to prevent scorching.

- 1 tablespoon water
- ½ cup popcorn kernels
- 2 tablespoons extra-virgin olive oil
- 1 teaspoon salt
- ½ teaspoon pepper

Heat Dutch oven over medium-high heat for 2 minutes. Add water and popcorn, cover, and cook, shaking frequently, until first few kernels begin to pop. Continue to cook, shaking vigorously, until popping has mostly stopped. Pour popcorn immediately into large bowl and toss with oil, salt, and pepper. Serve.

PER 2-CUP SERVING: Cal 90; **Fat** 4.5g; **Sat fat** 0.5g; **Chol** 0mg; **Carb** 10g; **Protein** 1g; **Fiber** 2g; **Sodium** 330mg

VARIATIONS

Popcorn with Warm Spices and Garlic
MAKES ABOUT 14 CUPS

When cooking the popcorn, be sure to keep the lid on tight and shake the pot vigorously to prevent scorching.

    2 tablespoons extra-virgin olive oil
    2 teaspoons garlic powder
    ½ teaspoon ground coriander
    ½ teaspoon ground cumin
    1 tablespoon water
    ½ cup popcorn kernels
    1 teaspoon salt
    ½ teaspoon pepper

1. Heat oil, garlic powder, coriander, and cumin together in 8-inch skillet over medium-low heat until warm and fragrant, about 1 minute. Remove from heat.

2. Heat Dutch oven over medium-high heat for 2 minutes. Add water and popcorn, cover, and cook, shaking frequently, until first few kernels begin to pop. Continue to cook, shaking vigorously, until popping has mostly stopped. Pour popcorn immediately into large bowl and toss with oil mixture, salt, and pepper. Serve.

PER 2-CUP SERVING: Cal 90; **Fat** 4.5g; **Sat fat** 0.5g; **Chol** 0mg; **Carb** 10g; **Protein** 2g; **Fiber** 2g; **Sodium** 330mg

Popcorn with Parmesan and Black Pepper
MAKES ABOUT 14 CUPS

When cooking the popcorn, be sure to keep the lid on tight and shake the pot vigorously to prevent scorching. We like to use a rasp-style grater for the Parmesan here because it makes small, delicate shreds of cheese that stick nicely to the warm popcorn.

    2 tablespoons extra-virgin olive oil
    ½ teaspoon pepper
    1 tablespoon water
    ½ cup popcorn kernels
    1 ounce Parmesan cheese, grated (½ cup)
    ¾ teaspoon salt

1. Heat oil and pepper together in 8-inch skillet over medium-low heat until warm and fragrant, about 1 minute. Remove from heat.

2. Heat Dutch oven over medium-high heat for 2 minutes. Add water and popcorn, cover, and cook, shaking frequently, until first few kernels begin to pop. Continue to cook, shaking vigorously, until popping has mostly stopped. Pour popcorn immediately into large bowl and toss with oil mixture, Parmesan, and salt. Serve.

PER 2-CUP SERVING: Cal 100; **Fat** 6g; **Sat fat** 1g; **Chol** 5mg; **Carb** 10g; **Protein** 3g; **Fiber** 2g; **Sodium** 300mg

Popcorn with Cinnamon and Sugar
MAKES ABOUT 14 CUPS

When cooking the popcorn, be sure to keep the lid on tight and shake the pot vigorously to prevent scorching.

    2 tablespoons canola oil
    2 tablespoons sugar
    1 teaspoon ground cinnamon
    1 tablespoon water
    ½ cup popcorn kernels
    ½ teaspoon salt

1. Heat oil, sugar, and cinnamon together in 8-inch skillet over medium-low heat until warm and fragrant, about 1 minute. Remove from heat.

2. Heat Dutch oven over medium-high heat for 2 minutes. Add water and popcorn, cover, and cook, shaking frequently, until first few kernels begin to pop. Continue to cook, shaking vigorously, until popping has mostly stopped. Pour popcorn immediately into large bowl and toss with oil mixture and salt. Serve.

PER 2-CUP SERVING: Cal 100; **Fat** 4.5g; **Sat fat** 0g; **Chol** 0mg; **Carb** 13g; **Protein** 1g; **Fiber** 2g; **Sodium** 170mg

QUINOA AND VEGETABLE STEW

SOUPS & STEWS

M = TEST KITCHEN MAKEOVER

CREAMLESS CREAMY TOMATO SOUP

A HEALTHY TOMATO SOUP SHOULD HAVE IT ALL: good looks, velvety smoothness, and a bright, tomatoey taste balanced by the fruit's natural sweetness. But poor versions of this classic are the norm, featuring either an acidic, watery broth or an overdose of cream. Though it's meant to tame tartness and lend body, we've always found that adding cream goes hand in hand with muting flavor. At the same time, it adds unnecessary fat and calories, often packing nearly a whopping 25 grams of fat and more than 400 calories per serving. We wanted a soup with rich tomato flavor, a satisfying texture, and a guilt-free ingredient list. We headed to the kitchen to see what we could do.

The first step in the process was to pass over fresh tomatoes for canned, which are almost always far better than your average supermarket tomato, boasting more consistently rich and concentrated flavor. Plus they're already peeled, which is a big timesaver. We quickly settled on whole tomatoes rather than diced or crushed; a few tests showed that the latter two types didn't break down completely, compromising the texture of the finished soup. From there we developed a simple working recipe, sautéing onions and garlic in a small amount of butter, stirring in the tomatoes and a can of chicken broth (we knew vegetable broth would make our soup too sweet), and then giving the whole thing a quick spin in the blender. The results were decent, but dull.

We started by making a few simple tweaks. If cream subdues tomato flavor, we figured the milk solids in the butter (even though it was only a small amount) were likely tamping it down as well. So we substituted extra-virgin olive oil, and the soup brightened as a result. A few more small changes—a bay leaf and a pinch of red pepper flakes sautéed with the onions—upped the flavor significantly. To compensate for the flavor the oil lost as it cooked, we drizzled a little more over the soup before it went into the blender. Most tasters also welcomed a couple of tablespoons of brandy.

Now that we had our flavor profile nailed down, we moved on to bigger problems: tartness and thin texture. Sugar is often used as a means to combat tartness. We preferred brown sugar to one-dimensional white sugar,

but sugar could take us only so far—add enough to tone down tartness and the soup became unpalatably sweet.

What we needed was a thickener that could also temper the acid. Fatty, flavor-dulling dairy ingredients were definitely out, but what about a starch? Cooking flour along with the onions to form a roux made for a thicker soup, but the texture turned slimy instead of creamy, and it did nothing for flavor. Cornstarch produced similar results. We scoured our cookbook library before we found inspiration in another tomato-based soup: gazpacho. This Spanish classic is made from tomatoes, olive oil, and garlic, along with an unusual element for thickening: bread. But gazpacho is served cold. Would bread work as a thickener for hot soup?

We tore several slices of sandwich bread into pieces and stirred them into the pot with the tomatoes and chicken broth as they simmered. When we processed the mixture in the blender, we ended up with bread chunks that swam in a sea of broth and resisted being sucked down into the blender's spinning blades. To cut back on the liquid in the blender, we decided to try leaving out the broth until the very end. For the next batch of soup, we pureed the tomatoes with the aromatics and bread before returning the mixture to the pan and whisking in the broth. One taste and we knew we'd hit on just the right solution.

Even without the cream, our tomato soup had the same velvety texture as the creamy kind, but with bright, fresh flavor. None of our tasters even guessed that our soup contained a secret ingredient in lieu of cream or that we had cut 14 grams of fat and 220 calories in the process. Only after the pot was empty did we divulge the truth behind our lightened tomato soup.

MAKEOVER SPOTLIGHT: CREAMY TOMATO SOUP

	CALORIES	FAT	SAT FAT	CHOLESTEROL
BEFORE	410	24g	16g	80mg
AFTER	190	10g	1.5g	0mg

Creamless Creamy Tomato Soup
SERVES 6

Some blenders will take a minute or more to blend the soup completely smooth. Adding the olive oil to the soup in the blender helps it emulsify.

1 onion, chopped fine

¼ cup extra-virgin olive oil

   Salt and pepper

3 garlic cloves, minced

1 bay leaf

   Pinch red pepper flakes

2 (28-ounce) cans whole peeled tomatoes

1 tablespoon brown sugar

3 slices hearty white sandwich bread, crusts removed, torn into 1-inch pieces

2 cups low-sodium chicken broth

2 tablespoons brandy

¼ cup minced fresh chives

1. Combine onion, 2 tablespoons oil, and ⅛ teaspoon salt in Dutch oven. Cover and cook over medium-low heat, stirring occasionally, until softened, 8 to 10 minutes. Stir in garlic, bay leaf, and red pepper flakes and cook until fragrant, about 30 seconds.

2. Stir in tomatoes. Using potato masher, mash tomatoes until no pieces are larger than 2 inches. Stir in sugar and bread, bring to simmer, and cook until bread begins to dissolve, about 5 minutes.

3. Discard bay leaf. Puree soup with remaining 2 tablespoons oil in blender, in batches, until smooth. Return soup to clean pot, stir in broth and brandy, and cook gently over medium-low heat until soup is hot. Season with salt and pepper to taste. Sprinkle individual bowls with chives before serving.

PER 1½-CUP SERVING: Cal 190; Fat 10g; Sat fat 1.5g; Chol 0mg; Carb 19g; Protein 3g; Fiber 3g; Sodium 760mg

NOTES FROM THE TEST KITCHEN

NO-MESS BLENDING
An immersion blender is a handy tool to have. Instead of awkwardly transferring hot soup to a blender to puree (and making a big mess along the way), you can simply stick the immersion blender into the pot and push a button. We tested eight models, priced from $25 to $100. The best performers had strong motors and cages around the blades that kept food close for blending but were wide enough to clean easily. We were happy to discover that our winner was also a bargain; the **Kalorik Sunny Morning Stick Mixer**, $29.95, was easy to use and clean and pureed like a champ.

SPLIT PEA AND HAM SOUP

SPLIT PEA SOUP HAS FRUGAL ORIGINS, BORN AS A way to use the highly flavorful bone and fatty chunks of meat left over from a roast ham. This peasant soup turns a minimal number of ingredients—generally just ham, dried peas, a few aromatics, and water—into a spoon-coating, richly flavored broth studded with tender shreds of sweet-smoky meat. But given the fatty chunks of meat as its starting point, traditional split pea soup doesn't exactly scream "healthy," not to mention that most recipes are time consuming and too often turn out an overly thick, green mash with one-note flavor. We wanted to revamp this classic into a weeknight soup that did not rely on having a ham bone on hand and was high on flavor and low on calories and fat.

Without a ham bone, we had to find an equally flavorful—yet healthier—replacement. Most of the recipes we came across swapped in ham hocks. While these sinewy knuckle pieces (we tried both fresh and smoked) had loads of flavor, they ultimately rendered our soup greasy and too fatty—not the outcome we were after. Plus, unless you find a particularly substantial specimen, hocks tend to be skimpy on meat.

We wanted plenty of ham strewn throughout the pot, so we made a point of shopping for leaner yet meatier alternatives. We returned to the test kitchen with Canadian bacon and ham steak. The Canadian bacon was disappointing. Unlike regular strip American bacon made from fat-streaked pork belly, the Canadian version comes from the lean loin region of the pig, and its meek flavor barely broke through the thick fog of peas. Ham steak, however, was a welcome addition to the pot; after we quartered the slab and let it simmer in the broth (a classic base of water fortified with sautéed onion and garlic, carrots and celery added midway through cooking to preserve their texture, bay leaves, and a pair of thyme sprigs) for about 45 minutes, the liquid had taken on significantly fuller pork flavor, and the ham itself was tender enough to pull into meaty shreds with a pair of forks.

But as our tasters rightly pointed out, the leaner ham steak was hardly an equal substitute for a bone. We all agreed that the soup was still lacking richness and could use more smokiness—a perfect job for American bacon. We hoped just a few strips added to the pot would get the job done without ramping up the fat too much. But the quick fix we were hoping for proved elusive.

SPLIT PEA AND HAM SOUP

We crisped a few pieces of bacon and added them to the pot, only to find that they overwhelmed the ham and peas. Instead, we found our solution by adding raw bacon to the soup along with the ham steak. The bacon steeped in the broth, permeating the soup with a pleasant but not overwhelming smoky flavor. We found that all the soup needed was a single strip, and best of all, the bacon could be fished out right before serving, eliminating a significant amount of fat but leaving behind plenty of smoky bacon flavor.

As for the peas, we knew from experience that the presoaking step in many recipes was not only unnecessary but also unfavorable. Unsoaked peas broke down just as readily as soaked peas, and the resulting soup was actually more flavorful, since they absorbed the pork-enriched broth.

All that was left to do was work up a few garnishes. A handful of fresh peas seemed appropriate; their sweetness popped against the smoky broth. Chopped fresh mint and a drizzle of good balsamic vinegar added freshness and sweetness, respectively, and punched up the flavors even more. At last, we had a deceptively healthy split pea soup, full of rich, meaty goodness.

Split Pea and Ham Soup

SERVES 6

Depending on the age and brand of split peas, the consistency of the soup may vary slightly. If the soup is too thin at the end of step 3, increase the heat and simmer, uncovered, until the desired consistency is reached. If it is too thick, thin it with a little water. Serve sprinkled with fresh peas, a grind of fresh pepper, chopped mint, and/or drizzled with aged balsamic vinegar, if desired.

- 1 onion, chopped fine
- 1 teaspoon canola oil
  Salt and pepper
- 2 garlic cloves, minced
- 7 cups water
- 12 ounces ham steak, rind removed, cut into quarters
- 1 slice bacon
- 1 pound (2 cups) green split peas, picked over and rinsed
- 2 sprigs fresh thyme
- 2 bay leaves
- 2 carrots, peeled and cut into ½-inch pieces
- 1 celery rib, cut into ½-inch pieces

1. Combine onion, oil, and ⅛ teaspoon salt in Dutch oven. Cover and cook over medium-low heat, stirring occasionally, until softened, 8 to 10 minutes. Add garlic and cook until fragrant, about 30 seconds. Add water, ham steak, bacon, peas, thyme, and bay leaves. Increase heat to high and bring to simmer, stirring frequently to keep peas from sticking to bottom. Reduce heat to low, cover, and simmer until peas are tender but not falling apart, about 45 minutes.

2. Remove ham steak, cover with aluminum foil or plastic wrap to prevent it from drying out, and set aside. Stir carrots and celery into pot and continue to simmer, covered, until vegetables are tender and peas have almost completely broken down, about 30 minutes longer.

3. When cool enough to handle, shred ham into small, bite-size pieces with 2 forks. Remove thyme sprigs, bay leaves, and bacon from pot. Stir ham back into soup and return to simmer to heat through. Season with salt and pepper to taste and serve.

PER 1⅔-CUP SERVING: Cal 360; Fat 5g; Sat fat 1.5g; Chol 25mg; Carb 51g; Protein 30g; Fiber 21g; Sodium 830mg

POTATO AND KALE SOUP

THERE'S NOTHING LIKE A SIMPLE YET HEARTY SOUP for warming you up during the winter months, but we wondered, could we make one that fit this criterion and was also healthy? We figured the best way to get started was to pick the starring components. Potatoes seemed like a good place to begin, as they are great for adding heft and thickening soups, and the addition of a winter green would add color, a complementary earthy flavor, and a good healthy component. A little research led us to two classic potato and hearty greens dishes: the Portuguese *caldo verde*, which adds sausage to the mix, and the Irish dish known as *colcannon*, which adds leeks as well as onions to the potato-greens combination. Though more of a challenge from a healthy-cooking perspective, we thought the addition of a little meaty flavor in the spirit of the Portuguese-style soup was just what we were after.

We started our testing with the greens. The traditional choice for this soup is *couve gallego*, a Galician cabbage native to the Iberian Peninsula. But since it isn't easily obtained in this country, we limited our tests to more available options: kale, collard greens, turnip greens, and Swiss chard. We began with a basic working recipe, browning a little chorizo, then adding onions, garlic, broth, and potatoes cut into large chunks (we worked with russets for now). We added the greens until closer to the end of cooking to avoid overcooking them.

Turnip greens fared the worst. Their tender leaves nearly fell apart and became slimy even after a brief stint in the stock. They also imparted an unpleasant sour and "dirty" flavor that was impossible to ignore. The collard greens were an improvement, as they added a lovely peppery flavor to the soup. The bad news was that the texture was similar to that of the turnip greens, which took them out of the running.

Swiss chard was next on the list. Tasters unanimously agreed its spinach-y, mineral-like flavor was out of place in this soup. Kale was our last hope, and luckily it pulled through. Because of its coarse, substantial texture, it resisted wilting and provided a more forgiving window of time in which it could cook. The kale also imparted a nice sweet cabbage flavor to the soup.

With the greens finally out of the way, we turned our sights to finding the best variety of potato for the job. The potatoes would be key for adding heft to our soup and acting as a thickener. We needed potatoes that would break down partially but not completely so that we could mash some yet still have an appealing chunky texture when we were through. Up until now, we had been using russets, but during our greens tests they fell apart completely and gave the soup a granular texture. Medium-starch Yukon Gold potatoes fared better texturally, but they were a little too sweet for this soup. Low-starch boiling potatoes, such as Red Bliss, worked best—even after a vigorous boiling and mashing, some potatoes held together to give our soup just the hearty texture we were after.

Finally, we tackled the meat. Most caldo verde recipes call for either the very garlicky Portuguese linguiça or smoky Spanish chorizo. We gave both a try, and surprisingly, the linguiça contributed little flavor to the soup. Chorizo, on the other hand, made a big impact. Its potent spices (chiefly smoked paprika) blended into the stock and gave it a very full, deep flavor, and we found that 4 ounces for the whole pot didn't push us over the edge nutritionally. Mexican chorizo (typically sold uncooked) worked as well. The sweet greens, pungent chorizo, and starchy potatoes came together to make a wonderfully balanced, deeply flavorful, and satisfying soup. But because we had cut down on the amount of chorizo found in most recipes, we felt our soup needed a little more protein. Though not traditional to caldo verde, nutty chickpeas were a welcome addition.

Last, we rounded out our soup's flavor with some cumin and red pepper flakes for heat and fresh oregano for herbal depth.

Potato and Kale Soup

SERVES 6

Either Mexican or Spanish chorizo can be used here; note that Spanish chorizo comes in both hot and mild varieties (either will work fine).

- 1 teaspoon canola oil
- 4 ounces chorizo, halved lengthwise and sliced crosswise ¼ inch thick
- 1 onion, chopped fine
- 4 garlic cloves, minced
- 1 teaspoon ground cumin
- Pinch red pepper flakes
- 6 cups low-sodium chicken broth
- 1½ pounds red potatoes, cut into ¾-inch chunks
- 1 (15-ounce) can chickpeas, rinsed
- 12 ounces kale, stemmed and leaves sliced ¼ inch thick
- 1 teaspoon minced fresh oregano or ¼ teaspoon dried
- Salt and pepper

1. Heat oil in Dutch oven over medium heat until shimmering. Add chorizo and cook until browned, 3 to 5 minutes. Transfer chorizo to plate.

2. Add onion to fat left in pot, reduce heat to medium-low, cover, and cook, stirring occasionally, until softened, 8 to 10 minutes. Stir in garlic, cumin, and pepper flakes and cook until fragrant, about 30 seconds.

3. Stir in broth, potatoes, and chickpeas and bring to simmer. Cover, reduce heat to medium-low, and cook until potatoes are almost tender, 15 to 20 minutes.

4. Stir in browned chorizo, kale, and oregano and continue to simmer until kale and potatoes are tender, about 10 minutes longer. Mash some of potatoes against side of pot with spoon to thicken soup slightly. Season with salt and pepper to taste and serve.

PER 1½-CUP SERVING: Cal 260; Fat 10g; Sat fat 3g; Chol 15mg; Carb 34g; Protein 12g; Fiber 5g; Sodium 960mg

MOROCCAN CHICKPEA SOUP

IT USED TO BE A GIVEN THAT MEAT (WHETHER BEEF, pork, or chicken) was a requirement on every American dinner plate, but these days that isn't necessarily the case. Now beans are often seen in the starring role, and it's no surprise—they are a great low-fat source of protein, and it doesn't hurt that they are also affordable. We wanted to come up with a healthy weeknight soup that made beans the main attraction.

In the test kitchen, we typically prefer using dried beans since they offer better flavor and texture than most canned varieties. But dried beans can be time-consuming to prepare, requiring presoaking and long cooking times. Could we develop a recipe that used convenient canned beans?

Out of the gate, we needed to determine which canned bean we would be using. After running through the options, we found that tasters' favorite was chickpeas for their buttery flavor. Chickpeas also fare well during the canning process, emerging from the can as whole, evenly cooked beans with unbroken skins. And because they are porous, they take on the flavors of a sauce or broth without breaking down or getting mushy.

With chickpeas as our bean of choice, now we needed to pick a flavor profile for our soup. Chickpeas are common in Moroccan dishes, so we decided to take our soup in that direction. Moroccan soups and stews are typically assertively flavored with the help of a combination of exotic spices, which meant the chickpeas in our soup would have the chance to soak up plenty of flavor. So we began by developing a flavor base. First we sautéed onions in a little oil, then we added garlic, vegetable broth, tomatoes, and the chickpeas. After simmering the mixture for about 30 minutes, we were off to a good start—the chickpeas had soaked up some flavor and the flavors had had some time to meld—but our soup definitely still needed help. Delving into the world of Moroccan cuisine, we came up with a list of highly flavorful ingredients to try, including saffron, preserved lemon, olives, dried fruit, ginger, and warm spices. Several options, like the preserved lemon, fell off the list simply because they were hard to find. Ultimately, hot paprika, saffron, ginger, and cumin—all readily available options—made the cut. We were getting closer, but still, our soup felt incomplete.

It needed a little more physical heft to match its big flavors, so we looked at some vegetables to add to the pot. We wanted to keep things simple, so we tested bell pepper, potato, zucchini, and cauliflower. We immediately ruled out the bell pepper; it became too soft during the simmer and its flavor seemed out of place. Cauliflower worked fine, but the winners turned out to be red potatoes and zucchini. The potatoes added bulk, and the zucchini lent a bright flavor and nice texture that kept our soup tasting fresh. Seeding the zucchini turned out to be an important step, as unseeded zucchini turned slimy by the end of cooking.

At this point, we were nearly there; our soup had a deep flavor from the spices and aromatics and good heft from the vegetables and chickpeas, but it had taken on an overly vegetal flavor. We knew from experience that vegetable broth can be tinny and overly sweet, so we tested side-by-side batches of our soup with all vegetable broth, half vegetable and half chicken broth, all chicken broth, and all water. Tasters unanimously chose the all chicken–broth version; the chicken broth lent a savory richness that was subtle yet present, and it nicely balanced the flavors of the other components in our soup.

NOTES FROM THE TEST KITCHEN

SEEDING SUMMER SQUASH OR ZUCCHINI
Both yellow squash and zucchini are filled with small translucent seeds that can have bitter taste and slimy texture. To avoid slippery squash in your final recipe, make sure to choose small to medium specimens that weigh 8 to 10 ounces (they contain fewer seeds), and then seed your squash using the following procedure.

Halve squash lengthwise, then use spoon or melon baller to scoop out seeds.

For a few finishing touches, tasters were evenly divided between parsley and mint as garnishes, so we kept both as options. And in lieu of the preserved lemon, we simply served our soup with lemon wedges to contribute a little brightness. This Moroccan-inspired soup offered so much flavor that it was just a bonus that it also happened to be a great healthy choice.

Moroccan Chickpea Soup

SERVES 8

If you don't have hot paprika, substitute ½ teaspoon of regular (or sweet) paprika and a pinch of cayenne pepper. You can substitute vegetable broth for the chicken broth to make this dish vegetarian.

- 1 onion, chopped fine
- 1 tablespoon canola oil
- 1 teaspoon sugar
  Salt and pepper
- 4 garlic cloves, minced
- ½ teaspoon hot paprika
- ¼ teaspoon saffron threads, crumbled
- ¼ teaspoon ground ginger
- ¼ teaspoon ground cumin
- 2 (15-ounce) cans chickpeas, rinsed
- 1 pound red potatoes, cut into ½-inch pieces
- 1 (14.5-ounce) can diced tomatoes
- 4 cups low-sodium chicken broth
- 1 zucchini, seeded and cut into ½-inch pieces
- ¼ cup minced fresh parsley and/or mint
  Lemon wedges

1. Combine onion, oil, sugar, and ⅛ teaspoon salt in Dutch oven. Cover and cook over medium-low heat, stirring occasionally, until softened, 8 to 10 minutes. Stir in garlic, paprika, saffron, ginger, and cumin and cook until fragrant, about 30 seconds.

2. Stir in chickpeas, potatoes, tomatoes, and broth. Bring to simmer, partially cover, and cook until potatoes are tender, about 20 minutes. Stir in zucchini and continue to simmer until tender, 5 to 10 minutes longer.

3. Mash some of potatoes against side of pot with spoon to thicken soup slightly. Stir in parsley and season with salt and pepper to taste. Serve with lemon wedges.

PER 1⅓-CUP SERVING: Cal 150; Fat 3.5g; Sat fat 0g; Chol 0mg; Carb 25g; Protein 6g; Fiber 5g; Sodium 540mg

WINTER SQUASH CHOWDER

VEGETABLE CHOWDERS AREN'T LIMITED TO CORN. Consider winter squash, a great candidate since its sweet, subtle flavor pairs well with many ingredients, especially warm spices (and, on the less healthy end of the spectrum, smoky bacon). Plus it offers myriad health benefits: It is high in fiber, low in fat, and full of vitamin B6 (which supports the heart, brain, and nervous system). Although squash can take a relatively long time to cook when roasted whole, bite-size pieces cook more quickly—making it perfect for a light and healthy soup that doesn't take hours to prepare.

Our main concern was how to best accentuate the mild, sweet flavor of the squash without overpowering it. We'd also have to carefully consider the aromatics and other ingredients to be incorporated; while we worried that a heavy hand with any one spice might negate the flavor of the squash, we were also aware that the squash's sweetness could easily take over. The success of our chowder rested on properly balancing the sweet and savory elements.

We tackled the squash first, narrowing down the varieties that would be suitable for chowder. Acorn squash can be sour and stringy, so it was nixed. Easy-to-find butternut squash, with its smooth, buttery flavor, seemed like a good candidate. Carnival and delicata squashes, which are starting to gain in popularity, also seemed like strong contenders. Carnival squash is creamy, delicate, buttery, and sweet, and delicata, which is also sweet, has a pleasant flavor reminiscent of corn. We made them our alternates to the butternut since they can be harder to find. Other varieties, such as sugar pumpkin and spaghetti, were cut from the running, as they can be too fibrous.

With our squash choices settled, we set out to select aromatics and a few other key ingredients that could provide the proper flavor backdrop for the squash. For a meaty base, we started by cooking a small amount of bacon. Then we sautéed onion, garlic, and a little thyme in the rendered fat before stirring in some broth along with a bay leaf. At this point, we added the squash, cut into small pieces, and let it simmer until tender.

After trying our first attempt, tasters commented that they appreciated the smokiness contributed by the bacon but thought it was starting to take over the chowder. Looking for a more subtle inclusion, we hit on pancetta, an unsmoked Italian bacon. It provided the same meaty, salty undertones, and with just 2 ounces in the recipe, we were still well within our healthy-cooking limits.

For spices and herbs, our teaspoon of thyme and bay leaf were essential, but we needed to look for additional seasonings that would pair well with the squash. Warm nutmeg and slightly bitter sage provided just the right savory notes that the soup needed. We also found that a small amount of dark brown sugar added some rich, caramel notes that worked very well with the squash's natural sweetness.

For the broth, we settled on a combination of chicken broth and vegetable broth; a little sweetness from vegetable broth complemented the delicate flavors in our recipe, and the chicken broth brought it into balance. We also needed to address the broth's consistency because at this point it was too thin to be considered a chowder. We had been hoping that some of the squash's natural starch would thicken the soup, but that hadn't been the case. To properly thicken the base, we had to stir in some flour. We started with just 1 tablespoon and worked our way up in single-tablespoon increments until we achieved the right consistency. A third of a cup gave the chowder a thick, but not gloppy, consistency that tasters approved. As for the requisite dairy for our chowder, we tried batches with heavy cream, half-and-half, and milk. The milk was too thin and had a tendency to break. We settled on half-and-half because it imparted richness and lent a velvety texture without feeling too heavy or making our chowder too fatty.

Tasters were mostly happy at this point, but some felt the chowder could use another vegetable to round it out. Specifically, they wanted a hearty green that would provide a nice foil to the sweetness of the soup. Bitter kale was the answer. It held up well to simmering, getting tender and nicely wilted without completely melting away.

With balanced flavors and textures and just 6 grams of fat and less than 200 calories per serving, the hearty chowder had it all.

NOTES FROM THE TEST KITCHEN

PREPARING BUTTERNUT SQUASH

1. After removing stem and root ends, cut squash in half crosswise where thinner neck meets thicker base.

2. Use vegetable peeler or paring knife to peel skin from squash, then cut base in half to expose seeds.

3. Use large spoon to scrape seeds and stringy pulp from base of squash. Chop each piece of squash as desired.

PREPARING SWISS CHARD, KALE, OR BOK CHOY

1. Cut away leafy green portion from either side of stalk or stem using chef's knife.

2. Stack several leaves on top of one another, and either slice leaves crosswise or chop them into pieces (as directed in recipe). Wash and dry leaves after they are cut, using salad spinner.

3. We often like to include bok choy stalks and chard stems in our recipes. To prepare either, wash stems thoroughly, then trim and cut them into small pieces (or as directed in each recipe).

WINTER SQUASH CHOWDER

Winter Squash Chowder

SERVES 8

We prefer squash that is smaller in size because it has a more concentrated flavor and finer texture than larger squash does. Delicata or carnival squash can be substituted for the butternut squash. Serve with grated Parmesan cheese, if desired.

    2   ounces pancetta, cut into ¼-inch pieces
    1   onion, chopped fine
    2   teaspoons canola oil
    3   garlic cloves, minced
    1   teaspoon minced fresh thyme or ¼ teaspoon dried
        Pinch ground nutmeg, plus extra to taste
    ⅓   cup all-purpose flour
    4   cups low-sodium chicken broth
    3   cups vegetable broth
    3   pounds butternut squash, peeled, seeded, and cut
        into ½-inch pieces (8 cups) (see page 37)
    1   bay leaf
    8   ounces kale, stemmed and leaves sliced
        ¼ inch thick
    ½   cup half-and-half
    1   tablespoon minced fresh sage
    1   teaspoon dark brown sugar
        Salt and pepper

1. Cook pancetta in Dutch oven over medium heat until crisp, 5 to 7 minutes. Reduce heat to medium-low, stir in onion and oil, cover, and cook until onion is softened, 8 to 10 minutes. Stir in garlic, thyme, and nutmeg and cook until fragrant, about 30 seconds. Stir in flour and cook for 2 minutes.

2. Gradually whisk in chicken broth and vegetable broth, scraping up any browned bits and smoothing out any lumps. Stir in squash and bay leaf and bring to boil. Cover, reduce to simmer, and cook until squash begins to soften, 10 to 15 minutes.

3. Stir in kale and continue to simmer, covered, until squash and kale are tender, about 10 minutes longer.

4. Off heat, remove bay leaf and stir in half-and-half, sage, and sugar. Season with salt, pepper, and nutmeg to taste and serve.

PER 1½-CUP SERVING: Cal 190; Fat 6g; Sat fat 2g; Chol 10mg; Carb 32g; Protein 6g; Fiber 5g; Sodium 670mg

RHODE ISLAND RED CLAM CHOWDER

WHILE CLAM CHOWDER AFICIONADOS DEBATE THE relative merits of white (and often flour-thickened) New England Chowder versus the tomato-based Manhattan-style red chowder, in Rhode Island you can find yet more spins on this controversial stew. There, locals enjoy both a broth-based clear clam chowder as well as Rhode Island red, a version that distinguishes itself by the addition of tomato puree to a clam broth base. With its combination of chopped fresh clams, tender chunks of potato, and a richly flavored, creamy base achieved without adding any high-fat dairy products, this lesser-known red version seemed like a great choice for our healthy collection.

Most of the recipes we found that were touted as "authentic" and "original" turned out a simple, if not particularly inspiring, chowder. Many start with cooking salt pork in a large pot until the fat is rendered. To this fat, onions are added and cooked until softened, then tomato puree, clam juice, and water go into the pot to form the base of the soup. Next up are the diced potatoes, which are simmered until tender, followed, finally, by chopped clams. We found that the resulting chowders tasted thin and sharp, a far cry from the creamy-tasting, rich, tomatoey clam soup that Rhode Islanders hold so dear. We decided to tackle the ingredients, one by one, in our effort to make a better bowl. We started with the clams.

Most of the recipes we found called for chopped clams, which leaves it up in the air as to whether you should shuck them yourself, buy them already cooked and chopped from a fishmonger, or, heaven forbid, choose canned chopped clams. We knew that starting with fresh, live clams would be key to getting great flavor. From test kitchen experience, we already knew that our favorite chowder clam, the cherrystone, offers great flavor and value, so it would be our clam of choice here. All we would need to do was steam the clams in water, stirring them halfway through to ensure that they cooked evenly. Checking the pot every few minutes to remove clams as they opened would ensure that every one was perfectly cooked and none turned tough or chewy.

What separates a good bowl of Rhode Island red clam chowder from a great one is the broth, so that was next on our list. We were after a broth that looked and tasted creamy (without the addition of cream) and perfectly balanced the flavors of clams and tomatoes. However, most recipes we tested produced either a tomato soup with clams or a clam-rich broth with just a hint of tomato. Addressing the clam flavor, we found that using all the steaming liquid from the clams resulted in an unpalatably salty base. Instead, we found that a combination of 2 cups of the clams' steaming liquid and 3 cups of bottled clam juice yielded a chowder base with great clam flavor minus the salt lick.

Next we tackled the tomato flavor. Most of the recipes we uncovered called for tomato puree, but we found that it produced a sharp, harsh-tasting chowder, with little tomato richness. We rounded up all of our other tomato options: fresh, diced, crushed, and whole. We pureed them until smooth and then added each to a batch of our clam broth. Tasters unanimously preferred the batch made with whole canned tomatoes, praising it for its true tomato flavor. Still, tasters felt that the chowder needed more tomato presence and complexity.

There was one tomato-based ingredient we had overlooked up to this point: tomato paste. One recipe called for sautéing the tomato paste, tomatoes, and some onion until dry and browned to concentrate the flavors. We gave it a shot, adding our clam broth to the browned tomato mixture before pureeing it a blender until completely smooth. Not only did this base have incredible tomato flavor, but it was also surprisingly creamy.

When it came to the potatoes, Yukon Golds were our favorite, besting both super-starchy russets (which crumbled into mashed potatoes) and high-moisture red potatoes (which absorbed little of the chowder's flavor). Most Rhode Island red clam chowders call for salt pork to add meaty flavor, but our tasters preferred the gentle smokiness of bacon. Since crisping the bacon and then pureeing it with the rest of the broth ingredients left the soup with an odd grainy texture, we borrowed a trick from our Split Pea and Ham Soup (page 31), adding whole slices of raw bacon (two did the trick) to the chowder as it simmered, then removing them prior to serving. This gave our chowder just the right amount of smoky bacon flavor and aroma without the added fat or calories. And although untraditional in the Ocean State, we found that a splash of sherry added a nice brightness and complexity. Our guilt-free Rhode Island Red Clam Chowder was ready for its big introduction.

NOTES FROM THE TEST KITCHEN

REMOVING CLAM MEAT FROM THE SHELL

1. Steam clams until they just open, as seen on right, rather than completely open, as shown on left.

2. Carefully use paring knife to open clam shell.

3. Once open, discard top shell and use knife to cut clam from bottom shell.

Rhode Island Red Clam Chowder
SERVES 6

Be sure to use fresh clams for this soup. This soup is typically served with oyster crackers.

- 3 cups water
- 6 pounds medium hard-shell clams, such as cherrystones, scrubbed
- 2 teaspoons canola oil
- 1 (28-ounce) can whole tomatoes, drained with juice reserved
- 1 onion, chopped fine
- 1 tablespoon tomato paste
- 4 garlic cloves, minced
- 3 (8-ounce) bottles clam juice
- 1½ pounds Yukon Gold potatoes, peeled and cut into ½-inch pieces

2 slices bacon

1 bay leaf

2 tablespoons minced fresh parsley

2 teaspoons dry sherry

½ teaspoon sugar

   Salt and pepper

1. Bring water to boil in Dutch oven. Add clams, cover, and cook for 5 minutes. Stir clams thoroughly, cover, and continue to cook until just beginning to open, 2 to 5 minutes longer. As clams open, transfer to large bowl and let cool slightly. Discard any unopened clams.

2. Measure out and reserve 2 cups of clam steaming liquid, avoiding any gritty sediment that has settled on bottom of pot. Remove clam meat from shells and chop coarse.

3. In clean Dutch oven, heat oil over medium heat. Add tomatoes, onion, and tomato paste and cook until dry and beginning to brown, 11 to 13 minutes. Stir in garlic and cook until fragrant, about 30 seconds. Stir in reserved clam steaming liquid, reserved tomato juice, and bottled clam juice, scraping up any browned bits.

4. Working in batches, puree soup until smooth, 1 to 2 minutes. Return soup to clean pot. Stir in potatoes, bacon slices, and bay leaf and bring to boil. Reduce to gentle simmer and cook until potatoes are tender, 20 to 25 minutes.

5. Off heat, remove bacon slices and bay leaf. Stir in parsley, sherry, and sugar and season with salt and pepper to taste. Stir in chopped clams, cover, and let stand until warmed through, about 1 minute. Serve.

PER 1½-CUP SERVING: Cal 270; Fat 4.5g; Sat fat 1g; Chol 50mg; Carb 33g; Protein 22g; Fiber 3g; Sodium 600mg

QUINOA AND VEGETABLE STEW

QUINOA IS AN ANCIENT GRAIN THAT HAS GAINED A lot of popularity in the United States over the past several years because of its healthy profile: It has a high protein content (it is considered a complete protein, which means it contains all of the essential amino acids that are necessary for growth, making it especially great for vegetarians), and it provides a number of vitamins and minerals. In countries along the Andean highlands,

this "super food" plays a starring role in many dishes, among them a quinoa stew. It traditionally includes a good mix of vegetables, with potatoes and corn at the forefront, and while some recipes might also call for meat, many rely solely on the quinoa for protein. The meatless version struck us as a great healthy vegetarian stew to add to our collection.

Most of the traditional recipes we found followed the same basic cooking method. First, a mix of cumin, coriander, and annatto powder was toasted in oil until fragrant. Next, onion, garlic, green pepper, and tomato were added and sautéed to form the background notes before broth, water, or a combination of the two was stirred into the pot along with native potatoes and giant kernels of Andean corn. When these were almost tender, quinoa was added and simmered until cooked through. Garnished with diced avocado, cilantro, and salty queso fresco, the authentic stews were hearty, delicious, and filling. This method seemed like the right place to start, but we needed to find a way to work around the obscure ingredients, such as annatto powder and Peruvian varieties of potatoes and corn, to make a recipe with an ingredient list that was manageable for American home cooks.

After cooking a few batches of the stew, we were able to identify what exactly the annatto powder contributed. We found it to be slightly sweet and earthy, with just a hint of peppery bitterness. Although its flavor can be somewhat subtle, the color it lends to foods is anything but. Just a teaspoon or two was enough to turn a pot of our stew a rich shade of crimson. We quickly realized that annatto powder has a flavor profile and color similar to those of sweet paprika, an easy switch for us to make. The cumin and coriander found in traditional recipes also made good additions that rounded out the flavor. To prevent our spices from burning (which happened in many of the recipes we tested), we added them to the pot only after we had sautéed our aromatics.

For our aromatics, the traditional combination of onion, green bell pepper, tomato, and garlic was OK, but tasters complained about the texture and flavor of the pepper, which turned army green and flavorless by the time the stew was done. Red bell pepper, on the other hand, remained sweet and fire-engine red. Tasters also felt the tomato flavor was spent by the end of cooking, so we waited to stir fresh tomatoes (preferred over canned since we had several other fresh vegetables in our recipe) into the pot until the end, just so they could warm through. With that tweak, they provided a welcome burst of freshness and clean tomato flavor. After adding a few cups of vegetable broth (which united the varying elements of the stew and was more flavorful than water alone or in combination) to the softened aromatics, we had to make a decision about the other vegetables that would give our stew its South American feel.

Without access to native Peruvian potatoes or Andean corn at our local supermarkets, we had to find acceptable substitutes. After getting our hands on some Peruvian potatoes and doing some comparing with our own domestic varieties, we found the texture of red potatoes to be the closest option. As for the corn, nothing came close to the dense, chewy, and nutty Andean corn, but tasters almost unanimously preferred the sweeter stew made with our own locally grown corn anyway. Finally, to round out our vegetable selection and add some green to the pot, we stirred in some frozen peas. Happy with the hearty mix of vegetables, next we focused on the quinoa.

We've cooked a fair bit of quinoa in the test kitchen before, so we knew it can go from crunchy to mushy almost instantly. Wary of overcooking the quinoa, we

added it to the pot only after the potatoes had softened (instead of until they were almost tender, as in the traditional recipes). After about 10 minutes, we were rewarded with firm yet cushy bites of quinoa, but tasters felt the broth lacked body. One colleague suggested stretching the cooking time of the quinoa as far as we could, just a few extra minutes, in the hope that the quinoa would release additional starch into the stew without softening too much. After a few more minutes of gentle simmering, the quinoa offered a slight chew and had also given up sufficient starch so the broth had good body.

To finish, we liked creamy avocado and citrusy cilantro (we were careful not to go overboard on the avocado to keep our recipe healthy). Some wanted salty queso fresco so we made it optional. This quinoa stew was the best of both worlds: a humble ode to its authentic roots and a streamlined yet flavorful offering ready for modern-day tastes.

Quinoa and Vegetable Stew

SERVES 6

This stew tends to thicken as it sits; add additional warm vegetable broth as needed before serving to loosen. Be sure to rinse the quinoa to remove its bitter coating (known as saponin) before cooking. You can also garnish this stew with queso fresco, if desired.

- 1 onion, chopped fine
- 1 red bell pepper, stemmed, seeded, and cut into ½-inch pieces
- 2 teaspoons canola oil
  Salt and pepper
- 5 garlic cloves, minced
- 1 tablespoon paprika
- 2 teaspoons ground coriander
- 1½ teaspoons ground cumin
- 6 cups vegetable broth
- 1 pound red potatoes, cut into ½-inch pieces
- 1 cup quinoa, rinsed
- 1 large ear corn, kernels cut from cob, or 1 cup frozen
- 2 tomatoes, cored and chopped coarse
- 1 cup frozen peas
- ½ cup minced fresh cilantro
- 1 avocado, halved, pitted, and cut into ½-inch pieces

NOTES FROM THE TEST KITCHEN

RINSING GRAINS AND RICE

Place grains or rice in fine-mesh strainer and rinse under cool water until water runs clear, occasionally stirring grains or rice around lightly with your hand. Let drain briefly.

CUTTING CORN OFF THE COB

Standing ear of corn upright inside large bowl, carefully cut kernels from cob using paring knife.

1. Combine onion, bell pepper, oil, and ⅛ teaspoon salt in Dutch oven. Cover and cook over medium-low heat, stirring occasionally, until softened, 8 to 10 minutes. Stir in garlic, paprika, coriander, and cumin and cook until fragrant, about 30 seconds. Stir in broth and potatoes and bring to boil. Reduce to gentle simmer and cook for 10 minutes.

2. Stir in quinoa and continue to simmer for 8 minutes. Stir in corn and continue to simmer until potatoes and quinoa are just tender, 5 to 7 minutes. Stir in tomatoes and peas and let heat through, about 2 minutes.

3. Off heat, stir in cilantro and season with salt and pepper to taste. Garnish individual bowls with avocado before serving.

PER 1⅔-CUP SERVING: Cal 330; Fat 9g; Sat fat 1g; Chol 0mg; Carb 54g; Protein 9g; Fiber 9g; Sodium 650mg

ARTICHOKE, BELL PEPPER, AND CHICKPEA TAGINE

TAGINES ARE A NORTH AFRICAN SPECIALTY. THESE exotically spiced, assertively flavored stews are slow-cooked in earthenware vessels of the same name. They can include all manner of meats, vegetables, and fruits. Given tagines' complex flavor profile, it's not surprising that vegetable tagines are no less delicious than their meat-centric cousins. We wanted a healthy vegetable tagine with a hearty mix of vegetables that could stand on their own, without the need for meat.

We decided to start by picking our key ingredients. The earthy flavor of artichokes, a popular Mediterranean vegetable, came to mind first. We also liked the idea of chickpeas, another mainstay of Mediterranean cooking, as they could contribute additional heartiness and a nutty flavor. We envisioned a stew overflowing with big, rich chunks of artichokes and tender chickpeas, enlivened with pungent garlic, warm spices, briny olives, and tangy lemon. With this lineup, we knew we were on track for making a tagine that would be a speedy but flavorful weeknight supper.

Starting with the artichokes, we considered all the available options: fresh, frozen, jarred, and canned. Fresh artichokes were quickly scratched off the list. Though they taste great, fresh artichokes are just too time-consuming to prepare. Canned artichokes were too

waterlogged for a stew no matter how well we drained them or how long we browned them, and so they were also eliminated. Jarred artichokes, which are packed in vinaigrette, seemed like a possibility, as we thought the flavors of the marinade might complement the traditional tagine herbs and spices. However, we couldn't have been more wrong—in a quick test using a basic working recipe, the marinade dominated our tagine, even when we thoroughly rinsed the artichokes first. Finally, we moved on to frozen artichokes. After thawing them and draining off the excess liquid, we patted them dry and sautéed them to drive off any remaining moisture. These artichokes—deep golden brown in color, with an intense, earthy flavor—were the clear winner.

Next we moved on to the chickpeas, opting to use canned to keep with our speedy theme. Two cans provided ample heartiness. For more substance and a stronger vegetable presence, we added two bell peppers, cut into matchsticks for visual appeal. Tasters preferred the sweet flavor of red or yellow bell peppers over the more overtly vegetal green peppers.

At this point, we referred back to previous tagines the test kitchen had developed to help narrow down the aromatics, cooking liquid, and spices. An onion was essential; it mellowed into a sweet, subtle flavor when cooked. As for the garlic, eight cloves offered the ideal amount of headiness and depth. For the liquid component, we used a few cups of store-bought vegetable broth to keep with our vegetable theme. Thickened with just 2 tablespoons of flour, the broth was the perfect consistency to coat the vegetables. A tablespoon of honey, stirred in with the broth, maintained the balance of sweet and savory we were after.

The lemon flavor in authentic tagines comes from preserved lemons, which are difficult to find and impossible to make at home in a reasonable amount of time. However, we found that sautéing several strips of lemon zest contributed similar flavor to our speedy tagine. We thought adding lemon juice might boost the brightness, but we found that its acidity stood out too much against the mild vegetables. Grated lemon zest, on the other hand, imparted bright lemon flavor that complemented the strips of zest. For the olives, we tried several kinds of green and black Mediterranean olives, and tasters preferred the more subdued flavor of kalamata olives. They weren't too salty or too briny, and they matched the other components nicely.

As for the spices, garam masala—a spice blend of coriander, cloves, cardamom, cumin, cinnamon, black pepper, and nutmeg—gave our tagine the complexity and warmth we were seeking. Paprika gave it a subtle sweetness and a deep, exotic red hue. Tasters wanted more pronounced sweetness, and since dried fruits are often found in tagines, that seemed like the obvious route to take. Dates, figs, and apricots each offered interesting flavor, but ultimately we liked the look and subdued sweetness of golden raisins the best. A little cilantro added the right fresh flavor.

Our stew was close, but it tasted a little lean. Looking for ways to enrich it without adding too much fat, we landed on yogurt. Stirring ⅓ cup of plain low-fat yogurt into the pot was good, but plain 2 percent Greek yogurt, with its fuller, richer flavor and texture, was even better. At last, we had a vegetable tagine that tasted every bit as bright and exotic as its meaty counterparts—and was just as satisfying.

Artichoke, Bell Pepper, and Chickpea Tagine

SERVES 6

Serve with couscous or rice. Do not substitute regular yogurt for the Greek because the sauce will not be as thick and creamy.

3	tablespoons olive oil
18	ounces frozen artichoke hearts, thawed, patted dry, and halved
2	yellow or red bell peppers, stemmed, seeded, and cut into ¼-inch-wide strips
1	onion, chopped fine
4	(3-inch) strips lemon zest plus 1 teaspoon grated zest
2½	teaspoons paprika
2	teaspoons garam masala
8	garlic cloves, minced
2	tablespoons all-purpose flour
3	cups vegetable broth
1	tablespoon honey
2	(15-ounce) cans chickpeas, rinsed
½	cup pitted kalamata olives, halved
½	cup golden raisins
⅓	cup 2 percent Greek yogurt
½	cup minced fresh cilantro
	Salt and pepper

1. Heat 1 tablespoon oil in Dutch oven over medium heat until shimmering. Add artichokes and cook until golden brown, 5 to 7 minutes; transfer to bowl.

2. Add 1 tablespoon oil to pot and return to medium heat until shimmering. Add bell peppers, onion, and lemon zest strips and cook until vegetables are softened and lightly browned, 5 to 7 minutes.

3. Stir in paprika, garam masala, and three-quarters of garlic and cook until fragrant, about 30 seconds. Stir in flour and cook for 1 minute. Slowly stir in broth and honey, scraping up any browned bits and smoothing out any lumps.

4. Stir in browned artichokes, chickpeas, olives, and raisins and bring to simmer. Reduce heat to medium-low, cover, and cook, stirring occasionally, until liquid has thickened slightly and vegetables are tender, about 15 minutes.

5. Off heat, remove lemon zest strips. Stir ½ cup of sauce from pot into yogurt to temper, then stir yogurt mixture into pot. Stir in remaining 1 tablespoon oil, remaining garlic, grated lemon zest, and cilantro. Season with salt and pepper to taste and serve.

PER 1½-CUP SERVING: Cal 330; Fat 11g; Sat fat 1.5g; Chol 0mg; Carb 49g; Protein 10g; Fiber 11g; Sodium 540mg

NOTES FROM THE TEST KITCHEN

VEGETABLE BROTH
There are a slew of vegetable broth options available today, but how do they all taste? We sampled 10 broths, heated and served plain and also cooked into soups and risotto. Flavors ranged from bland to overpowering; some broths were astonishingly salty or sweet, others oddly sour, and many tasted nothing like vegetables. What we learned is that broths listing vegetable content (whether from fresh whole vegetables or extracts) first on the ingredient list fared best. Also important were generous amounts of flavor-enhancing additives (such as MSG) and salt. Of the ten brands, Swanson Vegetarian Vegetable Broth was the overall winner; tasters praised its "good balance of vegetable flavors." But with 940 milligrams of sodium per cup, it was too sodium-laden for healthier recipes. We used our runner-up, **College Inn Garden Vegetable Broth**, which was deemed "one of the best," with only 590 milligrams of sodium per cup.

ARTICHOKE, BELL PEPPER, AND CHICKPEA TAGINE

CHICKEN AND LEEK SOUP

RUMORED TO BE A FAVORITE OF MARY QUEEN OF Scots, the chicken and leek soup known as cock-a-leekie has a serious pedigree—the first recorded version of this recipe dates back to the late 1500s. And after you give it a try, you can certainly see why it has withstood the test of time. The best versions finesse a rich, hearty, and surprisingly luxurious soup out of just a few simple ingredients. We thought this naturally light soup would be a great candidate for a modern take.

All of the recipes we uncovered in our research called for chicken, chicken broth, and leeks, but that's where the similarities ended. Many recipes disagreed about how much of a role the leeks should play. Some recipes called for simmering an entire bunch of leeks with the chicken, resulting in a bitter soup, while other recipes treated the ingredient as a garnish, with just a smattering added at the end. Also, some recipes called for the use of a grain, such as barley, oats, or rice, for thickness; others included prunes for sweetness. After trying out some rather laborious renditions, we decided a little American modernization would go a long way toward making an authentic-tasting yet streamlined cock-a-leekie.

The first step in many traditional recipes is stewing a rooster for up to 8 hours to create a flavorful stock. Searching for an easier path, we bucked tradition and turned to a technique we have used in the past when simplifying chicken soups: fortifying store-bought chicken broth. First we browned bone-in skin-on chicken breasts, which left a nice fond on the bottom of the pot that would serve as a good flavor base. After we removed the chicken from the pot and added the broth and leeks, the chicken breasts (skin removed) went into the soup to poach whole. Once they were cooked through, we removed them from the pot to let the soup finish cooking. By cooking the chicken this way, we ensured that the meat remained moist and tender, and our soup had a deeper, more chicken-y flavor. In a side-by-side tasting of simple bowls of stock and chicken, tasters preferred shredded chicken to cubes or strips, so once the meat was poached, we shredded it into bite-size pieces and simply stirred the pieces back into the broth to warm through before serving.

It was now time to consider the other starring ingredient, the leeks. We knew we didn't want a bitter, overly leek-y soup, but we also didn't want to relegate the leeks to a simple garnish. We wanted a soup somewhere in the middle: The leek flavor had to be persistent but pleasant, and the leeks themselves had to contribute some texture. To start, we sliced a few leeks and sautéed them after browning the chicken. After about 10 minutes of being cooked with the cover on, our leeks had released a great deal of flavor, and the resulting soup was rich, with a subtle sweetness that tasters appreciated. However, there was no leek texture by the time they made it into the serving bowl, so we added a few more sliced leeks to the pot after we added the broth. This second bunch of leeks didn't have as much time to soften, so they provided the texture we were looking for, as well as an additional burst of fresh leek flavor.

It was time to consider whether we wanted to add a grain as many of the older recipes did. While we generally appreciate the texture and heartiness that grains add to brothy soups, we found that in this recipe they muddied the clean leek flavor that we had worked so hard to achieve. Cloves also featured heavily in a number of recipes, and while tasters found too much overpowered the leek flavor, a pinch of ground cloves, added with a couple of cloves of minced garlic, provided just the right amount of warm spice flavor.

Prunes, another fairly common addition, originally served the purpose of disguising the often-gamy flavor of the rooster. While gaminess was clearly not a problem for us, tasters actually preferred the soups that included prunes, noting that their flavor was more balanced and complex. In some recipes the prunes were cooked for hours; in others, they were chopped fine and added as a garnish. Once again, we settled in the middle, preferring to cut the prunes into larger pieces (small pieces just disintegrated) and adding them to the soup with the shredded chicken to simmer for just a few minutes. This technique allowed the prunes to soften slightly but still maintain their shape, ensuring rich, sweet bites of prune throughout.

With a full, rich leek flavor, sweetness from a handful of prunes, and a hearty texture from the two additions of leeks, our cock-a-leekie soup seemed destined for many more years of popularity.

Chicken and Leek Soup

SERVES 8

Look for leeks with large white and light green parts. If your leeks are small, you may need a few extra for this recipe.

- 2 (12-ounce) bone-in split chicken breasts, trimmed of all visible fat
  Salt and pepper
- 1 teaspoon canola oil
- 3 pounds leeks, white and light green parts only, halved lengthwise, sliced ¼ inch thick, and washed thoroughly
- 2 garlic cloves, minced
  Pinch ground cloves
- 8 cups low-sodium chicken broth
- 10 pitted prunes, chopped
- 2 tablespoons minced fresh parsley

NOTES FROM THE TEST KITCHEN

PREPARING LEEKS

1. Trim root and dark green leaves.

2. Cut trimmed leek base in half lengthwise, then slice crosswise into ¼-inch pieces.

3. Rinse cut leeks thoroughly to remove dirt and sand using either salad spinner or bowl of water.

1. Pat chicken dry with paper towels and season with ⅛ teaspoon salt and ⅛ teaspoon pepper. Heat oil in Dutch oven over medium-high heat until just smoking. Carefully lay chicken, skin side down, in pot and cook until well browned on first side, about 5 minutes. Transfer chicken to plate and remove and discard skin.

2. Reduce heat to medium-low and add half of leeks and ⅛ teaspoon salt. Cover and cook until very soft, 8 to 10 minutes. Stir in garlic and cloves and cook until fragrant, about 30 seconds. Stir in broth, scraping up any browned bits, and bring to simmer. Add chicken and continue to simmer until chicken registers 160 degrees, about 15 minutes longer. Transfer chicken to plate and let cool slightly. Using 2 forks, shred chicken into bite-size pieces, discarding bones.

3. Stir in remaining leeks and gently simmer until leeks are just tender, 5 to 7 minutes. Stir in shredded chicken and prunes and let heat through, about 2 minutes. Off heat, stir in parsley, season with salt and pepper to taste, and serve.

PER 1½-CUP SERVING: Cal 160; Fat 2g; Sat fat 0g; Chol 30mg; Carb 20g; Protein 15g; Fiber 2g; Sodium 690mg

ULTIMATE BEEF CHILI

FULL OF TENDER CHUNKS OF MEAT AND CREAMY beans coated with a rich, heady, spice-laden sauce, chili is the epitome of comfort food. While the details vary from region to region, one thing does stay the same—it is not a dish to be taken lightly, literally. Each serving can tally more than 600 calories and 20 grams of fat. We had recently perfected a recipe for our favorite chili; could we develop a lighter, healthier version that still hit the spot?

TEST KITCHEN
MAKEOVER

When developing our recent recipe—which featured diced beef, pinto beans, tomatoes, onions, jalapeños, and garlic—we had made a few key discoveries. In lieu of chili powder, which gave the chili a gritty, dusty texture and a subpar flavor, we found we were far better off making our own chili powder. Of all the dried chiles that are available in most supermarkets, we chose anchos for their earthiness and árbols for their smooth heat. We removed the stems and seeds, then toasted the anchos in a dry skillet until they were fragrant (the very thin árbols burned when we tried to toast them). After cooling the anchos, we pulverized them in the food processor with the árbols, 2 teaspoons each of cumin and oregano, and a couple of tablespoons of cornmeal, a surprise ingredient that added a great subtle corn flavor to our chili along with its thickening power. Adding a bit of broth to the food processor encouraged the chile pieces to engage with the blade rather than simply fly around the bowl. The chili made with our homemade blend not only was much more deeply flavored but also had a remarkably smooth sauce.

We also tested countless "secret ingredients" that you often see cited online and in winning competition chili recipes. Most didn't make the cut: Guinness, coffee (both too bitter), wine, prunes, and Coca-Cola were all out. Peanut butter was a good thickener but had an odd aftertaste, and flour and brown sugar were both OK for thickening and flavor, respectively, but boring). Ingredients intended to enhance meaty flavor (anchovies, soy sauce, mushrooms, and even Marmite) threw the chili out of balance by overpowering the chiles and aromatics, so they too were off the list. Meanwhile, lighter lager beer was in, as it complemented the aromatics nicely, and molasses lent a good earthy, smoky depth. Several recipes out there suggested members of the chocolate family, including unsweetened chocolate, unsweetened cocoa, and bittersweet chocolate. All performed well, and tasters appreciated the complexity that each provided, but in the end tasters deemed unsweetened cocoa the winner.

So after quick-soaking our beans, we prepared the chili paste, sautéed the aromatics (onion, garlic, and jalapeño), then added the chili paste, some canned diced tomatoes, and molasses to the pot. To that we added our beans and chicken broth (which offered better balance than beef broth) and brought it all to a simmer. Meanwhile, we separately browned beef in batches, deglazed the pan with some beer, and added it all to the pot. After about 90 minutes in the oven both the meat and beans were tender. Tasty, of course; healthy, not really.

The culprit was the beef. Our earlier tests had run brisket, chuck-eye roast, blade steak, and short ribs, all cut in ¾-inch dice, through the kitchen. Though the short ribs were extremely tender, some tasters felt that they tasted too much like pot roast, and they are way too fatty for a healthy chili anyway. The brisket was wonderfully beefy but simply too lean and turned a bit tough. The two favorites were chuck-eye roast and blade steaks, both favored for their tenderness and rich flavor. In the end we chose blade steaks because of their easier prep. But our original recipe called for a full 3½ pounds of beef, way too much for a healthy chili serving about six folks.

In the past we have had great success substituting mushrooms for beef to lend meaty flavor and texture without the fat and calories. For our original recipe, we had tested adding them to the pot, but that was when we were using the full amount of beef. It seemed likely, however, that swapping out one for the other, rather than simply adding on, would work. We cut our beef down to 2 pounds (which, once completely trimmed and cubed, was only about 1½ pounds), and after browning the beef, we browned a pound of mushrooms. We tested white, cremini, portobello, and shiitake, and meaty portobellos were the hands-down winner. They actually resembled the blade steak so well that it took some tasters a few minutes to realize the swap. This substitution also allowed us to cut down the amount of oil from 3 tablespoons to just 3 teaspoons for browning purposes.

Now, clocking in at 450 calories and 12 grams of fat, we had a chili that was healthy and at the same time comforting.

MAKEOVER SPOTLIGHT: ULTIMATE BEEF CHILI

	CALORIES	FAT	SAT FAT	CHOLESTEROL
BEFORE	610	23g	7g	120mg
AFTER	450	12g	3.5g	65mg

Ultimate Beef Chili

SERVES 6

To quick salt-soak the beans, combine 2 quarts water, beans, and 1½ tablespoons salt in Dutch oven and bring to boil over high heat. Remove pot from heat, cover, and let stand for 1 hour. Drain and rinse well. If you prefer a chili with milder spiciness, omit one of the jalapeño chiles and use the lesser amount of arbol chiles.

Salt and pepper

8 ounces (1¼ cups) dried pinto beans, picked over
and rinsed

6 dried ancho chiles, stemmed, seeded, and torn
into 1-inch pieces

2–4 dried árbol chiles, stemmed and seeded

3 tablespoons cornmeal

2 teaspoons dried oregano

2 teaspoons ground cumin

2 teaspoons cocoa

3 cups low-sodium chicken broth

2 onions, chopped coarse

3 small jalapeño chiles, stemmed, seeded, and chopped

3 teaspoons canola oil

4 garlic cloves, minced

1 (14.5-ounce) can diced tomatoes

2 teaspoons light molasses

2 pounds blade steaks, trimmed of gristle and all visible
fat, and cut into ¾-inch pieces

1 (12-ounce) bottle mild lager, such as Budweiser

1 pound portobello mushroom caps, cut into ¾-inch
pieces

1. Dissolve 1½ tablespoons salt in 2 quarts cold water in large bowl or container. Add beans and soak at room temperature for at least 8 hours or up to 24 hours. Drain and rinse well.

2. Adjust oven rack to lower-middle position and heat oven to 300 degrees. Toast ancho chiles in 12-inch skillet over medium-high heat, stirring frequently, until flesh is fragrant, 4 to 6 minutes, reducing heat if chiles begin to smoke. Transfer to bowl and let cool. Do not wash skillet.

3. Process toasted ancho chiles, árbol chiles, cornmeal, oregano, cumin, and cocoa together in food processor until finely ground, about 2 minutes. With processor running, very slowly add ½ cup broth until smooth paste forms, about 45 seconds, scraping down bowl as needed. Transfer paste to small bowl. Pulse onions and jalapeños together in now-empty processor until consistency of chunky salsa, about 6 pulses, scraping down bowl as needed.

4. Heat 1 teaspoon oil in Dutch oven over medium-high heat. Add onion mixture and cook, stirring occasionally, until moisture has evaporated and vegetables are softened, 7 to 9 minutes. Add garlic and cook until

fragrant, about 30 seconds. Stir in chili paste, tomatoes, and molasses until thoroughly combined. Add drained beans and remaining 2½ cups broth; bring to boil, then reduce heat to simmer.

5. Meanwhile, pat beef dry with paper towels and season with ⅛ teaspoon salt and ⅛ teaspoon pepper. Heat 1 teaspoon oil in 12-inch skillet over medium-high heat until shimmering. Brown beef on all sides, about 10 minutes; transfer to Dutch oven. Add ½ bottle lager to skillet, scraping up any browned bits, and bring to simmer. Transfer lager to Dutch oven.

6. Add remaining 1 teaspoon oil and mushrooms to now-empty skillet, cover, and cook over medium heat until mushrooms are very wet, about 5 minutes. Uncover and continue to cook until mushrooms are dry and browned, 5 to 10 minutes; transfer to Dutch oven. Add remaining lager to skillet, scraping up any browned bits, and bring to simmer; transfer to Dutch oven and stir to combine. Bring back to simmer.

7. Cover pot and transfer to oven. Cook until meat and beans are fully tender, 1½ to 2 hours. Let chili stand, uncovered, for 10 minutes. Stir well, season with salt to taste, and serve. (Chili can be refrigerated for up to 3 days.)

PER 1½-CUP SERVING: Cal 450; Fat 12g; Sat fat 3.5g; Chol 65mg; Carb 47g; Protein 36g; Fiber 9g; Sodium 700mg

NOTES FROM THE TEST KITCHEN

TRIMMING BLADE STEAKS

1. Halve each steak lengthwise, leaving gristle on one half.

2. Cut away gristle from half to which it is attached.

THAI-STYLE RED CURRY WITH CHICKEN

THAI-STYLE RED CURRY

COMBINING A PROTEIN AND VEGETABLES IN A highly flavorful base that balances sweet, salty, spicy, and sour at once, Thai curries are a great one-dish meal. Unlike Indian curries that require a mix of dried spices for potent, aromatic flavor, Thai curries depend on a paste, usually made with garlic, ginger, shallots, lemon grass, kaffir lime leaves, galangal, shrimp paste, and chiles, for flavor. These curry pastes can be quite involved, requiring a good amount of time (up to an hour of preparation) and a well-stocked pantry (or refrigerator). But on the upside, once the paste is prepared, the curries themselves come together rather quickly. With the ingredient list and cooking method front of mind, we set out to develop a streamlined Thai curry that would boast bold flavors but not pack on the calories.

We started our testing with the paste, which is typically either red or green, featuring dried red chiles for the former and fresh green chiles for the latter. Unfortunately, the only good paste recipes we found included hard-to-find ingredients; the shortcut recipes all failed miserably. Luckily, we have found in the test kitchen that store-bought curry pastes can be just as good as, or even better than, those that take an hour to prepare. Additionally, many curries use only a small amount of the paste, which made the store-bought paste even more appealing. We decided to develop a boldly flavored red curry with chicken.

Next, we moved on to building the rest of our curry. Often coconut milk is used as the main liquid component for Thai curries, as its sweet flavor and cooling, silky texture balance the curry paste. However, regular coconut milk packed on too much fat and too many calories for our healthy recipe. Could we get the flavor and texture we were after using light coconut milk?

We began by sautéing the curry paste in the pot to deepen its flavor, then we whisked in a can of light coconut milk. The resulting sauce was, not surprisingly, somewhat thin compared to that of a full-fat curry. We solved the issue by adding a teaspoon of cornstarch, which helped thicken it up to the right consistency without adding fat. To give our curry base some balance and more authentic flavor, we added a few tablespoons of fish sauce and a tablespoon of light brown sugar, a salty-sweet combination that lent the contrasting notes and flavor profile our curry needed. We wondered with all these flavors, could we make the base even lighter?

We tried swapping out some of the coconut milk for chicken broth and found most tasters didn't even notice.

For the meat, we quickly settled on boneless, skinless breasts. While bone-in breasts have the added advantage of staying extra-moist, we knew that if we poached the chicken in our curry's base, they would not only stay moist but would also soak up good flavor. Once they were cooked, we removed them from the liquid and shredded the meat into bite-size pieces, to be returned to the curry to warm through just before serving.

With our protein in place, we moved on to the vegetables, which typically go into the pot after poaching the chicken. Traditional Thai curries can include a wide range of native vegetables such as eggplant, bell pepper, snap peas, squash, onions, and mushrooms, so we gave them each a fair shot. Tasters were not wild about the eggplant or mushrooms. The eggplant turned unappealingly mushy, and the mushrooms were slimy and rubbery. The squash fared well but still struck some tasters as a little too soft. Onions, red bell peppers, and snap peas were the winners, each providing bright, fresh flavor and a nice textural contrast to the chicken and sauce.

To put the finishing touches on our curry, we stirred in chopped basil for freshness and a splash of lime juice that lent the trademark sour note. It was easy from there to come up with variations using shrimp and tofu in lieu of the chicken. With that, we had three lighter Thai curries with authentic flavor, but without all the fuss.

Thai-Style Red Curry with Chicken
SERVES 4

Red curry paste is spicy; if you prefer a milder curry, feel free to use the lesser amount called for. Or you can substitute 4 teaspoons of green curry paste (which is much milder than red) for the red curry paste if desired.

- 1½ teaspoons canola oil
- 1-2 teaspoons red curry paste
- 1 (14-ounce) can light coconut milk
- 2 tablespoons fish sauce
- 1 tablespoon light brown sugar
- 1 pound boneless, skinless chicken breasts, trimmed of all visible fat
- ½ cup low-sodium chicken broth
- 1 teaspoon cornstarch
- 2 red bell peppers, stemmed, seeded, and cut into ¼-inch-wide strips

8 ounces snap peas, strings removed and sliced in half on bias

1 onion, halved and sliced ½ inch thick

½ cup chopped fresh basil

1 tablespoon lime juice

Salt

1. Heat oil in Dutch oven over medium heat until shimmering. Add curry paste and cook until fragrant, about 30 seconds. Whisk in coconut milk, fish sauce, and sugar.

2. Add chicken and bring to simmer. Cover, reduce heat to medium-low, and simmer until chicken registers 160 degrees, 12 to 18 minutes, flipping breasts over halfway through cooking. Transfer chicken to plate and let cool slightly. Using 2 forks, shred chicken into bite-size pieces.

3. Return sauce in pot to simmer over medium heat. Whisk broth and cornstarch together, then whisk mixture into pot. Stir in bell peppers, snap peas, and onion and simmer until vegetables are crisp-tender and sauce has thickened slightly, 8 to 10 minutes.

4. Return shredded chicken and any accumulated juice to pot and simmer until heated through, about 2 minutes. Off heat, stir in basil and lime juice. Season with salt to taste and serve.

PER 1½-CUP SERVING: Cal 290; Fat 9g; Sat fat 4g; Chol 65mg; Carb 21g; Protein 30g; Fiber 4g; Sodium 580mg

VARIATIONS

Thai-Style Red Curry with Shrimp
Omit chicken and skip step 2. Add 1 pound peeled and deveined extra-large shrimp (21 to 25 per pound) to pot after cooking vegetables in step 3; continue to simmer until shrimp are fully cooked, 3 to 5 minutes longer.

PER 1½-CUP SERVING: Cal 250; Fat 9g; Sat fat 4g; Chol 130mg; Carb 22g; Protein 21g; Fiber 4g; Sodium 640mg

Thai-Style Red Curry with Tofu
Omit chicken and skip step 2. Add 14 ounces extra-firm tofu, pressed dry with paper towels and cut into ¾-inch cubes, to pot after cooking vegetables in step 3; continue to simmer until tofu is heated through, 3 to 5 minutes longer.

PER 1½-CUP SERVING: Cal 250; Fat 12g; Sat fat 3.5g; Chol 0mg; Carb 23g; Protein 13g; Fiber 5g; Sodium 510mg

PORK AND HOMINY STEW

WE HAD ALREADY DEVELOPED A FEW HEALTHY soups and stews with bold flavors inspired by various international cuisines, so we decided to keep traveling the global menu in search of another recipe. We landed on *posole*, a hearty, chile-spiced Mexican stew featuring pork and hominy. We hoped to make this warming, mildly spicy, and wholly satisfying stew in our own kitchen, with a few added caveats: It had to be light and healthy, and it had to be easy to prepare and avoid obscure, hard-to-find ingredients.

We knew we had our work cut out for us. Some very traditional versions of posole that we found ran over three pages and called for 15-plus ingredients, including three (or more) types of dried chiles, a variety of Mexican hominy we couldn't find, unfamiliar spices, and seemingly every part of the pig. Other sources dumbed down the dish beyond recognition, relying on prepared salsa, taco seasoning mix, and ground pork. We tested posoles from easy to exacting and our colleagues gave us this directive: Keep all the mysterious, complex layers of flavor, but eliminate as many obscure ingredients and labor-intensive steps as you can.

How simple could we go? Hominy, dried corn that's been soaked in lye to remove its skin, was obviously essential. (The word *posole* also means "hominy" in Spanish.) So we dumped a few cans of hominy into a pot along with boneless country-style pork ribs (a fair compromise for now between the fattier and leaner cuts of pork on either end of the spectrum) and the standards: onions, garlic, spices, chili powder, and lots of water. After everything had simmered for about two hours, we fished out the meat, shredded it, and returned it to the pot. This posole was simple, all right, but it was also harsh, one-dimensional, and fattier than we liked.

Our first step was switching from water to chicken broth, and the payoff in flavor and body was high. Next, we pitted posole made with chili powder against a version made with dried ancho chiles (which you can find at any supermarket). The dried chiles gave unmatchable depth but required toasting to bring out their flavor. A few minutes in a skillet did the trick. Once they were cool, we steeped them in hot chicken broth, where they picked up even more flavor. Some recipes for posole call for complicated assemblies of spices, but we limited ourselves to cumin and oregano, which we figured most people keep in their cupboards, and got fine results.

Still, the soup was fattier than we wanted and the flavor needed some work. Clearly, country-style ribs were out, and in their place pork tenderloin went in. But we traded one problem for a few new ones. Not only did this lessen the meaty flavor in our stew, but it also took away from the body that had developed during the long simmering time necessary to turn the ribs tender. We came up with a two-pronged solution. First, we borrowed a trick from our Split Pea and Ham Soup (page 31), namely, poaching bacon in the soup and then discarding it before serving. This added plenty of smoky pork flavor without rendering all of the fat into the soup. The second solution came from an unlikely source: Chinese cuisine. Velveting is a traditional Chinese technique that involves coating protein (typically chicken or pork) in a thin cornstarch and egg white or oil mixture. The coating forms a barrier that keeps precious moisture inside, which in turn makes the pork seem more tender. The pork was not only juicy and tender, but it also developed an attractive golden brown coating. Meanwhile, the cornstarch thickened the soup just enough to resemble the consistency of the longer-cooked versions.

We had one last trick up our sleeve. We had been introducing the chopped onions and garlic to the pot raw. When we sautéed them first and pureed them with the chiles, they contributed a gentle, caramelized sweetness that had come through in some of the more challenging posole recipes.

Posole is served with a slew of additions: avocado, cabbage, radishes, cilantro, and limes are all traditional, and we had no reason to buck the trend in our new healthy version. Our stew had body and complexity, and it didn't hurt that it was a snap to make.

Pork and Hominy Stew

SERVES 8

Don't use store-bought chili powder: Dried ancho chiles make all the difference. Serve the stew with sliced radishes and green cabbage, chopped avocado, cilantro, hot sauce, and lime wedges.

3 dried ancho chiles, stemmed and seeded
7 cups low-sodium chicken broth
5 teaspoons canola oil
1 tablespoon cornstarch
1 tablespoon all-purpose flour
2 teaspoons water
2 (1-pound) pork tenderloins, trimmed of all visible fat and sliced thin
3 (15-ounce) cans white hominy, rinsed
2 onions, chopped fine
5 garlic cloves, minced
2 slices bacon
1 tablespoon minced fresh oregano
1 tablespoon lime juice
  Salt and pepper

1. Toast ancho chiles in 12-inch skillet over medium-high heat, stirring frequently, until flesh is fragrant, 4 to 6 minutes, reducing heat if chiles begin to smoke. Transfer to bowl and let cool. Combine chiles and 1 cup broth in bowl, cover, and microwave until bubbling, about 2 minutes. Let stand until softened, 10 to 15 minutes.

2. Whisk 2 teaspoons oil, cornstarch, flour, and water together in medium bowl until smooth, then stir in pork until evenly coated.

3. Heat 1 teaspoon oil in Dutch oven over medium-high heat until just smoking. Add half of pork, break up any clumps, and cook, without stirring, for 1 minute. Stir pork and continue to cook until lightly browned, 1 to 2 minutes longer; transfer to clean bowl. Repeat with 1 teaspoon oil and remaining pork; transfer to bowl.

4. Add hominy to now-empty pot and cook, stirring frequently, until fragrant and hominy begins to darken, 2 to 3 minutes. Transfer hominy to separate bowl.

5. Heat remaining 1 teaspoon oil in now-empty pot over medium-low heat until shimmering. Add onions, cover, and cook, stirring occasionally, until softened, 8 to 10 minutes. Stir in garlic and cook until fragrant, about 30 seconds. Puree onion mixture with softened chile mixture in blender until mostly smooth.

6. Combine remaining 6 cups broth, pureed onion-chile mixture, bacon, oregano, and ½ teaspoon pepper in now-empty pot and bring to boil. Reduce heat to low, add hominy to pot, and simmer, covered, until tender, about 30 minutes.

7. Return pork to pot and cook until heated through, 2 to 3 minutes. Off heat, remove bacon. Stir in lime juice, season with salt and pepper to taste, and serve.

PER 1½-CUP SERVING: Cal 280; Fat 8g; Sat fat 1.5g; Chol 75mg; Carb 23g; Protein 27g; Fiber 4g; Sodium 810mg

PERUVIAN GARLIC-LIME CHICKEN

CHAPTER 3

POULTRY

M = TEST KITCHEN MAKEOVER

THE BEST WEEKNIGHT CHICKEN

YOU'RE DRIVING HOME FROM WORK. YOU SWING by the supermarket to grab a "family pack" of chicken parts for supper. You set the oven to 350, put the pieces in a baking dish with a few shakes of salt and pepper, and bake until done. A pretty typical weeknight meal, though when we tried this method recently, we found that while it was simple, it left us with chicken that had hardly any flavor. We refused to choose between simple cooking and great flavor. We wanted a chicken recipe that was fast and easy but delivered flavorful, juicy results.

We settled quickly on 3 pounds of chicken—enough to feed a family of four. Breasts alone rather than a combination of breasts, thighs, and drumsticks were not only a lighter choice but also a faster-cooking one. Since lean white meat is a prime candidate for drying out, we decided to cook the chicken with the skin on. While the skin contains the majority of the fat, it would protect the meat during its time in the oven, helping it to retain moisture. After the chicken was cooked, we would simply remove the skin (or leave it on if we wanted to treat ourselves with a little more richness).

As for a cooking method, we began by considering our end goal. What method would guarantee juicy meat and crisp skin? Could pan-roasting be our answer? This technique, in which food is browned on the stovetop, then cooked through in the even heat of a hot oven, takes advantage of the benefits from both techniques. The direct heat from the stovetop creates ideal browning, and the ambient heat from the oven cooks the chicken quickly and evenly, ensuring tender, juicy meat. Pan-roasting can be a great help at speeding up otherwise time-intensive recipes. We set out for the kitchen, skillet in hand, ready to perfect our pan-roasted chicken.

Our plan was fairly simple: To make handling the chicken easier we would cut the split breasts in half, then brown the meat on both sides on the stovetop, and, finally, slide the chicken, skillet and all, into a hot oven to finish cooking. Typically when this technique is used in professional kitchens, the chicken is brined first, which both protects it from drying out and gives it flavor. But since our goal was making a supper that we could get on the table fast, we ruled out brining. The same went for marinating. And unfortunately, without those techniques, our chicken was dry and flavorless.

After some brainstorming, we got the idea to add liquid to the pan: It would be simple and fast, and we hoped it would keep the chicken moist in the oven. We started by adding broth to the pan after browning the chicken, taking care to add just enough to come up the sides of the chicken—submerging the chicken would have certainly washed away all of the browning we had developed. One taste proved that this addition was a big help, acting as a buffer to keep the meat from drying out. However, the flavor still needed some work.

Keeping the amount of liquid the same—we had been using about 2 cups—we replaced half of the broth with some dry white wine for a nice hint of acidity. For more flavor, we also sprinkled in some minced fresh thyme and a few smashed garlic cloves. Now bland chicken was nowhere to be seen. And the cooking liquid, which had partly evaporated in the hot oven and hence concentrated in flavor, struck us as a great base for a flavorful sauce to dress up the chicken. We set ourselves a few criteria first: Any sauce would have to be dead easy to make, plus we wanted to keep things light while still maintaining the silky consistency of a rich sauce.

We set the chicken aside, quickly defatted the juices left in the pan, and returned them to the skillet to reduce and intensify further. For most pan sauces, at this point you would simply whisk in a few pats of butter and call it a day—not a step we were about to take with our healthy recipe. In the past we have successfully used thickeners, usually flour or cornstarch, to help develop the consistency of a rich sauce without all the fat. We gave both a try, whisking each with a small amount of the broth to create a thin slurry free of lumps. We then whisked the flour and cornstarch slurries into separate batches of pan juices and brought the mixtures to a

simmer to fully thicken. Side by side, tasters preferred the smoother texture of the sauce made with cornstarch over the slightly grainy flour-thickened sauce. We were a step closer, but still we felt that something was missing. Everyone agreed that adding a small amount of butter was a must, but we found that with the help of the cornstarch we needed only 1 tablespoon to get the gloss and richness we wanted, which didn't add too much fat to push our servings over our healthy limits.

After about 30 minutes, very little of which was hands-on time, we were ready to sit down to a satisfying and uncomplicated chicken dinner—one that was, truth be told, worth eating any day of the week.

The Best Weeknight Chicken

SERVES 4

Make sure to use a 12-inch ovensafe skillet for this recipe.

- 1 cup low-sodium chicken broth
- 1½ teaspoons cornstarch
- 1 cup dry white wine
- 4 garlic cloves, peeled and smashed
- 2 teaspoons minced fresh thyme
- 4 (10-ounce) bone-in split chicken breasts, ribs trimmed (see page 56), trimmed of all visible fat, and halved crosswise
  Salt and pepper
- 1 teaspoon canola oil
- 1 tablespoon unsalted butter, chilled

1. Adjust oven rack to middle position and heat oven to 450 degrees. Whisk 2 tablespoons broth and cornstarch together in bowl until no lumps remain; set aside. Combine remaining broth, wine, garlic, and thyme in 4-cup liquid measuring cup.

2. Pat chicken dry with paper towels and season with ⅛ teaspoon salt and ⅛ teaspoon pepper. Heat oil in 12-inch ovensafe skillet over medium-high heat until just smoking. Place chicken, skin side down, in skillet and brown well on first side, 6 to 8 minutes. Flip chicken and continue to cook until lightly browned on second side, about 2 minutes longer.

3. Slowly pour broth-wine mixture into skillet and bring to boil. Transfer skillet to oven and roast until chicken registers 160 degrees, 12 to 18 minutes.

4. Using potholders (skillet handle will be hot),

remove skillet from oven. Transfer chicken to serving platter; remove and discard skin if desired. Tent loosely with aluminum foil and lest rest while finishing sauce.

5. Being careful of hot skillet handle, discard garlic. Let pan juices settle for 5 minutes, then remove fat from surface using large spoon. Measure out and reserve 1½ cups of defatted pan juices; discard remaining liquid. Add reserved liquid to now-empty skillet, bring to simmer, and cook until liquid is reduced to 1 cup, 5 to 7 minutes. Whisk reserved cornstarch mixture to recombine, then whisk into sauce; return to simmer and cook until sauce is slightly thickened, about 2 minutes. Off heat, whisk in butter and season with salt and pepper to taste. Serve chicken, passing sauce separately.

PER SERVING (WITHOUT SKIN): Cal 300; Fat 6g; Sat fat 2.5g; Chol 115mg; Carb 4g; Protein 43g; Fiber 0g; Sodium 340mg

PER SERVING (WITH SKIN): Cal 490; Fat 25g; Sat fat 8g; Chol 155mg; Carb 4g; Protein 48g; Fiber 0g; Sodium 360mg

CHICKEN CHOPPED SALAD

CHOPPED SALADS HAD THEIR HEYDAY IN THE 1950s as a popular light menu item for ladies who lunched. If you encounter a good version, it's easy to see why they're making a comeback. The best are lively, thoughtfully chosen compositions of lettuce, vegetables, and sometimes fruit cut into bite-size pieces, offering a variety of tastes, textures, and visual appeal. Unfortunately, we've had more experience with the mediocre kind. These are little better than random collections of cut-up produce from the crisper drawer exuding moisture that turns the salad watery and bland. To make matters worse, the whole thing is doused in a dressing overloaded with oil and topped with handfuls of fatty nuts and cheese. This dish would need some serious work to return to its lighter past. We headed to the test kitchen, set on creating a simple version that was light and flavorful, with a mixture of crisp, colorful vegetables tossed in a bright, well-balanced dressing. And while we were at it, we would add some chicken to turn it into a well-rounded meal.

Since one of the key problems we had encountered with poor versions of this salad was a random mishmash of ingredients, we made sure to start by choosing a collection of cohesive major players right at the start. We settled on a mix of fresh flavors and crisp texture, selecting cucumber, fennel, apples, and some crisp romaine. Red onion was also a natural choice, and a modest amount of some crumbled goat cheese offered a nice creamy textural contrast.

Salad ingredients selected, we were ready to address the issue of sogginess that had been prevalent in the recipes we had tasted. The cucumber had the potential to be the main offender in our lineup, so we focused our attention there. We started by salting it to remove excess moisture. We halved the cucumber and scooped out its watery seeds before dicing it, tossing it with salt, and allowing it to drain in a colander. After 15 minutes, the cucumber had shed a full tablespoon of water.

The apples, fennel, and romaine didn't release much liquid, so we quickly got chopping. Tasters liked them best in smaller pieces that were easily picked up by their forks. Slices worked great for the apples and fennel, and ½-inch pieces were preferred for the romaine.

With our vegetables and fruit ready to go, we moved on to the chicken. We wanted it to be fresh and moist, but we didn't want to make preparing it a production. We sought the flavor and color from browning, but browning both sides of the chicken breasts required more oil than we wanted to use, and it gave our chicken a tougher texture than we wanted. We found our answer in a half-sautéing, half-poaching method that required very little fat. First we browned the chicken on one side in 1 teaspoon of oil, then we flipped the chicken over, added water to the skillet, reduced the heat, and covered the skillet until the chicken was cooked through. This method yielded moist, flavorful chicken breasts. Once the breasts were cool, we cut them into chunks and combined the pieces with the other salad ingredients.

We were ready to tackle the dressing. After some early tests, it became clear that the dressings in most recipes weren't doing anything for the salads except weighing them down. Most called for a ratio of 3 parts oil to 1 part vinegar. This proportion is optimal for dressing tender, subtly flavored leafy greens, but it wasn't quite right here. Working with extra-virgin olive oil and cider vinegar, we found that a more assertive blend of equal parts oil and vinegar—3 tablespoons of each for now—was far better at delivering the bright, acidic kick needed in this hearty, chunky salad. But we had a big roadblock: While this ratio worked well at dressing our salad, it was weighing it down with fat and calories. We needed a creative way to reduce the oil without taking away from the unctuous consistency of the dressing.

As we reviewed our ingredient list, our gaze settled on the ¾ cup of goat cheese that we planned to sprinkle over the salad before serving. What if we whisked some of it into the dressing in place of some of the oil? We tried multiple batches with varying amounts of the goat cheese, and the idea was getting there—we had a dressing that was creamy and rich with 7 grams less fat—but even with the full amount of cheese and only 1 tablespoon of oil, the dressing was missing some liveliness. Adding a handful of chopped tarragon did the trick.

Looking to enhance our salad further, we wondered if we could use the dressing to even greater advantage. We found that marinating the heartier ingredients in the dressing for just five minutes before adding the romaine infused every component with flavor while still keeping it fresh and light.

Fennel, Apple, and Chicken Chopped Salad
SERVES 4

Use any sweet apple here such as Fuji, Jonagold, Pink Lady, Jonathan, Macoun, or Gala.

- 1 cucumber, peeled, halved lengthwise, seeded, and sliced ½ inch thick
   Salt and pepper
- 1 pound boneless, skinless chicken breasts, trimmed of all visible fat
- 1 teaspoon canola oil
- 3 ounces goat cheese, crumbled (¾ cup)
- ¼ cup cider vinegar
- ¼ cup minced fresh tarragon
- 1 tablespoon extra-virgin olive oil
- 2 apples, cored, quartered, and sliced crosswise ¼ inch thick
- 1 fennel bulb, stalks discarded, bulb halved, cored, and sliced ¼ inch thick (see page 60)
- ½ cup finely chopped red onion
- 1 romaine lettuce heart (6 ounces), cut into ½-inch pieces

1. Toss cucumber and ½ teaspoon salt together and let drain in colander for 15 to 30 minutes.

2. Meanwhile, pat chicken dry with paper towels and season with ⅛ teaspoon salt and ⅛ teaspoon pepper. Heat canola oil in 12-inch skillet over medium-high heat until just smoking. Brown chicken well on first side, 6 to 8 minutes. Flip chicken over, add ½ cup

FENNEL, APPLE, AND CHICKEN CHOPPED SALAD

water, and reduce heat to medium-low. Cover and continue to cook until chicken registers 160 degrees, 5 to 7 minutes longer.

3. Transfer chicken to cutting board, let rest for 5 minutes, then cut into ½-inch pieces.

4. Whisk goat cheese, vinegar, tarragon, and olive oil together in large bowl. Add drained cucumber, chicken, apples, fennel, and onion and toss to combine. Let sit at room temperature until flavors meld, about 5 minutes. Add romaine and toss gently to coat. Season with salt and pepper to taste and serve.

PER SERVING: Cal 320; **Fat** 11g; **Sat fat** 4g; **Chol** 75mg; **Carb** 22g; **Protein** 32g; **Fiber** 5g; **Sodium** 550mg

---

NOTES FROM THE TEST KITCHEN

PREPARING FENNEL

1. Cut off stems and feathery fronds.

2. Trim very thin slice from base and remove any tough or blemished outer layers from bulb.

3. Cut bulb in half through base, then use small, sharp knife to remove pyramid-shaped core.

4. Slice each half into thin strips and, if called for in recipe, chop strips crosswise.

PERUVIAN GARLIC-LIME CHICKEN

PERUVIAN CHICKEN JOINTS HAVE DEVELOPED A BIT of a cult following recently in the United States, and for good reason. The rotisserie bird that they serve is deeply bronzed from its slow rotation in a wood-fired oven and is impressively seasoned with garlic, spices, lime juice, chiles, and mint. Off the spit, this flavorful chicken is carved and served with a garlicky, faintly spicy, mayonnaise-like sauce. Just thinking about the flavors had us eager to try our hand at a version we could make at home, though we hoped to simplify ours a bit by skipping the rotisserie and using bone-in chicken pieces. And on the way, we would look for ways to trim excess fat and calories.

Choosing the right chicken pieces was the first order of business, and we quickly sided with bone-in, skin-on chicken breasts—a lighter choice than thighs and drumsticks. We also made the crucial decision to roast the chicken with the skin on. While the skin contains the majority of the fat, it would protect the meat during its time in the oven, guarding it from drying out. After the chicken was cooked, we would simply remove the skin before eating.

Chicken in hand, we began by salting the breasts, a technique we use often in the test kitchen for sealing in juices. Then, taking cues from recipes we had found, we coated the exterior of the breasts with a simple paste of mint, garlic, lime juice, and cumin. We also added 1 tablespoon of olive oil to help bloom the dry cumin. After setting the chicken on a baking sheet, we placed it in a blazing 450-degree oven with the hope of replicating the rotisserie flame. About 40 minutes later the chicken was brown, all right—but only on one side. What's more, despite the marinating treatment, the punchy flavors from the paste were literally skin-deep at best.

Actually, the lack of flavor made sense. Through a recent test, we had learned that none of the flavors in a marinade (including garlic, spices, and acids) penetrate much beyond the exterior of the meat, no matter how long the meat soaks—with one exception. Only salt and other compounds of sodium travel farther into the meat the longer it sits. The flavors of our current wet paste would never be more than superficial no matter how long we let the chicken marinate, so two things—salt and plenty of time—would be key to heightening those heady flavors and seasoning the meat.

Since both the salt and the paste were being rubbed onto the chicken, we combined the two components into one step. We also kicked up the flavors further with the addition of some dried oregano, grated lime zest, pepper, sugar, and a teaspoon of finely minced habanero chile. Instead of merely rubbing it over the skin, we spread the paste under the skin directly against the meat for maximum penetration; we then let the chicken rest for six hours before roasting. The result? The salt and additional flavors in the paste had worked their magic and ramped up the chicken's flavor from skin to bone.

Next up: even browning. While we knew that for a light recipe most home cooks would throw away the skin, we still wanted to achieve the best browning possible, for those times when people wanted to treat themselves. One option was to flip the chicken during cooking, but all that handling caused the flavorful paste to stick to the baking sheet and not the chicken. Our other idea was to use a wire rack, a trick we've used before to elevate chicken pieces and allow even circulation of heat. For the next test, we set a wire rack in a baking sheet, placed the chicken breasts on the rack, then transferred them to the oven to cook. This worked much better: The chicken browned evenly and still held on to the paste. As for achieving the subtle smokiness of a rotisserie, we knew our roasting technique wasn't going to help, so we turned to our spice cabinet instead. Two teaspoons of smoked paprika mixed into the paste turned out to be a pretty close approximation of the real thing.

Finally, there was the sauce. The ideal texture is thinner than traditional mayonnaise but still viscous enough to coat the chicken when dunked. Most recipes have you whip a whole egg and vegetable oil (nearly 1 cup) in the food processor with onion, lime juice, cilantro, pickled jalapeño, yellow mustard, and garlic, but we sought a lighter route. We exchanged the egg and oil for some light mayonnaise that we thinned with a little water, then we stirred in the remaining ingredients. Our lighter version was just as vibrant and creamy as the original but contained a lot less fat. We had a hunch our version of this Peruvian mainstay would be developing a following of its own.

NOTES FROM THE TEST KITCHEN

THE BEST KITCHEN SHEARS
Kitchen shears are a critical all-around tool, useful for butterflying or quartering chicken, trimming pie dough, shaping parchment to line pans, snipping herbs, or cutting lengths of kitchen twine. We set out to find a pair that aced all of these tasks; had powerful, sharp blades that were easy to maneuver and slip-resistant, comfortable handles; and were easy to clean. We wanted shears that would work for most cooks whatever their hand size or strength—and also work for lefties.

In the end, we found two pairs we liked. **Shun Classic Kitchen Shears** (left), $39.99, have very sharp blades. Testers praised these for their precision and economy of motion. While they separate for cleaning, the blades stay together until opened to 120 degrees. They work for both right- and left-handed users and feel sturdy and well engineered. Although these shears aren't cheap, their lifetime guarantee salves some of the sting. We also liked **J. A. Henckels International Take-Apart Kitchen Shears** (right), which are solid and sharp, and at $14.95, are the best buy.

Peruvian Garlic-Lime Chicken
SERVES 4

If habanero chiles are unavailable, 1 tablespoon of minced serrano chile can be substituted. Wear gloves when working with hot chiles. Serve with Spicy Mayonnaise (recipe follows), if desired.

- ¼ cup fresh mint leaves
- 6 garlic cloves, chopped coarse
- 1 tablespoon extra-virgin olive oil
- 1 tablespoon pepper
- 1 tablespoon ground cumin
- 1 tablespoon sugar
- 2 teaspoons smoked paprika
- 2 teaspoons dried oregano
- 2 teaspoons grated lime zest plus ¼ cup juice (2 limes)
- 1 teaspoon salt
- 1 teaspoon minced habanero chile
- 4 (10-ounce) bone-in split chicken breasts, ribs trimmed (see page 56) and trimmed of all visible fat

1. Process all ingredients except chicken in blender until smooth paste forms, 10 to 20 seconds. Using your fingers, gently loosen skin covering each breast; place 1 tablespoon of paste under skin, directly on meat of each breast. Gently press on skin to distribute paste over meat.

Rub remaining paste evenly over exterior surface of breasts. Place chicken in 1-gallon zipper-lock bag and refrigerate for at least 6 hours or up to 24 hours.

2. Adjust oven rack to middle position and heat oven to 425 degrees. Set wire rack in rimmed baking sheet lined with aluminum foil. Lay chicken, skin side up, on prepared rack and roast until skin is lightly charred and crisp and chicken registers 160 degrees, 30 to 40 minutes, rotating sheet halfway through roasting.

3. Transfer chicken to serving platter, remove and discard skin if desired, and let rest for 5 minutes before serving.

PER SERVING (WITHOUT SKIN): **Cal** 280; **Fat** 6g; **Sat fat** 1g; **Chol** 105mg; **Carb** 9g; **Protein** 44g; **Fiber** 2g; **Sodium** 720mg

PER SERVING (WITH SKIN): **Cal** 460; **Fat** 25g; **Sat fat** 7g; **Chol** 145mg; **Carb** 9g; **Protein** 48g; **Fiber** 2g; **Sodium** 740mg

Spicy Mayonnaise

MAKES ABOUT ½ CUP

- ¼ cup light mayonnaise
- 2 tablespoons water
- 1 small shallot, minced
- 1 tablespoon lime juice
- 1 tablespoon minced fresh cilantro
- 1 tablespoon minced jarred jalapeños
- 1 garlic clove, minced
- 1 teaspoon yellow mustard
- ¼ teaspoon salt

Combine all ingredients in bowl, cover, and refrigerate until flavors meld, about 30 minutes.

PER 2-TABLESPOON SERVING: **Cal** 40; **Fat** 3.5g; **Sat fat** 0.5g; **Chol** 5mg; **Carb** 2g; **Protein** 0g; **Fiber** 0g; **Sodium** 300mg

HERB ROAST CHICKEN

A CLASSIC ROAST CHICKEN CAN BE A DELICIOUS, satisfying meal. And when it's seasoned with the right combination of herbs, each juicy bite of chicken is packed with flavor, taking an ordinary bird to a sublime level. Herbs are also a great way to infuse a lot of flavor into a recipe without adding a lot of calories or fat. Unfortunately, achieving such perfection isn't as simple as some recipes would have you believe.

Having roasted quite a few chickens in the past, we decided to stick with one of our tried-and-true methods. This way we could focus all of our attention on herb flavor. Past tests had shown us that roasting whole chickens breast side down during the first half of cooking, then breast side up for the remaining time, helped to ensure that the white and dark meat finished at the same time. With that in mind, we started our basic roasting technique by placing two chickens—enough to serve eight people—breast side down on a V-rack set in a roasting pan. After roasting them for about 40 minutes in a 450-degree oven, we flipped the chickens and allowed them to finish cooking through.

Now we were ready for the herbs. Most recipes we found called for one of three methods: stuffing the bird's cavity with herbs; putting an herb butter under the skin; or applying a paste of herbs and oil, either under or on top of the skin. We decided to test them all. Stuffing the cavity with herbs delivered no herb flavor—not surprising, since no herbs actually touched the meat. In the oven, the herb butter melted and ran down the sides of the chicken, taking the herbs with it. As for the oil-based paste, it stayed on top of the meat and seemed most promising, but the flavor, like the paste, stayed on top. How could we get the herb flavor into the meat?

For our Peruvian Garlic-Lime Chicken (page 60), we had found that salting the meat helped to achieve deeper flavor in the chicken. By that logic, we knew that putting salt in our herb paste would accomplish the same thing. But we wondered if the fat in our paste was helping or hindering its effectiveness. After all, brines and dry rubs don't typically contain oil. To find out, we made two batches of paste using a basic combination of herbs plus salt (we'd perfect the combination later). For one batch, we combined the herb-salt mixture with oil; for the other, we left it alone. We slathered chickens under the skin with each batch of paste and roasted them. The herb-salt mixture without oil was the clear winner, with more penetrating herb flavor and juicier, better-seasoned meat—a plus for us since we wanted to cut fat anyway.

We had also learned when making our Peruvian chicken that patience was key. Allowing the flavoring plenty of time to work really made a difference, so for experiment's sake we roasted one paste-rubbed chicken right away, we let another sit for 30 minutes before cooking, and we let a third sit for an hour. Not surprisingly, the chicken placed immediately in the oven was a dud, with the least pronounced flavor. The chicken allowed to sit for 30 minutes had some penetrating herb flavor but also a residue of salt just below the skin. Chicken number three easily had the deepest, most pronounced herb flavor, and with no salty layer.

Subsequent tests showed that tasters still appreciated a small amount of the herb paste rubbed on the exterior of the chicken. Using a tablespoon of olive oil on the skin helped distribute the rub and assisted in browning.

With the cooking technique settled, we turned our attention to the best herb combinations. Dried herbs failed to pass, as their potency weakened dramatically during roasting and their texture turned gritty. For a balance of flavors and textures, we tried pairings of soft, delicately flavored herbs like parsley, cilantro, basil, tarragon, and chives with tougher, potent herbs like rosemary, oregano, thyme, and sage. After numerous tests we settled on a base herb: parsley. It contributed a fresh, grassy flavor that everybody liked. Then, for more pungent notes, we combined it with rosemary and thyme, two other herbs tasters favored, and a little minced garlic for an extra boost.

Just to make sure that every bite of chicken was bursting with herb flavor, we decided to make a simple, light sauce from the pan drippings. Because the small amount of drippings evaporated before the chickens finished cooking, we found that adding 1 cup of water to the pan midway through roasting saved the drippings without causing the skin to steam. Just that 1 cup, though, left the drippings too concentrated, so we added low-sodium chicken broth to balance the flavors and wine for acidity. Thickening the sauce with a little cornstarch enabled us to obtain a rich texture with only 1 tablespoon of butter whisked in at the end. To finish, we whisked in 1 teaspoon of herb paste for fresh flavor. With or without the skin, this Herb Roast Chicken and accompanying sauce were bursting with flavor.

NOTES FROM THE TEST KITCHEN

APPLYING HERB PASTE

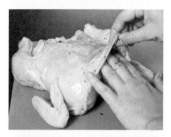

1. Carefully separate skin from meat on breast, thigh, and drumstick areas. Rub herb paste under skin and directly onto meat, distributing it evenly.

2. Apply herb paste mixed with oil to exterior of each chicken.

REMOTE THERMOMETER

So that we're not stuck holding a lonely vigil in the kitchen, we turn to a remote thermometer. Our favorite is the **Taylor Wireless Thermometer with Remote Pager Plus Timer**, $21.95. We found this two-part device—a temperature probe attached to a base that rests outside the oven or grill and a pager you carry—to be incredibly accurate and easy to set. Plus, it doesn't have preset doneness temperatures that are hard to override, like other models we've seen (a feature that often leads to overcooked meat). However, the Taylor does have a downside: Its pager does not have a temperature display. Instead it vibrates when the food is 10 degrees away from being done, then again when it's fully cooked. So while it does allow you to roam—more than 100 feet—you just can't go too far.

Herb Roast Chicken

SERVES 8

Do not substitute dried herbs for the fresh; they lose potency during cooking and turn the dish gritty.

- 1 cup minced fresh parsley
- 2 tablespoons minced fresh thyme
- 1 tablespoon minced fresh rosemary
- 2 garlic cloves, chopped coarse
  Salt and pepper
- 1 tablespoon olive oil
- 2 (4-pound) whole chickens, giblets discarded, trimmed of all visible fat
- 1 cup plus 2 tablespoons water
- 1¼ cups low-sodium chicken broth
- ¼ cup dry white wine
- 2 teaspoons cornstarch
- 1 tablespoon unsalted butter, chilled

1. Process parsley, thyme, rosemary, garlic, 1 teaspoon salt, and 1 teaspoon pepper in food processor until coarse paste forms, about 2 minutes, scraping down bowl as needed. Measure out and reserve 1 teaspoon herb paste for sauce. Combine 2 tablespoons herb paste with oil in bowl. Set aside remaining herb paste for under skin.

2. Pat chickens dry with paper towels. Using your fingers, gently loosen skin covering breast, thighs, and drumsticks of each chicken; place remaining herb paste evenly under skin, directly on meat of breast, thighs, and drumsticks. Gently press on skin to distribute paste over meat. Rub herb-oil mixture evenly over exterior surface of chickens. Tie legs together with kitchen twine and tuck wings behind backs. Transfer chickens to large platter, cover, and refrigerate for 1 hour.

3. Adjust oven rack to middle position and heat oven to 450 degrees. Set V-rack in roasting pan. Place chickens 2 inches apart, breast side down, on prepared V-rack, with legs pointing in opposite directions. Roast chickens until thighs register 135 to 140 degrees, 35 to 40 minutes.

4. Remove pan from oven. Using 2 large wads of paper towels, rotate chickens breast side up and add 1 cup water to pan. Return pan to oven and continue roasting until breasts register 160 degrees and thighs register 175 degrees, 25 to 30 minutes. Transfer chickens to carving board and let rest while making sauce.

5. Pour pan juices and any accumulated chicken juices into fat separator; allow liquid to settle for 5 minutes. Pour ½ cup of juices into medium saucepan; discard remaining liquid. Stir in broth and wine, bring to simmer, and cook until sauce is slightly thickened and reduced to 1¼ cups, 8 to 10 minutes. Whisk cornstarch and remaining 2 tablespoons water together in bowl until no lumps remain, then whisk into sauce. Return sauce to simmer and cook until thickened, 3 to 5 minutes.

6. Off heat, whisk in butter and reserved 1 teaspoon herb paste. Season with salt and pepper to taste. Carve chickens, removing and discarding skin if desired. Serve, passing sauce separately.

PER SERVING (WITHOUT SKIN): Cal 300; Fat 10g; Sat fat 3g; Chol 155mg; Carb 2g; Protein 47g; Fiber 0g; Sodium 550mg

PER SERVING (WITH SKIN): Cal 690; Fat 48g; Sat fat 14g; Chol 230mg; Carb 2g; Protein 56g; Fiber 0g; Sodium 600mg

QUICK CHICKEN FRICASSEE

THERE'S A REASON LEGENDARY CHEFS FROM Auguste Escoffier to Fannie Farmer to Julia Child and James Beard published recipes for chicken fricassee: Made the classic French way by poaching chicken pieces, mushrooms, and pearl onions in stock and saucing them with a cream-enriched reduction of the cooking liquid, the dish captures both richness and clean chicken flavor all on one platter. There's also a reason the dish has fallen out of favor: It's a bit bland for modern tastes, and many versions feel fussy and time consuming. This is especially true for recipes in which the chicken is browned before poaching—a crucial contemporary update that ensures deep, savory flavor in today's lean, bland, mass-produced birds.

Still, we were intrigued by this old-fashioned dish with its lush texture and straightforward chicken flavor, and we had ideas for a few refinements, namely, a streamlined technique that would give the dish weeknight potential and a brighter, more complex sauce—one that was also lighter but still had the hallmark creamy, rich flavor and consistency.

First up: The thick bone-in chicken parts would have to go. They took up too much room to brown in a single batch and required nearly 30 minutes of poaching. Instead, we decided to try the busy cook's favorite timesaver: boneless, skinless chicken pieces (we chose leaner breasts over thighs). These thinner pieces of meat not only fit nicely into our 12-inch skillet, but they were mostly cooked through after the initial sear.

That was the good news. The bad news was that doing without skin and bones meant losing the chicken's two primary sources of flavor. And while cooking the meat in 2 teaspoons of oil was enough to brown its exterior, it wasn't adding much richness. Plus, sautéing the skinless meat left very few browned bits (called fond) in the pan for creating a flavorful sauce. We started searching for ways to add flavor without overcomplicating our recipe.

In the past we've built up savory flavor by allowing vegetables to thoroughly brown until they developed their own fond. This method struck us as a potential solution here as well. As such, we made two key changes to the traditional fricassee components: First, we swapped the pearl onions for a regular chopped onion, which would provide more surface area for browning and caramelization. Second, because mushrooms are an excellent source of glutamates (compounds that significantly boost meaty umami flavor in food), we upped their amount from 12 ounces to a full pound.

Without much oil left in the skillet after browning the chicken, the vegetables struggled to soften and brown before scorching. Looking to avoid the addition of more oil, we tried adding some moisture—wine seemed like a great choice—to help jump-start the softening process. Sure enough, the steam created by the wine helped the mushrooms and onion quickly soften and brown. Now, after about 10 minutes, our pan was coated with a layer of dark browned bits. Just before deglazing with chicken broth, we stirred in a little minced garlic as well as 1 tablespoon of flour to help lightly thicken the sauce. Finally, we slid the chicken back into the skillet to finish cooking. Within 10 minutes, the breast meat was up to temperature and the poaching liquid had reduced to savory gravy.

The final step was to finish the sauce with dairy. Heavy cream is traditional in this sauce, but we knew it wouldn't work in our lighter version. We started by stirring in half-and-half, and while it added richness, it left the sauce thin. Light sour cream was a better choice but still didn't contribute as much creaminess as we wanted. In the end, we found that light cream cheese worked best, adding plenty of body and a pleasant tang. To ensure that our sauce remained satiny smooth without curdling, we whisked a portion of the thickened broth into the cream cheese before incorporating the mixture back into the skillet. All that was left was to add a spritz of lemon juice, grated nutmeg, and minced tarragon to lend a little more complexity.

Earlier generations might not consider our light, streamlined approach a true "fricassee," but they couldn't take issue with this quick dish's deep, rich chicken flavor and smooth, creamy sauce.

Quick Chicken Fricassee

SERVES 4

Two tablespoons of minced fresh parsley may be substituted for the tarragon in this recipe. Make sure to soften the cream cheese; firm cream cheese will be difficult to whisk into the sauce.

- **4** (6-ounce) boneless, skinless chicken breasts, trimmed of all visible fat
   Salt and pepper
- **2** teaspoons canola oil
- **1** pound cremini mushrooms, trimmed and sliced ¼ inch thick
- **1** onion, chopped fine
- **¼** cup dry white wine
- **1** tablespoon all-purpose flour
- **1** garlic clove, minced
- **1½** cups low-sodium chicken broth
- **2** ounces light cream cheese, softened
- **2** teaspoons lemon juice
- **2** teaspoons minced fresh tarragon
- **¼** teaspoon ground nutmeg

1. Pat chicken dry with paper towels and season with ⅛ teaspoon salt and ⅛ teaspoon pepper. Heat oil in 12-inch skillet over medium-high heat until just smoking. Brown chicken well on both sides, about 8 minutes; transfer to plate.

2. Add mushrooms, onion, and wine to now-empty skillet and cook over medium heat, stirring occasionally, until liquid has evaporated and mushrooms are browned, 8 to 10 minutes. Add flour and garlic and cook, stirring constantly, for 1 minute. Slowly whisk in broth, scraping up any browned bits, and bring mixture to boil. Return chicken and any accumulated juices to skillet. Reduce heat to medium-low, cover, and cook until chicken registers 160 degrees, about 10 minutes.

3. Transfer chicken to serving platter and tent loosely with aluminum foil. Whisk ½ cup of sauce from pan into cream cheese to temper, then stir cream cheese mixture back into pan. Stir in lemon juice, tarragon, and nutmeg and return sauce to brief simmer. Season with salt and pepper to taste. Pour sauce over chicken and serve.

PER SERVING: Cal 300; Fat 7g; Sat fat 2.5g; Chol 105mg; Carb 11g; Protein 44g; Fiber 1g; Sodium 480mg

CRISPY CHICKEN NUGGETS

WE'VE ALL EATEN CHICKEN NUGGETS, WHETHER they were from the drive-through or surreptitiously plucked from a child's plate (consider us guilty on both counts). Unfortunately, their terrific breaded coating is usually the result of frying the chicken pieces in a good amount of oil, a process that's not only calorie-laden but time consuming as well. Sure, there are lots of recipes for low-fat or "un-fried" chicken nuggets, but none that we tried even came close to the flavor, color, or crispness of a traditional fried recipe. These nuggets, with their flavorless, washed-out crusts, literally paled in comparison. We wondered if we could develop a better, lighter version, one actually worth eating. And since we knew we'd have to find an alternative to frying, we hoped that our lighter version would be streamlined as well.

Setting the issue of the crispy crust aside for now, we started with the chicken itself. Most nugget manufacturers use the least desirable parts of the bird and feed these "off cuts" through a grinder. While we did try a recipe that used ground breast meat (nuggets are usually white meat), the pasty texture persuaded us to instead cut nuggets from the breast. While tender, the meat from boneless, skinless breasts was bland and, if even slightly overcooked, dry. Happily, we discovered that a brief stint in a pungent, salty marinade made from Worcestershire sauce, onion powder, and garlic powder ensured that the nuggets had plenty of flavor and moisture.

While our chicken marinated, we turned to the coating. Obviously, deep-frying and pan-frying the nuggets were both out—these methods used too much oil. That left us with the oven. Homing in on the issue of oven temperature first, we found that baking the chicken nuggets for 8 to 10 minutes at 475 degrees produced the most tender and juicy chicken. Baking the chicken on a wire rack set in the baking sheet—a successful technique we have used in the past—quickly solved the soggy bottom issue, and spraying the tops with vegetable oil spray helped the breading on top of the nuggets crisp up nicely. We still, however, had issues with the bland flavor and pale color of the coating.

The test kitchen has often used baking soda to achieve additional browning while baking. We gave it a try with our nuggets, adding ½ teaspoon to our flour, and found that it encouraged the crust to take on more color during its time in the oven, but still not enough.

Then it hit us: What if we toasted the bread crumbs to a golden color before breading the nuggets? We toasted the bread crumbs in a skillet over medium heat until golden, then breaded the nuggets, sprayed the tops with vegetable oil, and baked them on the rack. These nuggets were a big improvement, with an even golden color and crisp, fried texture. Adding 2 tablespoons of canola oil to the crumbs as they toasted gave them a nice "fried" flavor without turning them greasy or adding too much fat or too many calories.

Testing the differences among store-bought dried bread crumbs, fresh bread crumbs, and panko, tasters universally disliked the old, ground cardboard flavor of the store-bought dried bread crumbs. Both the fresh bread crumbs and the panko were well liked; however, tasters preferred the ultra-crisp texture of panko to that of the fresh bread crumbs.

Now that we had flavorful, crisp, golden, oven-fried chicken nuggets, all we needed were some dipping sauces to go with them. We stuck to the classics, creating a vibrant sweet orange sauce and a tangy honey-mustard sauce that could be made in 10 minutes or less. Dipped in our simple homemade sauces, our crunchy chicken nuggets were a whole—and comparatively a far more wholesome—new take on a fast-food favorite.

Crispy Chicken Nuggets
SERVES 4

To make cutting the chicken easier, freeze it for 15 minutes. Avoid using kosher chicken in this recipe or it will be too salty. Serve with dipping sauces (recipes follow), if desired.

1½ **pounds boneless, skinless chicken breasts, tenderloins removed, trimmed of all visible fat**

2 **tablespoons Worcestershire sauce**

2 **teaspoons onion powder**

½ **teaspoon garlic powder**

½ **teaspoon salt**

3 **cups panko bread crumbs**

2 **tablespoons canola oil**

½ **cup all-purpose flour**

½ **teaspoon baking soda**

3 **large egg whites**

   Vegetable oil spray

¼ **teaspoon pepper**

1. Cut each chicken breast on bias into thirds. Working with largest piece, slice crosswise into ½-inch-thick pieces. Slice two smaller thirds crosswise on bias into ½-inch-thick pieces. Toss chicken pieces with Worcestershire, onion powder, garlic powder, and salt in bowl, cover, and refrigerate for 30 minutes.

2. Adjust oven rack to middle position and heat oven to 475 degrees. Combine panko and oil in 12-inch skillet and toast over medium heat, stirring often, until golden brown, 8 to 10 minutes. Transfer crumbs to shallow dish and let cool slightly. Combine flour and baking soda in second dish. In third dish, lightly beat egg whites until foamy.

3. Spray wire rack with oil spray and set in rimmed baking sheet. Remove chicken from marinade, pat dry with paper towels, and season with pepper. Working with few pieces of chicken at a time, dredge in flour, shaking off excess, then coat with egg mixture, allowing excess to drip off. Coat all sides with toasted crumbs, pressing gently so that crumbs adhere. Transfer chicken pieces to prepared wire rack and let sit for 10 minutes.

4. Spray tops of chicken pieces lightly with oil spray. Bake until chicken registers 160 degrees, 10 to 12 minutes. Serve.

PER SERVING: **Cal** 360; **Fat** 8g; **Sat fat** 1g; **Chol** 100mg; **Carb** 23g; **Protein** 45g; **Fiber** 1g; **Sodium** 650mg

Sweet Orange Dipping Sauce
MAKES ABOUT ¾ CUP

Store-bought orange juice works fine here, but freshly squeezed orange juice takes this sauce up a notch.

- ¾ cup orange juice
- ¼ cup orange marmalade
- 1 tablespoon honey
- 2 teaspoons cornstarch
-    Pinch ground ginger
-    Pinch garlic powder
-    Lemon juice
-    Salt

Whisk orange juice, marmalade, honey, cornstarch, ginger, and garlic powder together in small saucepan and bring to simmer over medium-high heat, whisking constantly. Reduce heat to medium-low and continue to simmer gently, stirring occasionally, until slightly thickened, 3 to 5 minutes. Off heat, season with lemon juice and salt to taste. Let cool to room temperature before serving.

PER 2-TABLESPOON SERVING: **Cal** 60; **Fat** 0g; **Sat fat** 0g; **Chol** 0mg; **Carb** 16g; **Protein** 0g; **Fiber** 0g; **Sodium** 10mg

Honey-Mustard Dipping Sauce
MAKES ABOUT ¾ CUP

Add more honey to make this dip sweeter or more mustard to make it spicier.

- ½ cup yellow mustard
- ⅓ cup honey
-    Salt and pepper

Mix mustard and honey together until smooth and season with salt and pepper to taste. Serve.

PER 2-TABLESPOON SERVING: **Cal** 70; **Fat** 1g; **Sat fat** 0g; **Chol** 0mg; **Carb** 16g; **Protein** 1g; **Fiber** 1g; **Sodium** 230mg

---

NOTES FROM THE TEST KITCHEN

CUTTING CHICKEN BREASTS FOR NUGGETS

1. Cut each chicken breast diagonally into thirds.

2. Slice largest piece crosswise into ½-inch-thick pieces.

3. Slice two smaller thirds crosswise on bias into ½-inch-thick pieces.

NUT-CRUSTED CHICKEN BREASTS

NUT-CRUSTED CHICKEN BREASTS

FOR ANYONE WHO WANTS TO EAT HEALTHIER, boneless, skinless chicken breasts are certain to frequent the weekly meal plans. They are packed with protein and virtually fat-free—and they are also affordable and exceptionally easy to prepare. Problem is, on their own, they can become pretty boring and bland.

We were looking for a departure from the humdrum, and while breading chicken breasts adds texture and flavor (we had just developed a fun and healthy take on this idea with our Crispy Chicken Nuggets, page 66), was there a way we could make the typical coating even more interesting? Incorporating chopped nuts into a coating for boneless, skinless chicken breasts struck us as a great way to add an unusual flavor element and boost the crust's crunch factor. Nuts can be a healthy food when used in moderation, so we would just need to keep an eye on the amount we added to ensure they weren't contributing too much fat.

While most recipes for nut-crusted chicken called for deep-frying or pan-frying, we hoped to minimize additional fat and calories by achieving a crisp crust in the oven. This seemed ideal in theory, but it would be no small challenge. Achieving a tender, moist breast with a crunchy nut crust in the oven was going to take some creativity. Fortunately, we already had two successful tools in our arsenal gained from our Crispy Chicken Nuggets tests: pretoasting the crumbs to achieve better browning and baking on a wire rack to avoid sogginess.

But before we even tackled the crust, we needed to ensure juicy, flavorful meat. We settled on salting, a technique that had previously proven successful in our Peruvian Garlic-Lime Chicken (page 60) and Herb Roast Chicken (page 62) recipes. Like brining, salting changes the structure of meat proteins, helping them to retain more moisture as they cook. Ideally, chicken should be salted for at least six hours to ensure full penetration and juiciness. But boneless, skinless breasts are supposed to be quick and easy, so we weren't willing to commit more than 30 extra minutes to the process. Poking holes in the meat with a fork created channels for the salt to reach the interior, maximizing the short salting time and making the interior even juicier.

As for the crust, we knew we wanted a combination of nuts and bread crumbs to help maintain a healthy profile that also offered great flavor and texture. Starting with the nuts, we chose almonds (a healthy choice among nuts since they are high in monounsaturated fats) and pulsed them in a food processor. For the bread crumbs, we tested several varieties: store-bought dried crumbs, fresh crumbs, and panko. Tasters quickly eliminated the store-bought dried bread crumbs for their stale flavor. Fresh bread crumbs and panko both had appeal, but in the end, the ultra-crisp texture of panko was the winner (not a big surprise since they had already won the top spot in our testing for our chicken nugget coating). Looking for a ratio of chopped almonds to panko that produced a crisp coating and was also within the proper range of fat, we found a mixture of half nuts and half toasted panko worked best.

Toasting the panko before breading the chicken gave the crumbs a head start in achieving a golden brown "fried" color in the oven—simply using them right out of the box was a no-go, producing a sad, pale coating. To improve flavor, we also added 1 tablespoon of canola oil to the crumbs as they toasted to give them a rich flavor without turning them greasy. With our crumb mixture ready, we dredged the breasts in flour, dipped them in beaten egg whites, then dragged them through the nut-panko mixture.

Taking a cue once again from our chicken nuggets, we baked the coated chicken breasts on a wire rack set over a baking sheet to help avoid sogginess, and we sprayed the tops with vegetable oil spray to achieve an even golden color and crisp texture. After baking in a 350-degree oven for about 20 minutes, the chicken emerged juicy and shrouded in an even, crisp crust—but with sadly modest nut flavor.

What could we do to boost the flavor of the nuts without adding more of them? In countless baking recipes we toast nuts to deepen their flavor. We were already toasting the bread crumbs, so why not toast the nuts along with them? For our next test we gave it a shot, stirring the nuts and panko, along with a minced shallot for a little zing, together in the skillet until the mixture was fragrant and russet-colored. We'd hit the target; our tasters couldn't stop reaching for second helpings of this latest batch.

With our technique settled, we made some final adjustments to flavor, adding Dijon mustard to the egg wash and lemon zest, fresh thyme, and a dash of cayenne to the nut-crumb mixture. Served with a squeeze of lemon, our nut-crusted chicken breasts were far from ordinary and certain to be a hit at any dinner table.

Nut-Crusted Chicken Breasts

SERVES 4

This recipe is best with almonds but also works well with pecans, pistachios, or walnuts. Serve with lemon wedges.

Vegetable oil spray

4 (6-ounce) boneless, skinless chicken breasts, tenderloins removed, trimmed of all visible fat

Salt and pepper

⅔ cup sliced almonds

⅔ cup panko bread crumbs

1 shallot, minced

1 tablespoon canola oil

1½ teaspoons grated lemon zest

¾ teaspoon minced fresh thyme

⅛ teaspoon cayenne pepper

½ cup all-purpose flour

3 large egg whites

2 teaspoons Dijon mustard

1. Adjust oven rack to lower-middle position and heat oven to 350 degrees. Spray wire rack with oil spray and set in rimmed baking sheet. Pat chicken dry with paper towels. Using fork, poke thicker half of each breast 5 to 6 times and sprinkle with ¼ teaspoon salt. Transfer breasts to prepared wire rack and refrigerate, uncovered, while preparing coating.

2. Pulse nuts in food processor until they resemble coarse meal, about 20 pulses. Combine processed nuts, panko, shallot, and oil in 12-inch skillet and toast over medium heat, stirring often, until golden brown, 8 to 10 minutes. Transfer crumb mixture to shallow dish, stir in lemon zest, thyme, ½ teaspoon salt, and cayenne, and let mixture cool slightly. Place flour in second dish. In third dish, lightly beat egg whites, mustard, and ¼ teaspoon pepper together.

3. Pat chicken dry with paper towels. Working with 1 breast at a time, dredge in flour, shaking off excess, then coat with egg mixture, allowing excess to drip off. Coat all sides of breast with toasted crumb mixture, pressing gently so that crumbs adhere. Return nut-breaded breasts to wire rack and let sit for 10 minutes.

4. Spray tops of chicken lightly with oil spray. Bake until chicken registers 160 degrees, 20 to 25 minutes. Let chicken rest for 5 minutes before serving.

PER SERVING: Cal 370; Fat 14g; Sat fat 1.5g; Chol 100mg; Carb 13g; Protein 46g; Fiber 2g; Sodium 620mg

CRUNCHY BUTTERMILK BAKED CHICKEN

THE RECIPES FOR BUTTERMILK BAKED CHICKEN are almost formulaic: You soak bone-in chicken pieces in buttermilk, roll them in crumbs, and bake them, undisturbed, for 40 to 45 minutes at 375 degrees, give or take. Just as appealing as the tangy flavor and crunchy coating is the uncomplicated, weeknight-friendly nature of the dish. Plus, baked chicken is a great option for those looking to avoid excess fat and calories.

Our tasters were excited when we called them to sample the half-dozen recipes we'd prepared, but their excitement was short-lived. In some of the versions, the chicken was bland and dry with nary a hint of buttermilk bite. Worse still were pasty, soggy, and sandy coatings. These versions certainly weren't going to cut it. We headed for the kitchen in search of big buttermilk flavor and a crisp, hearty crust.

While most of the recipes we had sampled called for a variety of bone-in chicken pieces—breasts, thighs, and drumsticks—we decided to single out breasts since they are the leaner cut of choice. Cutting the breasts in half gave us more manageable pieces when it came time for the breading, plus the additional surface area meant more room for the coating to stick.

We were now ready to work on bumping up the buttermilk flavor. Buttermilk is pretty lean on its own (just 110 calories and 2.5 grams of fat per cup), so working with it didn't raise many concerns. However, pouring 2 quarts of buttermilk—a typical amount in recipes we had found—down the drain did, so we cut it back to 2 cups. To add extra flavor, we had a secret ingredient up our sleeves: buttermilk powder. Adding it to the buttermilk upped the flavor in our chicken considerably. But we didn't stop there. One test cook suggested swapping out the buttermilk powder for powdered ranch seasoning mix, which is basically buttermilk powder plus seasonings. That change, plus a little salt, gave us chicken infused to the bone with big, bright flavor.

On to the coating. In our initial testing, toasted fresh bread crumbs had shown the most promise, but we found them a bit bland and they struggled to stay on the chicken. Our tasters wanted a livelier coating—and more of it. Mixing some of the ranch dressing powder with the crumbs gave them the flavor boost they sorely needed. To help them stick to the chicken, we tried slathering the chicken with light mayonnaise

(mayonnaise is often used as a "glue" in the test kitchen) after its buttermilk bath, but this turned the coating gummy. We found we were better off stirring the mayonnaise into the buttermilk mixture—the light coating left on the exterior of the chicken after its soak was enough to help the bread crumbs properly adhere. To further enhance the buttermilk tang, we found we could easily replace the light mayonnaise with low-fat sour cream. Last, we discarded the chicken skin; it wouldn't crisp when saturated with marinade and covered with crumbs, plus this move cut 11 grams of fat per serving.

At this point the chicken was well coated, but the proper crispness was still lacking. Toasting the crumbs in the oven with a little oil helped, but not enough. While the chicken baked, the crumbs absorbed moisture released by the chicken and buttermilk and quickly turned soggy. Looking at the coatings we had been using for our Crispy Chicken Nuggets (page 66) and our Nut-Crusted Chicken Breasts (page 69), we wondered if adding flour and egg wash layers between the chicken and bread crumbs would create a buffer zone that would prevent the crumbs from turning soggy. We gave it a try. When this chicken came out of the oven, we held our breath. Success! The crust was crisp and dry and still firmly bonded to the chicken.

Before our chicken was ready for the dinner table, we still needed to iron out a few cooking details. Up until this point, we had been baking our chicken directly on a rimmed baking sheet set on the lowest rack in our oven. To our surprise, this method worked better at ensuring a crisp bottom crust than placing the chicken on a wire rack, a technique we had relied on for our Crispy Chicken Nuggets (page 66) and Nut-Crusted Chicken Breasts (page 69). This was due in part to the fact that we were using fresh bread crumbs, not panko, but still, it wasn't perfect, as it caused the breast pieces to cook unevenly. The portion against the baking sheet was often overcooked. After fiddling with rack position and oven temperature, we finally arrived at a solution: To maintain a crisp bottom, we sprayed the baking sheet with vegetable oil spray, then started the chicken on the lowest rack in a scorching-hot 450-degree oven. After about 10 minutes, we moved the chicken to the middle rack and turned down the oven to 400 so that the chicken could cook through evenly. Gathering our tasters once again, we waited for any comments but didn't get any—they were too busy devouring the crispy, flavorful chicken.

Crunchy Buttermilk Baked Chicken
SERVES 4

Avoid using kosher chicken in this recipe or it will be too salty.

- 2 cups buttermilk
- ¼ cup low-fat sour cream
- 1 (1-ounce) envelope ranch seasoning mix
- 1 teaspoon salt
- 4 (10-ounce) bone-in split chicken breasts, skin removed, ribs trimmed (see page 56), trimmed of all visible fat, and halved crosswise
- 5 slices hearty white sandwich bread, torn into quarters
- 2 tablespoons canola oil
- ½ cup all-purpose flour
- 3 large egg whites

1. Whisk buttermilk, sour cream, 2 tablespoons seasoning mix, and salt together in large bowl. Add chicken pieces and turn to coat. Cover and refrigerate for at least 30 minutes or up to 1 hour.

2. Meanwhile, adjust oven racks to lowest and middle positions and heat oven to 450 degrees. Pulse bread in food processor to fine crumbs, about 15 pulses. Transfer crumbs to medium bowl and toss with oil and remaining seasoning mix. Spread crumbs on rimmed baking sheet and bake on middle rack, stirring occasionally, until golden brown and dry, about 5 minutes. Transfer crumbs to shallow dish and let cool slightly. Place flour in second dish. In third dish, lightly beat egg whites until foamy.

3. Line baking sheet with aluminum foil and spray with vegetable oil spray. Working with 1 piece of chicken at a time, remove from marinade and allow excess to drip off. Dredge in flour, shaking off excess, then coat with egg mixture, allowing excess to drip off. Coat all sides with toasted crumb mixture, pressing gently so that crumbs adhere; transfer to prepared baking sheet.

4. Bake on lowest rack until bottom of chicken is golden brown, about 10 minutes. Move baking sheet to middle rack and reduce oven temperature to 400 degrees. Continue to bake until top of chicken is golden brown and chicken registers 160 degrees, 20 to 25 minutes longer. Serve.

PER SERVING: Cal 380; Fat 9g; Sat fat 1.5g; Chol 110mg; Carb 22g; Protein 49g; Fiber 1g; Sodium 740mg

CHICKEN POT PIE

TEST KITCHEN
MAKEOVER

FEW DISHES CAN WHET THE APPETITE LIKE CHICKEN pot pie. Those three little words conjure images of buttery, flaky crust set atop moist chicken enveloped by rich, creamy sauce and surrounded by sweet peas and tender carrots. Recently, our fantasy of pot pie had led us to develop a streamlined casserole-style version that we could put on the table quickly. The fast lane became wide open to us once we used quickly poached chicken breasts, a simple sauce with sautéed vegetables, and an unfussy crumble topping. But, while we love this version, that tender chicken enveloped in a rich, creamy sauce and buttery crumble topping comes with a price tag of about 720 calories and 40 grams of fat per serving. Could we cut down on fat and calories and still keep the richness and flavor?

First, we needed to settle the method for cooking the chicken. Our original recipe called for boneless, skinless breasts or thighs, so we limited ourselves to the lower-fat breasts. In our initial testing, we had discovered that poaching the meat in chicken broth, rather than water, infused the chicken with flavor and helped keep it moist, so we followed suit. As an added bonus, that poaching liquid provided the base for a velvety, fairly full-bodied sauce that didn't need reducing. All we had to do now was shred the chicken into bite-size pieces.

For the vegetables, we saw no reason to change the traditional medley of mushrooms, onions, carrots, celery, and peas that had been used in our full-fat version. Cooking the chicken together with the vegetables, while undeniably efficient, had resulted in meat and sauce that tasted like vegetable soup base, and vegetables that turned mushy and didn't taste like much. Cooking the two elements separately—the chicken in broth, the vegetables in oil—was the only way to tease out and maintain their distinct flavors and textures in the pie. To keep the oil to a minimum for our lighter version, we found that if we covered the vegetables while they cooked, the pot needed only 1 teaspoon of oil, rather than the 1 tablespoon called for in our original. After the vegetables had cooked down, we removed the lid and increased the heat to cook off any liquid and allow the vegetables to brown. Waiting to stir in the peas until the end prevented them from overcooking.

For the sauce, traditional recipes (and our original version) relied on a roux, a combination of butter and flour, for thickening power. But for our lighter version, we needed a low-fat alternative. We first experimented with using flour alone. We started by toasting the flour in a dry, empty pot, then let it cool before whisking in the broth and milk and returning it to the heat. We were pleased to find that toasting the flour gave it just the nutty color you would find in a traditional roux, and it cooked out the flour's raw flavor. Once it was combined with the liquids and brought to a simmer, we had a thick, rich sauce—without any butter.

Our sauce now tasted clean and nicely chicken-y, but it lacked a certain savory depth. Fortunately, our full-fat recipe for pot pie quickly pointed us in the right direction. Heading to the pantry, we grabbed tomato paste and soy sauce, two ingredients that are rich in flavor compounds called glutamates that enhance savory qualities. Added to our vegetable mixture, these ingredients caramelized and helped to enhance the flavor of our filling. And with only 1 teaspoon of each, no one even guessed they were in the mix. A spritz of lemon and some fresh parsley rounded out the sauce.

With the filling ready to go, we focused on the crust. Our previous tests had led us to skip the tedious traditional pie dough crusts and biscuits for a savory crumble topping. It was a snap to prepare—we just rubbed butter into flour, salt, and leavening; tossed in some grated Parmesan, pepper, and cayenne; and bound it all together with cream to make a cohesive topping. Prebaking the crumbles prior to topping the pie had ensured they stayed crisp once scattered over the filling. However, with 6 tablespoons of butter and about ¾ cup of heavy cream, this topping was far too fatty. Could we successfully cut back on fat but keep the original appeal?

NOTES FROM THE TEST KITCHEN

MAKING THE CRUMBLE TOPPING

Prebaking the crumbles before sprinkling them over the pie ensures they stay crisp.

Crumble topping mixture into irregularly shaped pieces onto parchment-lined rimmed baking sheet and bake in 450-degree oven until they start to brown, 10 to 13 minutes.

CHICKEN POT PIE

Testing various ratios of butter and liquid to flour, we were surprised by how much fat we could omit from our crumble dough without compromising its richness. We found we could use a minimal amount of butter—only 4 tablespoons—and still produce flaky crumbles by melting the butter instead of rubbing it into the flour. This method distributed the butter more evenly and allowed us to use less of it. And instead of the cream, we used buttermilk, which is creamy, flavorful, and naturally low fat. After preparing the filling and parbaking our now-lighter crumble topping, we assembled our pie and moved it to the oven.

After a mere 15 minutes, our pot pie was browned and bubbling up the sides. Time check? Not even 90 minutes. Instead of merely imagining pot pie's rich, homey appeal, we had a quick version containing only 470 calories and 14 grams of fat that we could actually dig into without a shred of guilt.

MAKEOVER SPOTLIGHT: CHICKEN POT PIE

	CALORIES	FAT	SAT FAT	CHOLESTEROL
BEFORE	720	40g	24g	170mg
AFTER	470	14g	7g	95mg

Chicken Pot Pie

SERVES 6

This recipe relies on two unusual ingredients: soy sauce and tomato paste. Do not omit them. They don't convey their distinctive tastes but greatly deepen the savory flavor of the filling. We prefer to use finely grated Parmesan in this recipe so that it incorporates more easily. Do not substitute low-fat or skim milk for the whole milk in the filling.

CRUMBLE TOPPING

- 1¾ cups (8¾ ounces) all-purpose flour
- 1 ounce Parmesan cheese, finely grated (½ cup)
- 1½ teaspoons baking powder
- ½ teaspoon baking soda
- ½ teaspoon pepper
- ¼ teaspoon salt
- Pinch cayenne pepper
- ⅔ cup buttermilk
- 4 tablespoons unsalted butter, melted

FILLING

- ½ cup all-purpose flour
- 1½ pounds boneless, skinless chicken breasts, trimmed of all visible fat
- 3½ cups low-sodium chicken broth
- 1 cup water
- 10 ounces cremini mushrooms, trimmed and sliced thin
- 1 onion, chopped fine
- 3 carrots, peeled and sliced ¼ inch thick
- 1 celery rib, minced
- 1 tablespoon canola oil
- Salt and pepper
- 1 teaspoon low-sodium soy sauce
- 1 teaspoon tomato paste
- 1 cup whole milk
- 3 tablespoons minced fresh parsley
- 2 teaspoons lemon juice
- ¾ cup frozen peas

1. FOR THE TOPPING: Adjust oven rack to upper-middle position and heat oven to 450 degrees. Line rimmed baking sheet with parchment paper. Combine flour, Parmesan, baking powder, baking soda, pepper, salt, and cayenne in large bowl. Whisk buttermilk and melted butter together in another bowl. Add buttermilk mixture to flour mixture and stir until just combined and no pockets of flour remain. Crumble mixture into irregularly shaped pieces ranging from ¼ to ½ inch each onto prepared pan. Bake until fragrant and starting to brown, 10 to 13 minutes, rotating sheet halfway through baking. Set aside.

2. FOR THE FILLING: Toast flour in Dutch oven over medium-high heat, stirring often, until fragrant and light golden brown, 5 to 7 minutes; transfer to large bowl to cool. Wipe out pot with paper towels.

3. Bring chicken, broth, and water to simmer in now-empty pot. Reduce heat to medium-low, cover, and cook until chicken registers 160 degrees, 8 to 12 minutes. Transfer chicken to large bowl. Let cool slightly, then using 2 forks, shred chicken into bite-size pieces. Pour broth through fine-mesh strainer into 4-cup liquid measuring cup and reserve. Do not wash Dutch oven.

4. Combine mushrooms, onion, carrots, celery, oil, ¼ teaspoon salt, and ¼ teaspoon pepper in now-empty pot. Cover and cook over medium-low heat, stirring occasionally, until vegetables are softened, 8 to 10 minutes. Uncover and stir in soy sauce and tomato paste. Increase heat to medium-high and continue to cook, stirring occasionally, until vegetables are lightly browned, 8 to 12 minutes longer. Transfer vegetables to bowl with chicken; set aside.

5. Whisk reserved chicken broth and milk into bowl of cooled, toasted flour until evenly combined. Bring broth mixture to simmer in now-empty pot, scraping up any browned bits, and cook until sauce thickens, about 1 minute. Off heat, stir in 2 tablespoons parsley and lemon juice, then stir in chicken mixture and peas. Season with salt and pepper to taste.

6. Pour chicken mixture into 13 by 9-inch baking dish. Scatter crumble topping evenly over filling. Place pot pie on rimmed baking sheet lined with aluminum foil and bake until filling is bubbling and topping is well browned, 12 to 15 minutes. Sprinkle with remaining 1 tablespoon parsley and serve.

PER SERVING: Cal 470; Fat 14g; Sat fat 7g; Chol 95mg; Carb 46g; Protein 38g; Fiber 4g; Sodium 990mg

TURKEY MEATLOAF

AFTER DEVELOPING A FANTASTIC LIGHTER TAKE ON Chicken Pot Pie (page 72), we wondered if we could tackle yet another homey favorite: meatloaf. In the test kitchen, we find that the most juicy, meaty meatloaves are made with a mixture of veal, beef, and pork (often sold as simply "meatloaf mix"). So it's not surprising that like a lot of other classic comfort foods, meatloaf has enough fat and calories to rule it out for everyday healthy dining. Enter turkey meatloaf. We wondered if it was possible to use naturally low-fat ground turkey in place of beef to make a meatloaf that was just as appealing.

We found a number of turkey meatloaf recipes, but most contained oddball ingredients like spinach and dried cranberries, which we felt were too far from the classic. We set out to develop a simple but flavorful all-American meatloaf. We began our tests with the ground turkey itself. There were three kinds of ground turkey meat to choose from: ground dark meat, ground turkey breast (labeled 99 percent fat free), and a combination of the two. Meatloaf made with all dark turkey was sufficiently moist and flavorful, but it was still so high

in fat and calories that we may as well have made it with ground beef. The meatloaf made with all white turkey was a total disaster; it was so dry and stiff that it resembled a foam block in both taste and texture. This left the combination of ground white and dark meat. This turkey produced a moist loaf that would satisfy even the most avid beef lover, and it cut a few calories and grams of fat from the numbers you'd get in a loaf using the typical meatloaf mix.

Most meatloaves rely on some sort of binder; we have found that those prepared without a binder are coarse-textured and dense, like a big hamburger. We tried a wide range of binders for our turkey meatloaf, from cereal and oatmeal to crackers and bread crumbs. After trying them all, we found that bread crumbs provided the best texture without adding an off-flavor or superfluous fat. We also found that a little bit of whole milk and two eggs helped to bind the meatloaf together and provided some added richness. Mashing the bread with the milk until it formed a smooth paste (known as a panade) helped to ensure an even distribution throughout.

As for flavorings, tasters unanimously approved of sautéed onion and several cloves of garlic. We found it was important to sweat these ingredients in a skillet before adding them to the meat mixture; otherwise their flavor was too overpowering. A healthy dose of minced thyme and parsley gave our meatloaf a pleasant herbal note, and a bit of Dijon mustard, Worcestershire sauce, and hot sauce helped contribute a fuller, more complex flavor.

Now that we were satisfied with the flavor of our meatloaf, all that was left was to determine the best cooking method. We knew from experience that baking a meatloaf in a traditional loaf pan would produce an unappealing loaf because the sides would steam rather than bake. We therefore followed our usual protocol and baked a free-form loaf on a wire rack set on a baking sheet that was covered in aluminum foil. This method allowed the top as well as the sides to get brown, creating a delicious caramelized exterior. For oven temperatures, we tried a wide range of heat levels (and times) and learned that it was optimal to cook our turkey meatloaf at a low temperature for a longer time since this helped ensure that it stayed juicy. In the end, we found that baking it in a 350-degree oven for about 1 hour worked best.

We were almost finished, but our healthier meatloaf still needed a sauce or a glaze. We experimented with a number of sweet and sticky ingredients, such as honey, syrup, jams, and preserves, but good old ketchup mixed with a little bit of brown sugar and cider vinegar turned out to be the winner. Brushed on the loaf before baking and then again partway through the cooking time, this glaze hugged the loaf and reminded us of the best full-fat meatloaf we had tasted.

Turkey Meatloaf with Brown Sugar–Ketchup Glaze

SERVES 8

Be sure to use ground turkey, not ground turkey breast (also labeled 99 percent fat free), in this recipe. Do not substitute low-fat or skim milk for the whole milk.

- 1 teaspoon canola oil
- 1 onion, chopped fine
- 2 garlic cloves, minced
- 2 teaspoons minced fresh thyme
- 1½ slices hearty white sandwich bread, crusts removed, torn into 1-inch pieces
- ½ cup whole milk
- 2 large eggs, lightly beaten
- ¼ cup minced fresh parsley
- 2 teaspoons Dijon mustard
- 2 teaspoons Worcestershire sauce
- ½ teaspoon salt
- ½ teaspoon pepper
- ¼ teaspoon hot sauce
- 2 pounds 93 percent lean ground turkey
- ½ cup ketchup
- 2 tablespoons light brown sugar
- 4 teaspoons cider vinegar

1. Adjust oven rack to middle position and heat oven to 350 degrees. Fold piece of aluminum foil into 10 by 6-inch rectangle, place in center of wire rack, and use skewer to poke holes in foil every ½ inch. Place wire rack in foil-lined rimmed baking sheet and spray foil with vegetable oil spray.

2. Heat oil in 10-inch nonstick skillet over medium-high heat until shimmering. Add onion and cook until softened and lightly browned, 5 to 7 minutes. Stir in

garlic and thyme and cook until fragrant, about 30 seconds; transfer to bowl to cool.

3. Mash bread and milk together into smooth paste in large bowl using fork. Stir in cooled onion mixture, eggs, parsley, mustard, Worcestershire, salt, pepper, and hot sauce until combined. Mix in ground turkey using hands until uniform.

4. Press mixture together into compact mass, then turn it out onto prepared foil on wire rack. Press meat to edges of foil and into tidy 2-inch-thick loaf.

5. Stir ketchup, sugar, and vinegar together in bowl, then brush half of mixture evenly over meatloaf. Bake for 45 minutes.

6. Brush meatloaf with remaining ketchup mixture and continue to bake until loaf registers 160 degrees, 15 to 20 minutes longer. Let rest for 20 minutes, then slice into 1¼-inch-thick pieces and serve.

PER 1¼-INCH-THICK SLICE: Cal 230; Fat 10g; Sat fat 3g; Chol 120mg; Carb 13g; Protein 25g; Fiber 1g; Sodium 490mg

---

NOTES FROM THE TEST KITCHEN

MAKING A MEATLOAF

1. Fold sheet of heavy-duty aluminum foil into 10 by 6-inch rectangle and place foil in center of wire rack placed in baking sheet.

2. Poke holes in prepared piece of foil every ½ inch with skewer or tip of sharp knife. (This will allow fat to drip down and away from meatloaf as it cooks.) Spray with vegetable oil spray.

3. Pat meatloaf mixture into cohesive mass, transfer it to prepared rack, and, using foil as guide, press into 10 by 6-inch loaf, about 2 inches thick.

TURKEY MEATLOAF WITH BROWN SUGAR-KETCHUP GLAZE

MEXICAN LASAGNA

TEST KITCHEN
MAKEOVER

WITH LAYERS OF GOOEY CHEESE, A HEARTY BEAN and meat sauce, and a smattering of vegetables plus bold seasoning all between corn tortillas, Mexican Lasagna is serious comfort food. Our test kitchen recipe for the casserole is easy to put together and nothing short of satisfying, but with 670 calories and 37 grams of fat per serving it falls solidly in the category of guilty pleasures. Could we find a way to lighten this treat?

We knew that most of our excess fat and calories were coming from the meaty filling and gooey cheese, so we tackled these components first. In our original recipe, we used 1½ pounds of ground pork for its subtle flavor and natural sweetness that paired well with the sweet and earthy corn tortillas. The problem with ground pork, however, is that various cuts go into each package and the amount of fat can vary greatly. So we experimented with some consistently lean ground meats: lean ground beef, ground chicken, and ground turkey. We found the beef flavor overwhelming and the chicken dry, but ground turkey, which mimicked both the texture and meaty subtlety of the pork, was perfect. To further reduce the total fat, we upped the amount of pinto beans from one can to two in place of ½ pound of the turkey, a move that brought the fat down to 23 grams.

From there, we moved on to our next major task: lightening up the cheese. Our original recipe called for almost 1 pound of Colby Jack, which was completely out of the question for our lightened version. We knew we'd need to both scale back the amount of cheese and also to choose a slimmer dairy product. First we tried using 2 ounces of light cheddar for meltability and 4 ounces of naturally low-fat queso fresco on top for flavor. While the cheddar indeed melted into the filling, creating a subtle cheesiness and cohesive filling, the queso fresco on top turned into brittle cheese rocks. Perhaps with all of the other flavors of the casserole we didn't need the extra boost from the queso fresco anyway. We tried swapping in a little more light cheddar, and it worked like a charm, melting over the top layer of tortilla chips (we swapped out the regular chips in our original version for the lower-fat baked variety, crumbling them for easy serving and eating). With that, the fat came down to only 12 grams per serving.

Now that we had made significant steps in the lightening department, we moved on to our remaining ingredients. In the original recipe, we liked corn, red peppers, and chipotle chiles, in addition to the ubiquitous tomatoes, onion, and garlic. For flavor, we had found that just 2 teaspoons of chili powder contributed spice without masking the more subtle flavor of the beans and vegetables. In addition, cilantro and lime juice were the natural Southwestern components to round out the flavor profile. All of these ingredients proved to be just as tasty in our lightened version as in the original, so we had nothing to tweak.

Finally, we moved on to the casserole's assembly. When developing our original recipe, we found that this was easier said than done. Simply layering tortillas between cups of filling and cheese as one would layer pasta in a traditional lasagna left us with completely disintegrated tortillas and dried-out filling on the inside, and a withered and toughened mess on the top. The tricks we had discovered then held true for our lightened version as well. First, to keep the liquid in the sauce and out of the tortillas, we found that adding a bit of flour to our filling did the trick since the liquid became bound up in the swollen starch granules. This helped the sauce remain saucy and kept the tortilla layers soft but not mushy. Second, we discovered that we could further improve the middle layers of tortillas by spraying them with vegetable oil spray and softening them in the oven before assembly. And finally, we found that baking our casserole in a hot oven (450 degrees) allowed just enough time for the flavors to meld and the cheese to melt without overcooking the tortillas.

Once assembled, it took just 10 short minutes in the oven before our Mexican Lasagna emerged with a hot, bubbling filling and, to our delight, a crisp and flavorful topping. And with only 400 calories and 12 grams of fat, our Tex-Mex casserole had truly crossed the line from guilty pleasure to flavor-packed everyday comfort food.

MAKEOVER SPOTLIGHT: MEXICAN LASAGNA

	CALORIES	FAT	SAT FAT	CHOLESTEROL
BEFORE	670	37g	15g	100mg
AFTER	400	12g	3g	40mg

Mexican Lasagna with Turkey, Corn, and Pinto Beans

SERVES 8

Be sure to use ground turkey, not ground turkey breast (also labeled 99 percent fat free). Don't be tempted to use either preshredded or nonfat cheddar cheese in this dish; the texture and flavor will suffer substantially. For best results, choose a low-fat cheddar cheese that is sold in block form and has roughly 50 percent of the fat and calories of regular cheddar cheese (we like Cabot and Cracker Barrel brands). Serve with salsa, avocados, low-fat sour cream, and/or scallions.

- 2 teaspoons canola oil
- 2 red bell peppers, stemmed, seeded, and cut into ½-inch pieces
- 1 onion, chopped fine
  Salt and pepper
- 3 garlic cloves, minced
- 1 tablespoon minced canned chipotle chile in adobo sauce
- 2 teaspoons chili powder
- 1 pound 93 percent lean ground turkey
- 2 tablespoons all-purpose flour
- 2 cups low-sodium chicken broth
- 2 (15-ounce) cans pinto beans, rinsed
- 2 cups frozen corn, thawed
- 1 (14.5-ounce) can diced tomatoes, drained
- 6 tablespoons minced fresh cilantro
- 2 tablespoons lime juice
- 12 (6-inch) corn tortillas
  Vegetable oil spray
- 4 ounces 50 percent light cheddar cheese, shredded (1 cup)
- 1 cup crushed baked tortilla chips

1. Adjust oven rack to middle position and heat oven to 350 degrees. Heat oil in Dutch oven over medium heat until shimmering. Add bell peppers, onion, and ½ teaspoon salt, cover, and cook until softened, 8 to 10 minutes.

2. Stir in garlic, chipotle, chili powder, and ¼ teaspoon pepper and cook until fragrant, about 30 seconds. Stir in turkey and cook, breaking up meat with wooden spoon, until no longer pink, 5 to 8 minutes. Stir in flour and cook for 1 minute.

3. Gradually stir in broth and bring to simmer. Stir in beans, corn, and tomatoes and simmer, uncovered, until mixture is slightly thickened and flavors have blended, about 10 minutes. Off heat, stir in ¼ cup cilantro and lime juice and season with salt and pepper to taste.

4. Meanwhile, lightly coat both sides of tortillas with oil spray. Place 6 tortillas on baking sheet and bake until tortillas are soft and pliable, 2 to 4 minutes; transfer to plate. Repeat with remaining 6 tortillas and transfer to plate. Increase oven temperature to 450 degrees.

5. Spread one-third of turkey mixture in 13 by 9-inch baking dish. Layer 6 tortillas on top of filling, overlapping as needed, and sprinkle with ⅓ cup cheddar. Repeat with half of remaining filling, remaining 6 tortillas, and ⅓ cup more cheddar. Spread remaining filling over top. Scatter chips over filling and sprinkle with remaining ⅓ cup cheddar.

6. Bake until filling is bubbling and cheese is melted, about 10 minutes. Let casserole cool for 10 minutes, then sprinkle with remaining 2 tablespoons cilantro. Serve.

PER SERVING: Cal 400; Fat 12g; Sat fat 3g; Chol 40mg; Carb 52g; Protein 24g; Fiber 9g; Sodium 720mg

---

NOTES FROM THE TEST KITCHEN

OUR FAVORITE DICED TOMATOES

Unlike most kinds of canned produce, which pale in comparison to their fresh counterparts, a great can of diced tomatoes offers flavor almost every bit as intense as ripe in-season fruit. But supermarket shelves are teeming with different brands of diced tomatoes. To make sense of the selection, we gathered 16 widely available styles and brands and tasted them plain and in tomato sauce, rating them on tomato flavor, saltiness, sweetness, texture, and overall appeal. To our surprise, nearly half of the brands fell short. We found that various factors, such as geography and additives, played into whether a sample rated highly. Our top-ranked tomatoes were grown in California, source of most of the world's tomatoes, where the dry, hot growing season develops sweet, complex flavor; the bottom-ranked brands came from the Midwest and Pennsylvania. In addition, tasters overwhelmingly favored those brands with more salt. In fact, the tomatoes with the least salt ranked last. In the end, one can, **Hunt's Diced Tomatoes**, stood out from the pack.

HERB-CRUSTED PORK TENDERLOIN WITH FENNEL, TOMATOES, AND ARTICHOKES

MEAT

M = TEST KITCHEN MAKEOVER

PERFECT PORK STIR-FRIES

FOR A FAST AND HEALTHY MEAL, STIR-FRYING CAN be a great choice. After all, stir-fries traditionally contain an ample portion of vegetables in addition to the lean protein, and they can be in and out of the skillet quickly. While recipes for pork stir-fries are easy to find, those for a *good* pork stir-fry are not. They typically suffer from the same problems that plague all types of stir-fries: tough, bland meat; nearly raw vegetables; and a greasy, slick, and unbalanced sauce. We wanted to make a few stir-fries that combined tender, flavorful pork and perfectly cooked vegetables with a balanced sauce. We wanted them to taste true to their Asian heritage, not like generic takeout. And, on top of all of this, they each had to be healthy and balanced. We had a challenging task in front of us; we decided to conquer the pork first.

Pork stir-fry recipes often call for pork shoulder, but pieces weighing less than several pounds can be hard to find. Not to mention, pork shoulder is quite fatty; to cook it quickly in a healthy stir-fry, we would need to remove the intramuscular fat and such a time-consuming step was out of the question for what we wanted. Instead, we chose pork tenderloin: Tender and yielding, it has the textural qualities of a filet mignon. In addition, pork tenderloin is one of the leanest cuts of pork available, so trimming away any excess fat was a breeze.

We figured the mild pork tenderloin would benefit from a bold flavor boost before hitting the skillet. Tossing the meat with low-sodium soy sauce worked well, providing a good subtle saltiness. But this did little to prevent the pork from drying out when stir-fried. We wondered if the technique called velveting, which we have used in the past when stir-frying chicken, was the answer. Velveting usually involves coating the meat with a thin mixture of cornstarch, flour, and oil to protect it from the high heat. Our original velveting method requires up to 1 tablespoon of oil, so we tested cutting the oil in half and upping the amount of the other liquids in our mixture to compensate. We combined 2 teaspoons of soy sauce with equal parts cornstarch, flour, and Chinese rice wine and stirred in just enough sesame oil and water (1½ teaspoons each) to make a smooth mixture. Our healthier velveted pork performed just as well as the velveted chicken, browning beautifully over high heat yet remaining moist, juicy, and full of flavor.

Next, we moved on to our vegetables, sauce, and flavorings. For our first stir-fry, we decided to pair our pork with a subtle combination of carrots and cabbage. We found that napa cabbage worked best for this stir-fry because it releases less liquid than its green cousin. As for the sauce, we knew that we wanted one with just enough substance and cling to coat our pork and vegetables without turning into a gloppy mess. To give it backbone without diluting flavor, we settled on chicken broth as our base, adding to it soy sauce, Chinese rice wine for a pop of flavor, a little sugar for balance. Plenty of ginger helped give this otherwise mild stir-fry some punch. Two teaspoons of cornstarch provided that clingy quality so the sauce lightly coated the pork and vegetables.

For a second variation, we set out to develop something more fiery. This time, scallions became our base vegetable, and they matched well with red bell peppers and edamame for a little extra protein. A spicy orange sauce contributed a sweetly pleasant heat that brought it all together. Finally, for a Thai-inspired version, we chose eggplant and onion, along with a huge hit of garlic (nine cloves) and black pepper. For the sauce, equal amounts of soy and fish sauce added depth, and lime juice lent a shot of bright acidity.

Now for putting it all together. Our standard test kitchen method for stir-fries requires preparing protein and vegetables in batches to ensure that each component is perfectly cooked. We usually use about 1½ teaspoons of oil per batch, but since we wanted to keep our total amount of fat as low as possible, we wondered how low we could go. We found that the minimum amount of oil we could use for each batch was 1 teaspoon; any less caused our vegetables to stick to the pan. To further boost flavor, we wanted to add aromatics (or more of them, in some cases), such as ginger and garlic. We already knew that simply adding aromatics at the beginning of cooking, as one does in a sauté, doesn't work for a stir-fry; the high heat will burn delicate garlic if it cooks for more than a minute or so. Instead, we made a paste with our aromatics. We cooked our protein in the skillet, then set it aside. The vegetables went into the pan, then we cleared the center and added a teaspoon of oil and the aromatic paste. Once it had cooked just until fragrant, we returned the pork to the pan, added our sauce, and stirred to coat.

A far cry from greasy, gloppy takeout, our trio of healthy pork stir-fries was balanced and vibrant.

Stir-Fried Pork and Napa Cabbage with Ginger Sauce

SERVES 4

To make it easier to slice the pork into thin strips, freeze it for 15 minutes (see at right for more information on slicing pork for stir-fries). The skillet will be quite full once the cabbage is added, but the cabbage will wilt down substantially. Serve with steamed white rice.

SAUCE

- ½ cup low-sodium chicken broth
- ¼ cup low-sodium soy sauce
- 2 tablespoons Chinese rice cooking wine or dry sherry
- 1 tablespoon sugar
- 2 teaspoons cornstarch
- 1 tablespoon grated fresh ginger

STIR-FRY

- 2 teaspoons cornstarch
- 2 teaspoons all-purpose flour
- 2 teaspoons low-sodium soy sauce
- 2 teaspoons Chinese rice cooking wine or dry sherry
- 1½ teaspoons toasted sesame oil
- 1½ teaspoons water
- 1 (12-ounce) pork tenderloin, trimmed of all visible fat and sliced into ¼-inch strips
- 4 teaspoons canola oil
- 3 scallions, minced
- 3 garlic cloves, minced
- 1 tablespoon grated fresh ginger
- 4 carrots, peeled and cut into 2-inch-long matchsticks
- ½ head napa cabbage, cored and shredded into 1-inch-wide pieces (5 cups)

1. FOR THE SAUCE: Whisk all ingredients together in bowl; set aside.

2. FOR THE STIR-FRY: Whisk cornstarch, flour, soy sauce, rice wine, sesame oil, and water together in bowl until smooth, then stir in pork until evenly coated. In another bowl, combine 1 teaspoon canola oil, scallions, garlic, and ginger.

3. Heat 1 teaspoon canola oil in 12-inch nonstick skillet over high heat until just smoking. Add pork, breaking up any clumps, and cook, without stirring, for 1 minute. Stir pork and continue to cook until lightly browned, about 1 minute longer; transfer to clean bowl.

SLICING PORK TENDERLOIN

Although some stir-fry recipes call for ground pork or thinly sliced boneless chops, we find that strips cut from pork tenderloin are the most tender and flavorful option, and it doesn't hurt that tenderloin is also very lean.

1. To make it easier to cut pork thin, place pork tenderloin in freezer for 15 minutes. Then place partially frozen tenderloin on clean, dry counter. Using sharp chef's knife, slice pork crosswise into ¼-inch-thick medallions.

2. Slice each medallion into ¼-inch-wide strips.

CUTTING CARROTS INTO MATCHSTICKS

1. Start by slicing carrot on bias into 2-inch-long, oval-shaped pieces.

2. Lay ovals flat on cutting board, then slice ovals into 2-inch-long matchsticks, about ¼ inch thick.

4. Add remaining 2 teaspoons canola oil to now-empty skillet and return to high heat until shimmering. Add carrots and cook until crisp-tender, 3 to 4 minutes. Stir in cabbage and cook, stirring constantly, until cabbage is slightly wilted and crisp-tender, about 2 minutes.

5. Clear center of skillet, add scallion mixture, and cook, mashing mixture into pan, until fragrant, about 30 seconds. Stir scallion mixture into vegetables.

6. Return pork, with any accumulated juices, to skillet. Whisk sauce to recombine, then add to skillet. Cook, stirring constantly, until sauce is thickened, about 30 seconds. Transfer to platter and serve.

PER SERVING: **Cal** 250; **Fat** 9g; **Sat fat** 1g; **Chol** 55mg; **Carb** 20g; **Protein** 22g; **Fiber** 3g; **Sodium** 810mg

VARIATIONS

Stir-Fried Pork, Scallions, and Edamame with Spicy Orange Sauce

SERVES 4

To make it easier to slice the pork into thin strips, freeze it for 15 minutes first. Sliced scallion whites and greens are used as a vegetable in this recipe; you will need about 2 bunches. Serve with steamed white rice.

SAUCE

- ¼ cup Chinese rice cooking wine or dry sherry
- 2 tablespoons low-sodium soy sauce
- 1 tablespoon Asian chili-garlic sauce
- 2 teaspoons sugar
- 2 teaspoons cornstarch
- 1 teaspoon grated orange zest plus ½ cup juice

STIR-FRY

- 2 teaspoons cornstarch
- 2 teaspoons all-purpose flour
- 2 teaspoons low-sodium soy sauce
- 2 teaspoons Chinese rice cooking wine or dry sherry
- 1½ teaspoons toasted sesame oil
- 1½ teaspoons water
- 1 (12-ounce) pork tenderloin, trimmed of all visible fat and sliced into ¼-inch strips (see page 83)
- 4 teaspoons canola oil
- 3 garlic cloves, minced
- 1 tablespoon grated fresh ginger
- 12 scallions, white and green parts separated, both parts sliced on bias into 1-inch pieces
- 2 red bell peppers, stemmed, seeded, and cut into ¼-inch-wide strips
- ¾ cup frozen shelled edamame beans

1. FOR THE SAUCE: Whisk all ingredients together in bowl.

2. FOR THE STIR-FRY: Whisk cornstarch, flour, soy sauce, rice wine, sesame oil, and water together in bowl until smooth, then stir in pork until evenly coated. In another bowl, combine 1 teaspoon canola oil, garlic, and ginger.

3. Heat 1 teaspoon canola oil in 12-inch nonstick skillet over high heat until just smoking. Add pork, breaking up any clumps, and cook, without stirring, for 1 minute. Stir pork and continue to cook until lightly browned, about 1 minute longer; transfer to clean bowl.

4. Add remaining 2 teaspoons canola oil to now-empty skillet and return to high heat until shimmering. Add scallion whites and cook until whites begin to soften, about 1 minute. Stir in bell peppers and edamame and cook until vegetables are crisp-tender, 3 to 4 minutes.

5. Clear center of skillet, add garlic mixture, and cook, mashing mixture into pan, until fragrant, about 30 seconds. Stir garlic mixture into vegetables.

6. Return pork, with any accumulated juices, to skillet. Stir in scallion greens. Whisk sauce to recombine, then add to skillet. Cook, stirring constantly, until sauce is thickened, about 30 seconds. Transfer to platter and serve.

PER SERVING: **Cal** 290; **Fat** 10g; **Sat fat** 1g; **Chol** 55mg; **Carb** 23g; **Protein** 25g; **Fiber** 5g; **Sodium** 530mg

---

NOTES FROM THE TEST KITCHEN

SLICING BELL PEPPERS INTO STRIPS

1. After slicing top and bottom off of pepper and removing seeds and stem, set pepper on cut end and slice down through side of pepper.

2. Lay pepper flat on cutting board and slice into ¼-inch-wide strips.

STIR-FRIED PORK, SCALLIONS, AND EDAMAME WITH SPICY ORANGE SAUCE

Stir-Fried Pork, Eggplant, and Onion with Garlic and Black Pepper

SERVES 4

This take on a classic Thai stir-fry is not for those with timid palates; it has an intense and slightly salty flavor. To make the pork easier to slice into thin strips, freeze it for 15 minutes first. Leaving the skin on the eggplant keeps the pieces intact during cooking. Serve with steamed white rice.

SAUCE

- ½ cup low-sodium chicken broth
- ¼ cup water
- 2½ tablespoons packed brown sugar
- 4 teaspoons fish sauce
- 4 teaspoons low-sodium soy sauce
- 2 teaspoons lime juice
- 2 teaspoons cornstarch

STIR-FRY

- 5½ teaspoons canola oil
- 2 teaspoons cornstarch
- 2 teaspoons all-purpose flour
- 2 teaspoons fish sauce
- 2 teaspoons Chinese rice cooking wine or dry sherry
- 1½ teaspoons water
- 1 (12-ounce) pork tenderloin, trimmed of all visible fat and sliced into ¼-inch strips (see page 83)
- 9 garlic cloves, minced
- 2 teaspoons pepper
- 1 pound eggplant, cut into ¾-inch cubes
- 1 large onion, halved and sliced into ¼-inch wedges
- ¼ cup chopped fresh cilantro

1. FOR THE SAUCE: Whisk all ingredients together in bowl.

2. FOR THE STIR-FRY: Whisk 1½ teaspoons oil, cornstarch, flour, fish sauce, rice wine, and water together in bowl until smooth, then stir in pork until evenly coated. In separate bowl, combine 1 teaspoon oil, garlic, and pepper.

3. Heat 1 teaspoon oil in 12-inch nonstick skillet over high heat until just smoking. Add pork, breaking up any clumps, and cook, without stirring, for 1 minute. Stir pork and continue to cook until lightly browned, about 1 minute longer; transfer to clean bowl.

4. Add 1 teaspoon oil to now-empty skillet and return to high heat until shimmering. Add eggplant and cook until eggplant begins to brown and is no longer spongy, 5 to 7 minutes. Transfer to bowl with pork.

5. Add remaining 1 teaspoon oil to now-empty skillet and return to high heat until shimmering. Add onion and cook until just softened and lightly browned, about 2 minutes. Clear center of skillet, add garlic mixture, and cook, mashing mixture into pan, until fragrant, about 30 seconds. Stir garlic mixture into onion.

6. Return cooked pork and eggplant, with any accumulated juices, to skillet. Whisk sauce to recombine, then add to skillet. Simmer, stirring constantly, until sauce is thickened, about 30 seconds. Transfer to platter, sprinkle with cilantro, and serve.

PER SERVING: Cal 270; Fat 9g; Sat fat 1g; Chol 55mg; Carb 28g; Protein 21g; Fiber 5g; Sodium 650mg

CIDER-GLAZED PORK CHOPS

BONELESS PORK CHOPS ARE A FAVORITE LIGHT weeknight meal since they are a quick-cooking and naturally lean, but they are easy to overcook and often turn out bland and stringy. Could we come up with a great pork chop recipe that was worth making? We'd need to choose our cooking method carefully and create a bold sauce to pair with the subtle flavor of the chops.

We knew from experience that a perfect counterpart for pork chops is a sweet, saucy glaze, and glazes are well suited to light cooking since they usually contain little to no additional fat. Boneless chops are such a quick-cooking protein that we'd want to formulate our glaze so it was ready at about the same time that the pork was ready for the table. We quickly came up with a working recipe as our starting point: We would brown and cook our chops, then build our glaze in the hot skillet (picking up all of the flavorful fond along the way) while the chops rested. It sounded easy enough to us.

We figured that cooking the pork chops properly would be the easy part. We put a little oil in our skillet, set it over medium-high heat, and once the oil was smoking we cooked the chops until they had even color on both sides. Unfortunately, we had trouble getting a rich sear on the lean chops without overcooking them. Then we thought maybe we could get away with searing one side of each chop pretty heavily and putting a quick sear on the second side. Although this worked, the timing was critical: A few extra seconds took the chops from perfectly tender to dry and tough. Although workable, we had been hoping for something a little more foolproof. We decided to put the pork chops on hold while we experimented with the glaze.

We started by whipping up a few simple test glazes. In terms of liquids we tried water, broth, and fruit juices, and for sweeteners we tested maple syrup, honey, granulated sugar, and brown sugar. Glazes made with water tasted, well, watery; and those made with broth tasted too much like gravy. Tasters felt the maple syrup was better saved for French toast and waffles, and honey tended to crystallize and become grainy. Apple cider, on the other hand, created pleasing depth of flavor with a touch of sweetness, and brown sugar added a complementary caramel-y note. A generous glug of apple cider vinegar lent a balancing acidity. Low-sodium soy sauce, Dijon mustard, and cayenne pepper finished the sauce perfectly. Once the cooked chops were set aside, we poured the mixture into the skillet and let it simmer until it was thick enough to coat our pork chops.

While this glaze was tasty, it was taking 10 to 15 minutes to reduce; by then our pork chops had grown cold. To streamline and save time, one taster suggested finding a method for adding the glaze to the pan before the chops finished cooking.

Not only did this work, but it also gave us the insurance we'd been missing in our cooking method. Finishing the chops over moderate heat (which was a must to avoid burning the glaze) slowed things down just enough to give us a better chance of getting them out of the pan while they were still juicy. What's more, unlike the high, relatively dry heat of searing, gently simmering the chops in the wet glaze over moderate heat helped them retain moisture. Once the meat reached 140 degrees, a five-minute rest on a platter let their internal temperature rise a bit and let the juices redistribute. Meanwhile, we let the glaze reduce, then returned the chops to the skillet to be coated by the glaze. *Voilà*—perfectly cooked glazed pork chops.

With our master recipe nailed down, we could develop some variations. First we made a pub-inspired version. We added some whole grain mustard for a crunchy, spicy kick, replaced the apple cider with beer for malty complexity, and added caraway and fresh thyme to round out the flavors. For a second variation, we took our chops in a Japanese-inspired direction: We swapped in rice vinegar for the cider vinegar, added orange juice and mirin for sweetness, ginger for a subtle kick, and sesame oil and sesame seeds to finish.

Finally, we had an easy, quick, and healthy weeknight meal ready to go.

Cider-Glazed Pork Chops
SERVES 4

These pork chops get a deep browning on only one side; this ensures that you get the benefits of browning without overcooking the chops.

GLAZE
- ½ cup cider vinegar
- ⅓ cup packed brown sugar
- ⅓ cup apple cider or apple juice
- 2 tablespoons Dijon mustard
- 1 tablespoon low-sodium soy sauce
-    Pinch cayenne pepper

PORK CHOPS
- 4 (6-ounce) boneless pork chops, ¾ to 1 inch thick, trimmed of all visible fat
- ⅛ teaspoon salt
- ⅛ teaspoon pepper
- 2 teaspoons vegetable oil

1. FOR THE GLAZE: Stir all ingredients together in bowl until well combined.

2. FOR THE PORK CHOPS: Pat pork chops dry with paper towels and season with salt and pepper. Heat oil in 12-inch skillet over medium-high heat until just smoking. Brown chops well on first side, 4 to 6 minutes. Flip chops and cook for 1 minute.

3. Reduce heat to medium and add glaze mixture. Simmer until pork registers 145 degrees, 5 to 8 minutes. Transfer chops to platter, tent loosely with aluminum foil, and let rest for 5 minutes.

4. Stir any accumulated meat juices into glaze left in skillet and bring to simmer over medium heat, whisking constantly, until glaze has thickened, about 5 minutes. Off heat, return chops to skillet and turn to coat both sides with glaze. Transfer chops back to platter, browned side up, pour remaining glaze over chops, and serve.

PER SERVING: Cal 330; Fat 9g; Sat fat 2g; Chol 115mg; Carb 23g; Protein 38g; Fiber 0g; Sodium 490mg

Orange-Glazed Pork Chops with Ginger and Sesame

SERVES 4

To quickly and easily grate the ginger, we prefer to use a rasp-style grater.

GLAZE

½ cup rice vinegar

⅓ cup packed brown sugar

3 tablespoons orange juice

3 tablespoons mirin

2 tablespoons Dijon mustard

1 tablespoon low-sodium soy sauce

1 teaspoon grated fresh ginger

Pinch cayenne pepper

PORK CHOPS

4 (6-ounce) boneless pork chops, ¾ to 1 inch thick, trimmed of all visible fat

⅛ teaspoon salt

⅛ teaspoon pepper

2 teaspoons vegetable oil

2 teaspoons rice vinegar

1 teaspoon toasted sesame oil

1 teaspoon toasted sesame seeds

1. FOR THE GLAZE: Stir all ingredients together in bowl until well combined.

2. FOR THE PORK CHOPS: Pat pork chops dry with paper towels and season with salt and pepper. Heat oil in 12-inch skillet over medium-high heat until just smoking. Brown chops well on first side, 4 to 6 minutes. Flip chops and cook for 1 minute.

3. Reduce heat to medium and add glaze mixture. Simmer until pork registers 145 degrees, 5 to 8 minutes. Transfer chops to platter, tent loosely with aluminum foil, and let rest for 5 minutes.

4. Stir rice vinegar and any accumulated meat juices into glaze left in skillet and bring to simmer over medium heat, whisking constantly, until glaze has thickened, about 5 minutes. Off heat, return chops to skillet and turn to coat both sides with glaze. Transfer chops back to platter, browned side up, pour remaining glaze over chops, sprinkle with sesame oil and sesame seeds, and serve.

PER SERVING: Cal 360; Fat 10g; Sat fat 2g; Chol 115mg; Carb 25g; Protein 38g; Fiber 0g; Sodium 490mg

NOTES FROM THE TEST KITCHEN

ENHANCED AND UNENHANCED PORK

Because modern pork is remarkably lean and therefore somewhat bland and prone to dryness if overcooked, a product called "enhanced" pork has overtaken the market. Enhanced pork has been injected with a solution of water, salt, sodium phosphates, sodium lactate, potassium lactate, sodium diacetate, and various flavor agents to bolster flavor and juiciness; these enhancing ingredients add 7 to 15 percent extra weight. (Pork containing additives must be labeled as such with a list of ingredients.) After several taste tests, we have concluded that, although enhanced pork is indeed juicier and more tender than unenhanced pork, the latter has more genuine pork flavor. Some tasters picked up artificial, salty flavors in enhanced pork. (Never brine enhanced pork, which only intensifies the saltiness, resulting in virtually inedible meat.) It can also leach juices that, once reduced, will result in overly salty sauces. We prefer natural pork, but the choice is up to you.

Mustard-Glazed Pork Chops with Beer and Caraway

SERVES 4

A lager-style beer, such as Budweiser, works well in this glaze.

GLAZE

½ cup cider vinegar

⅓ cup packed brown sugar

⅓ cup beer

3 tablespoons whole grain mustard

2 tablespoons Dijon mustard

1 tablespoon minced fresh thyme

2 teaspoons low-sodium soy sauce

¾ teaspoon caraway seeds, toasted and chopped coarse

PORK CHOPS

4 (6-ounce) boneless pork chops, ¾ to 1 inch thick, trimmed of all visible fat

⅛ teaspoon salt

⅛ teaspoon pepper

2 teaspoons vegetable oil

1. FOR THE GLAZE: Stir all ingredients together in bowl until well combined.

2. FOR THE PORK CHOPS: Pat pork chops dry with paper towels and season with salt and pepper. Heat oil in 12-inch skillet over medium-high heat until just smoking. Brown chops well on first side, 4 to 6 minutes. Flip chops and cook for 1 minute.

3. Reduce heat to medium and add glaze mixture. Simmer until pork registers 145 degrees, 5 to 8 minutes. Transfer chops to platter, tent loosely with aluminum foil, and let rest for 5 minutes.

4. Stir any accumulated meat juices into glaze left in skillet and bring to simmer over medium heat, whisking constantly, until glaze has thickened, about 5 minutes. Off heat, return chops to skillet and turn to coat both sides with glaze. Transfer chops back to platter, browned side up, pour remaining glaze over chops, and serve.

PER SERVING: **Cal** 360; **Fat** 10g; **Sat fat** 2g; **Chol** 115mg; **Carb** 21g; **Protein** 38g; **Fiber** 0g; **Sodium** 670mg

SPICY MEXICAN PORK AND RICE

THE SIMPLE TECHNIQUE OF COOKING RICE IN A flavorful liquid has been used to great effect by cultures the world over (think chicken and rice, paella, risotto, and pilaf). The rice acts like a sponge, absorbing richness and flavor from the broth. One of the test kitchen's favorite variations on this theme is a Mexican-style recipe we developed this past year incorporating chunks of pork butt into a pot of flavorful rice. Spiced with chipotle chiles and bathed in a tomatoey sauce, this dish was jam-packed with flavor but, unfortunately, also jam-packed with calories and fat. Our dish tipped the scales at 610 calories and 35 grams of fat (11 grams of it saturated) per serving. Could we slim down this favorite but still maintain its bold identity?

When developing our original pork and rice dish, we browned the pork, then simmered it in a combination of chicken broth and tomato sauce. We started it in a low oven, cooking the pork until it was falling-apart tender, then we stirred in rice and let it simmer in a higher-temperature oven until it absorbed all of the liquid. Flavoring the pot with onion, oregano, garlic, thyme, and canned chipotle chiles in adobo sauce ensured big flavor in every bite (canned chipotles are not only easier to use and locate than their dried brethren, but the adobo sauce in which they are packed adds smoke and depth).

TEST KITCHEN MAKEOVER

In our lightened version, we knew we wanted to maintain the same flavor profile as the original but cut back substantially on fat. Since our original choice of meat, pork butt, is a well-marbled cut (especially well suited to long cooking times), it was the main source of fat in our dish. We tried substituting everything from pork tenderloin to boneless country-style ribs, but nothing was quite right, so we had to stick with the pork butt. Trimming it of all the fat we could find was a start, and we decided to skip the browning step—there was so much flavor it didn't seem essential—which cut back on the amount of oil needed in the final dish. We also found that even with well-trimmed pork, the 2 pounds of meat used in the original recipe was too much for our makeover. We scaled the meat back to 1½ pounds, which cut the fat down to 6 grams per serving. To compensate, tasters approved of adding a can of pinto beans toward the end of cooking. These changes not only brought down our fat count, but they also slashed the calories by almost half.

In our original tests, we discovered that choosing the best rice for our dish was quite a challenge. We tested both medium-grain rice and long-grain rice (both are staples in the Mexican kitchen). We found that the long-grain rice was too fluffy for this substantial, homey dish, and medium-grain rice turned out a pot of Mexican-style risotto (not a good thing). In either case, we needed to modify the amount of liquid used from our standard ratio of 1½ cups liquid to 1 cup rice. Since it seemed easier to make the long-grain rice more dense than to make the medium-grain rice fluffier, we chose to add more liquid to the pot with long-grain.

For our original recipe, 2 cups of broth and 1 cup of rice had worked well, but our lighter version, it turned out, couldn't just follow suit. The cause of the problem was twofold: The beans were creating little nooks and crannies in which rice could hide, leading to some unevenly cooked rice grains, plus our well-trimmed pork exuded less liquid into the pot than the fattier version, which meant the final dish was too dry. We didn't want to lose the pleasantly dense consistency of the original, but we knew we'd need to make some serious modifications for our new version to work.

First, we increased the broth amount all the way up to 2½ cups. This helped the rice to cook more quickly and evenly, but, given the extra liquid, it was now too starchy. To fix this problem, we rinsed the extra starch off the grains before adding them to the pot. This rice

SPICY MEXICAN PORK AND RICE

was the best of both worlds: substantial without being pasty, and fluffy enough to balance the rich pork and sauce. Our rice conundrum solved, we moved on to some final touches.

To cut the pork's richness (even though there was less now), lime juice and fresh cilantro were musts, providing citrusy brightness as well as unmistakable Mexican character. Finally, we added sliced scallions to the mix for clean, subtle onion flavor. Other options for toppings that worked well were low-fat sour cream, queso fresco, and/or diced avocado. Any way we chose to garnish it, our new, lightened Mexican pork and rice was as bold as the original, and with 260 fewer calories and 29 grams less fat, it was just as much of a favorite.

MAKEOVER SPOTLIGHT: MEXICAN PORK AND RICE

	CALORIES	FAT	SAT FAT	CHOLESTEROL
BEFORE	610	35g	11g	105mg
AFTER	350	6g	1.5g	50mg

Spicy Mexican Pork and Rice
SERVES 6

Be sure to stir the rice gently when cooking in step 5; aggressive stirring will make the rice taste gluey. Boneless pork butt roast is often labeled Boston butt in the supermarket. Serve this dish with low-fat sour cream, avocado, and/or queso fresco, if desired.

- 1 teaspoon olive oil
- 2 onions, chopped fine
  Salt and pepper
- 5 garlic cloves, minced
- 1 tablespoon minced canned chipotle chile in adobo sauce
- 1 teaspoon minced fresh thyme
- ½ teaspoon dried oregano
- 2½ cups low-sodium chicken broth
- 1 (8-ounce) can tomato sauce
- 1½ pounds boneless pork butt roast, pulled apart at seams, trimmed of all visible fat, and cut into 1-inch pieces
- 1½ cups long-grain white rice, rinsed
- 1 (15-ounce) can pinto beans, rinsed
- ½ cup minced fresh cilantro
- 3 scallions, sliced thin
- 1 tablespoon lime juice plus lime wedges for serving

1. Adjust oven rack to lower-middle position and heat oven to 300 degrees.

2. Heat oil in Dutch oven over medium heat until shimmering. Add onion and ½ teaspoon salt, cover, and cook until onion is softened, 8 to 10 minutes. Uncover, stir in garlic, chipotle, thyme, and oregano, and cook until fragrant, about 30 seconds. Stir in broth and tomato sauce, scraping up any browned bits.

3. Add pork and bring to simmer, skimming off any foam that rises to surface. Cover, transfer pot to oven, and cook until fork slips easily in and out of pork, 75 to 90 minutes.

4. Remove pot from oven and increase oven temperature to 350 degrees. Let liquid settle for 5 minutes, then remove fat from surface using large spoon.

5. Bring defatted braising liquid to simmer and thoroughly stir in rice and beans. Cover and continue to cook in oven until rice is tender and all liquid has been absorbed, 20 to 30 minutes longer, gently stirring rice from bottom of pot to top every 10 minutes.

6. Stir in cilantro, scallions, and lime juice and season with salt and pepper to taste. Cover and let stand for 5 minutes. Serve with lime wedges.

PER 1½-CUP SERVING: Cal 350; Fat 6g; Sat fat 1.5g; Chol 50mg; Carb 50g; Protein 22g; Fiber 5g; Sodium 800mg

HERB-CRUSTED PORK TENDERLOIN

WHILE WE LOVE PORK CHOPS FOR AN EASY DINNER, there's another cut of pork that is equally suited to a quick meal: the tenderloin. Nothing can match the fine-grained, buttery-smooth texture of pork tenderloins when they're cooked properly, plus they're naturally lean. And because they are relatively long and thin, they cook quickly. These two pros, however, lead to a few cons. It is quite easy to overcook the tenderloin into a dry, flavorless shadow of a roast. To guarantee flavorful results, we knew we'd need to add bold seasoning and cook our pork with a watchful eye, and we wanted to develop a creative side dish to roast alongside.

When cooking pork tenderloin, we typically start by searing it on the stovetop to brown the exterior for both flavor and color. But we were looking for simplicity. What could do the job with minimal work? We wondered if a dry rub was the answer. Seasoning with salt and pepper provided a solid base, but we wanted a distinct flavor profile to guide the rest of the dish. Herbes de Provence, a dried herb blend that usually includes thyme, fennel, savory, marjoram, and lavender, would give a distinctively Mediterranean flavor profile to our pork without requiring a number of different herbs and spices. After a very potent first test, we learned that a little of this blend goes a long way; a mere 2 teaspoons was sufficient to flavor and coat two tenderloins without overwhelming the pork.

Because pork tenderloins tend to be long, thin, and lean, a relatively brief stay in a hot oven works best to avoid overcooking. We found that roasting the tenderloins at 450 degrees for about 30 minutes was all that was needed to bring the interior of the pork to a rosy 140 degrees. To optimize browning on the exterior of the pork, we turned the tenderloins over halfway through the cooking time.

Finding a vegetable accompaniment for such a quick-cooking meat was tricky; after just 30 minutes of roasting time, most root vegetables are still raw, yet more delicate vegetables, such as green beans or asparagus, are totally overcooked. Thinking again about our Mediterranean-inspired rub, we wondered if fennel might work, since its sweet, delicate flavor would be the perfect complement to our pork tenderloin. However, we knew from previous experience that 30 minutes is not quite enough time to cook fennel to its tender best. So we decided to give it a jump start in the microwave.

After five minutes, the fennel was just beginning to soften and was ready to go in the oven. We tossed it with artichoke hearts, niçoise olives, and 2 tablespoons of olive oil, spread the mixture in the roasting pan, and placed the tenderloins on top.

After 30 minutes, the pork was finished, but the vegetables were dry and flavorless, and the fennel still had a little too much crunch. The cooking time was easy to fix: We knew that the pork needed to rest for about 10 minutes before serving, and in that amount of time, the fennel was tender. But the vegetable mixture still needed more flavor and more moisture. For acidity and brightness, we decided to add tomatoes and lemon (in the form of both juice and zest) to the mix. Since the tomatoes didn't need to cook quite as long as the fennel, we waited to stir them in until we flipped the pork over halfway through cooking. To fix the dryness, we stirred in a little chicken broth when we removed the pork. Finally, to finish, we added a generous sprinkling of fresh parsley and a light drizzle of olive oil.

In less than an hour, we were transported to Provence with a dinner that was low on fuss but high on flavor.

Herb-Crusted Pork Tenderloin with Fennel, Tomatoes, and Artichokes
SERVES 6

Be sure to thoroughly thaw and pat dry the frozen artichokes; otherwise, their moisture will inhibit the browning of the vegetables. Herbes de Provence, a blend of dried herbs such as rosemary, basil, marjoram, fennel, thyme, and lavender, is available in the spice aisle of supermarkets.

- 2 (1-pound) pork tenderloins, trimmed of all visible fat
- 2 teaspoons dried herbes de Provence
  Salt and pepper
- 2 large fennel bulbs, stalks discarded, halved, cored, and cut into ½-inch-thick slices (see page 60)
- 12 ounces frozen artichoke hearts, thawed and patted dry
- ⅓ cup pitted niçoise or kalamata olives, chopped coarse
- 8 teaspoons extra-virgin olive oil
- 4 garlic cloves, minced
- 1 pound cherry tomatoes, halved
- ½ cup low-sodium chicken broth
- 1 tablespoon grated lemon zest plus 2 tablespoons juice
- 2 tablespoons minced fresh parsley

1. Adjust oven rack to lower-middle position and heat oven to 450 degrees. Pat pork dry with paper towels, then season with herbes de Provence, ⅛ teaspoon salt, and ⅛ teaspoon pepper.

2. Combine fennel and 2 tablespoons water in bowl, cover, and microwave until softened, about 5 minutes. Drain fennel well and toss with artichokes, olives, 2 tablespoons oil, garlic, ¼ teaspoon salt, and pepper to taste.

3. Spread vegetables in large roasting pan. Lay pork on top of vegetables. Roast pork and vegetables for 15 minutes. Turn pork over and add tomatoes to roasting pan. Continue to roast pork and vegetables until meat registers 145 degrees, 10 to 15 minutes longer.

4. Transfer pork to carving board, tent loosely with aluminum foil, and let rest for 10 minutes. Meanwhile, stir broth and lemon zest into vegetables and continue to roast until fennel is tender and tomatoes have softened, about 10 minutes.

5. Stir remaining 2 teaspoons oil, lemon juice, and parsley into roasted vegetables and season with salt and pepper to taste. Slice pork ½ inch thick and serve with vegetables.

PER SERVING: Cal 340; Fat 13g; Sat fat 2g; Chol 100mg; Carb 21g; Protein 36g; Fiber 9g; Sodium 540mg

ROAST PORK LOIN WITH SWEET POTATOES AND CILANTRO SAUCE

UNASSUMING AND SIMPLE TO PREPARE, A BONELESS pork roast is hearty fare for a Sunday dinner. When cooked correctly, the meat is tender and juicy, its flavor sweet and mild—usually so mild that a spicy rub or tangy sauce is welcome. In addition, these roasts are naturally lean, so they make for nearly effortless light cooking. Our goals for the roast were simple: We wanted a foolproof method for cooking the meat without drying it out; we wanted a boldly flavored, low-fat sauce that would complement the pork without overwhelming it; and we wanted a healthy side dish that we could roast alongside the pork. We thought of a recipe we had recently developed for Roast Pork Loin and Sweet Potatoes with a bright cilantro sauce. It seemed like a great candidate for lightening up.

Since the flavor of the sauce can guide the rest of the dish, we decided to start there when developing our original recipe. We knew that we wanted to keep the sauce simple with just a few basic ingredients and minimal prep. A no-cook sauce sounded promising; a mixture along the lines of a fresh salsa or pesto would be flavorful and light, and it would give our meal some direction. While brainstorming ideas, one of our test cooks recalled a Cuban dish she particularly enjoyed: tender pork served with a tangy cilantro sauce.

The sauce our colleague described was fresh and light, similar to a loose pesto. While this was fine for our original recipe, for our lighter version it wouldn't do. The problem with a sauce of this type is that it is typically made by combining herbs with a good amount of oil. In fact, our original recipe contained ½ cup of extra-virgin olive oil. Simply taking out most of the oil and substituting water threw everything out of balance, so we revisited the ingredients. Drawing from a test kitchen recipe for a light mint relish, we combined minced cilantro with 2 tablespoons each of water and olive oil and 1 tablespoon of lime juice. We added a bit of garlic and scallion for complexity and a touch of sugar for balance. Our sauce was tangy, refreshing, and just loose enough to drizzle over a roast.

While we were pleased with our sauce, we knew that no matter how good it was, it could never disguise a dry, overcooked pork loin, so next we turned our attention to creating a juicy and flavorful pork roast. In our original recipe, we started by brining the pork (soaking it in a saltwater solution), which is a technique we often use in the test kitchen to season and boost the juiciness of meat. And brining did indeed yield tender, juicy, well-seasoned pork, but we quickly learned that it didn't protect the pork from overcooking and drying out if roasted at too high a temperature. After much trial and error, we found that we got the best results from cooking the roast in a moderate 375-degree oven until it registered 140 degrees. The temperature of the roast continued to rise out of the oven, and it reached its ideal serving temperature of 145 degrees while resting on a carving board before slicing.

In many test kitchen recipes for large roasts, we brown the meat first before placing it in the oven. This step helps to develop meaty flavor, but it also introduces extra fat and extra work. Luckily, in our original recipe, our goal had been simplicity and we had skipped the browning. Instead, we used a dry rub that complemented our Cuban-inspired sauce and lent visual appeal. A mixture of ground coriander, cumin, salt, and pepper gave the pork's exterior both color and flavor, and it also complemented our lively cilantro sauce.

With our pork loin and sauce perfected, we could look at rounding out the meal. We considered several options but eventually settled on creamy, rich sweet potatoes. For our original recipe we tossed sweet potato chunks with 3 tablespoons of oil and a pinch of cayenne pepper and roasted them with the pork. Could we cut back on the oil? When we reduced it to 1 tablespoon, we ended up with undercooked potatoes that stuck to the roasting pan. We tried switching to a nonstick roasting pan, but the dark color of the pan caused our potatoes to burn in the time it took to cook them through. We decided that we would need to go up a little on oil (to 2 tablespoons), and for extra assurance, we lined our pan with parchment paper (we had tried aluminum foil, but it was more difficult to work with). To make sure that the potatoes cooked through, we left them in the oven for an extra 10 to 15 minutes after we took the pork out to rest.

With that, both elements of our walk-away pork roast dinner were ready to be drizzled with the fresh cilantro sauce. Making a light, well-rounded, and flavor-packed Sunday dinner couldn't get much easier than this.

NOTES FROM THE TEST KITCHEN

TYING A PORK ROAST
Most pork loin roasts are unevenly shaped, which makes it challenging to cook them evenly. Tying the roast helps by holding the meat in a more even shape, which in turn evens out the cooking. It also tidies slumped roasts into neat, round ones, making for a nice presentation and easier slicing. Here's how to do it:

Wrap 1 piece of butcher's twine around roast and tie with double knot. Snip off excess and repeat down length of roast, spacing each tie 1 to 1½ inches apart. Knots should be snug but not so tight that twine cuts into meat.

Roast Pork Loin with Sweet Potatoes and Cilantro Sauce
SERVES 8

To prevent sticking, you will need to use a rimmed baking sheet lined with parchment paper. A ⅛-inch-thick layer of fat on top of the roast is ideal; if your roast has a thicker fat cap, trim it back accordingly. If the pork is enhanced, skip step 1 and season the roast with ⅛ teaspoon salt in step 2 (see page 88 for more about enhanced pork).

PORK AND POTATOES
- ¼ cup sugar
- Salt and pepper
- 1 (3-pound) boneless pork loin roast, fat trimmed to ⅛-inch thickness and tied at 1-inch intervals
- 1 teaspoon ground coriander
- 1 teaspoon ground cumin
- 3 pounds sweet potatoes, peeled, quartered, and cut into 2-inch pieces
- 2 tablespoons vegetable oil
- ⅛ teaspoon cayenne pepper

CILANTRO SAUCE
- ½ cup minced fresh cilantro
- 2 tablespoons water
- 2 tablespoons extra-virgin olive oil
- 1 tablespoon lime juice
- 1 teaspoon sugar
- ½ small shallot, minced
- 1 garlic clove, minced
- Salt and pepper

1. FOR THE PORK AND POTATOES: Dissolve sugar and ¼ cup salt in 2 quarts water in large container. Submerge pork in brine, cover, and refrigerate for 1½ to 2 hours.

2. Adjust oven rack to lower-middle position and heat oven to 375 degrees. Line rimmed baking sheet with parchment paper and spray with vegetable oil spray. Remove pork from brine and pat dry with paper towels. Season pork with coriander, cumin, and ½ teaspoon pepper and place in center of prepared sheet.

3. Toss sweet potatoes with ¼ teaspoon salt, oil, and cayenne, then spread evenly on pan around pork. Roast pork and potatoes until pork registers 140 degrees, 50 to 70 minutes, turning roast over and stirring potatoes halfway through roasting.

4. FOR THE CILANTRO SAUCE: Meanwhile, stir all ingredients together in bowl until well combined. Season with pepper to taste.

5. Transfer pork to carving board, tent loosely with aluminum foil, and let rest for 15 minutes. Meanwhile, stir potatoes and continue to roast until spotty brown, 10 to 15 minutes longer. Slice pork ¼ inch thick and serve with potatoes and cilantro sauce.

PER SERVING: **Cal** 420; **Fat** 14g; **Sat fat** 2.5g; **Chol** 115mg; **Carb** 31g; **Protein** 40g; **Fiber** 5g; **Sodium** 410mg

PERFECT FILETS MIGNONS

WHEN IT COMES TO ENJOYING A GOOD STEAK, Americans prize tenderness above all, and filet mignon is the most tender steak there is. At restaurants, filets are usually served rare, with a deeply seared crust and adorned with a rich, luxurious pan sauce. Since they are naturally very lean, filets make for a great celebratory food for the health-conscious cook—as long as you skip the butter-laden pan sauce. We wanted to bring the filet out of the restaurant kitchen and into the home, creating an easy, healthy method of preparation, along with a sauce that could enhance the steak without enhancing our waistlines.

To replicate the best restaurant filets at home, we would need to develop a deeply browned, rich crust on both sides of each steak without overcooking the interior. We would also need to avoid scorching the drippings in the pan, since the drippings would go on to serve as the basis for our sauce. To that end, we investigated the finer points of both the steaks themselves and the cooking process.

Filets are thick (usually 1¼ to 2 inches), boneless steaks, cut from the slender, super-tender, ultra-lean tenderloin muscle, which rests under the animal's spine. The muscle remains tender because the animal doesn't use it to move about, and it is both lean and mildly flavored because it has little marbling. To determine the optimal thickness for filets, we cooked steaks cut 1 and 2 inches thick and at ¼-inch intervals in between. Tasters preferred the steaks cut 1¼ inches thick, which was thick enough to allow for a perfect medium-rare center and a good crust, but still small enough to ensure a healthy (i.e., 6-ounce) portion.

Grilling is a good option for filets, but because we also wanted to make a pan sauce, we decided to cook our filets indoors. The recipes we looked at suggested a few options, including broiling, high-roasting (oven-roasting at high heat), and pan-searing (stovetop cooking over high heat), all of which we tried. Pan-searing ended up being the winner. It developed the best deep brown, caramelized crust, which is critical to the flavor of both the meat and the sauce, since bits of the crust left behind in the pan (the fond) flavor the pan sauce. Right off the bat we confirmed our suspicion that filets are best cooked rare to medium-rare. In our opinion, cooking them to medium begins to compromise their tenderness, which is, after all, their raison d'être.

Since our aim was to cook as healthfully as possible, we first tried searing our well-dried filets in a dry pan (drying the steaks thoroughly with paper towels aids development of a crust). Unfortunately, this method gave us a brittle and barely-there crust and no fond left behind in the pan. Some fat was key. We added small amounts of oil to the pan, 1 teaspoon at a time, until we reached a happy medium between a lean profile and a satisfying crust, landing at 4 teaspoons of oil. In the midst of this test, we also found that the best results—a good crust and a perfectly cooked center—were achieved when we rubbed the steaks with 2 teaspoons of the oil rather than adding all the oil directly to the pan. Rubbing the steaks with the oil prevented splattering, created an even coating, and provided just enough fat to produce the proper satisfying crust.

In our tests of different heat levels, we found that a crust formed over consistently high heat was better developed than that produced by a medium-high flame. But this approach also created a problem. Over such high heat, the fond was often scorched by the time the meat reached medium-rare, giving the sauce a bitter flavor.

In an attempt to fix this problem, first we tried switching from the 12-inch skillet we'd been using to cook our steaks to a smaller 10-inch model. The decreased surface area between the steaks helped protect the fond. Second, we revisited the high-roasting method and decided our best bet was combining it with our searing method. We seared the steaks first on the stovetop, then transferred the seared steaks to a preheated baking sheet set in a hot oven to cook through. This ensured that the fond was saved from burning by being exposed to heat for too long.

With our steaks finishing in the oven, we moved on to our sauces. We knew going into testing that making a light pan sauce would be challenging. After all, test kitchen recipes for pan sauces contain up to 3 tablespoons of butter for just four servings, and pan sauces served at restaurants can contain much more. We'd need to be creative. For our first sauce, we made a teriyaki-style sauce flavored with low-sodium soy sauce, mirin, ginger, and garlic. We added cornstarch for thickening power and simmered the mixture in our skillet until thickened, making sure to incorporate all of the flavorful bits of fond left over from browning the steaks. For a second, more vegetal sauce, we sautéed red bell pepper, onion, garlic, and thyme in our skillet, added chicken broth for our liquid element, and finished with balsamic vinegar for a subtle sweetness. Served alongside our tender steaks, either of these sauces enhanced the luscious filets without taking the meal over the edge.

Perfect Filets Mignons

SERVES 4

We prefer these steaks cooked to medium-rare, but if you prefer them more or less done, see our guidelines on page 183. Serve with Teriyaki Steak Sauce or Bell Pepper and Vinegar Steak Sauce (recipes follow), if desired. If serving with a pan sauce, make sure not to clean out the skillet after transferring the steaks to the baking sheet since you will want the fond left behind for the sauce.

    4 (6-ounce) center-cut filets mignons, about 1¼ inches
        thick, trimmed of all visible fat
    4 teaspoons canola oil
    ⅛ teaspoon salt
    ⅛ teaspoon pepper

1. Adjust oven rack to lower-middle position, place rimmed baking sheet on rack, and heat oven to 450 degrees.

2. Pat steaks dry with paper towels, rub each steak with ½ teaspoon oil, and season with salt and pepper.

Heat remaining 2 teaspoons oil in 10-inch skillet over high heat until just smoking. Brown steaks well on both sides, about 6 minutes.

3. Transfer steaks to hot sheet in oven (do not clean out skillet if serving with pan sauce). Roast until meat registers 120 to 125 degrees (for medium-rare), 6 to 8 minutes.

4. Transfer steaks to platter, tent loosely with aluminum foil, and let rest for 5 minutes before serving.

PER SERVING: Cal 300; Fat 16g; Sat fat 4.5g; Chol 115mg; Carb 0g; Protein 38g; Fiber 0g; Sodium 170mg

Teriyaki Steak Sauce

MAKES ½ CUP

The key to a great pan sauce is to not wash the pan after searing the steaks—those remaining browned bits add important flavor to the sauce. Make the sauce while the steaks are resting, after they have been removed from the oven.

    ½ cup water
    ¼ cup low-sodium soy sauce
    ¼ cup sugar
    1 tablespoon mirin
    2 teaspoons cornstarch
    1 teaspoon grated fresh ginger
    1 garlic clove, minced
       Salt and pepper

Whisk all ingredients together in bowl to dissolve cornstarch, then add mixture to skillet, scraping up any browned bits. Simmer over medium-high heat until sauce has thickened and measures about ½ cup, 1 to 2 minutes. Season with salt and pepper to taste and serve with steaks.

PER 2-TABLESPOON SERVING: Cal 70; Fat 0g; Sat fat 0g; Chol 0mg; Carb 17g; Protein 1g; Fiber 0g; Sodium 530mg

Bell Pepper and Vinegar Steak Sauce

MAKES 1½ CUPS

The key to a great pan sauce is to not wash the pan after searing the steaks—those remaining browned bits add important flavor to the sauce. Make the sauce while the steaks are resting, after they have been removed from the oven.

PERFECT FILET MIGNON WITH BELL PEPPER AND VINEGAR STEAK SAUCE

2   teaspoons canola oil

1   red bell pepper, stemmed, seeded, and sliced into
    2-inch-long matchsticks

1   small red onion, halved and sliced thin

2   garlic cloves, minced

1   teaspoon minced fresh thyme

1   cup low-sodium chicken broth

1   tablespoon balsamic vinegar
    Salt and pepper

1. Add oil to skillet and return to medium-high heat until shimmering. Add bell pepper and onion and cook until softened, 5 to 7 minutes. Stir in garlic and thyme and cook until fragrant, about 30 seconds.

2. Stir in broth and any accumulated meat juices, scraping up any browned bits, and simmer until sauce has thickened, about 6 minutes. Off heat, stir in vinegar, season with salt and pepper to taste, and serve with steaks.

PER 6-TABLESPOON SERVING: Cal 45; Fat 2.5g; Sat fat 0g; Chol 0mg; Carb 5g; Protein 1g; Fiber 1g; Sodium 150mg

NOTES FROM THE TEST KITCHEN

A SUPERIOR SKILLET

We use our skillets all the time, for everything from pan-roasting chicken breasts and sautéing fish to preparing one-skillet meals. When it comes to traditional skillets, the variation in price is dizzying—pans can cost anywhere from $30 to $150 or more. Preliminary tests of traditional skillets confirmed our suspicions that cheap was not the way to go, but how much do you really need to spend? We zeroed in on a group of eight pans from well-known manufacturers. All of the pans tested had flared sides, and most had uncoated stainless steel cooking surfaces, which we prize for promoting a fond (the browned, sticky bits that cling to the interior of the pan when food is sautéed and that help flavor sauces).

We concluded that medium-weight pans are ideal—they brown food beautifully and most testers handled them comfortably. These pans have enough heft for heat retention and structural integrity, but not so much that they are difficult to manipulate. For its combination of excellent performance, optimum weight and balance, and overall ease of use, the **All-Clad Stainless Fry Pan**, which comes in 8-inch ($85), 10-inch ($100), and 12-inch ($110) diameters, was the hands-down winner.

SPICE-RUBBED FLANK STEAK WITH TOASTED CORN AND BLACK BEAN SALSA

HAVING DEVELOPED A SUCCESSFUL LIGHT RECIPE for restaurant-caliber filets mignons, next we wanted to see if we could expand our healthy repertoire by bringing grill-friendly flank steak indoors. Like other cuts from the chest and side of the cow, flank steak has a rich, full, beefy flavor. It is also a great addition to any light repertoire since it is relatively lean. We wanted to find a reliable way to cook flank steak indoors that didn't add unnecessary fat, and we wanted to make a healthy side dish to serve alongside our steak.

We began with our cooking method. Since we love the dark, browned crust a flank steak develops from the intense heat of the grill, we first decided to try and replicate that using the oven's broiler. The heat of the broiler did succeed in browning the exterior of the meat, but this didn't occur until the steak's interior was overcooked. Additionally, between flipping the steak and checking for doneness, we ended up having to monitor the steak constantly. Standing around outside while you grill is one thing, but hovering by the oven door was not what we had in mind.

Considering other methods, we thought about an oven-roasting method we'd used with flank steak recently, but this required the use of far too much oil to prevent the steak from sticking to a sheet pan. Instead, we moved to the stovetop. We found that if we used a nonstick skillet, we could sear our steak using only 2 teaspoons of oil without any sticking. We were getting closer, but we wanted a better crust still.

We wondered if a spice rub might help to create a good crust, not to mention improve the flavor. The idea of a bold, deep red Southwestern chili-based rub won approval from tasters, so we settled on a mixture of chili powder, coriander, cumin, and cinnamon to add just the right amount of heat and complexity to our meaty flank steak. After about 10 to 15 minutes in our skillet, the rub formed an attractive and flavorful dark mahogany crust. To promote caramelization and boost flavor even further we added a little sugar.

Our flank steak perfected, we set to work on our side dish. Since we had already developed a Southwestern flavor profile with our rub, we settled on a corn and black bean salsa. Looking for the simplest recipe possible, we stirred together thawed frozen corn, rinsed canned black beans, and a lime- and cilantro-based dressing. The result: a bland and boring mess. From there we made a few changes to liven things up. Toasting the corn in the skillet before cooking our steak allowed the natural sugars in the corn to caramelize, giving it an appealing nuttiness and slight crunch. We tested frozen corn, canned corn, and fresh corn, but only the fresh corn browned properly, and its superior flavor was worth the small amount of additional preparation.

In addition, we added chopped red bell pepper for sweetness, crunch, and color; half a jalapeño for a hint of heat; and one scallion for a little oniony zing. For the dressing, we found that the typical ratio of 1 part acid to 3 parts oil was much too mild (and required far too much extra oil) for our hearty salsa. Instead, we liked a little more lime juice than oil, which delivered the right amount of fresh brightness. We tossed the corn, beans, and pepper with the dressing before cooking the steak to let the flavors meld. The salsa's bright, refreshing flavor was an ideal complement to the spice-rubbed steak. This was by far the best steak dinner that never saw the grill.

Spice-Rubbed Flank Steak with Toasted Corn and Black Bean Salsa

SERVES 4

Do not substitute frozen corn for the fresh corn here. Be sure to use a nonstick skillet when toasting the corn. To make the salsa spicier, add the chile seeds. We prefer this steak cooked to medium-rare, but if you prefer it more or less done, see our guidelines on page 183.

SALSA

4½ teaspoons extra-virgin olive oil
 1 ear corn, kernels cut from cob (see page 42)
 ¾ cup canned black beans, rinsed
 1 red bell pepper, stemmed, seeded, and chopped fine
 ½ jalapeño chile, stemmed, seeds reserved, and minced
 2 tablespoons minced fresh cilantro
 2 tablespoons lime juice
 1 scallion, sliced thin
 2 garlic cloves, minced
   Salt and pepper

STEAK

 1 (1½-pound) flank steak, trimmed of all visible fat
 2 teaspoons ground cumin

 2 teaspoons chili powder
 1 teaspoon ground coriander
 ⅛ teaspoon salt
 ⅛ teaspoon pepper
 ⅛ teaspoon ground cinnamon
 ⅛ teaspoon sugar
 2 teaspoons canola oil

1. FOR THE SALSA: Heat 1½ teaspoons oil in 12-inch nonstick skillet over medium-high heat until shimmering. Add corn and cook, stirring occasionally, until golden brown, about 4 minutes.

2. Transfer corn to bowl, stir in remaining 1 tablespoon oil, beans, bell pepper, jalapeño, cilantro, lime juice, scallion, and garlic and season with salt and pepper to taste. Cover and let sit while cooking steak.

3. FOR THE STEAK: Wipe out skillet with paper towels. Pat steak dry with paper towels. Mix cumin, chili powder, coriander, salt, pepper, cinnamon, and sugar together in bowl, then rub spice mixture evenly over meat.

4. Heat oil in now-empty skillet over medium-high heat until just smoking. Brown steak well on first side, 3 to 5 minutes. Flip steak, reduce heat to medium, and cook until meat registers 120 to 125 degrees (for medium-rare), 5 to 10 minutes longer.

5. Transfer steak to carving board and let rest for 5 minutes. Slice steak thin against grain and serve with corn and black bean salsa.

PER SERVING: Cal 400; Fat 18g; Sat fat 4.5g; Chol 55mg; Carb 16g; Protein 41g; Fiber 5g; Sodium 330mg

---

NOTES FROM THE TEST KITCHEN

SLICING STEAK AGAINST THE GRAIN
The "grain" of a piece of meat is determined by the direction in which the muscle fibers run within a certain cut. In a flank steak, it is easy to determine; the fibers run parallel to each other. Cutting against the grain means slicing the meat perpendicular to these striations.

Once steak has rested for 5 minutes, slice meat across grain into thin pieces.

STEAK TACOS

BEEF TACOS MADE INDOORS ARE TYPICALLY THE pedestrian ground-beef kind, stuffed into a hard corn tortilla shell and loaded with cheese and shredded lettuce. More an invention of time-strapped American home cooks than Mexican tradition, this type of taco is not only ho-hum, but between the greasy filling, sodium-laden taco seasoning, and fatty, caloric toppings it is also far from healthy family fare. We wanted a healthier, more interesting, and more flavorful beef taco.

To start, we decided we would do away with the ground beef, and instead take a cue from Mexican *carne asada*. Carne asada typically calls for a thin cut of beef, like flank steak, which is marinated, then grilled, cut into pieces, and served in a soft corn tortilla with simple garnishes. Done properly, the meat has rich, grilled flavor, and the tacos themselves are simple to throw together. This choice of ingredients already held advantages for lightening: Flank steak is a relatively lean cut of beef (and much tastier than lean ground beef), and the requisite soft corn tortillas are significantly lower in fat and calories than their fried brethren. However, we knew that we wanted to keep this recipe viable for year-round cooking, and in order to do so we'd need to skip the grill.

We had already had some experience with testing cooking methods for flank steak (see our spice-rubbed flank steak recipe on page 98), so we knew that the broiler, while it seems like a good idea, would only lead to overcooked meat. Pan-searing was the way to go. But we wanted more of a charred outside. We tried increasing the surface area by butterflying the steak, but this was a tedious process that didn't yield significantly better results. Next we experimented with cutting the steak lengthwise with the grain into four long strips about 2½ inches wide and 1 inch thick. The results were great. Because the strips were relatively thick, we could brown them on four sides instead of two, which gave us even more exposed edges that became crisp and super-flavorful.

Unadorned, the flank steak was good, but we wondered if we could render the meat even juicier. Recalling a test kitchen recipe for grilled flank steak, we found that sprinkling the meat with salt and allowing it to sit for an hour markedly boosted juiciness. We were able to reduce that time to just 30 minutes by poking holes into the steak with a fork, which allowed the salt to sink more quickly into the meat's interior. To promote caramelization and boost flavor even further, we sprinkled the steak pieces with a little sugar before browning.

With a successful cooking method squared away, we now looked at adding some complexity to the steak. While looking into traditional carne asada recipes, we saw that many called for marinades. We liked the idea of a wet rub or paste, provided it was removed before cooking so that it wouldn't impede browning. We quickly settled on a combination of cilantro, scallions, garlic, and jalapeño. Processed into a pestolike paste with some oil, this marinade added fresh flavors throughout the steak. We reserved some of the marinade to toss with the steak after it was sliced. This brightened the flavor and presentation considerably.

For healthy garnishes, we chose raw onion, cilantro leaves, and lime wedges, all of which echoed the flavors in the marinade. Tasters also liked thinly sliced radishes and cucumber for the contrast to the steak's texture they provided. Last, we experimented with making some quick pickled vegetables, which we loosely based on *curtido* (a relish commonly served in Latin America). Tasters loved the onions we "pickled" in a mixture of sugar and red wine vinegar enlivened by a couple of jalapeños. We now had a great-tasting and healthy alternative to the ubiquitous ground beef taco—one that could even be made in the middle of winter and in no time at all.

Steak Tacos

SERVES 4

To make this dish spicier, add the chile seeds. We prefer this steak cooked to medium-rare, but if you prefer it more or less done, see our guidelines on page 183. Serve with Sweet and Spicy Pickled Onions (recipe follows), thinly sliced radishes or cucumber, or salsa.

- ¾ cup fresh cilantro leaves
- 3 scallions, chopped coarse
- 3 garlic cloves, peeled
- 1 jalapeño chile, stemmed, seeds reserved, and chopped coarse
- ½ teaspoon ground cumin
- 2 tablespoons canola oil
- 1 tablespoon lime juice

1 **(1½-pound) flank steak, trimmed of all visible fat and cut with grain into 4 equal pieces**
  Salt and pepper
½ **teaspoon sugar**
12 **(6-inch) corn tortillas, warmed**
1 **small onion, minced**
  Lime wedges

1. Pulse ½ cup cilantro, scallions, garlic, jalapeño, cumin, and 4 teaspoons oil in food processor until paste-like, 10 to 12 pulses. Transfer 2 tablespoons of herb paste to bowl, whisk in lime juice, and reserve for serving.

2. Using dinner fork, poke each piece of steak 10 to 12 times on each side. Pat steaks dry with paper towels, season with ⅛ teaspoon salt, and place in large baking dish. Coat steak thoroughly with remaining herb paste, cover, and refrigerate for at least 30 minutes or up to 1 hour.

3. Scrape herb paste off steak. Sprinkle all sides of each piece evenly with sugar and season with ⅛ teaspoon pepper. Heat remaining 2 teaspoons oil in 12-inch nonstick skillet over medium-high heat until just smoking. Brown steaks well on all sides and cook until meat registers 120 to 125 degrees (for medium-rare), 7 to 14 minutes. Transfer steaks to carving board and let rest for 5 minutes.

4. Slice each steak thin across grain and transfer to bowl. Toss steak with reserved herb–lime juice mixture and season with salt and pepper to taste. Serve with remaining ¼ cup cilantro, warm tortillas, onion, and lime wedges.

PER SERVING: **Cal** 530; **Fat** 19g; **Sat fat** 4g; **Chol** 55mg; **Carb** 47g; **Protein** 40g; **Fiber** 4g; **Sodium** 280mg

Sweet and Spicy Pickled Onions

MAKES ABOUT 2 CUPS

These sweet, tart onions are the perfect accompaniment not only to Steak Tacos but also to most any grilled meat or poultry. To make this dish less spicy, remove the chile seeds.

1 **red onion, halved and sliced thin**
1 **cup red wine vinegar**
⅓ **cup sugar**
2 **jalapeño chiles, stemmed and cut into thin rings**
¼ **teaspoon salt**

Place onions in heat-resistant bowl. Bring vinegar, sugar, jalapeños, and salt to simmer in small saucepan over medium-high heat, stirring occasionally, until sugar dissolves. Pour vinegar mixture over onions, cover loosely with plastic wrap, and let cool to room temperature, about 30 minutes. Once cool, drain onions and discard liquid. (Pickled onions can be refrigerated for up to 1 week.)

PER ¼-CUP SERVING: **Cal** 45; **Fat** 0g; **Sat fat** 0g; **Chol** 0mg; **Carb** 10g; **Protein** 0g; **Fiber** 0g; **Sodium** 75mg

NOTES FROM THE TEST KITCHEN

CORN TORTILLAS
We tasted six brands of corn tortillas and found that thicker tortillas did not brown as well in the oven and became more chewy than crisp. Thin tortillas, either white or yellow, quickly became feather-light and crisp when oven-fried. The same applied to steaming; the thicker varieties quickly became leathery as they cooled. Flavor differences among brands were slight, but locally made tortillas did pack a bit more corn flavor than national brands. Our advice? Purchase the thinnest tortillas you can find and choose a locally made brand, if possible.

THICK
Too Chewy

THIN
Just Right

THE BEST RED WINE VINEGAR
As with balsamic vinegars, the number of red wine vinegars in the condiment aisle has exploded in the past decade. Given the variety available, we decided to take a look at red wine vinegars and asked tasters to sample 10 brands plain, in a simple vinaigrette, and in pickled onions. In the plain tasting, tasters liked full flavor and a little sharpness. And while the vinaigrette tasting told us that a good vinegar needs some muscle in the form of acidity to tease out all the flavors, the highly acidic vinegars lost out in our plain and pickled onion tests. In the end, we found vinegars that were blends to be a good bet, as multiple varieties of grapes create vinegar with a complex and pleasing taste—aging not necessarily required. For everyday red wine vinegar, our winner, **Laurent du Clos Red Wine Vinegar**, is hard to beat. At 35 cents per ounce, it's not the least expensive brand we tasted, but that's a reasonable price for a vinegar that doesn't compromise on flavor.

SOY-MUSTARD GLAZED SALMON

CHAPTER 5

FISH AND SHELLFISH

M = TEST KITCHEN MAKEOVER

OVEN-ROASTED SALMON FILLETS

SALMON'S POPULARITY AS A HEALTHY PROTEIN IS no surprise. It has a rich, yet not aggressively fishy flavor and a buttery texture, and it is full of heart-healthy omega-3 fatty acids. Steaming and poaching are two favorite methods for bringing out its silky texture, while pan-searing is the best way to produce a flavorful, caramelized crust. But what if you want both qualities: moist, succulent flesh inside, and contrasting texture on the outside? Recipes for roasting salmon promise just that.

A few tests quickly proved that roasting at a high temperature (from 400 to 475 degrees) created a lightly browned exterior, but by the time that point was reached, we had a well-done piece of salmon. Slow-roasting at a very gentle temperature, between 250 and 300 degrees, seemed like the direction to go next. Cooking our fillets at 275 degrees for about 20 minutes resulted in moist, near-translucent flesh, just as we had hoped, but the fish was a little mushy, and—no surprise—there was no contrast in texture whatsoever.

Perhaps a hybrid cooking technique combining high and low heat, as we often use when roasting chicken to achieve crisp skin and tender, juicy meat, would work. After a bit of experimentation, we settled on a starting temperature of 500 degrees, which we reduced to 275 degrees immediately after we placed the fish in the oven. The initial blast of high heat firmed the exterior of the salmon and helped render some of the excess fat that had made the slower-roasted fish mushy. Then our fish gently cooked through while the oven temperature

slowly dropped. To prevent the oven temperature from dropping too rapidly, we also preheated the baking sheet, and to keep the bottoms of our fillets from overcooking the minute they hit the preheated sheet, we left the skin on to provide a barrier. Now we were closer, but this fish tasted a little too fatty. This turned out to be an easy fix. Making several slits through the skin before placing the fillets on the baking sheet allowed the fat residing directly beneath the skin to render onto the baking sheet.

Though the oven temperature was never really in a range that we would consider true slow-roasting, this technique did rely on a declining ambient temperature to slowly cook the fish. It worked beautifully; we now had salmon with a little firmness on the outside and a lot of moist, succulent meat on the inside.

Next we wanted to dress it up to make it more company worthy. Compound butters and vinaigrettes with lots of oil were too fatty for a light and healthy meal. We tried several marinades, but their impact was more subtle than we wanted. In the end, quick salsas and easy, no-cook relishes were the answer. After trying dozens of combinations, we found that those with an acidic element worked best to balance the richness of the fish. Tasters liked a tangy tangerine and ginger combo, a tart grapefruit-basil pairing, and a tomato-basil relish. In addition to bright flavor, each relish provided a further contrast in texture to complement the salmon's silkiness. This dinner was so elegant and appealing, the fact that it was also healthy was just an added bonus.

NOTES FROM THE TEST KITCHEN

SCORING SALMON FILLETS

Keeping the skin on salmon prevents the fish from falling apart and losing moisture as it cooks, but you need to score the skin to keep it from buckling.

Using sharp or serrated knife, cut 4 or 5 shallow slashes diagonally, about 1 inch apart, through skin of each piece of salmon, being careful not to cut into flesh.

Oven-Roasted Salmon Fillets with Tangerine and Ginger Relish

SERVES 4

Use center-cut salmon fillets of similar thickness so that they cook at the same rate. The best way to ensure uniformity is to buy a 1½-pound whole center-cut fillet and cut it into 4 pieces. For more information on cutting tangerines into pieces, see page 196.

TANGERINE AND GINGER RELISH

- 4 tangerines
- 2 teaspoons lemon juice
- 2 teaspoons extra-virgin olive oil
- 1 scallion, sliced thin
- 1½ teaspoons grated fresh ginger
  Salt and pepper

SALMON

4 (6-ounce) skin-on salmon fillets, about 1½ inches thick, skin scored

2 teaspoons olive oil

⅛ teaspoon salt

⅛ teaspoon pepper

1. FOR THE TANGERINE RELISH: Cut away peel and pith from tangerines. Quarter tangerines, then slice crosswise into ½-inch-thick pieces. Place tangerines in strainer set over bowl and let drain for 15 minutes, reserving 1 tablespoon of drained juice.

2. Combine reserved tangerine juice, lemon juice, oil, scallion, and ginger in bowl. Stir in drained tangerines and season with salt and pepper to taste.

3. FOR THE SALMON: Adjust oven rack to lowest position, place rimmed baking sheet on rack, and heat oven to 500 degrees. Pat salmon dry with paper towels. Rub fillets evenly with oil and season with salt and pepper. Reduce oven temperature to 275 degrees and remove baking sheet. Carefully place salmon, skin side down, on hot baking sheet. Roast until center is still translucent when checked with tip of paring knife and registers 125 degrees (for medium-rare), 9 to 13 minutes.

4. Gently transfer fish to individual plates and serve with relish.

PER SERVING WITH ¼ CUP RELISH (WILD SALMON): Cal 330; Fat 16g; Sat fat 2.5g; Chol 95mg; Carb 12g; Protein 35g; Fiber 2g; Sodium 150mg

PER SERVING WITH ¼ CUP RELISH (FARMED SALMON): Cal 400; Fat 23g; Sat fat 4.5g; Chol 100mg; Carb 12g; Protein 35g; Fiber 2g; Sodium 180mg

VARIATIONS

Oven-Roasted Salmon Fillets with Grapefruit and Basil Relish

Substitute the following for Tangerine and Ginger Relish: 2 Ruby Red grapefruits, 2 tablespoons chopped fresh basil, 1 small minced shallot, 2 teaspoons lemon juice, and 2 teaspoons extra-virgin olive oil.

PER SERVING WITH ¼ CUP RELISH (WILD SALMON): Cal 330; Fat 16g; Sat fat 2.5g; Chol 95mg; Carb 13g; Protein 34g; Fiber 2g; Sodium 150mg

PER SERVING WITH ¼ CUP RELISH (FARMED SALMON): Cal 400; Fat 23g; Sat fat 4.5g; Chol 100mg; Carb 13g; Protein 35g; Fiber 2g; Sodium 170mg

Oven-Roasted Salmon Fillets with Fresh Tomato Relish

Skip step 1 and substitute the following for Tangerine and Ginger Relish: 2 chopped cored and seeded tomatoes, 2 tablespoons chopped fresh basil, 1 tablespoon extra-virgin olive oil, 1 small minced shallot, 1 teaspoon red wine vinegar, and 1 minced garlic clove.

PER SERVING WITH ¼ CUP RELISH (WILD SALMON): Cal 310; Fat 17g; Sat fat 2.5g; Chol 95mg; Carb 4g; Protein 35g; Fiber 1g; Sodium 150mg

PER SERVING WITH ¼ CUP RELISH (FARMED SALMON): Cal 380; Fat 24g; Sat fat 4.5g; Chol 100mg; Carb 4g; Protein 35g; Fiber 1g; Sodium 180mg

GLAZED SALMON

WITH A GREAT RECIPE FOR OVEN-ROASTED SALMON (see page 104) under our belts, we all agreed that one more healthy, foolproof method for cooking this favorite fish was a good idea. Why not balance the salmon's rich flavor with a sweet-tart glaze? We set out to see what we could do.

In most recipes for glazed salmon, the fish is brushed with a sticky mixture, then placed a few inches from the broiler element and basted every minute or so to ensure a substantial coating. Of course, we didn't relish the idea of repeatedly reaching into a hot oven, but the method seemed viable enough. When we tried it, however, the sugary glaze charred, and a band of leathery, overcooked flesh developed on the outside of the fish, with only the very center of the salmon exhibiting the translucent, buttery texture we were looking for.

The problem was the broiler; it was simply too hard to pinpoint the proper doneness using such extreme heat, and repeatedly opening and closing the oven door to apply the glaze only complicated matters. We already knew from our oven-roasted salmon tests that slow-roasting the fish in a lower-temperature oven would lead to fish that was moist; could we work this into our method for glazing salmon? We put our salmon in a nonstick skillet (the best choice here since we'd need to cook the glaze and salmon together later) and placed it in a low oven—we'd address the glaze later. After 10 minutes at 300 degrees, the salmon was cooked perfectly. However, tasters missed the slightly crusty, flavorful browned exterior of the broiled fish. To address this, we seared each side of the fish in the skillet on the stovetop before transferring it to the low oven. While this crust looked the part, one bite revealed that we had virtually negated the benefits of our slow-cooking technique, as the several minutes that it took to develop a good crust had turned the outer layer of the fish tough and dry.

We needed to more rapidly caramelize the exterior of the fillets without the risk of turning them tough and leathery. We turned to a favorite test kitchen technique: We lightly sprinkled the flesh with brown sugar (a better match here than white sugar because of its subtle molasses flavor), then seared the fish. This time, it took only a minute for a delicate, flavorful crust to form. We then seared the skin side of the fish for another minute to promote even cooking and transferred the skillet to the oven. Seven minutes later, we had just what we wanted: a golden brown exterior and a pink, wonderfully moist interior.

That just left us with the glaze. We combined more brown sugar with vinegar, then added mirin, soy sauce, and mustard to create a teriyaki-inspired varnish that would serve as a perfect foil to the rich, fatty salmon. We brought the mixture to a boil in a saucepan, reduced it for five minutes, then spooned it over the seared salmon fillets. But even before we got the fish into the oven, much of the glaze slid off and pooled in the bottom of the pan. Basting the salmon every couple of minutes would certainly have helped, but we hated to go that tedious route. Adding 1 teaspoon of cornstarch to the glaze was a step in the right direction, but too much of the sauce still dribbled down the sides of the fish. Adding more cornstarch was not an option; any more than 1 teaspoon rendered our glaze gummy and gloppy.

We were running out of ideas when an altogether different approach occurred to us: What if instead of trying to create a tackier glaze, we worked on getting the salmon itself to have more "stickability"? We had a hunch that rubbing cornstarch on the surface of the fish would add texture, essentially creating tiny nooks and crannies to trap the glaze.

Fingers crossed, we combined ¼ teaspoon of cornstarch with the brown sugar we were already rubbing on the fish, plus ⅛ teaspoon of salt for seasoning, and then seared the fillets. As we'd hoped, the surface was now quite coarse, mottled all over with tiny peaks and valleys. We proceeded with the recipe, spooning the glossy glaze over the salmon and then transferring it to the low oven. This time the mixture stuck, resulting in a glistening, well-lacquered exterior and no need to stand watch basting the fish.

With our glaze holding fast, we knew we were in good shape, so from there we whipped up three more variations: a salty, citrusy orange-miso version; an Asian barbecue mixture drawing sweetness from hoisin sauce and tartness from rice vinegar; and a fruity pomegranate version spiked with balsamic vinegar. Now we had a healthy, foolproof dinner that we could get on the table in about 20 minutes.

Soy-Mustard Glazed Salmon
SERVES 4

Use center-cut salmon fillets of similar thickness so that they cook at the same rate. The best way to ensure uniformity is to buy a 1½-pound whole center-cut fillet and cut it into 4 pieces. If your nonstick skillet isn't ovensafe, sear the salmon as directed in step 3, then transfer it to a rimmed baking sheet, glaze it, and bake it as directed in step 4.

SOY-MUSTARD GLAZE
- 3 tablespoons light brown sugar
- 2 tablespoons low-sodium soy sauce
- 2 tablespoons mirin
- 1 tablespoon sherry vinegar
- 1 tablespoon whole grain mustard
- 1 tablespoon water
- 1 teaspoon cornstarch
- ⅛ teaspoon red pepper flakes

SALMON
- 1 teaspoon light brown sugar
- ¼ teaspoon cornstarch
- ⅛ teaspoon salt
- ⅛ teaspoon pepper
- 4 (6-ounce) skin-on salmon fillets, about 1½ inches thick
- 1 teaspoon canola oil

1. FOR THE SOY-MUSTARD GLAZE: Whisk all ingredients together in small saucepan. Bring to boil over medium-high heat and simmer, whisking often, until thickened, about 1 minute. Remove from heat and cover to keep warm.

2. FOR THE SALMON: Adjust oven rack to middle position and heat oven to 300 degrees. Combine sugar, cornstarch, salt, and pepper in small bowl. Pat salmon dry with paper towels and sprinkle sugar mixture evenly over flesh side of salmon, rubbing to distribute.

3. Heat oil in 12-inch ovensafe nonstick skillet over medium-high heat until just smoking. Place salmon, flesh side down, in skillet and cook until well browned, about 1 minute. Using tongs, carefully flip salmon and cook on skin side for 1 minute.

4. Off heat, spoon glaze evenly over salmon fillets. Transfer skillet to oven and cook until center is still translucent when checked with tip of paring knife and registers 125 degrees (for medium-rare), 7 to 10 minutes. Gently transfer fillets to individual plates and serve.

PER SERVING (WILD SALMON): **Cal** 330; **Fat** 12g; **Sat fat** 2g; **Chol** 95mg; **Carb** 15g; **Protein** 35g; **Fiber** 0g; **Sodium** 880mg

PER SERVING (FARMED SALMON): **Cal** 400; **Fat** 20g; **Sat fat** 4g; **Chol** 100mg; **Carb** 15g; **Protein** 35g; **Fiber** 0g; **Sodium** 910mg

VARIATIONS

Orange-Miso Glazed Salmon

Substitute the following mixture for Soy-Mustard Glaze: ¼ cup orange juice, 2 tablespoons white miso, 1 tablespoon light brown sugar, 1 tablespoon rice vinegar, 1 tablespoon whole grain mustard, 1 teaspoon grated orange zest, ¾ teaspoon cornstarch, and pinch cayenne. Prepare as directed in step 1.

PER SERVING (WILD SALMON): **Cal** 300; **Fat** 13g; **Sat fat** 2g; **Chol** 95mg; **Carb** 10g; **Protein** 35g; **Fiber** 0g; **Sodium** 460mg

PER SERVING (FARMED SALMON): **Cal** 370; **Fat** 20g; **Sat fat** 4g; **Chol** 100mg; **Carb** 10g; **Protein** 35g; **Fiber** 0g; **Sodium** 480mg

Asian Barbecue Glazed Salmon

Substitute the following mixture for Soy-Mustard Glaze: 2 tablespoons ketchup, 2 tablespoons hoisin sauce, 2 tablespoons rice vinegar, 2 tablespoons light brown sugar, 1 tablespoon low-sodium soy sauce, 2 teaspoons Asian chili-garlic sauce, 1 teaspoon toasted sesame oil, and 1 teaspoon grated fresh ginger. Prepare as directed in step 1, increasing cooking time to about 3 minutes.

PER SERVING (WILD SALMON): **Cal** 320; **Fat** 13g; **Sat fat** 2g; **Chol** 95mg; **Carb** 15g; **Protein** 34g; **Fiber** 0g; **Sodium** 710mg

PER SERVING (FARMED SALMON): **Cal** 390; **Fat** 21g; **Sat fat** 4g; **Chol** 100mg; **Carb** 15g; **Protein** 34g; **Fiber** 0g; **Sodium** 740mg

Pomegranate-Balsamic Glazed Salmon

Substitute the following mixture for Soy-Mustard Glaze: 3 tablespoons light brown sugar, 3 tablespoons pomegranate juice, 2 tablespoons balsamic vinegar, 1 tablespoon whole grain mustard, 1 teaspoon cornstarch, and pinch cayenne. Prepare as directed in step 1.

PER SERVING (WILD SALMON): **Cal** 320; **Fat** 12g; **Sat fat** 2g; **Chol** 95mg; **Carb** 15g; **Protein** 34g; **Fiber** 0g; **Sodium** 230mg

PER SERVING (FARMED SALMON): **Cal** 390; **Fat** 20g; **Sat fat** 4g; **Chol** 100mg; **Carb** 15g; **Protein** 34g; **Fiber** 0g; **Sodium** 250mg

BAKED SOLE FILLETS

SOLE IS PRIZED IN PARTICULAR FOR ITS MILD FLAVOR and, like most fish, it is a great choice for eating healthfully. It is also thin and cooks up fast. Altogether, it sounds like a perfect candidate for a healthy weeknight meal. We wanted a fuss-free, foolproof recipe for sole that was suitable for a quick meal yet worthy of company.

Before we even sharpened our knives we realized our goals were easier said than done. Most cooking methods presented drawbacks. Both sautéing and pan-frying sole would yield nice golden color, but both methods typically require a significant amount of butter or oil. Plus, depending on a hot skillet means the thin fillets can overcook in a flash, and because sole's footprint is wide, fillets must be sautéed or pan-fried in batches. Poaching, while gentler, is also downright bland without a flavorful poaching liquid and sauce for serving. We didn't want to fuss with either of those things.

Baking, however, struck us as a forgiving, convenient, and healthy route to take, though this technique, too, was not without fault. Of the recipes we turned up, most were uninspired (coated with plain bread crumbs) or overwrought (wrapped artfully around blanched asparagus). We selected a few of the more sensible options and gave them a go.

Simply laying the fillets flat on a baking sheet to bake seemed promising—until they broke into pieces when we transferred them to dinner plates. Rolling them into compact bundles eased the transport from baking dish to plate, but the trade-off was a thicker piece of fish that cooked unevenly. But the technique itself—baking rolled fillets—showed promise, so we experimented with oven temperatures (300 to 450 degrees) to even out the cooking. After 30 minutes at 325 degrees, the fillets were nicely done from edge to center, and covering the baking dish with foil offered the delicate fish further protection from the drying heat of the oven.

With the cooking method settled, we set out to ramp up the flavor. We sprinkled the fillets with salt and pepper, minced fresh herbs, and lemon zest, drizzled them with a little melted butter, rolled them, drizzled a little more butter over, and put them in the oven. The flavor? Better, but still mild, and tasters felt we could cut back on the butter. We reduced the butter from 4 tablespoons to 2, and once we worked a clove of minced garlic into the butter and put a slather of Dijon mustard over each fillet, the flavor popped.

All we had left to address? The baked fillets' one-dimensional texture and unappetizing pallor. A topping of panko (Japanese-style bread crumbs) toasted in just a single tablespoon of butter along with garlic offered a possible solution to both issues. But when to add the panko posed a problem. They absorbed moisture and lost their lovely crispness when added at the outset, but they lacked cohesion with the fish when sprinkled on after cooking. We compromised with a hybrid technique, removing the foil with 5 to 10 minutes remaining in the cooking time, basting the fillets with pan juices, topping them with most of the toasted crumbs, and then returning them to the oven uncovered. Just before serving, we sprinkled on the remaining crumbs. This way, most of the crumbs fused to the fish during baking, and the final showering offered delicate crispness. Adding a measure of herbs to the panko lent some much-needed freshness.

Fuss-free and foolproof, these panko-topped, herb-filled fillets were exactly what we had hoped to create: fish suitable for a healthy weeknight dinner, impressive and elegant enough to serve to company.

Baked Sole Fillets with Herbs and Bread Crumbs

SERVES 6

Flounder can be substituted for the sole. Try to purchase fillets of similar size. If using smaller fillets (about 3 ounces each), serve 2 fillets per person and reduce the baking time in step 3 to 20 minutes. We strongly advise against using frozen fish in this recipe; freezing can undermine the texture of the fish, making it hard to roll. Fresh basil or dill can be used in place of the tarragon.

3 tablespoons minced fresh parsley
3 tablespoons minced fresh chives
1 tablespoon minced fresh tarragon
1 teaspoon grated lemon zest
3 tablespoons unsalted butter
2 garlic cloves, minced
6 (6-ounce) skinless sole fillets
  Salt and pepper
1 tablespoon Dijon mustard
½ cup panko bread crumbs
  Lemon wedges

1. Adjust oven rack to middle position and heat oven to 325 degrees. Combine parsley, chives, and tarragon in small bowl. Measure out 1 tablespoon of herb mixture and set aside. Stir lemon zest into remaining herbs.

2. Melt 2 tablespoons butter in 8-inch skillet over medium heat. Add 1 teaspoon garlic and cook, stirring often, until fragrant, about 1 minute. Set skillet aside.

3. Pat fillets dry with paper towels and season with ⅛ teaspoon salt and ⅛ teaspoon pepper. Turn fillets skinned side up with tail end pointing away from you. Spread ½ teaspoon mustard on each fillet, sprinkle each evenly with 1 tablespoon herb–lemon zest mixture, and drizzle each with ½ teaspoon garlic butter. Tightly roll fillets from thick end to form cylinders. Set fillets seam side down in 13 by 9-inch baking dish. Drizzle remaining garlic butter evenly over fillets, cover baking dish with aluminum foil, and bake for 25 minutes.

4. Meanwhile, wipe out skillet and melt remaining 1 tablespoon butter over medium heat. Add panko and cook, stirring often, until crumbs are deep golden brown, 5 to 8 minutes. Reduce heat to low, add remaining garlic, and cook, stirring constantly, until garlic is fragrant and evenly distributed throughout panko, about 30 seconds. Transfer to small bowl and stir in ¼ teaspoon salt and pepper to taste. Let cool, then stir in reserved 1 tablespoon herb mixture.

5. Remove baking dish from oven. Baste fillets with melted garlic butter from baking dish, then sprinkle with all but 3 tablespoons of panko mixture. Continue to bake, uncovered, until fish flakes apart when gently prodded with paring knife and registers 140 degrees, 6 to 10 minutes longer. Using thin metal spatula, transfer fillets to individual plates, sprinkle with remaining 3 tablespoons panko mixture, and serve with lemon wedges.

PER SERVING: Cal 230; Fat 8g; Sat fat 4.5g; Chol 95mg; Carb 4g; Protein 33g; Fiber 0g; Sodium 360mg

BAKED SOLE FILLETS WITH HERBS AND BREAD CRUMBS

PAN-SEARED TUNA

PERFECTLY SEARED TUNA IS A THING OF BEAUTY and an expression of contrasts. The outside has a deeply seared crust that envelops a tender, moist, plum-red interior—a sort of culinary ying and yang. One bite confirms the harmony these opposites can achieve when they come together. Unfortunately, we've had as many poorly prepared versions of pan-seared tuna as we've had great ones. The checklist of potential problems includes tuna that is crustless, tuna that is overcooked, and tuna that tastes fishy. We wanted to find a method that would avoid all of these problems and produce a quick and easy, healthy dinner entrée at the same time.

We began our testing by comparing pan-seared tuna steaks (we used a basic working method for now) that were ¾ inch thick and those that were 1 inch thick. We all recognized that the thin steaks cooked too quickly and lost their rare look, feel, and taste. The extra ¼ inch in the 1-inch-thick steaks made a big difference; after a few minutes in the pan, the centers of these steaks

NOTES FROM THE TEST KITCHEN

SPATULAS WORTH FLIPPING OVER
A good spatula is indispensable, whether you're flipping burgers or transferring delicate fish fillets. We scooped up nearly two dozen tools costing between $2 and $38: traditional squared-off metal turners, thin-bladed fish spatulas with long heads and short grips, even a spatula made entirely of wires. We ran them through a battery of tests, including maneuvering fried eggs, sliding them under cookies, and lifting burgers and pancakes. A good spatula, we found, must have a slim, but not too narrow, front edge that can slip under food with ease. A rectangular, well-proportioned head offers support without compromising dexterity. Handles measuring roughly 6 inches and a total length of about 11 inches provide enough distance to keep us safe while letting the spatula maneuver naturally. We preferred only a slight offset to the grip. A little stiffness in the spatula head was preferred; spatulas that were too flexible threatened to drop their cargo. Our favorites were the fish spatulas, in particular the metal **Wüsthof Gourmet Fish Spatula** (right), $29.95, and the plastic **Matfer Bourgeat Pelton Spatula** (left), $7.50.

were still rare, just what we were after. To see which type of tuna would work best, we purchased the four most likely contenders: bigeye, bluefin, yellowfin, and albacore. When the results were tallied, yellowfin was the clear favorite.

Next, we tackled the crust. We figured we were off to a good start by using a very hot skillet and 2 table-spoons of oil. But after 1½ minutes on each side, the tuna did not develop the deep brown crust that we were after. And if we cooked it any longer, our perfectly rare centers were in jeopardy. We couldn't afford adding more oil, but then a colleague suggested that we first dip the fish in balsamic vinegar to coat it. This idea seemed to have merit; we imagined that the sugar in the vinegar would help caramelize the crust and at the same time it would add concentrated flavor. But this tuna also disappointed. While the crust was much darker in color—almost burnt-looking, in fact—the crunch was still missing.

We realized that the only way our tuna steaks could get the textural appeal we were after was to use some sort of coating. Inspired by similar beef steak recipes, we started by testing crushed peppercorns, putting a liberal coat on both sides of the steaks and cooking them for 1½ minutes on each side. But the flavor of the pepper-corns was overpowering and the high heat caused them to burn. These steaks needed a more neutral-flavored coating. On the upside, we had learned two things from the tests with peppercorns. First, a nonstick skillet was going to be necessary to prevent scorching and sticking. Second, it was best to rub the tuna with a bit of oil to help the coating adhere, and then use just a bit more oil in the hot pan to cook the fish.

For our next test, we created a coating with a blend of aromatic spices that included cumin, coriander, and mustard seed. This time, with our nonstick skillet and extra oil, the spices stayed put on the steaks and they didn't burn in the pan. However, while some tasters loved the bold blend of flavors, others thought we needed something a little more approachable. That's when we hit on the idea of sesame seeds: simple, easy to find, and neutral enough to pair with a range of other flavorings. Once again we coated some steaks in a little oil, dredged them in the seeds, heated up the pan, and seared both sides for a few minutes. This time we'd nailed it. The contrast between the crisp, crunchy, beautifully browned crust and the tender, rare interior was exactly right.

All our tuna needed was a little something to brighten it up. The answer was a light wasabi dressing. Its pungent flavor and even heat complemented the rich flavor of the tuna and the nutty sesame seeds. This was a foolproof recipe that was in perfect balance.

Sesame-Crusted Tuna with Wasabi Dressing

SERVES 4

We prefer the flavor and texture of yellowfin tuna, here but any type will work. Note that different types of tuna have significantly different amounts of fat and calories; the nutritional analysis for this recipe was done using yellowfin. Try to purchase tuna steaks that are about 1 inch thick; if they are thicker or thinner, adjust the cooking time as needed. We prefer our tuna rare; if you prefer your tuna cooked medium-rare, cook it on the second side until it is opaque at the perimeter and reddish pink at the center when checked with the tip of a paring knife and registers 125 degrees, about 3 minutes.

- ¼ **cup light mayonnaise**
- 2 **tablespoons water**
- 1 **tablespoon wasabi paste**
- 1 **tablespoon lime juice**
   Salt and pepper
- 3 **tablespoons sesame seeds**
- 4 **(6-ounce) tuna steaks, about 1 inch thick**
- 4 **teaspoons canola oil**

1. Whisk mayonnaise, water, wasabi paste, and lime juice together in bowl and season with salt and pepper to taste.

2. Spread sesame seeds in shallow dish. Pat tuna dry with paper towels, then coat with 2 teaspoons oil and season with ⅛ teaspoon salt and ⅛ teaspoon pepper. Press both sides of each steak into sesame seeds to coat.

3. Heat remaining 2 teaspoons oil in 12-inch non-stick skillet over medium-high heat until just smoking. Gently lay tuna in pan and cook until seeds are golden brown, about 2 minutes. Carefully flip fish and continue to cook until just golden brown on second side, opaque at perimeter and translucent red at center when checked with tip of paring knife, and registers 110 degrees (rare), about 1½ minutes. Gently transfer fish to carving board and slice on bias. Serve with wasabi dressing.

PER SERVING: Cal 320; Fat 14g; Sat fat 1g; Chol 80mg; Carb 2g; Protein 41g; Fiber 1g; Sodium 420mg

GREEK SHRIMP WITH FETA

THE TEST KITCHEN RECENTLY DEVELOPED A RECIPE called Greek-Style Shrimp with Tomatoes and Feta. Based on shrimp *saganaki*, a classic Greek dish of shrimp baked in a tomato sauce under crumbles of feta cheese, this recipe sounded like a flavorful, worthy addition to our light cooking repertoire. We headed to the kitchen to revisit our own version and see where we could lighten it up. We wanted a healthy take on this classic Mediterranean meal that combined sweet shrimp with briny feta, all swathed in a sweet-tart tomato sauce.

Admittedly, not everyone had been sold on a dish that included both seafood and cheese. In the bad versions we had come across, tough, rubbery shrimp were hidden under store-bought tomato sauce and an unhealthy layer of salty cheese. Since shrimp are incredibly easy to overcook, our main challenge in our original testing had been to get them just right—that is, tender, juicy, and just cooked through, not tough and rubbery. The modern approach for this dish—layering the tomato sauce and shrimp in a baking dish, sprinkling feta over the top, and slipping the dish into a hot oven—produced an unexpected problem: The shrimp around the perimeter cooked more quickly and were noticeably tougher than the ones in the center.

From there we decided we'd have better luck if we turned this into a quick and easy skillet dish. For our next attempt, we quickly seared the shrimp in a hot skillet, then we added the sauce and feta. Simple, for sure, but tasters remarked that the flavors hadn't melded; all we had was tough shrimp topped with tomato sauce and cheese. We hoped one change would fix both problems. For our next test, we added the shrimp raw to the tomato sauce and briefly simmered them on medium-low. The lower heat increased the cooking time, allowing the flavors to blend better. And the shrimp, cooked gently at the barest simmer, were tender and succulent.

While the shrimp now were cooked just right (perfectly tender but not underdone), they still tasted a little dull. Our experience cooking stir-fries had taught us that a quick, simple marinade can do a lot to boost flavors, and tossing the shrimp in this recipe with some minced garlic, lemon zest, salt, pepper, and a little olive oil and letting them sit for a few minutes was a great start here. The shrimp had more flavor, but still, they were not distinctively Greek tasting. Adding just a tablespoon of ouzo, a lightly sweet, anise-based Greek liqueur, to the marinade brought a welcome complexity of flavor and aroma, an undeniable improvement.

For the tomato sauce, we experimented with various forms of tomato—fresh, canned whole, and canned diced—and settled on canned diced, which were not only the most convenient but also had more intense flavor than fresh supermarket tomatoes. As for flavorings, some more minced garlic and diced onion sautéed in a bare minimum of olive oil were naturals for this Mediterranean sauce. Still, it needed more enhancement. After making more than a dozen variations, we settled on adding half a diced red bell pepper for natural sweetness, half a diced green bell pepper for earthy vegetal notes, red pepper flakes for a little enlivening heat, and a small measure of dry white wine for a touch of acidity. We also tried stirring fresh and dried oregano into the sauce, but both made it taste pizzalike. Grassy fresh parsley was a better option. To finish with a Greek flourish, we added a couple of extra tablespoons of the ouzo.

Now, what about the feta? At first we simply crumbled it over and gave it a few moments to soften, but we wondered if the added step of browning the cheese under a broiler or in an extra-hot oven would give the dish another dimension. A few tries and we had the answer: no. Feta is not a cheese that browns easily or takes on toasty notes when caramelized. Besides, the high heat overrode the gentle heat we had used to cook the shrimp and toughened them up. As for the amount, our original recipe called for a full 6 ounces. Could we cut this back but still keep the creamy profile of the dish? Indeed we could; in fact, we found we could cut it all the way down to 2 ounces and tasters were still satisfied with its creamy, briny contribution.

As final touches, we drizzled a teaspoon of extra-virgin olive oil over the dish (down from the original tablespoon) for a rich fruitiness, then sprinkled a little dill over the top. Its unique grassy, tangy notes had the big benefit of tasting distinctly Greek. With that, we had yet another dish successfully lightened for our collection of healthy weeknight favorites.

Greek-Style Shrimp with Tomatoes and Feta
SERVES 4

This recipe works equally well with jumbo shrimp, but the cooking times in step 3 will increase slightly. For more information on buying shrimp, see page 120. Serve this recipe with crusty bread or white rice.

- 1½ pounds extra-large shrimp (21 to 25 per pound), peeled and deveined, tails removed if desired
- 3 tablespoons ouzo
- 5 garlic cloves, minced
- 1 tablespoon extra-virgin olive oil
- 1 teaspoon grated lemon zest
  Salt and pepper
- 1 small onion, chopped
- ½ red bell pepper, stemmed, seeded, and cut into ½-inch pieces
- ½ green bell pepper, stemmed, seeded, and cut into ½-inch pieces
- ¼ teaspoon red pepper flakes
- 1 (28-ounce) can diced tomatoes, drained with ⅓ cup juice reserved
- ¼ cup dry white wine
- 2 tablespoons minced fresh parsley
- 2 ounces feta cheese, crumbled (½ cup)
- 2 tablespoons minced fresh dill

1. Toss shrimp, 1 tablespoon ouzo, 1 teaspoon garlic, 1 teaspoon oil, lemon zest, ⅛ teaspoon salt, and ⅛ teaspoon pepper in bowl until well combined; set aside.

2. Combine 1 teaspoon oil, onion, red and green bell pepper, and ⅛ teaspoon salt in 12-inch skillet. Cover and cook over medium-low heat, stirring occasionally, until softened, 8 to 10 minutes. Add remaining garlic and red pepper flakes and cook until fragrant, about 1 minute.

3. Add remaining 2 tablespoons ouzo, tomatoes and reserved juice, and wine. Increase heat to medium, bring to simmer, and cook, uncovered, stirring occasionally, until sauce is slightly thickened (sauce should not be completely dry), 5 to 8 minutes. Stir in parsley and season with salt and pepper to taste.

4. Reduce heat to medium-low and stir in shrimp. Cover and cook, stirring occasionally, until shrimp are opaque throughout, 6 to 9 minutes. Off heat, sprinkle evenly with feta and dill, and drizzle remaining 1 teaspoon oil evenly over top. Serve immediately.

PER SERVING: Cal 300; Fat 9g; Sat fat 3g; Chol 205mg; Carb 16g; Protein 30g; Fiber 4g; Sodium 930mg

SHRIMP STIR-FRIES

WE ALREADY KNEW THAT WHEN IT COMES TO QUICK and healthy meals, it's hard to beat stir-fries since they are composed primarily of lean protein and healthy vegetables. We'd just developed several stir-fries featuring pork (see pages 82–86), so we thought, Why not create a few with shrimp as our protein of choice? Our goal was to avoid the all-too-common mistakes: rubbery shrimp, vegetables that are either raw or way overcooked, and greasy, gloppy sauce. We wanted to put a few great-tasting, healthy shrimp stir-fries on the table with minimal fuss.

We had used a solid test kitchen method for making our pork stir-fry recipes: Batch-cook the meat followed by the vegetables in a hot skillet, add the aromatics, then finish with a flavorful, quick-simmered sauce. We figured this process would work just as well with shrimp, though we did decide to make one tweak for our first tests using shrimp instead of pork. Our pork recipes rely on a process called velveting to keep the meat tender and moist. We wouldn't need to employ that process with shrimp, but we thought a quick, simple marinade would be a smart move to help boost the shrimp's flavor. We gave our revised method a shot and quickly found it wouldn't be quite so simple. After choking down batches of tightly curled, rubbery shrimp, we realized that meat and shrimp are not interchangeable. To begin with, the shrimp cooked faster than the meat. Second, marinades seemed to roll right off their tightly grained flesh and ended up burning in the hot skillet. We clearly needed to customize our stir-fry technique to make it work for shrimp.

To solve the problem of overcooked shrimp, we took a step back from our meat stir-fry technique and reconsidered the super-hot fire. Traditionally, high heat serves two purposes: speed and flavorful browning. The time and temperature window for perfectly plump, just-firm shrimp, however, is particularly narrow. A few degrees too much and the shrimp turn into rubber erasers. Substantial browning, meanwhile, doesn't occur until well above 300 degrees—a surefire path to overcooking. Since shrimp stir-fries usually call for an assertive sauce, we wondered if tasters would miss the browning.

To find out, we turned down the burner to medium-low and gently parcooked a batch of shrimp, removed them from the skillet, then turned up the heat to sear the vegetables, sauté the aromatics, and finish cooking the shrimp with the sauce. This worked beautifully. No one missed a browned exterior, instead commenting on the shrimp's supreme tenderness. A few more tests uncovered an even better method. Reversing the approach—cooking the veggies followed by the aromatics over high heat, then turning the heat down before adding the shrimp—made the process more efficient.

Next, it was time to think more deeply about the marinade. A basic mixture of Chinese rice wine and soy sauce (ingredients we had used to season the meat in our pork stir-fries) wasn't doing much for the shrimp. In fact, it merely overwhelmed their sweet taste. Instead, we tried another common Chinese texture-boosting technique, which we hoped would also improve flavor: soaking the shrimp in a saltwater brine, which both seasons and hydrates the flesh. Their texture became noticeably juicier, but we still wanted more flavor in the shrimp themselves. The idea of adding aromatics, particularly garlic, won votes from tasters, but we knew that infusing the brine with garlic wouldn't work since the clove's flavorful compounds are mostly oil-soluble and thus don't come through in a watery solution.

So was there any need to introduce water at all? In the past, we have had success marinating shrimp in a combination of oil, salt, and minced garlic. The salt not only helps the shrimp retain moisture as they cook, but it also draws flavorful compounds out of the garlic's cells, which then dissolve in the oil and spread evenly around the shellfish. Sure enough, this method worked like a charm. (And even better, the technique lent itself to a flavor variation with ginger.)

As for an assertive sauce, the heavily soy-based brews were too runny and salty. Better suited to the shrimp (and more traditional in Chinese cuisine anyway) were sweeter or spicier sauces that were reduced to a consistency that tightly adhered to the shellfish. We then let our sauces inspire the vegetables for each stir-fry. For a vinegar-based hot and sour sauce, we settled on crisp snow peas and red bell peppers. An intense garlic sauce was complemented well by a mix of creamy eggplant, bright scallions, and the richness of cashews. And finally, a spicy Sichuan-style sauce called for mild zucchini, sweet red bell pepper, and salty peanuts for balance.

By combining Chinese traditions with new techniques, we developed three distinctly different healthy stir-fries full of tender shrimp and complementary vegetables. These shrimp stir-fries certainly wouldn't play second fiddle to their land-based counterparts.

Stir-Fried Shrimp with Snow Peas and Bell Peppers in Hot and Sour Sauce

SERVES 4

Serve over plain white or brown rice. For more information on buying shrimp, see page 120.

SAUCE

- 3 tablespoons sugar
- 3 tablespoons white vinegar
- 1 tablespoon Asian chili-garlic sauce
- 1 tablespoon dry sherry or Chinese rice cooking wine
- 1 tablespoon ketchup
- 2 teaspoons toasted sesame oil
- 1 teaspoon cornstarch
- 1 teaspoon low-sodium soy sauce

STIR-FRY

- 1 tablespoon canola oil
- 1 tablespoon grated fresh ginger
- 2 garlic cloves, 1 minced and 1 sliced thin
- ⅛ teaspoon salt
- 1 pound extra-large shrimp (21 to 25 per pound), peeled, deveined, and tails removed
- 1 large shallot, sliced thin
- 8 ounces snow peas or snap peas, strings removed
- 1 red bell pepper, stemmed, seeded, and cut into ¾-inch pieces

1. FOR THE SAUCE: Whisk all ingredients together in bowl; set aside.

2. FOR THE STIR-FRY: Stir 1 teaspoon oil, ginger, minced garlic, and salt together in medium bowl. Stir in shrimp until evenly coated; let marinate at room temperature for 30 minutes. In separate bowl, combine 1 teaspoon oil, sliced garlic, and shallot.

3. Heat remaining 1 teaspoon oil in 12-inch nonstick skillet over high heat until just smoking. Add snow peas and bell pepper and cook, stirring frequently, until vegetables begin to brown and are crisp-tender, 1½ to 2 minutes; transfer to bowl.

4. Add shallot mixture to now-empty skillet, return to high heat, and cook, stirring frequently, until just beginning to brown, about 30 seconds. Add shrimp, reduce heat to medium-low, and cook, stirring frequently, until shrimp are light pink on both sides, 1 to 1½ minutes.

5. Whisk sauce to recombine, then add to skillet. Increase heat to high and cook, stirring constantly, until sauce is thickened and shrimp are cooked through, 1 to 2 minutes. Return vegetables to skillet and toss to combine. Transfer to platter and serve.

PER SERVING: Cal 230; Fat 8g; Sat fat 1g; Chol 130mg; Carb 21g; Protein 20g; Fiber 2g; Sodium 400mg

VARIATIONS

Stir-Fried Sichuan-Style Shrimp with Zucchini, Bell Pepper, and Peanuts

SERVES 4

Broad bean chili paste is also referred to as chili bean sauce or horse bean chili paste. If you can't find it, increase the amount of Asian chili-garlic sauce by 1 teaspoon. Sichuan peppercorns, available at Asian markets and some supermarkets, have purplish-red husks and shiny black seeds; it is preferable to buy them with the seeds removed, as it's the husk that provides the aromatic, gently floral fragrance (and the notable numbing effect on the tongue). Serve over plain white or brown rice. For more information on buying shrimp, see page 120.

SAUCE

- 2 tablespoons dry sherry or Chinese rice cooking wine
- 1 tablespoon broad bean chili paste
- 1 tablespoon Asian chili-garlic sauce
- 1 tablespoon white vinegar or Chinese black vinegar
- 2 teaspoons water
- 1 teaspoon chili oil or toasted sesame oil
- 1 teaspoon sugar
- 1 teaspoon cornstarch
- ½ teaspoon Sichuan peppercorns, toasted and ground (optional)

STIR-FRY

- 1 tablespoon canola oil
- 2 garlic cloves, 1 minced and 1 sliced thin
- ⅛ teaspoon salt
- 1 pound extra-large shrimp (21 to 25 per pound), peeled, deveined, and tails removed
- ¼ cup dry-roasted peanuts
- 1 jalapeño chile, stemmed, halved, seeded, and sliced thin on bias
- 1 small zucchini, cut into ¾-inch pieces
- 1 red bell pepper, stemmed, seeded, and cut into ¾-inch pieces
- ½ cup fresh cilantro leaves

1. FOR THE SAUCE: Whisk all ingredients together in bowl; set aside.

2. FOR THE STIR-FRY: Stir 1 teaspoon oil, minced garlic, and salt together in medium bowl. Stir in shrimp until evenly coated; let marinate at room temperature for 30 minutes. Combine 1 teaspoon oil, sliced garlic, peanuts, and jalapeño in small bowl.

3. Heat remaining 1 teaspoon oil in 12-inch nonstick skillet over high heat until just smoking. Add zucchini and bell pepper and cook, stirring frequently, until zucchini is tender and well browned, 2 to 4 minutes; transfer to bowl.

4. Add peanut mixture to now-empty skillet, return to high heat, and cook, stirring frequently, until just beginning to brown, about 30 seconds. Add shrimp, reduce heat to medium-low, and cook, stirring frequently, until shrimp are light pink on both sides, 1 to 1½ minutes.

5. Whisk sauce to recombine, then add to skillet. Increase heat to high and cook, stirring constantly, until sauce is thickened and shrimp are cooked through, 1 to 2 minutes. Return vegetables to skillet, add cilantro, and toss to combine. Transfer to platter and serve.

PER SERVING: **Cal** 230; **Fat** 11g; **Sat fat** 1.5g; **Chol** 130mg; **Carb** 10g; **Protein** 21g; **Fiber** 2g; **Sodium** 480mg

---

NOTES FROM THE TEST KITCHEN

SHRIMP VERSUS PRAWN: WHAT'S THE DIFFERENCE?

It may seem as if restaurant menus and supermarkets advertise both prawns and shrimp interchangeably, but are they the same thing? Biologically speaking, there is a difference between shrimp and prawns, and it's mainly about gill structure—a distinguishing feature that is hard for the consumer to spot and is typically lost during processing and cooking. This simple fact may be why the terms are often used interchangeably or can vary depending on factors as random as custom and geography. "Prawn" is a term often used in the southern United States, for example, while Northerners might refer to the same specimen as "shrimp." In Britain and in many Asian countries, it's all about size: Small crustaceans are called shrimp; larger ones, prawns. Size is actually not a good indication of a true shrimp or a true prawn, as each comes in a wide range of sizes, depending on the species. Taste won't provide a clue either: We found in testing that each type can sometimes taste more or less sweet, again depending on the species.

The bottom line: We found no problem substituting one for the other in any recipe. The most important thing is to make sure that the count per pound (which indicates the size) is correct so that the same cooking times will apply.

Stir-Fried Shrimp with Garlicky Eggplant, Scallions, and Cashews

SERVES 4

Serve over plain white or brown rice. For more information on buying shrimp, see page 120.

SAUCE

- 2 tablespoons low-sodium soy sauce
- 2 tablespoons oyster sauce
- 2 tablespoons dry sherry or Chinese rice cooking wine
- 2 tablespoons sugar
- 1 tablespoon white vinegar
- 2 teaspoons cornstarch
- 1 teaspoon toasted sesame oil
- ⅛ teaspoon red pepper flakes

STIR-FRY

- 1 tablespoon canola oil
- 6 garlic cloves, 1 minced and 5 sliced thin
- ⅛ teaspoon salt
- 1 pound extra-large shrimp (21 to 25 per pound), peeled, deveined, and tails removed
- 6 large scallions, whites sliced thin and greens cut into 1-inch pieces
- ¼ cup cashews
- 12 ounces eggplant, cut into ¾-inch pieces

1. FOR THE SAUCE: Whisk all ingredients together in bowl; set aside.

2. FOR THE STIR-FRY: Stir 1 teaspoon oil, minced garlic, and salt together in medium bowl. Stir in shrimp until evenly coated; let marinate at room temperature for 30 minutes. Combine 1 teaspoon oil, sliced garlic, scallion whites, and cashews in small bowl.

3. Heat remaining 1 teaspoon oil in 12-inch nonstick skillet over high heat until just smoking. Add eggplant and cook until eggplant begins to brown and is no longer spongy, 5 to 7 minutes. Add scallion greens and continue to cook until scallion greens begin to brown and eggplant is fully tender, 1 to 2 minutes longer; transfer to bowl.

4. Add scallion white mixture to now-empty skillet, return to high heat, and cook, stirring frequently, until just beginning to brown, about 30 seconds. Add shrimp, reduce heat to medium-low, and cook, stirring frequently, until shrimp are light pink on both sides, 1 to 1½ minutes.

5. Whisk sauce to recombine, then add to skillet. Increase heat to high and cook, stirring constantly, until sauce is thickened and shrimp are cooked through, 1 to 2 minutes. Return vegetables to skillet and toss to combine. Transfer to platter and serve.

PER SERVING: Cal 270; Fat 10g; Sat fat 1.5g; Chol 130mg; Carb 22g; Protein 22g; Fiber 4g; Sodium 810mg

INDONESIAN FRIED RICE

FRIED RICE IS EASY TO MAKE AND EVEN EASIER TO make badly, as evidenced by greasy, uninspired boxes from countless Chinese takeout restaurants. A simple way to use up leftovers, the recipe is straightforward: Take cold cooked rice; stir-fry it with whatever meat, vegetables, and aromatics are on hand; and toss it in a sauce that lightly coats the mixture and rehydrates the grains. When done well (which is rare), the result can be a satisfying, but fat- and sodium-laden, one-dish meal. In fact, some of the recipes we tested packed a whopping 23 grams of fat and almost 1,400 milligrams of sodium per serving! These Chinese versions are far from healthy, but Indonesia's spin on the approach, called *nasi goreng*, inspired us to rethink fried rice. In this rendition, the grains themselves are thoroughly seasoned with a pungent chili paste called *sambal*, along with fermented shrimp paste and a syrupy-sweet soy sauce known as *kecap manis*. The rice is garnished with fried shallots, egg, and crisp fresh vegetables. The final product boasts so much complexity in flavor and texture that it hardly seems like the typical afterthought. We had recently developed a recipe for this style of fried rice in the test kitchen. Once again, we were excited about the challenge of taking the stigma—and for our light version, most of the fat and sodium—out of fried rice, but could we do it without losing all the flavor?

A quick survey of Indonesian fried rice recipes confirmed the source of this dish's heady flavor: chili paste. This coarse mixture is nothing more than a puree of shallots, garlic, and fresh Thai chiles. In most recipes, sautéing the chili paste in oil is the first step in the process; the paste develops complexity and heat before the other ingredients hit the pan. The chili paste was easy to reproduce and a snap to make, requiring just a few quick pulses in the food processor. Reducing the

TEST KITCHEN **MAKEOVER**

amount of oil we used to sauté the paste in our original recipe from 3 tablespoons down to 4 teaspoons was the first step in lightening the dish.

We knew that duplicating the flavors of the super-salty shrimp paste while keeping sodium levels in check would be difficult. Fishy-tasting anchovies were a non-starter, and intensely flavored fish sauce was simply too salty and lacked body. We had discovered in our original recipe that the best option was going to the source and simply sautéing chopped shrimp to make the paste, but the flavor still wasn't quite strong enough. We returned to fish sauce, finding that just 2 tablespoons bumped up the intensity of the shrimp paste without sending our sodium levels through the roof. While table salt is added to both the chili and shrimp pastes in other versions of nasi goreng, we found that we could lean on the fish sauce to keep things flavorful without the additional salt.

Next up was finding a reasonable substitute for the kecap manis. Bottled versions consist of palm sugar, which has a rich, almost caramelized flavor, and soy sauce. Simply adding brown sugar, which also has caramel notes, to soy sauce didn't quite replicate this condiment's complex flavor and viscosity. We had the best luck sweetening the soy with equal amounts of dark brown sugar and molasses. For our lighter version, switching to low-sodium soy sauce was a no-brainer.

We toasted the paste, then added the shrimp, followed by the sweet soy mixture (including the fish sauce) and, finally, the rice. Each bite of this fried rice revealed that famously addictive balance of sweetness, heat, and pungency. A squirt of lime juice gave it a fresh finish.

With the flavors of this dish locked down, we moved on to tackle a more fundamental fried rice problem: hastening the crucial rice-chilling step. Unlike freshly cooked rice, which forms soft, mushy clumps when stir-fried, chilled rice undergoes a process called retrogradation, in which the starch molecules form crystalline structures that make the grains firm enough to withstand a second round of cooking. That's why this dish is tailor-made for last night's leftover rice: After hours in the fridge, the grains are cold and firm. To approximate the texture of leftover rice, we tried cooking and chilling rice for varying lengths of time to achieve the right consistency, but none of our attempts came close to that of rice chilled overnight.

Since we couldn't figure out a way to speed up retrogradation, we tried to produce similarly firm, dry results by cooking the rice in less water. The standard 3:2 ratio of water to rice was saturating the grains too much, so we tested draining varying amounts of water from the pot. We achieved rice with the ideal texture using just ⅓ cup less liquid. Then we briefly let it rest with a dish towel under the lid (to absorb excess moisture), spread the rice on a baking sheet, and popped the tray in the fridge. Twenty minutes later, the rice felt almost as firm as the overnight-chilled batches. The only holdup: The grains were a bit sticky. The two-pronged solution? Rinsing the raw rice to remove starch and briefly sautéing it in some oil to form a barrier before adding the water. Our original recipe had used 2 tablespoons of oil, but we found we could drop down to 1 tablespoon and still get good results.

All that remained were the traditional trimmings: frizzled shallots, a fried egg or omelet, and fresh-cut cucumbers and tomatoes. The latter two were no problem, but the shallot and egg required some slimming. We agreed that deep-frying shallots was out of the question in our light version, so we brainstormed other options before asking whether the dish really needed them at all. While everyone loved their savory crunch, the final version was so flavorful without them that our tasters didn't miss them that much.

The eggs weren't quite as easy. In our original recipe we had agreed that avoiding the last-minute work of egg frying would be a plus. So we decided to go the omelet route, and for our healthy version we'd do the same, with a slight detour. Instead of using four whole eggs, we opted for five whites and one whole egg cooked in a nonstick pan coated with vegetable oil spray (rather than the teaspoon of oil our original recipe used). Our healthy omelet slid out of the pan clean and lean, ready to be rolled into a tight log and sliced into spirals.

With its sweet-salty flavors, spicy kick, and contrasting textures, this lighter take on fried rice was anything but humdrum. By making some calculated changes, we reduced the fat of our original recipe by almost two-thirds and the sodium by almost half. And since we didn't even have to wait a day to make it, it was a recipe that we'd turn to again and again.

MAKEOVER SPOTLIGHT: INDONESIAN FRIED RICE

	CALORIES	FAT	SAT FAT	CHOLESTEROL
BEFORE	590	23g	2.5g	205mg
AFTER	420	8g	1g	120mg

Indonesian-Style Fried Rice

SERVES 6

If Thai chiles are unavailable, substitute one serrano or jalapeño. You can make this dish less spicy by removing the ribs and seeds from the chiles. This dish progresses very quickly at step 4; it's imperative that your ingredients be in place by then and ready to go. If desired, serve the rice with sliced cucumbers and tomato wedges.

RICE

- 1 tablespoon canola oil
- 2 cups jasmine or long-grain white rice, rinsed
- 2⅔ cups water

STIR-FRY

- 6 ounces shallots, peeled
- 4 garlic cloves, peeled
- 3 green or red Thai chiles, stemmed
- 3 tablespoons low-sodium soy sauce
- 2 tablespoons molasses
- 2 tablespoons fish sauce
- 2 tablespoons packed dark brown sugar
- 1 large egg plus 5 egg whites
- ⅛ teaspoon salt
- 4 teaspoons canola oil
- 1 pound extra-large shrimp (21 to 25 per pound), peeled, deveined, tails removed, and cut crosswise into thirds
- 4 scallions, sliced thin
  Lime wedges

1. FOR THE RICE: Heat oil in large saucepan over medium heat until shimmering. Add rice and stir to coat grains with oil, about 30 seconds. Add water, increase heat to high, and bring to boil. Reduce heat to low, cover, and simmer until all liquid is absorbed, about 18 minutes.

2. Off heat, remove lid and place clean kitchen towel folded in half over saucepan; replace lid. Let stand until rice is just tender, about 8 minutes. Spread cooked rice on rimmed baking sheet, set on wire rack, and cool for 10 minutes. Transfer to refrigerator and chill for 20 minutes.

3. FOR THE STIR-FRY: Pulse shallots, garlic, and chiles together in food processor until coarse paste forms, about 15 pulses, scraping down bowl as necessary. Transfer mixture to small bowl and set aside. In second small bowl, stir together soy sauce, molasses, fish sauce, and sugar. Whisk egg, egg whites, and salt together in medium bowl.

4. Spray 12-inch nonstick skillet with vegetable oil spray and heat over medium heat. Add half of egg mixture to skillet, gently tilting pan to evenly coat bottom. Cover and cook until bottom of omelet is spotty golden brown and top is just set, about 1½ minutes. Slide omelet onto cutting board and gently roll up into tight log. Using sharp knife, cut log crosswise into 1-inch segments (leaving segments rolled). Spray pan with oil spray and repeat with remaining egg mixture.

5. Remove rice from refrigerator and break up any large clumps with fingers. Heat oil in now-empty skillet over medium heat until just shimmering. Add shallot mixture and cook until mixture turns golden, 3 to 5 minutes. Add shrimp, increase heat to medium-high, and cook, stirring constantly, until exterior of shrimp is just opaque, about 2 minutes. Push shrimp to sides of skillet to clear center; stir soy sauce mixture to recombine, then pour into center of skillet. When soy sauce mixture bubbles, add rice and cook, stirring and folding constantly, until shrimp is cooked, rice is heated through, and mixture is evenly coated, about 3 minutes.

6. Stir in scallions, remove from heat, and transfer to serving platter. Garnish with egg roll segments and lime wedges and serve.

PER 1½-CUP SERVING: Cal 420; Fat 8g; Sat fat 1g; Chol 120mg; Carb 66g; Protein 22g; Fiber 1g; Sodium 710mg

SHRIMP BURGERS

BENEATH THEIR SHELLS, SHRIMP CONCEAL SWEET, briny flesh that is high in protein but low in fat and calories. These days they're also extremely convenient, available year-round in your supermarket's freezer. We had already developed a great Greek-inspired skillet shrimp supper and a handful of shrimp stir-fries. Was there another application worth exploring? After a little research, we found ourselves leaning toward Southern-inspired shrimp burgers as a simple preparation that would highlight their sweet flavor. Unfortunately, many of the shrimp burgers we tried were reminiscent of fish-flavored rubber patties; others were more bread ball than shrimp burger. With these pitfalls in mind, we set out to develop a recipe for our ideal indoor shrimp burger: moist, with distinguishable pieces of shrimp yet still cohesive, and with seasonings that complemented the sweet shrimp flavor without overpowering it.

We started with the shrimp. We typically prefer to buy shell-on shrimp because we find them to be firmer and sweeter than prepeeled ones. After some early tests, we decided we needed a combination of textures— finely chopped shrimp to help bind the burgers, and some larger, bite-size chunks. We peeled and thoroughly dried 1 pound of shrimp, tossed half in the food processor until finely minced, then chopped the other half by hand. This worked well, but after a few tests we realized we could eliminate a step and pulse it all in the food processor, which resulted in the inconsistent texture we were after.

As for a binder, we wanted to use as little as possible to ensure the shrimp flavor was at the forefront. Most recipes we found used some combination of mayonnaise, egg, and bread crumbs, but these recipes all yielded burgers with shrimp swathed in a soggy, unappealing mush. The mayonnaise was adding much-needed fat and moisture (unlike beef, shrimp have little fat of their own), but the egg seemed less helpful—it only made the burgers wet, requiring more bread crumbs. We made a batch of burgers without the egg and decreased the bread crumbs to a single slice of bread, which proved to be just the right amount of binder to keep them together without detracting from the flavor or texture.

We discovered that overpacking the patties makes them rubbery, so we handled them as little as possible, then allowed them to firm up in the refrigerator for 30 minutes. Despite the small amount of binder, we were surprised at how well these burgers held together. Even better, they stayed together in the pan.

For seasonings, there were a lot to choose from, some better than others. Chunky vegetables like celery and bell peppers caused the burgers to break apart during cooking, so they were out. Tasters agreed that aggressively flavored ingredients like mustard, Old Bay, and hot sauces detracted from the shrimp flavor. Ultimately, tasters preferred simplicity: some minced scallion and parsley, as well as lemon zest, which accentuated the sweetness of the shrimp, and a touch of cayenne pepper.

To seal the deal, we whipped up a low-fat creamy chipotle sauce to top our perfectly cooked burgers. Some light mayonnaise, low-fat sour cream, lime juice, cilantro, and garlic, mixed together with some chipotle, made the perfect blend. The mild, smoky heat paired perfectly with the briny sweetness of the burgers. On a toasted bun with tomato, lettuce, and our sauce, these healthy shrimp burgers are sure to disappear fast.

SHRIMP BURGERS

Shrimp Burgers

SERVES 4

For more information on buying shrimp, see below. Serve with your favorite traditional burger toppings and our Creamy Chipotle Chile Sauce (recipe follows).

- 1 **slice hearty white sandwich bread, torn into 1-inch pieces**
- 1 **pound extra-large shrimp (21 to 25 per pound), peeled, deveined, and tails removed**
- 3 **tablespoons light mayonnaise**
- 2 **scallions, sliced thin**
- 2 **tablespoons minced fresh parsley**
- 1 **teaspoon grated lemon zest**
- ⅛ **teaspoon salt**
- ⅛ **teaspoon pepper**
  Pinch cayenne pepper
- 2 **teaspoons canola oil**
- 4 **hamburger buns, toasted**

1. Pulse bread in food processor to coarse crumbs, about 4 pulses, and transfer to bowl (you should have about ¾ cup crumbs). Wipe food processor clean and pulse shrimp until there is an even mix of finely minced and coarsely chopped pieces, about 7 pulses.

2. Whisk mayonnaise, scallions, parsley, lemon zest, salt, pepper, and cayenne together in large bowl until uniform. Gently fold in processed shrimp and bread crumbs until just combined.

3. Scrape shrimp mixture onto small baking sheet, divide into 4 equal portions, and loosely pack each into 1-inch-thick patty. Cover with plastic wrap and refrigerate for 30 minutes.

4. Heat oil in 12-inch nonstick skillet over medium-high heat until shimmering. Gently lay shrimp burgers in skillet and cook until crisp and browned on both sides, 8 to 10 minutes. Place burgers on buns and serve.

PER SERVING: **Cal** 280; **Fat** 9g; **Sat fat** 1.5g; **Chol** 130mg; **Carb** 26g; **Protein** 22g; **Fiber** 1g; **Sodium** 540mg

---

NOTES FROM THE TEST KITCHEN

DEVEINING SHRIMP

Although the vein running along the back of shrimp has no adverse effect on flavor or texture, removing it can improve the appearance of the shrimp.

1. After removing shell, use paring knife to make shallow cut along back of shrimp so that vein is exposed.

2. Use tip of knife to lift vein out of shrimp. Discard vein by wiping blade against paper towel.

BUYING SHRIMP

Virtually all of the shrimp sold today in supermarkets have been previously frozen, either in large blocks of ice or with a method called "individually quick frozen (IQF)." Supermarkets defrost the shrimp before displaying them on ice at the fish counter, where they look as though they are freshly plucked from the sea. Generally, we recommend buying bags of still-frozen, shell-on IQF shrimp and defrosting them as needed, since there is no telling how long shrimp at the market may have been kept on ice. IQF shrimp have a better flavor and texture than shrimp frozen in blocks. IQF shrimp are available both with and without their shells, but we find the shell-on shrimp to be firmer and sweeter. Shrimp should be the only ingredient listed; some packagers add sodium-based preservatives, but we find that these shrimp have a strange translucency and rubbery texture. Shrimp are sold by size as well as by the number needed to make 1 pound. Choosing by number per pound is more accurate.

SIZE OF SHRIMP	NUMBER PER POUND
Small	51 to 60
Medium	41 to 50
Medium-Large	31 to 40
Large	26 to 30
Extra-Large	21 to 25
Jumbo	16 to 20

Creamy Chipotle Chile Sauce

MAKES ABOUT ½ CUP

¼ cup light mayonnaise

2 tablespoons low-fat sour cream

1 tablespoon lime juice

2 teaspoons minced fresh cilantro

1 garlic clove, minced

½ teaspoon minced canned chipotle chile in adobo sauce

Water

Salt and pepper

Combine mayonnaise, sour cream, lime juice, cilantro, garlic, and chipotle in bowl. Add water as needed to thin sauce consistency and season with salt and pepper to taste. Cover and refrigerate for 30 minutes before serving.

PER 2-TABLESPOON SERVING: Cal 45; Fat 4g; Sat fat 0.5g; Chol 5mg; Carb 2g; Protein 0g; Fiber 0g; Sodium 135mg

SEAFOOD RISOTTO

SEAFOOD RISOTTO BEGINS WITH NATURALLY LOW-fat shellfish paired with Arborio rice and either broth or fumet (a concentrated fish stock). So why does this healthy- and minimalist-sounding dish get such a bad rap? First of all, it tends to entail a lot of work, traditionally demanding 30 minutes of diligent attention and stirring to produce evenly cooked, ultra-creamy rice. Hot broth is ladled into the pot in small amounts while the cook stirs almost constantly until the rice is tender but still maintains a slight bite. Time-consuming, yes, but unhealthy? Unfortunately, in many seafood risotto recipes the "creaminess" of the rice's naturally occurring starch is also buoyed with heavy cream and high-fat cheeses. Our goal was to create a rich-tasting weeknight seafood risotto without breaking the scale or the bank. We also wanted to keep dirty dishes to a minimum and develop a more hands-off approach.

We started with streamlining. Medium-grain rice is the best choice since it is higher than both short- and long-grain rice in an important starch called amylopectin, the key to what gives risotto a creamy consistency. Stirring the rice in hot broth releases the surface starches that dissolve into, and thicken, the broth. Since stirring is paramount to this technique, we knew that

eliminating it entirely wasn't an option, but we were hopeful we could reduce the amount required. To see how infrequently we could add broth and stir and still get the creamy results we desired, we made dozens of batches of risotto tweaking both factors. Batches stirred roughly half of the time were hard to distinguish from those stirred constantly. In the end, we settled on a technique of adding almost half of the liquid at the beginning and stirring infrequently for the first 13 to 17 minutes. The remaining broth is then added in 1-cup increments, and the rice is stirred frequently (but not constantly) for the final 13 to 17 minutes.

While some seafood risotto recipes opt for plain water, our tasters found the resulting risotto thin and bland. Substituting bottled clam juice for a portion of the water was more promising, offering a welcome briny hit, but it came at a price: Bottled clam juice is high in sodium, and the four bottles we added knocked our sodium numbers off the charts. In addition, the broth still lacked depth. Stepping away from the sea for a moment, we tried substituting store-bought low-sodium chicken broth for some of the water. This was certainly our richest batch yet, but tasters were missing a certain seafood essence.

At this point, a fellow test cook pointed out that since we knew we wanted our risotto to include shrimp, we could use their shells to add the missing seafood flavor to the broth. We tried simmering the broth with the shells from ½ pound of shrimp, along with onion, bay leaves, and peppercorns (a few classic broth additions). Simmering the shells for just 15 minutes infused the broth with a light but distinct seafood flavor that was potent enough to allow us to reduce the clam juice from four bottles to three, which got us into an appropriate range for sodium. Final touches of saffron and drained diced tomatoes added color and acidity to the rice.

Next we focused on the seafood and when to add it to the pot. In addition to the shrimp, we decided to include squid, which tasters liked for its mild flavor and gentle bite. We cut the bodies into rings but left the tentacles whole to showcase their unique texture and visual appeal. In the end, we excluded clams and mussels (their steaming would require another pot and we wanted to keep our risotto simple), but scallops lent their trademark gentle brininess and sweetness and were easy to prepare. We chose small bay scallops over large sea scallops because they cooked quickly and fit on a fork with a bite of rice. Now we just needed to find the best way to cook the seafood.

We tested a number of recipes that called for adding the seafood to the rice as it stood off the heat for a few minutes. We liked the idea here, relying on residual heat to gently cook the seafood, but we found it often produced rare shrimp and squid. We found it was necessary to keep the pot on the heat for about three minutes before taking it off. Stirring during this brief period ensured that every bite of seafood cooked at the same rate. With a richly flavored pot of perfectly cooked rice and seafood, we addressed a few final touches.

Since fish and cheese are rarely combined in Italian cooking, we weren't tempted to enrich this risotto with cheese, not to mention that it would only hurt the healthy profile. But we did want to add some richness and body. A single minced anchovy added with the aromatics and just 1 tablespoon of butter stirred in once the rice had finished cooking did the trick. The anchovy lent a savory character, and the butter gave the rice a voluptuous feel without loading it down with cream or cheese.

With just a few labor- and pot-saving techniques, we now had a deceptively light seafood risotto that even a figure-conscious mermaid would love.

Seafood Risotto

SERVES 6

Do not buy peeled shrimp; you will need the shrimp shells in order to make the broth. For more information on buying shrimp, see page 120. You can substitute ½ pound sea scallops, quartered, for the bay scallops. We recommend buying "dry" scallops, those without chemical additives. Dry scallops will look ivory or pinkish and feel tacky; "wet" scallops look bright white and feel slippery. If using wet scallops, soak them in a solution of 1 quart water, ¼ cup lemon juice, and 2 tablespoons salt for 30 minutes before step 5.

BROTH

- 3 (8-ounce) bottles clam juice
- 3 cups water
- 2 cups low-sodium chicken broth
- 1 (14.5-ounce) can diced tomatoes, drained
  Shells from ½ pound shrimp (see risotto ingredients)
- 1 onion, chopped coarse
- 10 black peppercorns
- 2 bay leaves
- ⅛ teaspoon saffron threads, crumbled
  Hot water

RISOTTO

- 2 tablespoons unsalted butter
- 1 onion, chopped fine
  Salt and pepper
- 5 garlic cloves, minced
- 1 teaspoon minced fresh thyme or ¼ teaspoon dried
- 1 anchovy fillet, rinsed and minced
- 2 cups Arborio rice
- 1 cup dry white wine
- ½ pound large shrimp (31 to 40 per pound), peeled and deveined (shells reserved)
- ½ pound small bay scallops, tendons removed
- ½ pound squid, bodies cut crosswise into ½-inch rings, tentacles left whole
- 1 tablespoon lemon juice
- 2 tablespoons minced fresh parsley

1. FOR THE BROTH: Combine all ingredients except water in large saucepan over medium-high heat and bring to boil. Reduce heat to medium-low and simmer for 15 minutes. Strain broth through fine-mesh strainer into large measuring cup, pressing on solids to extract as much liquid as possible. (You should have 8 cups of broth; if not, add hot water as needed.) Discard solids and transfer stock to clean saucepan; return saucepan to lowest possible heat to keep broth warm.

2. FOR THE RISOTTO: Melt 1 tablespoon butter in Dutch oven over medium-low heat. Add onion and ¼ teaspoon salt, cover, and cook, stirring occasionally, until softened, 8 to 10 minutes. Stir in garlic, thyme, and anchovy and cook until fragrant, about 30 seconds. Increase heat to medium, stir in rice, and cook, stirring frequently, until grains are translucent around edges, about 3 minutes.

NOTES FROM THE TEST KITCHEN

PREPARING SCALLOPS

The small, crescent-shaped muscle that is sometimes attached to scallops will be incredibly tough when cooked. Use your fingers to peel it away from side of each scallop before cooking.

---

3. Stir in wine and cook, stirring frequently, until fully absorbed, 2 to 3 minutes. Stir in 3½ cups of warm broth. Bring to simmer and cook, stirring about every 3 minutes, until broth is absorbed and bottom of pot is dry, 13 to 17 minutes.

4. Continue to cook rice, stirring frequently and adding more hot broth, 1 cup at a time, every few minutes as pan bottom turns dry, until rice is cooked through but still somewhat firm in center, 13 to 17 minutes.

5. Stir in shrimp, scallops, and squid and continue to cook, stirring frequently, until seafood is just cooked through, about 3 minutes longer. Remove pot from heat, cover, and let stand for 5 minutes.

6. Stir in remaining 1 tablespoon butter, lemon juice, and parsley and season with salt and pepper to taste. If desired, add remaining broth, ¼ cup at a time, to loosen consistency of risotto before serving.

PER 1½-CUP SERVING: Cal 470; Fat 7g; Sat fat 3.5g; Chol 160mg; Carb 69g; Protein 27g; Fiber 3g; Sodium 820mg

STEAMED MUSSELS

SERVED AS A REFRESHING APPETIZER OR LIGHT meal, bowls of steamed mussels in a flavorful broth have proliferated as a favorite menu item at upscale restaurants and neighborhood bistros. We knew that with a little know-how, these mollusks could be just as easily prepared at home. After all, most recipes for steamed mussels contain just a few ingredients: mussels, some aromatics, broth or wine, herbs, and a hefty dose of cream or at the least butter. When cooked together, the result is a dish that is more than the sum of its parts: a bowl full of steaming shellfish bathed in a fragrant and flavorful broth. The butter or cream adds richness and texture to the broth, but it is also what takes typical mussels recipes out of the running for quick, healthy meals. We wanted to develop a quick and simple mussels recipe with a rich, flavorful broth, but without the fat.

We started with the starring ingredient. Most mussels today are farmed either on ropes or along seabeds. You may occasionally also see "wild" mussels, which are caught the old-fashioned way—by dredging along the seafloor. In our tests, we found them extremely muddy and not worth the bother. Rope-cultured mussels can be as much as twice the cost of wild or bottom-cultured mussels, but we found them to be free of grit, and since

mussels are generally inexpensive anyway (no more than a few dollars a pound), we think clean mussels are worth the extra money. Look for tags, usually attached to the bag containing the mussels, that indicate how and where the mussels have been grown.

When shopping, look for tightly closed mussels; you want to avoid any that are gaping since they may be dying or dead and should not be eaten. Store mussels in a bowl in the refrigerator and use within a day or two. (Do not store in a sealed container, as this will cause them to die.) Mussels may need scrubbing to remove any grit from their shells (you don't want it to end up in your broth) as well as debearding, which simply means pulling off the weedy protrusion attached to the mussel. We found this was most easily done using a paring knife (see page 125 for more about debearding). Note that mussels should be debearded just before you are ready to cook them, since the process can be traumatic and potentially kill the mussels.

Next, we turned our attention to the cooking process. Typical recipes call for sautéing some aromatics, adding cooking liquid such as broth or wine plus some herbs, dropping in the mussels, then putting on a lid and steaming them until they open, which signals that they are cooked. Usually, once the mussels open, the cooking liquid is enriched with butter and perhaps some cream—but obviously that wouldn't be happening in our lightened recipe. Aside from that detail, we saw no reason to change this method, just perfect it.

We wanted to develop a classically flavored mussels recipe first. There were many steaming liquid options to choose from, including water, broth, coconut milk, wine, and beer. The assertive flavors of the beer and coconut milk didn't seem like a fit here, but we thought it was worth seeing how fish stock and wine would fare. In a side-by-side test of mussels steamed in white wine and mussels steamed in fish stock, tasters agreed that the stock made the dish overly fishy; the bright acidity of the wine proved a better choice, as it offset the briny flavor of the mussels. While it is possible to steam 4 pounds of bivalves in less than a cup of liquid, we agreed we'd like to have enough for dunking bread or for saucing rice. We settled on using 2 cups of white wine to cook 4 pounds of mussels. As for flavorings, 4 cloves of garlic as well as 3 whole shallots, a few sprigs of thyme, and a bay leaf added the right depth. Once the mussels opened, they expelled their own liquid into the broth, bringing to it the right briny notes.

ASIAN-STYLE STEAMED MUSSELS

This is typically the point at which you would remove the mussels from the pot and finish the broth with butter and/or cream. Was there a lower-fat but equally flavorful alternative? We tested batches made with a whole slew of finishing ingredients. We tried adding only 1 tablespoon of butter (as opposed to the typical 4 tablespoons), replacing the butter with light cream cheese, using half-and-half instead of the typical cream, and even thickening the broth with a cornstarch slurry. While tasters thought the half-and-half had potential, they preferred the flavor of the mussels and the broth in this recipe as is. The additional ingredients masked or conflicted with the shellfish's sweet, briny flavor here. We settled on just stirring some minced parsley into the pot, then pouring the finished broth over the mussels.

With our master recipe squared away, we felt some quick variations were in order. An Italian-inspired recipe with tomato and basil, a creamy tarragon version, and a spicy Asian-style recipe with coconut milk and cilantro were the favorites, each one producing tender mussels and a highly flavorful broth. We agreed that these recipes were best served with some crusty bread to mop up every last drop of the broth, though we'd argue the mussels themselves were just as delicious.

Steamed Mussels with White Wine and Garlic
SERVES 4

You can substitute littlenecks or cherrystone clams for the mussels. This dish serves 4 as a main course or 8 as an appetizer. Serve with plenty of crusty bread to dunk in the flavorful broth. You will need at least a 6-quart Dutch oven for this recipe.

    1 teaspoon olive oil
    3 shallots, minced
    4 garlic cloves, peeled and smashed
    2 cups dry white wine
    3 sprigs fresh thyme
    1 bay leaf
    4 pounds mussels, scrubbed and debearded
    ½ cup minced fresh parsley

1. Heat oil in Dutch oven over medium-low heat until shimmering. Add shallots and cook until softened, about 2 minutes. Stir in garlic and cook until fragrant, about 30 seconds. Increase heat to high, add wine, thyme, and bay leaf, and simmer to blend flavors, about 3 minutes.

2. Add mussels, cover, and cook, stirring occasionally, until mussels open, 4 to 8 minutes.

3. Use slotted spoon to transfer mussels to large serving bowl, discarding any that have not opened. Stir parsley into broth and pour broth over mussels before serving.

PER SERVING: Cal 520; Fat 11g; Sat fat 2g; Chol 125mg; Carb 25g; Protein 55g; Fiber 0g; Sodium 1310mg

VARIATIONS
Steamed Mussels with Tomato and Basil
Omit parsley. Substitute 2 cups crushed tomatoes for 1 cup of wine and ½ cup chopped fresh basil for thyme sprigs.

PER SERVING: Cal 510; Fat 11g; Sat fat 2g; Chol 125mg; Carb 31g; Protein 57g; Fiber 2g; Sodium 1490mg

Steamed Mussels with Cream Sauce and Tarragon
Add ½ cup half-and-half to pot after removing cooked mussels and continue to simmer cooking liquid over medium-high heat until thickened, about 5 minutes. Add 1 tablespoon lemon juice and 1 tablespoon minced fresh tarragon along with parsley.

PER SERVING: Cal 560; Fat 15g; Sat fat 4g; Chol 140mg; Carb 27g; Protein 56g; Fiber 0g; Sodium 1320mg

Asian-Style Steamed Mussels
Add 2 sliced jalapeño chiles with shallots. Substitute 1 cup light coconut milk and 1 (14.5-ounce) can diced tomatoes, drained, for wine. Substitute ½ cup minced fresh cilantro for parsley. Season broth with brown sugar and fish sauce to taste before pouring it over mussels. Serve with lime wedges.

PER SERVING: Cal 470; Fat 14g; Sat fat 4g; Chol 125mg; Carb 28g; Protein 55g; Fiber 2g; Sodium 1510mg

---

NOTES FROM THE TEST KITCHEN

DEBEARDING MUSSELS
Occasionally, mussels have a harmless weedy piece (known as the beard) protruding from between shells.

To remove beard from mussels before cooking, grasp beard between thumb and butter knife or flat side of paring knife and quickly tug.

FOOLPROOF THIN-CRUST PIZZA

PIZZA & PASTA

M = TEST KITCHEN MAKEOVER

FOOLPROOF THIN-CRUST PIZZA

WHEN WE PICTURE LIGHT AND HEALTHY MEALS, cheese pizza certainly isn't the first thing that comes to mind. Nevertheless, we had recently developed a fantastic recipe for a New York–style thin-crust pizza and were hoping that with some adjustments, we could get it into the healthy range. Luckily, after we sat down and actually crunched the numbers, we found that it didn't need that much work after all. This was a simple, thin-crust cheese pizza; there were no fatty toppings (the usual culprits in making a pizza unhealthy), and the cheese in our original recipe was sprinkled on with a light hand. We decided to walk through our original tests, review what we had learned, and see if there were any places we might want to lighten things up.

Most of our initial effort went into perfecting the pizza dough, which, after all, makes or breaks a homemade pizza recipe. Pizza dough is made from just flour, water, salt, and yeast, so each element has to count. We first took a look at the flour. For a slightly chewy and spottily charred pie, we found that high-protein bread flour was our best choice. The higher protein in the bread flour encourages gluten development and browning, as well as firmer, stronger dough; this extra elasticity came in handy when it was time to stretch and shape it.

Our dough was promising great things so far, but we knew that pizza perfection was a long way away. First off, instead of being thin and just a little floppy, the crust was bready and overinflated, with a texture more like that of focaccia than pizza. Plus, the dough lacked any kind of flavor, save for the strong yeastiness. Simply reducing the yeast would help to reduce the puffy crust, but it would also wipe out what little flavor the dough had. Could we keep the same amount of yeast and somehow fix the puffy crust problem? We needed to think outside the box.

NOTES FROM THE TEST KITCHEN

SHAPING DOUGH FOR THIN-CRUST PIZZA

1. Halve proofed dough and shape into balls. Place on lightly greased baking sheet and cover with greased plastic wrap. Let rest for 1 hour to allow dough to return to room temperature.

2. On well-floured counter and using fingertips, gently flatten dough into 8-inch disk, leaving outer edge slightly thicker than center to create fatter "handle."

3. Using hands, stretch dough into 12-inch round, working along edges and giving dough quarter turns. Transfer to well-floured peel and stretch to 13-inch round.

SHREDDING SEMISOFT CHEESES

Mozzarella and other semisoft cheeses can stick to a box grater and cause a real mess. Here's how to keep the holes on the grater from becoming clogged.

Lightly coat side of box grater with large holes with vegetable oil spray, then shred cheese.

THE BEST PIZZA STONE

Baking stones simulate a brick oven in your home oven, absorbing and radiating intense, consistent heat to produce crisp, golden brown crusts on pizza, calzones, and bread. Of the five stones we tested, **The Baker's Catalogue Pizza Baking Stone by Old Stone Oven**, $54.95, won out for being roomy but not cumbersome, with ridged "feet" that lift the edge for a comfortable grip. Pizza and calzones emerged evenly golden brown and crisp.

We knew that when the ingredients for pizza dough are first mixed, tiny "seed" bubbles form. These then expand at two different points in the procedure: once when the dough is "proofed" (when the dough is first given time to rise) and again during the first few minutes of baking. Logically, the larger the bubbles in the dough prior to baking, the more open and puffy the final crust will be. We realized that dough proofed at room temperature has much larger air bubbles than dough that is chilled, so instead of letting our dough proof on the counter, we decided to try sticking it in the refrigerator to proof. The next day, we pulled it out, divided and shaped it into rounds, and let it warm to room temperature while the baking stone was preheating. Bingo! This gave us just the thin crust we wanted, plus we got a few added bonuses out of the deal. The dough proved much easier to work with because the colder temperature slowed down the gluten development, making the dough looser and more pliable. Chilling also had the added benefit of creating a more flavorful dough. Why? Because at lower temperatures, yeast produces not only less carbon dioxide (aka air bubbles) but also more of the side products—sugar, alcohol, and acids—that contribute to flavor.

Then we wondered, if 24 hours of cold fermentation had such a dramatic effect, what would happen if we refrigerated the dough even longer? Three days later, we had a more flavorful crust, but any longer and the yeast would start producing too much carbon dioxide, rendering the dough too puffy. While this method wasn't exactly quick, the dough was a snap to pull together. Plus, the long rest wasn't altogether inconvenient; with a little planning, it was a great make-ahead recipe.

With our perfect crust ready to go, all we had left to do was evaluate the toppings in our original recipe and steer them in the direction of a pie lighter and healthier than your average greasy pizza. With a simple mix of canned tomatoes, extra-virgin olive oil, red wine vinegar, and garlic, the no-cook sauce developed for the original recipe was flavorful and didn't need any adjusting from our light-cooking point of view. As for the cheese, the original used whole-milk mozzarella. In a side-by-side test, our tasters couldn't tell the difference when we switched to part-skim, so we happily trimmed a little bit of fat with that simple swap. Our original pizza also included a handful of sharp, salty grated Parmesan cheese to balance the creamy, mild mozzarella.

Only a quarter of a cup went on each pie, and the flavor it added was well worth it, so we left it alone.

With just a few well-chosen modifications, we had a recipe for a delicious thin-crust pie ready to make for our next pizza night.

Foolproof Thin-Crust Pizza
SERVES 6

You can shape the second dough ball while the first pizza bakes, but don't top the pizza until right before you bake it. You can substitute a rimless baking sheet or inverted rimmed baking sheet, preheated for 30 minutes, for the baking stone. You can likewise substitute a floured rimless or inverted baking sheet for the peel. Make sure to use ice water in the dough to prevent overheating it while in the food processor. Greasing the bowls and plastic wrap lightly is important to prevent the dough from sticking and to allow it to rise properly.

DOUGH
- 3 cups (16½ ounces) bread flour
- 2 teaspoons sugar
- ½ teaspoon instant or rapid-rise yeast
- 1⅓ cups ice water
- 1 tablespoon canola oil
- 1¼ teaspoons salt

SAUCE
- 1 (14.5-ounce) can whole peeled tomatoes, drained
- 1½ teaspoons extra-virgin olive oil
- ½ teaspoon red wine vinegar
- 1 garlic clove, minced
- ½ teaspoon dried oregano
-    Salt and pepper

- 1 ounce Parmesan cheese, grated (½ cup)
- 8 ounces part-skim mozzarella cheese, shredded (2 cups)

1. FOR THE DOUGH: Process flour, sugar, and yeast together in food processor until combined, about 2 seconds. With processor running, slowly add water until dough is just combined and no dry flour remains, about 10 seconds. Let dough sit for 10 minutes.

2. Add oil and salt and process until dough forms satiny, sticky ball that clears sides of bowl, 30 to

60 seconds. Transfer dough to lightly greased counter and knead briefly until smooth, about 1 minute, then shape dough into ball. Place dough in greased bowl and cover tightly with greased plastic wrap. Refrigerate for at least 24 hours or up to 3 days.

3. FOR THE SAUCE: Process all ingredients together in food processor until smooth, about 20 seconds. Season with salt and pepper to taste. Transfer sauce to bowl and refrigerate until ready to use.

4. Position oven rack 4½ inches from top of oven, set pizza stone on rack, and heat oven to 500 degrees. Let stone heat for 1 hour. Meanwhile, remove dough from refrigerator and divide in half. Shape each piece into smooth ball and place on greased baking sheet, spaced at least 3 inches apart. Cover loosely with greased plastic wrap; let stand for 1 hour.

5. Coat 1 ball of dough generously with flour and place on well-floured counter. Using fingertips, gently flatten into 8-inch disk, leaving 1 inch of outer edge slightly thicker than center. Using hands, gently stretch disk into 12-inch round, working along edges and giving disk quarter turns as you stretch. Transfer dough to well-floured peel and stretch into 13-inch round.

6. Spread ½ cup of tomato sauce over dough, leaving ¼-inch border around edge. Sprinkle with ¼ cup Parmesan, followed by 1 cup mozzarella. Slide pizza carefully onto stone and bake until crust is well browned and cheese is bubbly and beginning to brown, 10 to 12 minutes, rotating pizza halfway through baking. Remove pizza and place on wire rack for 5 minutes before slicing and serving. Repeat steps 5 and 6 to shape, top, and bake second pizza.

PER SERVING (2 SLICES): Cal 440; **Fat** 14g; **Sat fat** 6g; **Chol** 25mg; **Carb** 63g; **Protein** 22g; **Fiber** 2g; **Sodium** 920mg

SPAGHETTI AL LIMONE

SPAGHETTI AL LIMONE, A STAPLE OF SOUTHERN Italy, is a simply flavored pasta dish that puts the emphasis on bright lemony flavor, with a few key background ingredients to support it. Sure, it sounds like the ideal light and healthy pasta dish. Yet traditional recipes, and the version we had recently developed in the test kitchen, rely on heavy cream, Parmesan cheese, and a generous amount of olive oil to create a sauce that just barely clings to each strand of spaghetti.

We already knew from testing our original full-fat recipe that the right amount of fat (from both dairy and oil) serves a dual purpose. First, it dampens the sourness of the lemon by neutralizing some of the acids in the juice. Second, it actually changes the part of the lemon's flavor profile (the oils) responsible for the fruity, floral notes by working in tandem with the olive oil to emulsify those flavors into a form that really coats the taste buds. We couldn't exactly afford the 23 grams of fat that went into this pasta thanks to the heavy cream, extra-virgin olive oil, and Parmesan, but without the rich ingredients to tame the bracing acidity of the lemon, the flavor was thrown totally out of balance.

We started by looking at what kinds of low-fat dairy might work to replace the heavy cream. Fat-free evaporated milk came to mind first since it has a rich, silken texture, but tasters found it too sweet and overpowering here. Regular low-fat milk was pretty unimpressive also. Weak in flavor, it was easily overpowered by the lemon, and its thin consistency meant it didn't coat the pasta but rather sat at the bottom of the pot in a puddle. Half-and-half certainly had the desired richness and was our best bet, but it wasn't quite able to cling to each strand of spaghetti the way we wanted. We needed to find another ingredient to work as a thickener.

A little bit of light cream cheese seemed like a logical choice since it would maintain the dairy profile. Combined with the half-and-half, it gave the sauce more body, but tasters found that the one-dimensional and "generic cheese flavor" competed with the purer ingredients in the dish like the lemon and Parmesan. Cornstarch or flour often helps thicken sauces in the test kitchen, so that angle seemed like our next stop. We tried mixing just ¼ teaspoon of cornstarch into our half-and-half. We added the mixture to the pot and brought it up to a simmer with some of the starchy water we used to cook our spaghetti to give a little more volume, and voilà, we had a clean, silky sauce that lightly coated our pasta and really allowed the lemon to shine.

To finish our pasta, we added a little chopped basil and a minced shallot for depth and to give the pasta a delicate and subtle sweetness, plus a hint of color. At this point, our numbers were so low we didn't need to change anything else about our original recipe. We happily kept the ½ cup of Parmesan cheese, as it lent a nutty, salty tang and really brought our dish to life. This was one pasta that tasted luxurious and rich without any guilt.

Spaghetti al Limone
SERVES 6

Let the pasta rest briefly before serving so the flavors develop and the sauce thickens.

- 1 pound spaghetti
- Salt and pepper
- 2 tablespoons extra-virgin olive oil
- 1 shallot, minced
- ¼ teaspoon cornstarch
- ¼ cup half-and-half
- 2 teaspoons finely grated lemon zest plus ¼ cup juice (2 lemons)
- 1 ounce finely grated Parmesan cheese (½ cup)
- 2 tablespoons shredded fresh basil

1. Bring 4 quarts water to boil in Dutch oven. Add pasta and 1 tablespoon salt and cook, stirring often, until al dente. Reserve 1¾ cups cooking water, then drain pasta and set aside.

2. Combine 1 teaspoon oil, shallot, and ½ teaspoon salt in now-empty pot. Cover and cook over medium-low heat, stirring occasionally, until softened, 3 to 5 minutes.

3. Whisk cornstarch into half-and-half, then whisk into pot along with 1½ cups reserved cooking water. Bring to simmer and cook for 2 minutes.

4. Off heat, add cooked pasta and toss until coated. Add remaining 5 teaspoons oil, lemon zest, lemon juice, Parmesan, and ½ teaspoon pepper and toss to combine. Cover and let stand for 2 minutes, tossing frequently. Before serving, add remaining ¼ cup cooking water as needed to adjust consistency, stir in basil, and season with salt and pepper to taste.

PER 1¼-CUP SERVING: **Cal** 350; **Fat** 8g; **Sat fat** 2.5g; **Chol** 5mg; **Carb** 59g; **Protein** 12g; **Fiber** 3g; **Sodium** 460mg

---

NOTES FROM THE TEST KITCHEN

NEW SCHOOL OLIVE OILS

California growers have spent the last two decades developing extra-virgin olive oils that might rival the best of Europe's. Because the quality of olive oil degrades over time, the benefit of buying domestically is built in. After running 10 California olive oils through several taste tests against our favorite from abroad, Columela, the former favorite still won out—but just by a mere half point. **California Olive Ranch Arbequina** won raves for its fresh, sweet, fruity flavor and pleasing bitterness.

SPRING VEGETABLE PASTA

PASTA PRIMAVERA: THE NAME ALONE INVOKES feelings of spring, the time when our favorite vegetables make their triumphant return to the local markets. But what we imagine the perfect pasta primavera to be—a light, creamy sauce to accompany the freshest vegetables we can get our hands on—unfortunately isn't what turns up on our plates. Recipes and restaurants alike typically turn out a random jumble of bland produce tossed with noodles in a flavor-deadening, heavy cream sauce. The test kitchen had just developed a pasta primavera that did away with the heavy cream sauce and overcooked produce, but when we looked at the numbers, we were shocked to discover that it wasn't that much healthier. Clearly, we needed to do a little investigating and reevaluate each component if we wanted a true light and healthy spring vegetable pasta.

We stayed with asparagus and green peas for the main vegetables since they had been carefully selected for their bright, grassy characteristics. Garlic and leeks also made the cut since they helped to lend an aromatic depth and sweetness. Minced chives, mint, and lemon zest and juice lent freshness, and red pepper flakes gave the dish a welcome bite we didn't want to miss, so we kept those components the same as well.

As for cooking the vegetables, many pasta primavera recipes call for blanching each individual vegetable, a tedious step that we found still delivered subpar results. We had found an easier, and faster, approach for our full-fat recipe. We sautéed the vegetables in stages with extra-virgin olive oil, a more controlled method that ensured the vegetables maintained their crisp-tender texture, plus they were able to take on a touch of flavorful browning. But this technique required 6 tablespoons of oil; here was the source of most of the fat in our recipe. We found that 4 teaspoons of oil was just barely enough to sauté the vegetables without causing any sticking or burning. But once the vegetables were combined with the pasta and seasoning, we found the results disappointing: The dish was too tart. Since all of the fat had been taken out, there was nothing there to balance the lemon juice, and aside from the bracing acidity, the dish tasted bland and lean.

We knew we had to add back a little oil, but this time we would be more strategic about where we put it. By using only 1 tablespoon to sweat our vegetables over lower heat (covered, to ensure that they wouldn't burn), we could still achieve the crisp-tender, lightly browned results of our original. We then used 1 more tablespoon of oil at the end to give a burst of fruity flavor and take care of the leanness as well.

What really set our original recipe apart from other versions was the "risotto" method used to cook the pasta. Instead of boiling pasta separately then combining it with the vegetables, we cooked it in a little wine and the fortified vegetable broth. This had a twofold benefit: The pasta took on more flavor, and the noodles released some of their starches into the liquid, which helped build a sauce with good body—no need for thickeners like heavy cream. We were on board with this idea, and just by simmering the trimmings we had left over from the leeks and asparagus, plus a couple of cloves of garlic, we added even more vegetable flavor.

Our original recipe called for stirring in ½ cup of Parmesan before serving, and we liked how it deepened the flavor of our vegetables and imparted some creaminess. We had planned on doing a few tests to reduce the cheese, but tasters agreed we had already cut sufficient fat to make this dish healthy; why make any sacrifices?

Tasters loved this lighter version; even with the oil reduced by a whopping two-thirds, they praised the pasta for its pure and balanced flavor.

NOTES FROM THE TEST KITCHEN

ONE GREAT ROTARY GRATER

When shredding cheese tableside, we prefer to do the job with a rotary grater rather than risk scraping our knuckles on a box or rasp-style grater. We asked testers to try four models priced from $9.99 to $34.99, handing them everything from hard Parmesan to semisoft cheddar, soft mozzarella, and even a chunk of chocolate. The biggest factor was the size of the barrel: Models with barrels smaller than 2 inches in diameter came in with sluggish grating times, while one of the widest-barreled graters (measuring 2⅝ inches) zipped through an ounce of cheddar in 15 seconds. Graters that disassembled quickly and contained fewer pieces of cheese made cleanup a breeze. We also much preferred classic designs, where one hand presses a clamp against the cheese to hold it in place while the other rotates the handle, instead of innovative (read: gimmicky) devices. Our winner was the **Zyliss All Cheese Grater**, $19.95, which produced perfect shredded mozzarella and Parmesan and is dishwasher- and lefty-friendly.

Spring Vegetable Pasta
SERVES 6

Campanelle is our pasta of choice in this dish, but farfalle and penne are acceptable substitutes. The test kitchen's preferred brand of vegetable broth is Swanson Vegetable Broth.

- 1½ pounds leeks, white and light green parts halved lengthwise, sliced ½ inch thick, and washed thoroughly; 3 cups dark green parts chopped coarse and washed thoroughly (see page 47)
- 1 pound asparagus, trimmed, tough ends reserved and chopped coarse, spears sliced ½ inch thick on bias
- 2 cups frozen baby peas, thawed
- 4 garlic cloves, minced
- 4 cups vegetable broth
- 1 cup water, plus extra as needed
- 2 tablespoons extra-virgin olive oil
  Salt and pepper
- ⅛ teaspoon red pepper flakes
- 1 pound campanelle
- 1 cup dry white wine
- 2 tablespoons minced fresh mint
- 2 tablespoons minced fresh chives
- ½ teaspoon grated lemon zest plus 1 tablespoon juice
- 1 ounce grated Parmesan cheese (½ cup)

1. Place dark green leek trimmings, asparagus trimmings, 1 cup peas, half of garlic, vegetable broth, and water in large saucepan. Bring to simmer and cook gently for 10 minutes. Strain broth through fine-mesh strainer into 8-cup liquid measuring cup, pressing on solids to extract as much liquid as possible; discard solids. (You should have 5 cups broth; add water as needed to measure 5 cups.) Return broth to saucepan, cover, and keep warm over low heat.

2. Combine sliced leeks, 1 teaspoon oil, and ⅛ teaspoon salt in Dutch oven. Cover and cook over medium-low heat, stirring occasionally, until just beginning to brown, about 5 minutes. Add asparagus pieces and cook until crisp-tender, 4 to 6 minutes. Add remaining garlic and pepper flakes and cook until fragrant, about 30 seconds. Add remaining 1 cup peas and continue to cook for 1 minute longer. Transfer vegetables to plate and set aside. Wipe out pot.

3. Heat 2 teaspoons oil in now-empty pot over medium heat until shimmering. Add pasta and cook, stirring frequently, until just beginning to brown, about 5 minutes. Add wine and cook, stirring constantly, until absorbed, about 2 minutes.

4. Add warm broth, increase heat to medium-high, and bring to boil. Cook, stirring frequently, until most of liquid is absorbed and pasta is al dente, 8 to 10 minutes. Meanwhile, combine mint, chives, and lemon zest in small bowl.

5. Off heat, stir in cooked vegetables, remaining 1 tablespoon oil, half of herb mixture, lemon juice, and Parmesan. Season with salt and pepper to taste. Serve, passing remaining herb mixture separately.

PER 2-CUP SERVING: **Cal** 470; **Fat** 7g; **Sat fat** 1.5g; **Chol** 5mg; **Carb** 78g; **Protein** 16g; **Fiber** 7g; **Sodium** 520mg

PENNE WITH KALE AND WHITE BEANS

A HEARTY PASTA DISH FEATURING WINTER GREENS and creamy, tender beans is a staple in Tuscany. Both naturally healthy and satisfying, it seemed like a great addition to our light pasta collection, but the starring ingredients traditionally take time to prepare: Dried beans are soaked and cooked, and the greens usually go through a lengthy precooking process to tame their bitterness. Plus, with so few ingredients it is important to make sure that the subtle, light sauce boasts appealing flavor. Still, if we could find a few shortcuts and flavorful additions, this dish could easily become a regular at the healthy weeknight dinner table.

Beans are a great match for pasta since they contribute lean protein and fiber to the meal, and cannellini beans have an appealing creamy, velvety texture that we thought would be perfect here. Traditionally, beans are gently simmered for about an hour until tender, so the first shortcut we took was opting for canned beans over dried. Though dried typically offer superior flavor and texture, the hour required to prepare the beans wasn't an option for the easy weeknight dinner we had in mind. We knew that given the mildness of the canned beans, we would need to incorporate some additional bold flavors. So we moved on to the greens, knowing we'd then need to address the finishing aromatics.

Hearty greens would be key for adding texture, flavor, and a prominent healthy component, so we needed to make sure we chose wisely. Turnip, dandelion, and mustard greens, as well as chicory, broccoli rabe, collards, and kale, were all on the table. But several of these would require an involved cooking process to reduce their bitterness to a palatable range: Many winter greens require blanching, shocking, squeezing dry, chopping, and finally sautéing. This process was too time consuming and fussy for this recipe. Kale and collard greens stood out because of their appealing mineral-like qualities and milder flavor, which meant they were our top options. Surely they could handle a more straightforward cooking method. And, indeed, just a quick sauté was enough. We agreed that kale was a better fit for the Mediterranean profile of our recipe, so we started our testing with 1½ pounds. To avoid cooking the greens in batches, we used a Dutch oven. Just 2 cups of broth would be enough to quickly braise the kale, and the broth could also serve as the base for a sauce. So we added our broth and white beans to the pot, brought everything up to a simmer, then added the kale and covered it to let it wilt. Once the kale was tender, however, we found that it was soaking up a lot of the liquid that we would need to sauce the pasta. Reducing the greens to 1 pound solved the problem and still provided the dish with plenty of heft.

Next, we addressed the few but essential flavor additions that would really bring our dish to the next level. Garlic was a must, giving the meal a clear Tuscan flavor profile, and we didn't want to be shy with it either. Twelve cloves of this aromatic powerhouse went into the pot. A pinch of red pepper flakes lent a much-needed bit of heat, and a little bacon added saltiness and meatiness. Stirring in a little Parmesan at the end gave one last salty and nutty punch of flavor.

Finally, we needed to figure out what we were going to do about our pasta. Throughout our testing, we had been using plain penne. While it was fine, tasters felt it wasn't bringing anything to the table. Looking back at past test kitchen notes, we recalled that whole wheat pasta is a natural complement to sauces like this one (in contrast, tomato-based sauces are a poor match because they are often too acidic and clash with the whole wheat flavor). We decided to give it a try, and tasters were immediately won over by its distinct rustic flavor that stood up to the kale and beans. The whole wheat penne turned out to be the missing link that gave our pasta the complexity and heartier flavor it needed—and we didn't have to spend any extra time cooking to make it happen.

WHOLE WHEAT PENNE WITH KALE AND WHITE BEANS

Whole Wheat Penne with Kale and White Beans

SERVES 6

The kale may look like a lot at first, but it wilts down substantially as it cooks. To make this dish vegetarian, omit the bacon and substitute vegetable broth for the chicken broth.

- 1 slice bacon, chopped fine
- 4 teaspoons extra-virgin olive oil
- 2 onions, chopped fine
- 12 garlic cloves, minced
- 1 teaspoon minced fresh thyme
- ⅛ teaspoon red pepper flakes
- 2 (15-ounce) cans cannellini beans, rinsed
- 2 cups low-sodium chicken broth
- 1 pound kale, stemmed and leaves cut into 1-inch pieces
  Salt and pepper
- 12 ounces whole wheat penne
- 1 ounce Parmesan cheese, grated (½ cup)

1. Cook bacon and 2 teaspoons oil in Dutch oven over medium heat until bacon is crisp, about 8 minutes. Stir in onions and cook until softened, about 5 minutes.

2. Stir in garlic, thyme, and pepper flakes and cook until fragrant, about 30 seconds. Stir in beans and broth. Bring to simmer and cook until sauce has thickened slightly, about 10 minutes.

3. Stir in kale, cover, and cook, stirring occasionally, until tender, 10 to 12 minutes. Off heat, mash some of beans against side of pot with wooden spoon to thicken sauce. Season with salt and pepper to taste.

4. Meanwhile, bring 4 quarts water to boil in large pot. Add pasta and 1 tablespoon salt and cook, stirring often, until al dente. Reserve ½ cup cooking water, then drain pasta.

5. Add remaining 2 teaspoons oil, cooked pasta, and ¼ cup Parmesan to kale-bean mixture and toss to combine. Before serving, add reserved cooking water as needed to adjust consistency, then sprinkle with remaining ¼ cup Parmesan.

PER 1⅔-CUP SERVING: Cal 390; Fat 9g; Sat fat 2g; Chol 5mg; Carb 62g; Protein 16g; Fiber 12g; Sodium 720mg

NOTES FROM THE TEST KITCHEN

THE BEST INEXPENSIVE DUTCH OVEN

Dutch ovens are kitchen workhorses, useful for making pasta dishes and for braising hearty greens, as well as making stews and soups. We tested several inexpensive Dutch ovens by making stew, rice, and French fries, hoping to find a more affordable alternative to our favorites by Le Creuset and All-Clad (which run roughly $270 and $295 respectively). The **Tramontina 6.5-Quart Cast Iron Dutch Oven** passed all of our tests with flying colors. Comparable in size to our pricier favorites and performing almost as well, it's hard to beat with its price tag of $54.95.

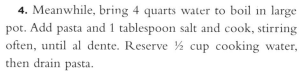

QUICK TOMATO-MUSHROOM RAGU

WHEN WE FIRST SET OUT TO LIGHTEN A RECENT test kitchen recipe for a quick tomato-mushroom ragu, we thought, given its name, that it would be quick and painless. We learned in short order that this weeknight pasta dinner was designed with speed and ease in mind, not necessarily waistlines. We did have to give the recipe credit, though; it managed to maintain this classic Tuscan dish's hearty and flavorful authenticity (most ragu recipes take hours to develop flavor) and still get on the table in less than 30 minutes. But at 20 grams of fat per serving, this recipe was going to need a little work from us to make it a healthy dinner option. With only a handful of key ingredients—mushrooms, tomatoes, pancetta, garlic, olive oil, broth, and rosemary—we were hesitant to change too much at the risk of throwing off the perfect balance; moderate adjustments here and there were going to be the key.

We started with the pancetta, reducing the original 4 ounces to 2. But when the pancetta was cut into ½-inch pieces as directed in our original recipe, bites of meaty flavor were rare. We found it was best to cut the pancetta into smaller ¼-inch pieces so that tasters would get a little bit of that unmistakable meatiness in every bite.

The mushrooms, a key ingredient in the recipe, obviously weren't contributing much fat. We had tested a few different fresh mushrooms for our original recipe, but we liked portobellos the most because they gave our sauce good meaty bulk. Meanwhile, dried mushrooms added concentrated flavor; we had settled on porcinis for their smoky quality that added another layer of complexity to the sauce. There was no need to make any adjustments to either of those components, so we looked at the cooking method.

For our original recipe we cooked the pancetta in the skillet first, then added the portobello and porcini mushrooms along with 3 tablespoons of olive oil (plus some garlic, tomato paste, and rosemary). The mixture was sautéed until the liquid from the mushrooms cooked off, then we added chicken broth and a can of whole tomatoes, crushed by hand (this provided a softer, heartier texture than chopped fresh tomatoes), to the pan. This was brought to a simmer and cooked for about 15 minutes until it was properly thickened. There wasn't much to work with in terms of fatty components other than the oil. So we tested gradually reducing the oil and found that just 1 tablespoon added to the pan in addition to the fat rendered from the pancetta (which we had already cut in half) gave us plenty of flavor and richness.

Last, our original ragu recipe called for a pound of spaghetti to feed four people, but we found that reducing the pasta to 12 ounces meant there would be a more healthfully balanced ratio of starchy noodles to healthy sauce.

At last we had a rib-sticking, ultra-savory sauce paired with the perfect amount of pasta—no one even missed the extra fat.

Quick Tomato-Mushroom Ragu with Spaghetti
SERVES 4

Use a spoon to scrape the dark brown gills from the portobellos. Serve with grated Pecorino Romano or Parmesan cheese if desired.

- 1 cup low-sodium chicken broth
- 1 ounce dried porcini mushrooms, rinsed
- 2 ounces pancetta, cut into ¼-inch pieces
- 2 large portobello mushroom caps, gills removed and caps cut into ½-inch pieces
- 4 garlic cloves, sliced thin
- 1 tablespoon extra-virgin olive oil
- 1 tablespoon tomato paste
- 2 teaspoons minced fresh rosemary
- 1 (14.5-ounce) can whole peeled tomatoes, drained with juice reserved, tomatoes coarsely crushed
  Salt and pepper
- 12 ounces spaghetti

1. Microwave broth and porcini mushrooms in covered bowl until steaming, about 1 minute. Let sit until softened, about 5 minutes. Drain mushrooms through fine-mesh strainer lined with coffee filter, reserve liquid, and finely chop mushrooms.

2. Cook pancetta in 12-inch skillet over medium heat, stirring occasionally, until rendered and crisp, 7 to 10 minutes. Add chopped porcinis, portobellos, garlic, oil, tomato paste, and rosemary and cook, stirring occasionally, until all liquid has evaporated and tomato paste starts to brown, 5 to 7 minutes. Stir in reserved liquid, crushed tomatoes, and reserved tomato juice, increase heat to high, and bring to simmer. Reduce heat to medium-low and simmer until thickened, 15 to 20 minutes. Season with salt and pepper to taste.

3. Meanwhile, bring 4 quarts water to boil in large pot. Add pasta and 1 tablespoon salt and cook, stirring often, until al dente. Reserve ½ cup cooking water, then drain pasta and return it to pot. Add sauce to pasta and toss to combine. Before serving, add reserved cooking water as needed to adjust consistency.

PER 1¾-CUP SERVING: Cal 470; Fat 9g; Sat fat 2.5g; Chol 10mg; Carb 76g; Protein 20g; Fiber 6g; Sodium 910mg

MUSSELS MARINARA

THERE'S A LOT TO LIKE ABOUT MUSSELS; THEY ARE quick cooking, flavorful, and low in fat. Advances in production have made them virtually free of sand and grit, so they also require minimal prep. We had already developed some simple steamed mussels recipes (see page 123); what about using them in a healthy one-pot pasta supper? One of our favorite preparations is mussels marinara, in which mussels are tossed in a spicy tomato sauce and served with pasta (or crusty bread). Since this dish is naturally pretty low in fat, all we had to do was find a way to bring our idea of a streamlined recipe to fruition. We had recently developed a method for cooking a full pasta dinner in a single pot, and that seemed like the mess- and fuss-free route we were looking for.

While the term "marinara" generally conjures images of a thick, smooth tomato sauce, most of the recipes we tested for mussels marinara produced brothier, chunkier sauces. Tasters generally disliked the few versions we tried that featured a smooth sauce, as they felt this style lacked any real contrast or texture when paired with the mussels. We agreed our ideal sauce was brothy with chunks of tomato, packed a little heat, and was rich with seafood brininess. We realized that this sauce had a lot in common with a recently developed test kitchen recipe for pasta puttanesca (a zesty sauce containing anchovies, garlic, olives, and capers). While testing that recipe, we had discovered that processing whole tomatoes with their juice produced a better sauce than just straight canned diced tomatoes. So we made a modified version of our puttanesca sauce, using two 28-ounce cans of whole tomatoes, some anchovies, red pepper flakes, and a fistful of garlic. This put us in very good shape. Using this sauce as the base of our working recipe, we turned our attention to the type of pasta we were going to use.

For our recently developed one-pot pasta method, we had found that we could eliminate cooking pasta in a separate pot of water. Instead, we cooked it right in the sauce. The added benefit (beyond simplicity) was that the pasta absorbed more flavor. Starch released by the pasta during simmering worked as a thickener, so creating a sauce that was slightly looser than we wanted in the final product was key. We added 3 cups of water to the sauce, then tested pairing our marinara base with a variety of pasta shapes, simmering them vigorously until the pasta was tender and the sauce thickened. Tasters preferred longer noodles, which grabbed more of the sauce. After testing linguine, spaghetti, vermicelli, capellini, and bucatini, we settled on spaghetti as the best complement. With our pasta of choice and a working tomato sauce recipe under our belts, we tackled the true star of this dish: the mussels.

We decided that 2 pounds of mussels was an ample amount for six people, so we examined our options for cooking them. A typical approach for clams and mussels is to steam them in a large pot until they open, using a little water or wine. Not wanting to stop now with our one-pot approach, we tried the obvious—adding the mussels directly to the pot as the pasta finished simmering. After a few tests, we found that it took just a couple of minutes for the shells to open and for the mussels to release their briny juice into the pot. This technique resulted in perfectly cooked mussels and pasta, with no additional cooking steps. With the finish line in sight, we took a final look at the flavors of our sauce.

While tasters liked the texture of our sauce, many found the anchovies to be too strong and the overall flavor too spicy. To ensure that the mussels remained the star, we cut the anchovies down to just one fillet and took the pepper flakes down to a more modest ½ teaspoon. This sauce offered better balance but lacked the brininess that tasters expected. Substituting a bottle of clam juice for some of the water was the clear and simple solution; it amped up the dish's brininess without overpowering the flavor of the mussels. We used 1 tablespoon of extra-virgin olive oil to sauté our onion, which gave the sauce a subtle sweetness, and, since we had a little wiggle room in the nutrition numbers, we added a much-needed second tablespoon of oil at the end to round out the flavors of the acidic tomatoes and briny clam juice. A handful of minced fresh parsley added some color and freshness. We finally had a simple, healthy, yet sensational one-pot mussels marinara.

Mussels Marinara with Spaghetti

SERVES 6

When adding the spaghetti in step 3, stir gently to avoid breaking the noodles; after a minute or two, they will soften enough to be stirred more easily. If necessary, add hot water, 1 tablespoon at a time, to adjust the consistency of the sauce before serving.

2 **(28-ounce) cans whole tomatoes**
1 **onion, minced**
2 **tablespoons extra-virgin olive oil**
6 **garlic cloves, minced**
1 **anchovy fillet, rinsed and minced**
½ **teaspoon red pepper flakes**
2 **cups water**
1 **(8-ounce) bottle clam juice**
1 **pound spaghetti**
2 **pounds mussels, scrubbed and debearded**
   (see page 125)
¼ **cup minced fresh parsley**
   Salt and pepper

1. Pulse tomatoes with their juice, 1 can at a time, in food processor until coarsely chopped and no large pieces remain, 6 to 8 pulses; transfer to large bowl.

2. Combine onion and 1 tablespoon oil in Dutch oven. Cover and cook over medium-low heat, stirring occasionally, until softened, 8 to 10 minutes. Stir in garlic, anchovy, and pepper flakes and cook until fragrant, about 30 seconds. Stir in processed tomatoes and simmer gently until tomatoes no longer taste raw, about 10 minutes.

3. Stir in water, clam juice, and spaghetti and bring to rapid simmer over medium-high heat. Cover and simmer vigorously, stirring often, for 12 minutes. Stir in mussels and continue to simmer vigorously, covered, until pasta is tender and mussels have opened, about 2 minutes longer.

4. Uncover, reduce heat to low, and stir in remaining 1 tablespoon oil and parsley. Cook, tossing pasta gently, until well coated with sauce, 1 to 2 minutes. Season with salt and pepper to taste and serve.

PER 1½-CUP SERVING WITH 8 MUSSELS: Calories 520; Fat 9g; Sat fat 1.5g; Chol 45mg; Carb 76g; Protein 31g; Fiber 5g; Sodium 1030mg

CHICKEN RIGGIES

TEST KITCHEN
MAKEOVER

THUS FAR WE HAD DEVELOPED A GOOD MIX OF healthy pasta dishes; now we craved something that offered heartiness and big, bold flavor, a meal perfect for a cold winter day. Combing through pasta recipes recently developed in the test kitchen, we came across Chicken Riggies. Formerly unknown to us, this dish hails from Utica, New York, where it is well celebrated (including an annual festival called "RiggieFest"). Uticans brim with hometown pride for this Italian-American specialty: rigatoni with tender, boneless chicken and vegetables in a spicy, creamy tomato sauce. Our recently developed version was creamy, piquant, and loaded with tender chicken, red peppers, mushrooms, and olives. It sounded just like what we were craving. However, when we crunched the numbers, we found that our original recipe tallied 30 grams of fat and 780 calories per serving. We would have to do some major overhauling in order to make this fit into our light and healthy parameters.

We started with the chicken. This was a boldly flavored dish, so the chicken had to fit into that picture; plain old chicken breasts wouldn't do. For our original recipe we had come up with an inventive, flavorful brine—a mixture of brine from a jar of pickled cherry peppers, a tablespoon of oil, and some salt—to imbue the chicken with the flavor it needed. For our first test, we tried doing away with the oil completely and just marinating the chicken in the cherry pepper brine and a smaller amount of salt. Taking away the oil, however, had its consequences; the chicken came out mushy.

The oil had been protecting the meat from essentially cooking in the otherwise high-acid marinade. Was there another trick we could use? In lieu of oil, for our next test we tried diluting the brine with 2 tablespoons of water. This did the trick: The chicken came out just as tender as the batch with oil in it, and it still had the unique cherry pepper flavor it needed.

Next, we looked to the vegetables. In our original recipe, 1 tablespoon of oil had been used to sauté the mushrooms and bell peppers, and another to sauté the onions before the sauce was built. We knew we could cut this back to just a teaspoon of oil per batch by covering the Dutch oven to let the vegetables steam, then uncovering it once the vegetables were cooked all the way through to brown them and add flavor.

After we sautéed the onions, it was time to build the sauce. We added minced cherry peppers for the kick that this dish is known for delivering, and five garlic cloves and a sprinkling of oregano gave it an Italian attitude. Adding cheese and cream to crushed tomatoes was key for creating the right richness in our original recipe. We were able to reduce the original 1¼ cups of grated Pecorino Romano cheese to a modest ½ cup without tasters complaining, but the ¾ cup of heavy cream posed more of a challenge. Reducing it sacrificed too much of the creamy texture. Looking back at our notes, we found that we had great luck with Spaghetti al Limone (page 130) when we combined half-and-half and a little cornstarch to create a sauce with a rich, thick consistency without relying on heavy cream. When we applied this technique to our Chicken Riggies, adding the mixture of half-and-half and cornstarch along with the can of crushed tomatoes, it thickened up nicely.

To finish up, we reduced the amount of kalamata olives stirred in at the end from the original ¾ cup to ¼ cup and chopped them instead of halving them for better distribution. With that last change, in total we had taken the fat from 30 grams per person down to 10 grams. With a few well-applied tricks, a creamy, cheesy pasta dish was clearly not out of the question even if we were trying to keep things on the lighter side.

MAKEOVER SPOTLIGHT: CHICKEN RIGGIES

	CALORIES	FAT	SAT FAT	CHOLESTEROL
BEFORE	780	30g	13g	120mg
AFTER	570	10g	4g	80mg

Chicken Riggies

SERVES 6

If you find only sweet cherry peppers, add ¼ to ½ teaspoon red pepper flakes with the garlic in step 3.

4 (6-ounce) boneless, skinless chicken breasts, cut into 1-inch pieces

2 tablespoons jarred sliced hot cherry peppers, chopped fine, plus 2 tablespoons cherry pepper brine

2 tablespoons water

Salt and pepper

10 ounces white mushrooms, trimmed and quartered

2 red bell peppers, stemmed, seeded, and cut into 1-inch pieces

2 teaspoons olive oil

1 onion, cut into 1-inch pieces

5 garlic cloves, minced

1½ teaspoons dried oregano

1 teaspoon cornstarch

¾ cup half-and-half

1 (28-ounce) can crushed tomatoes

¼ cup pitted kalamata olives, chopped

1 pound rigatoni

1 ounce Pecorino Romano cheese, grated (½ cup)

1. Combine chicken, 1 tablespoon cherry pepper brine, water, and ⅛ teaspoon salt in zipper-lock bag and refrigerate for 30 minutes or up to 1 hour.

2. Combine mushrooms, bell peppers, and 1 teaspoon oil in Dutch oven. Cover and cook over medium-low heat, stirring occasionally, until softened, 8 to 10 minutes. Uncover, increase heat to medium, and continue to cook until well browned, 8 to 10 minutes longer. Transfer vegetables to medium bowl and set aside.

3. Add onion and remaining 1 teaspoon oil to now-empty pot. Cover and cook over medium-low heat, stirring occasionally, until softened, 8 to 10 minutes. Stir in cherry peppers, garlic, and oregano and cook until fragrant, about 30 seconds.

4. Whisk cornstarch into half-and-half, then whisk into pot along with tomatoes and ½ teaspoon pepper and bring to boil. Reduce heat to medium and simmer, stirring occasionally, until sauce is thickened, 10 to 15 minutes. Stir in chicken and reserved vegetables, cover, and simmer, stirring occasionally, until chicken is cooked through, 6 to 8 minutes. Off heat, add olives and remaining cherry pepper brine; cover to keep warm.

5. Meanwhile, bring 4 quarts water to boil in large pot. Add pasta and 1 tablespoon salt and cook, stirring often, until al dente. Reserve ½ cup cooking water, then drain pasta and return to pot. Add sauce and cheese to pasta and toss to combine. Season with salt and pepper to taste. Before serving, add reserved cooking water as needed to adjust consistency.

PER 2½-CUP SERVING: Cal 570; Fat 10g; Sat fat 4g; Chol 80mg; Carb 73g; Protein 41g; Fiber 5g; Sodium 700mg

WEEKNIGHT BOLOGNESE

WITH ITS HEARTY COMBINATION OF VARIOUS MEATS in a thick, full-bodied, dairy-enriched tomato sauce, Bolognese is often considered the king of the Italian meat sauces—hardly worthy of a second thought (or first, for that matter) when trying to choose a light and healthy dinner. Still, when we were developing our test kitchen one-pot pasta-cooking technique this past year, our recipe for Weeknight Bolognese with Linguine was one of the most popular in the collection. And no wonder: Using a few clever tricks (including our method for cooking pasta right in the sauce), we could get our take on this hearty, meaty sauce plus pasta ready for the table in less than an hour. We decided to give ourselves our biggest challenge in terms of light and healthy cooking yet: We wanted to turn this popular recipe, which tallied 22 grams of fat per serving, into a low-fat dinner option without sacrificing richness or heartiness.

We knew that our biggest hurdle would be cutting fat while maintaining the rich, complex flavors that the sauce is known for. We decided to start by hitting the ingredient list where it really counted, which was the meat. Our original recipe called for 1 pound of meatloaf mix (a mixture of equal parts ground beef, veal, and pork). Turkey seemed like a healthier way to go, so we looked at our options: ground dark-meat turkey, which contains 15 to 20 percent fat (labeled 80 to 85 percent lean); ground white-meat turkey with 1 to 2 percent fat (98 to 99 percent lean); and a blend of the two (93 percent lean). A sauce made with all dark meat turned out to be moist and flavorful, but it was almost as high in fat as the original Bolognese so it wasn't any help in getting us closer to our lighter goal.

On the opposite end of the spectrum, we didn't have to worry about too much fat ending up in the sauce made with all-white-meat ground turkey, but it had an unmistakably bland flavor and a texture that was tough and grainy. It was clearly a nonstarter. The sauce made with a combination of white and dark meat turned out to be the clear crowd favorite. The combination turkey cut fat and some calories, yet it was flavorful enough to make us feel like we weren't eating diet food and it remained soft and moist throughout cooking.

We were off to a great start, but there were a few more challenges we would need to face before we could call this dish healthy. When we were developing the original recipe, we realized that browning the meat in the initial sauce-building step made the meat tough, and it took hours of simmering to retenderize it. When we skipped the browning step, the recipe moved more quickly (the whole thing could be made start to finish in about 45 minutes), but it left a void in terms of flavor and complexity. Instead of going back to browning, we found the answer in adding a puree of glutamate-rich ingredients—namely, pancetta, an anchovy, and dried porcini mushrooms—which lent a savory richness to our Bolognese without much work. We simply cooked the puree briefly, then added the meat, cooked it for about a minute, then continued with building the sauce. We wanted our lighter turkey Bolognese to be just as quick and easy, so we followed the same procedure with a little tweak. We tested cutting back on the 3 ounces of pancetta. Since the mixture was processed into a paste and evenly distributed throughout the sauce, one test proved that taking away an ounce of pancetta did not make a huge difference in the final results (any less than that and tasters noticed). This brought down our fat and sodium amounts, and the paste successfully elevated our turkey Bolognese to new heights of meatiness.

Milk is a traditional addition to Bolognese sauce, as it helps moisten and tenderize the meat during the simmering, and in our one-dish version it was added to the pot after the meat was briefly cooked, just before the other liquid components (wine, a can of whole tomatoes pulsed in the food processor, and water) and the pasta were stirred in and cooked through. We didn't want to lose this dairy component entirely, so in lieu of whole milk we tried using 2 percent low-fat milk.

Happily, it added a slight richness and kept the meat tender without adding too much fat.

Naturally, we wanted to get rid of as many excess calories as possible for our light version, but when we took out the 2 teaspoons of sugar that our original recipe called for, our sauce was thrown out of balance. The richness of the meat and the acidity of the wine and tomatoes had nothing to balance them, so we added a teaspoon of sugar back to our recipe and found our happy medium.

We also found that because this sauce was leaner than its predecessor, a little more water was needed to prevent the linguine from sticking to the bottom of our pot while it simmered. Stirring often was also an important step, since we found that the sauce could scorch easily if it was left simmering unattended for too long. Nevertheless, we didn't mind giving it a little extra attention, because we had at last found our way to a healthy one-pot Bolognese.

Weeknight Turkey Bolognese with Linguine
SERVES 6

When adding the linguine in step 5, stir gently to avoid breaking the noodles; after a minute or two they will soften enough to be stirred more easily. Make sure to stir the noodles often to prevent scorching. If necessary, add hot water, 1 tablespoon at a time, to adjust the consistency of the sauce before serving. Serve with grated Parmesan cheese if desired.

- 2 carrots, peeled and cut into 1-inch pieces
- 1 onion, cut into 1-inch pieces
- 2 ounces pancetta, cut into 1-inch pieces
- ½ ounce dried porcini mushrooms, rinsed
- 1 anchovy fillet, rinsed
- 1 (28-ounce) can whole tomatoes
- 1 tablespoon unsalted butter
  Salt and pepper
- 1 teaspoon sugar
- 1 garlic clove, minced
- 1 pound 93 percent lean ground turkey
- 1½ cups 2 percent low-fat milk
- 2 tablespoons tomato paste
- ½ cup dry white wine
- 4 cups water
- 1 pound linguine

WEEKNIGHT TURKEY BOLOGNESE WITH LINGUINE

1. Pulse carrots and onion in food processor until finely chopped, 10 to 15 pulses; transfer to bowl. Process pancetta, porcini mushrooms, and anchovy until finely chopped, 30 to 35 seconds; transfer to separate bowl. Pulse tomatoes with their juice until mostly smooth, about 8 pulses; transfer to separate bowl.

2. Melt butter in Dutch oven over medium heat. Add processed pancetta mixture and cook until browned, about 2 minutes. Stir in processed carrot mixture and 1 teaspoon salt, cover, and cook over medium-low heat, stirring occasionally, until softened, 8 to 10 minutes.

3. Stir in sugar and garlic and cook until fragrant, about 30 seconds. Stir in turkey, breaking up meat with wooden spoon, and cook for 1 minute. Stir in milk, scraping up any browned bits, and simmer, stirring occasionally, until nearly evaporated, 18 to 20 minutes.

4. Stir in tomato paste and cook for 1 minute. Add wine and simmer, stirring occasionally, until nearly evaporated, 8 to 10 minutes.

5. Stir in processed tomatoes, water, and linguine and bring to rapid simmer over medium-high heat. Cover and simmer vigorously, stirring often, until pasta is tender and sauce is thickened, 12 to 16 minutes. Off heat, season with salt and pepper to taste and serve.

PER 1¾-CUP SERVING: Cal 530; Fat 12g; Sat fat 5g; Chol 60mg; Carb 73g; Protein 32g; Fiber 5g; Sodium 750mg

ASIAN-STYLE NOODLE DINNERS

WE ALL REMEMBER THE INSTANT RAMEN NOODLES from our college days. They were cheap, cooked in about 10 minutes, and made a fine dinner for a hungry, time-pressed cook. But now the sodium-laden artificial seasoning packets and dehydrated vegetables sounded more like a nightmare than dinner. We were inspired by a test kitchen recipe that gave the old ramen dinner a fresh face-lift and used the familiar one-dish pasta technique (cooking the noodles right in the sauce), which meant this recipe was also streamlined. There were several variations of one-pot ramen dishes; we decided to start with a recipe featuring beef. We would retest it step by step and make tweaks as needed to ensure that it qualified for our healthy recipe collection.

Our original recipe started with cooking thin slices of flank steak (tossed with soy sauce for flavor and a little extra color) followed by shiitake mushrooms. These were set aside, then garlic, ginger, and chicken broth went into the pot. This made a great base for the sauce, and since we cooked the noodles in this broth, they too became infused with flavor.

Then we came to the noodles. Ramen noodles, we realized, even without the dehydrated vegetables and sodium-laden seasoning packet, weren't a healthy choice; the typical ramen noodles are packed with fat (15 grams per package). Parcooking the noodles—by deep-frying—at the factory is what makes them so convenient for the home cook since it means they take only a few minutes to rehydrate, but it spells disaster for a low-fat dinner.

So ramen were out of the question, but we weren't going to be easily discouraged. After all, we could still maintain the Asian flavor profile and character of our fresh take on ramen noodle dinners and just use a different noodle. We thought of other, healthier options that might work well as "ramen-style" noodles, and soba came to mind first. They are thin but still carry some heft. Soba noodles come in several varieties, such as buckwheat and whole wheat, but we agreed that our best choice of the bunch was a high-end variety called *chuka* (a more mildly flavored form of soba), because its flavor resembles ramen the most. But when we plugged them into our working recipe, tasters agreed that they were too thin-looking and didn't offer enough to justify running out to a specialty Asian market. We were hesitant to try any type of noodle we wouldn't be able to find at our local supermarket, so in the end, we settled on the easiest noodle of all to find: spaghetti.

We knew the spaghetti wouldn't be a simple substitution, however. In our original recipe, for instance, 3½ cups of low-sodium chicken broth were needed to rehydrate the ramen. In our case, since we were going to be cooking the spaghetti from its dry state, we knew it was going to take longer. We increased the amount of chicken broth to 5½ cups for our first test. While the ratio of liquid to pasta was perfect, the results were far too salty. We went back to the 3½ cups of chicken broth, and we added 2 cups of water to the pot. That, however, gave us a pasta dish that tasted watered-down. After a couple more tests, we found that 4 cups of broth to 1½ cups of water was the best ratio for a flavorful but not too salty base for our sauce. With the noodle situation taken care of, we turned our attention toward tweaking the other components.

We had already started a great base for our sauce with the garlic and ginger, so we just needed a few more ingredients to round out the Asian-inspired profile. We liked the spice of chili-garlic sauce but found it too overpowering. Switching to a pinch of red pepper flakes gave our recipe a little zip without taking over. When we added some hoisin sauce, more than one taster said our noodles tasted too much like the generic brown sauce you get with bad Chinese takeout. Oyster sauce fared much better, imparting a salty, complex richness the dish was otherwise lacking. A touch of toasted sesame oil, added at the end with the hoisin once the noodles had cooked through, perfumed every bite with its signature nutty flavor. Then we stirred the beef and mushrooms into the pot, followed by handfuls of baby spinach that we cooked just until wilted.

At this point we were happy with what we had accomplished, so we moved on to creating a few more recipes, substituting different proteins for the beef. We quickly settled on tofu and shrimp. After a few tests, we realized that the spinach wasn't a good fit with these substitutes; tasters wanted more texture. Lightly sautéed red bell peppers added texture and color with nice sweetness. In the end, we liked the peppers so much we decided to make the change to our beef recipe as well, dropping the spinach across the board.

The shrimp turned out to be a simple substitute for the beef, but the tofu took a little more work. When we seared it just as we had the shrimp and beef, the flavor was bland. Glazing the tofu first in a mixture of

broth, sugar, soy sauce, and ginger really dressed it up, and tossing it with some cornstarch before searing and glazing gave it a crispier texture that tasters welcomed.

Even though our Asian noodle dinners ended up being ramen-free, we didn't hear anyone complaining. They were too busy cleaning their plates.

Spaghetti with Beef, Shiitakes, and Red Bell Peppers
SERVES 6

When adding the spaghetti in step 3, stir gently to avoid breaking the noodles; after a minute or two they will soften enough to be stirred more easily. If necessary, add hot water, 1 tablespoon at a time, to adjust the consistency of the sauce before serving.

- 1 **pound flank steak, trimmed of all visible fat and sliced thin across grain on bias**
- 2 **tablespoons low-sodium soy sauce**
- ¼ **teaspoon pepper**
- 4 **teaspoons canola oil**
- 2 **red bell peppers, stemmed, seeded, and cut into ¼-inch-wide strips**
- 1 **pound shiitake mushrooms, stemmed and sliced thin**
- 8 **garlic cloves, minced**
- 2½ **tablespoons grated fresh ginger**
  Pinch red pepper flakes
- 4 **cups low-sodium chicken broth**
- 1½ **cups water**
- 1 **pound spaghetti**
- 3 **tablespoons oyster sauce**
- 1 **teaspoon toasted sesame oil**
- 4 **scallions, sliced thin**

1. Pat beef dry with paper towels and toss with 1 teaspoon soy sauce and pepper. Heat 1 teaspoon canola oil in Dutch oven over high heat until just smoking. Add beef, break up any clumps, and cook without stirring until beginning to brown, about 1 minute. Stir beef and continue to cook until nearly cooked through, about 1 minute longer. Transfer beef to bowl and cover to keep warm.

2. Add 1 teaspoon canola oil and bell peppers to now-empty pot, cover, and cook over medium-low heat until softened, 2 to 3 minutes. Transfer to bowl with beef. Add remaining 2 teaspoons canola oil and mushrooms to now-empty pot, cover, and cook over

medium heat until browned, about 6 minutes. Stir in garlic, ginger, and pepper flakes and cook until fragrant, about 30 seconds.

3. Stir in broth, water, and pasta and bring to rapid simmer over medium-high heat. Cover and simmer vigorously, stirring often, for 12 minutes.

4. Stir in remaining 5 teaspoons soy sauce, oyster sauce, and sesame oil and continue to simmer until sauce is thickened and pasta is tender, about 1 minute. Return beef-vegetable mixture to pot and cook until heated through, about 30 seconds. Sprinkle with scallions and serve.

PER 2-CUP SERVING: Cal 490; Fat 10g; Sat fat 2g; Chol 25mg; Carb 68g; Protein 31g; Fiber 4g; Sodium 950mg

VARIATIONS

Spaghetti with Shrimp, Shiitakes, and Red Bell Peppers

SERVES 6

Be sure not to cook the shrimp through completely in step 1, or they will overcook and turn rubbery when returned to the pot in step 4. When adding the spaghetti in step 3, stir gently to avoid breaking the noodles; after a minute or two they will soften enough to be stirred more easily. If necessary, add hot water, 1 tablespoon at a time, to adjust the consistency of the sauce before serving.

- 1 pound extra-large shrimp (21 to 25 per pound), peeled, deveined, and tails removed
- ¼ teaspoon pepper
- ⅛ teaspoon sugar
- 4 teaspoons canola oil
- 2 red bell peppers, stemmed, seeded, and cut into ¼-inch-wide strips
- 1 pound shiitake mushrooms, stemmed and sliced thin
- 8 garlic cloves, minced
- 2½ tablespoons grated fresh ginger
  Pinch red pepper flakes
- 4 cups low-sodium chicken broth
- 1½ cups water
- 1 pound spaghetti
- 3 tablespoons oyster sauce
- 2 tablespoons low-sodium soy sauce
- 1 teaspoon toasted sesame oil
- 4 scallions, sliced thin

1. Pat shrimp dry with paper towels and toss with pepper and sugar. Heat 1 teaspoon canola oil in Dutch oven over high heat until just smoking. Add shrimp and cook without stirring until beginning to brown, about 1 minute. Stir shrimp and continue to cook until nearly cooked through, about 1 minute longer. Transfer to bowl, cover, and set aside.

2. Add 1 teaspoon oil and bell peppers to now-empty pot, cover, and cook over medium-low heat until softened, 2 to 3 minutes. Transfer to bowl with shrimp. Add remaining 2 teaspoons canola oil and mushrooms to now-empty pot, cover, and cook over medium heat until browned, about 6 minutes. Stir in garlic, ginger, and pepper flakes and cook until fragrant, about 30 seconds.

3. Stir in broth, water, and pasta and bring to rapid simmer over medium-high heat. Cover and simmer vigorously, stirring often, for 12 minutes.

4. Stir in oyster sauce, soy sauce, and sesame oil and continue to simmer until sauce is thickened and pasta is tender, about 1 minute longer. Return shrimp-vegetable mixture to pot, toss to combine, and cook until heated through, about 30 seconds. Sprinkle with scallions and serve.

PER 2-CUP SERVING: Cal 430; Fat 7g; Sat fat 1g; Chol 85mg; Carb 67g; Protein 26g; Fiber 4g; Sodium 990mg

Spaghetti with Glazed Tofu, Shiitakes, and Red Bell Peppers

SERVES 6

When adding the spaghetti in step 3, stir gently to avoid breaking the noodles; after a minute or two they will soften enough to be stirred more easily. To make this dish vegetarian, substitute low-sodium vegetable broth for the chicken broth. If necessary, add hot water, 1 tablespoon at a time, to adjust the consistency of the sauce before serving.

TOFU
- ¼ cup low-sodium chicken broth
- 2 tablespoons low-sodium soy sauce
- 2 tablespoons sugar
- 5 teaspoons canola oil
- 2 garlic cloves, minced
- 1 tablespoon grated fresh ginger
- ⅓ cup cornstarch
- 1 (14-ounce) block extra-firm tofu, patted dry and cut into 1-inch cubes

PASTA

- **2** teaspoons canola oil
- **2** red bell peppers, stemmed, seeded, and cut into ¼-inch-wide strips
- **1** pound shiitake mushrooms, stemmed and sliced thin
- **5** garlic cloves, minced
- **2½** tablespoons grated fresh ginger
  Pinch red pepper flakes
- **4** cups low-sodium chicken broth
- **1½** cups water
- **1** pound spaghetti
- **3** tablespoons oyster sauce
- **1** tablespoon low-sodium soy sauce
- **1** teaspoon toasted sesame oil
- **4** scallions, sliced thin

1. FOR THE TOFU: Whisk broth, soy sauce, and sugar together in small bowl. In separate bowl, combine 1 teaspoon oil, garlic, and ginger. Place cornstarch in shallow dish. Coat tofu thoroughly with cornstarch, pressing to help it adhere, then transfer to plate.

2. Heat 2 teaspoons oil in 12-inch nonstick skillet over medium-high heat until just smoking. Add half of tofu and cook until crisp and browned on all sides, about 8 minutes, turning as needed; transfer to bowl. Repeat with remaining 2 teaspoons oil and remaining tofu. Return all tofu to skillet, add broth mixture, and cook until nicely glazed, 1 to 2 minutes. Transfer glazed tofu to clean bowl, cover, and set aside.

3. FOR THE PASTA: Combine 1 teaspoon canola oil and bell peppers in Dutch oven. Cover and cook over medium-low heat until softened, 3 to 5 minutes. Transfer to bowl with tofu. Add remaining 1 teaspoon canola oil and mushrooms to now-empty pot, cover, and cook over medium heat until browned, about 6 minutes. Stir in garlic, ginger, and pepper flakes and cook until fragrant, about 30 seconds.

4. Stir in broth, water, and pasta and bring to rapid simmer over medium-high heat. Cover and simmer vigorously, stirring often, for 12 minutes.

5. Stir in oyster sauce, soy sauce, and sesame oil and continue to simmer until sauce is thickened and pasta is tender, about 1 minute. Return tofu-vegetable mixture to pot, toss to combine, and cook until heated through, about 30 seconds. Sprinkle with scallions and serve.

PER 2-CUP SERVING: Cal 500; Fat 11g; Sat fat 1g; Chol 0mg; Carb 80g; Protein 21g; Fiber 5g; Sodium 1080mg

STUFFED SHELLS WITH MEAT SAUCE

GIVEN THEIR GREAT FLAVOR BUT HIGH FAT AND calorie content, stuffed shells have predictably inspired no shortage of lower-fat recipes. Some use novelty ingredients like pureed beans or squashed tofu as a primary filling. When we tested some of these recipes, we weren't too shocked that tasters put down their forks in boredom. Other versions we found relied on fat-free ricotta, chalky all-white-meat ground turkey, or nonfat cheese that gave the recipe a plastic texture. Tasters began to wonder if they were eating "real" food. Clearly, these recipes had gone too far; we would have to forge our own path to make low-fat stuffed shells taste as good as the full-fat version.

TEST KITCHEN
MAKEOVER

As a starting point for the filling, we used a full-fat test kitchen recipe that uses ricotta, Parmesan, shredded mozzarella, and two eggs. From there, we would slice and whittle where we could. Fortunately, in the process of trying the low-fat versions, we had come across one "diet" ingredient that really worked: fat-free cottage cheese. We usually (though not always) prefer reduced-fat products to fat-free products because they have better texture and no aftertaste from the stabilizers often added to nonfat ingredients. But in this case we found that when the fat-free cottage cheese was processed to a creamy puree, its smooth texture was indistinguishable from that of the higher-fat versions, and its flavor was clean and mild. So we substituted fat-free cottage cheese for the full-fat ricotta, and tasters agreed that the dish remained completely satisfying.

Next, we cut the Parmesan down little by little until we were left with half the amount we started with—its flavor is so strong, it didn't take much to make an impact. Using part-skim mozzarella was an easy switch from the full-fat version, and tasters thought it also offered up plenty of flavor even when we had reduced the amount by half a cup.

At this point, the filling was delicious but too soupy—it ran right out of the shells. We tried draining the cottage cheese, but even this was runnier than the ricotta had been, and adjusting the amounts and types of shredded cheeses in the filling had reduced their binding power as well. Removing the eggs made the raw filling firmer (and saved some calories), but it still wasn't firm enough to pipe into the shells. One at a time, we tested adding a handful of various low-fat ingredients such as cooked rice, instant potato flakes, and bread crumbs. Each gave the filling body, but in every case either the taste or the texture of the ingredient was notably wrong for stuffed shells. Finally, we reached for a box of saltines, thinking that their relatively neutral flavor might work in our favor. It did. When ground fine in the food processor with the cheeses, they disappeared into the filling, firming it up nicely and adding only a few calories and no fat per portion.

Now for the sauce. We knew we wanted to stick with beef for flavor. Most full-fat recipes use a pound or so of 85 percent lean ground beef. When we reduced the amount to 6 ounces, there was still enough beefy flavor but too much fat. Once we switched to 93 percent lean ground beef, we had hit our calorie mark, but the beef flavor was wan, and the texture was tough with so little fat. Adding a tablespoon of savory soy sauce to the raw meat boosted the beef flavor but failed to improve its texture.

As we had learned when making our one-pot turkey Bolognese sauce (see page 139), browning could be the reason the meat here was so tough. Indeed, cooking the meat gently until it was no longer pink—but not yet browned—did help a little. But since this sauce wasn't going to be simmered quite as long as the Bolognese would be, we were not totally satisfied with the finished product. We decided to try processing the raw beef (with the soy sauce to help move it along) in the food processor. This technique was just what was needed, as the blades cut the collagen into shorter fibers, resulting in more tender meat.

Since the rest of the sauce was so low in fat, and the stuffed shells finally had a rich, beefy flavor combined with good texture, we decided to stop there. We had cut the calories by 350 and the fat by 34 grams per serving. While the effort involved in making the traditional dish hadn't been reduced, neither had the flavor of the creamy filling and hearty sauce, so we were happy with our final result.

MAKEOVER SPOTLIGHT: STUFFED SHELLS

	CALORIES	FAT	SAT FAT	CHOLESTEROL
BEFORE	860	49g	25g	225mg
AFTER	510	15g	7g	55mg

Stuffed Shells with Meat Sauce
SERVES 6

You'll need a 24-ounce container of fat-free cottage cheese (don't use whipped). If it appears watery, drain it in a fine-mesh strainer for 15 minutes before you use it. Separate the pasta shells after draining them to keep them from sticking together. The tomatoes are the primary source of sodium in this recipe; if you are concerned about sodium intake, substitute low-sodium or salt-free canned tomatoes.

MEAT SAUCE

- 6 ounces 93 percent lean ground beef
- 1 tablespoon low-sodium soy sauce
- 3 (14.5-ounce) cans diced tomatoes
- 1 onion, chopped fine
- 1 tablespoon olive oil
- 2 tablespoons tomato paste
- 3 garlic cloves, minced
- ¼ teaspoon red pepper flakes
- ½ teaspoon salt
- ¼ cup chopped fresh basil

STUFFED SHELLS

- 1 (12-ounce) box jumbo pasta shells
  Salt
- 12 saltines, broken into pieces
- 20 ounces (2½ cups) fat-free cottage cheese, drained if necessary
- 8 ounces part-skim mozzarella cheese, shredded (2 cups)
- 1 ounce Parmesan cheese, grated (½ cup)
- 2 tablespoons chopped fresh basil
- 2 garlic cloves, minced

1. FOR THE MEAT SAUCE: Adjust oven rack to upper-middle position and heat oven to 375 degrees. Pulse beef and soy sauce together in food processor until well combined; transfer to medium bowl. Add tomatoes to processor and pulse until coarsely ground, 3 to 5 pulses.

2. Combine onion and oil in large saucepan. Cover and cook over medium-low heat, stirring occasionally, until softened, 8 to 10 minutes. Stir in beef mixture, breaking up meat with wooden spoon, and cook until no longer pink, about 3 minutes. Add tomato paste, garlic, and pepper flakes and cook until fragrant, about 1 minute. Stir in processed tomatoes and salt and simmer

STUFFED SHELLS WITH MEAT SAUCE

until sauce is slightly thickened, about 25 minutes. Off heat, stir in basil.

3. FOR THE STUFFED SHELLS: Meanwhile, bring 4 quarts water to boil in large pot. Add shells and 1 tablespoon salt and cook until al dente, 12 to 15 minutes. Drain shells and transfer to kitchen towel–lined baking sheet. Reserve 24 shells, discarding any that have broken.

4. Pulse saltines in clean food processor until finely ground. Add cottage cheese, 1½ cups mozzarella, Parmesan, basil, garlic, and ½ teaspoon salt and process until smooth; transfer to large zipper-lock bag. Using scissors, cut off 1 corner of bag and pipe 2 tablespoons of filling into each shell.

5. Spread half of meat sauce over bottom of 13 by 9-inch baking dish. Arrange filled shells, seam side up, over sauce in dish. Spread remaining meat sauce over shells. Cover with aluminum foil and bake until bubbling around edges, 35 to 40 minutes. Remove foil and sprinkle with remaining ½ cup mozzarella. Bake until cheese is melted, about 5 minutes. Let cool for 15 minutes before serving.

PER 4-SHELL SERVING: Cal 510; **Fat** 15g; **Sat fat** 7g; **Chol** 55mg; **Carb** 51g; **Protein** 38g; **Fiber** 4g; **Sodium** 1690mg

GREEK LASAGNA

TEST KITCHEN
MAKEOVER

THE CONSUMMATE GREEK COMFORT FOOD, *PASTITSIO* is a rich ground meat and pasta casserole often described as "Greek lasagna." To make it, elbow noodles are tossed in béchamel (a butter-and-flour thickened cream sauce), then spread in a casserole dish, topped with a meaty, cinnamon-spiced tomato sauce, and finished with a layer of more béchamel plus cheese. The test kitchen had recently developed a great version in which the noodles are bound with a simple whole milk–based béchamel, and the casserole is topped with a béchamel to which egg and yogurt have been added to create a custardy, tangy layer. This sauce swapped out traditional lamb for easier-to-find beef and stirred in 2 cups of Pecorino Romano cheese. It also tallied 610 calories and 30 grams of fat per serving. It clearly needed an overhaul to make the light and healthy grade. Nevertheless, we'd had great success lightening a hearty Bolognese (see page 139), which we had thought would be nearly impossible. so we were confident we could also make over our pastitsio and still deliver satisfying results.

The meat sauce was a good place to begin. For our original recipe, onions were sautéed in olive oil, then aromatics (garlic, dried oregano, and cinnamon) were added, followed by ground beef and tomato paste. So first, we swapped out the 93 percent lean ground beef used in the original recipe for ground turkey. We knew from past testing that a combination of white and dark meat turkey was a leaner alternative to beef yet was still moist and flavorful. We also found we could reduce the quantity from 1½ pounds to 1 pound and still have a lasagna with plenty of heartiness. Oil is always an ingredient we target when lightening recipes, and we found we could reduce the olive oil from 1 tablespoon to 1 teaspoon to sauté our aromatics. After these little changes, the sauce was in pretty good shape. We knew our real hurdle would be lightening the béchamel.

Our original béchamel was made with 5 cups of whole milk, 5 tablespoons of butter, three eggs, and ⅓ cup of full-fat Greek yogurt. This quickly became the focus of our makeover. We were able to cut fat by switching to low-fat milk, but tasters found this béchamel watery and bland-tasting. Next we tested béchamels made with a variety of dairy products, alone and in combination, to see what would restore the richness without too much fat. Tasters were finally satisfied when we hit on a combination of low-fat evaporated milk and 2 percent low-fat milk.

A traditional roux was out since we couldn't afford the butter, so we tried making our sauce with a butterless roux. We toasted the flour to deepen its flavor, then whisked in our milk mixture until combined and smooth. We then added the eggs as in the original recipe and switched out the full-fat yogurt for low-fat Greek yogurt. The results were not impressive: This béchamel came out too firm and springy and looked curdled. We took out the eggs one by one, thinking they were the cause, until we ended up with a sauce made with no eggs at all. While we were surprisingly satisfied with the taste of this eggless sauce, it still appeared grainy. We went back and reevaluated every single component of our sauce and finally realized that it was the flour separating from the milk that gave it a curdled appearance. We decided the flour had to go and started looking into thickening alternatives. Though concerned that cornstarch might make our sauce too gummy, we gave it a shot anyway, whisking 3 tablespoons into a portion of our cold milk to make a slurry before pouring it into the sauce. This worked perfectly. The cornstarch thickened the sauce and didn't taste at all starchy, and once the casserole was assembled and baked, the top layer of béchamel did not appear curdled at all.

With the biggest challenge crossed off the list, all we had left to do was some final trimming. We slowly reduced the amount of cheese until our tasters said we'd hit the minimum. We ended up getting away with just 1¼ cups of cheese, and we found we got more impact from it if we skipped putting most in the sauce as in the original recipe. Instead, we added ¾ cup to the béchamel and sprinkled the remaining ½ cup on top.

As we looked back at the full-fat Greek lasagna we had started with and compared it to where we were now, we were a little surprised. We had worked in leaner meat, less oil, and, most significantly a faux béchamel made with no butter or eggs, plus evaporated milk, low-fat milk, low-fat yogurt, and ¾ cup less cheese. We felt pretty good about the 18 grams of fat and 240 calories we had cut, but the best sign was that our lighter version disappeared in the test kitchen as quickly as the original.

MAKEOVER SPOTLIGHT: GREEK LASAGNA (PASTITSIO)

	CALORIES	FAT	SAT FAT	CHOLESTEROL
BEFORE	610	30g	17g	185mg
AFTER	370	12g	6g	55mg

Greek Lasagna (Pastitsio)

SERVES 8

Be sure to use 93 percent lean ground turkey, not ground turkey breast (also labeled 99 percent fat free), in this recipe.

MEAT SAUCE

- 1 onion, chopped fine
- 1 teaspoon olive oil
- Salt and pepper
- 2 tablespoons tomato paste
- 4 garlic cloves, minced
- 1½ teaspoons dried oregano
- 1 teaspoon ground cinnamon
- 1 pound 93 percent lean ground turkey
- ⅓ cup red wine
- 1 (15-ounce) can tomato sauce

PASTA AND BÉCHAMEL SAUCE

- 8 ounces elbow macaroni
- Salt and pepper
- 1 teaspoon olive oil
- 3 garlic cloves, minced
- 2½ cups 2 percent low-fat milk
- 1 (12-ounce) can low-fat evaporated milk
- 3 tablespoons cornstarch
- 2½ ounces Pecorino Romano cheese, grated (1¼ cups)
- ⅓ cup 2 percent Greek yogurt

1. FOR THE MEAT SAUCE: Adjust oven rack to middle position and heat oven to 375 degrees. Combine onion, oil, ⅛ teaspoon salt, and ¼ teaspoon pepper in large skillet. Cover and cook over medium-low heat, stirring occasionally, until softened, 8 to 10 minutes. Uncover, increase heat to medium, and stir in tomato paste, garlic, oregano, and cinnamon. Cook until tomato paste begins to darken, 1 to 2 minutes.

2. Stir in turkey, breaking up meat with wooden spoon, and cook until no longer pink, about 5 minutes. Stir in wine and cook until liquid is nearly evaporated, 2 to 4 minutes. Add tomato sauce, bring to simmer, and cook, stirring occasionally, until slightly thickened, 6 to 8 minutes; set aside.

3. FOR THE PASTA AND BÉCHAMEL SAUCE: Bring 4 quarts water to boil in Dutch oven. Add pasta and 1 tablespoon salt and cook until almost al dente, 3 to 4 minutes. Drain and rinse with cold water until cool. Drain pasta well and transfer to large bowl.

4. Heat oil in now-empty Dutch oven over medium-low heat until shimmering. Add garlic and cook until fragrant, about 30 seconds. Stir in 2 cups milk and evaporated milk and bring to simmer, stirring often.

5. Whisk cornstarch into remaining ½ cup milk, then whisk into pot. Continue to simmer, whisking constantly, until thickened, about 6 minutes. Off heat, stir in ¾ cup cheese and season with salt and pepper to taste.

6. Stir 1½ cups béchamel sauce into pasta until combined. Whisk yogurt into remaining béchamel. Transfer sauced pasta to 13 by 9-inch baking dish. Spread meat sauce over pasta and top with remaining béchamel. Sprinkle remaining ½ cup cheese evenly over top. Bake until golden brown, about 30 minutes. Let cool for 10 minutes before serving.

PER SERVING: Cal 370; Fat 12g; Sat fat 6g; Chol 55mg; Carb 38g; Protein 26g; Fiber 3g; Sodium 800mg

SLOW-COOKER SUPER VEGGIE BEEF STEW

SLOW COOKER

15-BEAN SOUP

SLOW COOKERS ARE GREAT FOR HANDS-FREE AND easy cooking, but the recipes that typically come to mind as slow-cooker favorites are rarely those of the light and healthy variety. Most often we picture stews, braises, and sauces made with fatty cuts of meat and numerous canned products, which are convenient but can also pile on the sodium. But we knew that not all slow-cooker recipes have to fit into that genre. In our search for a slow-cooker recipe with healthy-eating potential, 15-Bean Soup landed high on our list. We set out to see what we could do to make a well-rounded, flavorful, and healthy bean soup in our slow cooker.

Dried beans are a slow-cooker natural. You can find 15-bean soup mixes that offer convenience and variety, but made according to the packet, they are inevitably disappointing, as the dried seasonings included offer zero flavor, and the petrified bits of vegetables resemble astronaut food. Even the addition of more than a pound of fatty pork products (as directed on the packaging) is not enough to save them.

We already had a test kitchen recipe for a stovetop version of this soup that tackled many of these problems. It was also already on the right track in terms of lightening. We had ditched the flavoring packet from the mix and used only 4 ounces of bacon. However, at 11 grams of fat and 1100 milligrams of sodium, it still seemed a little off the mark for an almost meatless soup.

We started with the beans. In the past, we've learned that to cook beans evenly, it is best to salt-soak them. Since we were already taking advantage of the slow cooker's long cooking time, we wondered if we could skip this step for the sake of ease. When we added dried beans directly to the slow cooker, some emerged crunchy and others were blown out. So we returned to our salt soak. This version was much improved: The beans were now soft and creamy throughout.

For aromatics, we would include onion, garlic, and thyme as the base to keep our flavors simple yet strong. In our original stovetop recipe, the first step in building the soup's flavor was to sauté these aromatics. Since we were using the slow cooker and trying to limit additional cooking, we wondered if we even needed to bring out a sauté pan. We tried adding the aromatics raw, but even with a six- to eight-hour cooking time, the onions were still crunchy and the spices tasted dusty. We needed a different tactic.

In the past, we've used the microwave to parcook vegetables. Could we use that method for the aromatics here? We also thought we could take advantage of the microwave's more gentle heat and cut back the amount of oil. We mixed the onion, garlic, and thyme with 1 teaspoon oil, microwaved the mixture for five minutes, then added it to the slow cooker along with our beans and several cups of chicken broth. This time, the onions softened into the broth, and the aromatics mellowed.

Our stovetop recipe used bacon to add savory depth and a touch of smokiness. We knew we wanted to keep this flavor profile, but we hoped we could cut back on the four strips. We turned to a trick we'd used in several earlier light recipes: We scaled the bacon down to two slices, simmered it whole, and then removed it from the pot prior to serving. This infused the soup with plenty of bacon flavor, but the long cooking time threw us a curveball. The slices had broken apart by the end of cooking, and they were too difficult to remove. Instead of fighting the problem, we decided we were better off working with it. We reduced the amount of bacon to one slice, and we minced it so that it would simply disappear into the broth. Luckily this small amount of bacon still contributed enough pork flavor, and the small pieces melded seamlessly into the soup.

Next were the vegetables. We liked carrots for their subtle sweetness and white mushrooms for their meaty texture. We found that both could be added directly to the broth at the beginning of cooking. To further boost the mushroom flavor, we also added ½ ounce of minced dried porcini, which broke down and infused the broth with their rich, earthy flavor.

The carrots and mushrooms provided needed contrast to our soup, but tasters thought that still something was missing. To add color, we incorporated Swiss chard. For a final burst of brightness, we also added chopped canned tomatoes. Using just one can ensured the sodium stayed in check.

Up to this point, we had been using low-sodium chicken broth for our liquid base, as it added complexity to our relatively simple soup. We wondered whether we'd get more balanced flavor if we cut the broth with water. Starting with 5½ cups of broth and ½ cup of water, we gradually increased the water by the half-cup until we found the perfect ratio: 4 cups of broth to 2 cups of water. We liked this even more than the all-broth original, as it brought the flavors into unison. This soup was the epitome of healthy convenience.

Slow-Cooker 15-Bean Soup

SERVES 6

To quick salt-soak the beans, combine 2 quarts water, beans, and 1½ tablespoons salt in Dutch oven and bring to boil over high heat. Remove pot from heat, cover, and let stand for 1 hour. Drain and rinse well. *Cooking time: 9 to 11 hours on low or 5 to 7 hours on high*

> Salt and pepper
>
> 8 ounces (1¼ cups) 15-bean soup mix, flavoring packet discarded, picked over and rinsed
>
> 1 onion, chopped fine
>
> 6 garlic cloves, minced
>
> 2 teaspoons minced fresh thyme or ½ teaspoon dried
>
> 1 teaspoon canola oil
>
> 4 cups low-sodium chicken broth
>
> 12 ounces white mushrooms, trimmed and quartered
>
> 2 cups water
>
> 1 slice bacon, chopped fine
>
> ½ ounce dried porcini mushrooms, rinsed and minced
>
> 2 bay leaves
>
> 8 ounces Swiss chard, stemmed and leaves sliced ½ inch thick
>
> 1 (14.5-ounce) can whole peeled tomatoes, drained and chopped coarse

1. Dissolve 1½ tablespoons salt in 2 quarts cold water in large bowl or container. Add beans and soak at room temperature for at least 8 hours or up to 24 hours. Drain and rinse well.

2. Combine onion, garlic, thyme, and oil in bowl and microwave, stirring occasionally, until onion is softened, about 5 minutes; transfer to slow cooker.

3. Stir broth, white mushrooms, water, soaked beans, bacon, porcini mushrooms, and bay leaves into slow cooker. Cover and cook until beans are tender, 9 to 11 hours on low or 5 to 7 hours on high.

4. Let soup settle for 5 minutes, then remove fat from surface using large spoon. Remove bay leaves. Stir in chard and tomatoes, cover, and cook on high until chard is tender, 20 to 30 minutes. Season with salt and pepper to taste. Serve.

PER 1½-CUP SERVING: Cal 210; Fat 3.5g; Sat fat 1g; Chol 5mg; Carb 33g; Protein 12g; Fiber 5g; Sodium 680mg

---

NOTES FROM THE TEST KITCHEN

THE BEST SLOW COOKER

We recently pitted seven slow cookers, all priced under $200, against each other to see if we could save money without sacrificing performance. We limited our lineup mainly to oval slow cookers, which can fit a large roast, with capacities of 6 quarts or more, and we judged the cookers on design and performance. Six models had programmable timers and warming modes, features we liked. We also liked clear glass lids so that we could assess the food as it cooked. Ideally, a slow cooker should produce perfect results on all settings. But when we made pot roast, tomato sauce, and French onion soup, some of the models variously gave us pot roast with dry, tough meat or juicy, sliceable meat, and tomato sauces that were extra-thick or thin and watery. We devised a test to measure the temperatures of the models and found that some just didn't get hot enough, whereas others reached the boiling point; the best models fell somewhere in between. Our winner, the **Crock-Pot Touchscreen Slow Cooker**, $129.99, cooked our dinner perfectly. It also had the best control panel (with a timer that counted up to 20 hours, even on high); it was simple to set and clearly indicated when the cooker was programmed.

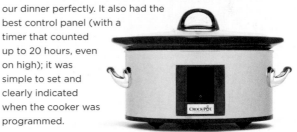

TURKEY AND RICE SOUP

NOW THAT WE HAD SUCCESSFULLY CREATED a great bean soup in the slow cooker, we wanted to develop a go-to slow-cooker soup that was comforting, convenient, and healthy. Soups like chicken noodle and chicken and rice are about as comforting as it gets, and since chicken noodle is typically in the limelight, we decided to focus on the rice version. We also decided to mix things up by swapping in turkey for the chicken. We figured that not only would this change-up add variety, but since turkey pieces are naturally larger than chicken pieces, they would also require less prep. The best poultry-based soups boast meaty flavor balanced with earthy vegetables in a clean, flavor-packed broth. Could we revamp this comfort classic into a creative, healthy dish? And could we do it all in our slow cooker?

To begin, we tackled the turkey. We knew we wanted to stick with a bone-in cut, since the bone would add both flavor and body to our soup. We gathered bone-in thighs, bone-in breasts, and turkey legs to find the best option. We hoped that the turkey breast would work since it contained only 2.5 grams of fat per serving. Unfortunately, we ran into multiple roadblocks: it barely fit in the slow cooker, the moist cooking environment was not enough to prevent the meat from drying out, and it gave us far too much meat. The legs were not much better. Again, we had a difficult time even fitting them in the cooker, and the meat itself turned stringy and tough. The thighs, luckily, worked perfectly. Two 1-pound pieces gave us the right amount of meat, and since thighs are made up entirely of dark meat, they added a great deal of rich turkey flavor. Best of all, they were nearly impossible to overcook. As long as we removed the skin and trimmed the meat well, our fat levels stayed at only 5 grams per serving.

Now that we had chosen our cut of turkey, we moved on to our aromatics and cooking liquid. Wanting to keep the soup simple and let the clean flavor of the turkey shine, we stuck with a classic *mirepoix* of onion, carrot, and celery for our aromatic base, with garlic, thyme, and a few bay leaves for brightness and herbal flavor. As we had learned to do with our Slow-Cooker 15-Bean Soup (page 152), we used the microwave to soften and bloom the aromatics. For the liquid base, we wondered if a combination of water and chicken broth would be the way to go, as it had been with the 15-Bean Soup. We started at 4 cups of each. However, given the subtle profile of this soup's starring ingredients, tasters wanted a stronger broth presence.

NOTES FROM THE TEST KITCHEN

THE BEST TOMATO PASTE

Tomato paste is the backbone of many tomato-based recipes, as well as non-tomato-based recipes, such as beef stew. It often acts as our secret ingredient because it's naturally full of glutamates, which bring out subtle flavors and savory notes. Could a better-tasting brand have an even bigger impact? We sampled 10 top-selling brands plain, cooked on their own, and cooked in marinara sauce. When we sampled our lineup uncooked, tasters' choices were split between brands that tasted bright and acidic, like fresh tomatoes, and those with deep cooked tomato flavor. Many tasters downgraded brands for dried herb notes. In the end, while better tomato pastes improved the taste of the marinara, no one brand ruined the dish. Our winner, **Goya**, boasted "bright, robust tomato flavor" with a "peppery kick."

We gradually substituted chicken broth for water, and as it turned out, the richer base made with all chicken broth was the tasters' favorite.

While our soup was on the right track, it was still missing the depth you find in the best chicken soups. If we were cooking our soup on the stovetop, we would have browned our turkey thighs to create a flavorful fond. However, since our goal was simplicity and convenience, we didn't want to bring out the skillet unless we needed to. We looked, instead, to umami-rich tomato paste. For many test kitchen stew recipes, we add tomato paste to the pot when sautéing aromatics to contribute deep, meaty flavor. In this case, we had to wonder whether the flavor of the paste would blend into the soup or stand out as an awkward addition, but it seemed like it was worth a shot. We hoped we could achieve the same effect as sautéing the paste by cooking it in the microwave with our aromatics. We added a tablespoon of tomato paste to the onions, garlic, thyme, and oil and microwaved the mixture for five minutes. We hesitated since we could smell the fragrant tomato scent as we added the aromatics to the slow cooker, but a few hours later we found we had created a broth that tasted full, rich, and not tomatoey in the slightest.

Finally, to round out our soup, we looked at our rice. We tried white long-grain rice, brown rice, and wild rice, as well as combinations of the three. Two varieties failed when added on their own: Brown rice took far too long to cook through and tended to blow out. Wild rice was too toothsome on its own. White rice was acceptable but a little boring. A combination of white and wild rice was perfect: The mild and soft white rice balanced the flavorful and chewy wild rice, giving us variety in every bite.

For a final burst of freshness, we stirred in minced parsley right before serving. Now our turkey soup was not only comforting but convenient and light enough for everyday cooking.

Slow-Cooker Turkey and Wild Rice Soup
SERVES 8

Do not substitute a turkey breast for the thighs; the breast will not cook at the same rate as the thighs and will produce too much meat for the soup. We like the flavor of a wild and white rice blend in this soup; however, you can substitute 1 cup of long-grain white rice if desired. *Cooking time: 6 to 8 hours on low or 5 to 7 hours on high*

2 onions, chopped fine

4 garlic cloves, minced

1 tablespoon tomato paste

2 teaspoons minced fresh thyme or ½ teaspoon dried

1 teaspoon canola oil

8 cups low-sodium chicken broth

3 carrots, peeled and sliced ¼ inch thick

2 celery ribs, chopped

2 bay leaves

2 (1-pound) bone-in turkey thighs, skin removed, trimmed of all visible fat

Salt and pepper

1 cup long-grain and wild rice blend

2 tablespoons minced fresh parsley

1. Combine onions, garlic, tomato paste, thyme, and oil in bowl and microwave, stirring occasionally, until onions are softened, about 5 minutes; transfer to slow cooker.

2. Stir broth, carrots, celery, and bay leaves into slow cooker. Season turkey with ⅛ teaspoon salt and ⅛ teaspoon pepper and nestle into slow cooker. Cover and cook until turkey is tender, 6 to 8 hours on low or 5 to 7 hours on high.

3. Transfer turkey to carving board, let cool slightly, then shred into bite-size pieces, discarding bones. Let soup settle for 5 minutes, then remove fat from surface using large spoon. Remove bay leaves. Stir in rice, cover, and cook on high until rice is tender, 30 to 40 minutes.

4. Stir in shredded turkey and let sit until heated through, about 5 minutes. Stir in parsley, season with salt and pepper to taste, and serve.

PER 1½-CUP SERVING: Cal 230; Fat 5g; Sat fat 1.5g; Chol 60mg; Carb 26g; Protein 20g; Fiber 2g; Sodium 710mg

TURKEY CHILI

CHILI SEEMS LIKE A NATURAL FIT FOR THE SLOW cooker given its long cooking time, but despite the myriad recipes for it, most versions turn out watery and bland. In addition, most of these not-so-successful recipes call for pounds upon pounds of fatty ground beef and multiple cans of sodium-laden tomato products. In an effort to counter these uninspiring chilies, we developed several test kitchen recipes for slow-cooker ground meat chilies, some with ground beef and others with turkey. Even the turkey recipes, however, contained

up to 16 grams of fat and 1,970 milligrams of sodium per serving. Could we transform our turkey chili from a once-a-year Super Bowl food to an everyday light and healthy recipe?

First we turned to the turkey. When developing our original slow-cooker chili recipes, we learned two key techniques for cooking with ground meat. First, while many slow-cooker recipes call for adding raw ground meat directly to the slow cooker, during testing we found it turned into unpleasantly fine grains. Browning the meat in a skillet before adding it to the cooker fixed the problem, giving us meat in more discernible pieces. Browning the meat, however, didn't keep it from drying out. To keep it moist, we borrowed a trick from the test kitchen's recipes for meatballs and meatloaves: We combined the turkey with a panade (a mixture of milk and bread) and browned the mixture before adding it to the slow cooker.

Given these findings, we tested our working recipe using a lineup of ground turkey options, pitting 85 percent lean (dark meat) turkey against both 93 percent lean (a mix of light and dark) and 99 percent lean (all light). We'd already worked with ground turkey in several light recipes, but we wondered if the slow cooker would give us different results. The light-meat turkey was nice and lean but far too dry; dark-meat turkey was tender but added too much fat. Ninety-three percent lean turkey, as we had suspected, was the perfect medium, giving us moist meat with only a marginal amount of fat. We were also able to reduce the original amount of oil needed for browning from 2 tablespoons to just 2 teaspoons by using a nonstick skillet. These changes reduced our fat count to only 8 grams per serving.

Since we had already brought out the skillet to brown the turkey, we decided to go ahead and sauté our aromatics and spices in the pan. Our original recipe contained a standard lineup of two onions, three cloves of garlic, 2 tablespoons of chili powder, 2 teaspoons of cumin and oregano, and a dash of red pepper flakes. Tasters still liked the quantity of onion and garlic, but the spices were now a little out of balance; since we had markedly lowered the amount of fat, the chili powder was harsh and overpowering. By reducing the amount by almost half, to 4 teaspoons, we brought the flavors back in line.

To add meaty depth to the chili, our original recipe called for 2 tablespoons each of tomato paste and soy sauce. We found that we needed to keep the full amount of tomato paste, browned in the skillet along with the aromatics, to maintain its presence in the final chili. We swapped in low-sodium soy sauce for the fully salted version, which helped us cut a good amount of sodium.

Next we moved on to the other core components: tomatoes and beans. While both of these ingredients are often the subject of much debate concerning their rightful presence in chili, we found that we liked both in this recipe. Canned diced tomatoes added much-needed brightness to such a long-cooked dish, and beans bulked up the lean protein. We found that one small can of diced tomatoes and one can of pinto beans were just the right amounts to complement but not overwhelm the meat. In addition, tasters liked the inclusion of tomato sauce for its complex flavor and silky texture. Since we knew that all of these ingredients would add a fair amount of sodium to our final dish, we removed almost all of the extra salt from the recipe, choosing to season to taste at the very end.

Even though we were generally pleased with the direction our turkey chili recipe was taking, we found the recipe a little dull. To spice it up a bit, we added some smoky heat with canned chipotle chiles in adobo sauce. Just 1 teaspoon added the complex background heat that our slow-cooker chili had been lacking. Finally, to further distinguish our chili, we stirred in a little tequila and lime for a Southwestern twist. Some honey helped bring out the tequila's sweetness, and lime zest contributed to the bright citrus flavor. This turkey chili was now not only lightened but also vibrant and exciting—a far cry from its bland cousins.

Slow-Cooker Tequila and Lime Turkey Chili

SERVES 6

Do not use ground turkey breast here (also labeled 99 percent fat free). Do not cook on high heat; the higher temperature will lead to tough and dry turkey. Serve with your favorite chili toppings, such as lime wedges, grated cheese, avocado, and low-fat sour cream.

Cooking time: 4 to 6 hours on low

- 1 slice hearty white sandwich bread, torn into quarters
- 2 tablespoons whole milk
- 1 pound 93 percent lean ground turkey

Salt and pepper
- 2 onions, chopped fine
- 2 teaspoons canola oil
- 2 tablespoons tomato paste
- 4 teaspoons chili powder
- 3 garlic cloves, minced
- 2 teaspoons ground cumin
- 2 teaspoons minced fresh oregano or ½ teaspoon dried
- ¼ teaspoon red pepper flakes
- 1 (15-ounce) can tomato sauce
- 1 (15-ounce) can pinto beans, rinsed
- 1 (14.5-ounce) can diced tomatoes
- ¼ cup tequila
- 1 tablespoon low-sodium soy sauce
- 1 tablespoon honey
- 1 teaspoon minced canned chipotle chile in adobo sauce
- 1 teaspoon grated lime zest plus 1 tablespoon juice

1. Mash bread and milk into smooth paste in large bowl using fork. Mix in ground turkey and ⅛ teaspoon pepper, using hands, until uniform.

2. Combine onions, oil, and ¼ teaspoon salt in 12-inch nonstick skillet. Cover and cook over medium-low heat, stirring occasionally, until softened, 8 to 10 minutes. Uncover, increase heat to medium, stir in tomato paste, chili powder, garlic, cumin, oregano, and pepper flakes, and cook until fragrant, about 30 seconds.

3. Stir in turkey mixture and cook, breaking up large pieces with wooden spoon, until no longer pink, about 3 minutes. Stir in tomato sauce, scraping up any browned bits, and cook until slightly reduced, about 1 minute; transfer to slow cooker.

4. Stir beans, tomatoes, 3 tablespoons tequila, soy sauce, honey, and chipotle into slow cooker. Cover and cook until turkey is tender, 4 to 6 hours on low.

5. Let chili settle for 5 minutes, then remove fat from surface using large spoon. Break up any remaining large pieces of turkey with spoon. Stir in remaining 1 tablespoon tequila, lime zest, and lime juice. Season with salt and pepper to taste and serve.

PER 1⅓-CUP SERVING: Cal 270; Fat 8g; Sat fat 1.5g; Chol 45mg; Carb 26g; Protein 21g; Fiber 7g; Sodium 960mg

SLOW-COOKER TEX-MEX CHICKEN STEW

TEX-MEX CHICKEN STEW

FROM DOWN-HOME CHICKEN AND DUMPLINGS TO refined chicken bouillabaisse, we have plenty of experience in the test kitchen cooking rich chicken stews on the stove. We wondered if this type of stew could be lightened up and prepared in a slow cooker. Our goals were threefold. First, we wanted a chicken stew that could be easily prepared and left to cook on its own but still boast bites of juicy chicken and tender vegetables draped in a velvety sauce. Second, we wanted to keep our stew light and healthy, yet still maintain its rich-tasting and full-bodied nature. Third, we wanted to mix up our chicken stew repertoire by incorporating bright and spicy Tex-Mex flavors.

Starting with the chicken, we decided to test both light and dark meat. We knew that we'd want to shred the meat after cooking, so, for the sake of ease, we first tried using boneless and skinless cuts of both thighs and breasts. These pieces of chicken were certainly easy to shred, but unfortunately, both cuts dried out during the long cooking time and contributed little in the way of flavor to our broth. Switching to bone-in, skinless cuts, we again pitted chicken breasts against chicken thighs. While the bone-in thighs were certainly tender and flavorful, we were surprised to find that, once shredded, the bone-in breasts offered comparable flavor and texture for about half the fat.

After a few tests, we found that cooking the chicken on the low setting yielded significantly more

---

NOTES FROM THE TEST KITCHEN

LIGHT AND HEALTHY SLOW COOKING
You might think of heavy stews and meaty sauces (read: far from light, healthy meals) as classic slow-cooker fare, but this appliance can actually be a great vehicle for healthy eating since food is essentially steamed. After developing a collection of slow-cooker recipes for this book, we learned a few tricks for ensuring success.

USE YOUR MICROWAVE: To save time, we microwaved aromatics (such as onion and garlic) and spices to bloom their flavors. This takes just five minutes and is much easier than getting out a skillet to cook these ingredients. We also used the microwave to parcook potatoes so they'd emerge from the slow cooker cooked through. Using the microwave also allowed us to cut back significantly on oil in many of our recipes, since very little is needed in such a moist cooking environment.

COOK CHICKEN ON LOW FOR UP TO SIX HOURS: Although in many slow-cooker recipes chicken is cooked all day, we found that method led to dry, stringy chicken that no one would really want to eat. Cooking chicken on low heat, and for only four to six hours, gave us perfectly juicy meat.

MAKE A FOIL PACKET: Depending on the recipe, the cooking time, and how the vegetables are cut, it is sometimes necessary to wrap vegetables in an aluminum foil packet to keep them from overcooking, as we did in our Super Veggie Beef Stew (page 167). The packet helps keep them out of the cooking liquid and slows down their cooking, protecting their flavors from fading. For more information about making a foil packet, see page 168.

ADD SOY SAUCE AND TOMATO PASTE FOR MEATY FLAVOR: We found that microwaving tomato paste with aromatics adds meaty richness to slow-cooker recipes with minimal work. Soy sauce (we use low-sodium to keep the numbers in line) appears in other (non-slow-cooker) recipes as well; just a small amount in chilis and stews adds surprising depth of flavor without calling attention to itself.

BROWN YOUR MEAT AND CHICKEN—SOMETIMES: There is no hard-and-fast rule about browning meat before placing it in the slow cooker. In some recipes, usually ones that use a lot of spicy or aromatic ingredients (such as our Curried Chicken Breasts, page 165), we found that we could get away with not browning. But there were instances when, in order to build a deep flavor base, we needed to get out the skillet and brown the meat (as for our Chicken Vesuvio, page 162). When it came to the ground turkey in our Tequila and Lime Turkey Chili (page 155), we found that browning was important to keep the meat tender and avoid an unappealing grainy texture.

USE THE RIGHT THICKENER: Since there is no opportunity for sauces and stews to thicken naturally in the moist environment of the slow cooker, thickeners are necessary for soups, stews, and braises. After years of testing flour, cornstarch, and tapioca, we found that for lightly thickened sauces, tapioca was the easiest solution and could be added right at the start. But if any more than ¼ cup was used, the tapioca pearls were too noticeable in the final dish. For very thick stews (like our Super Veggie Beef Stew, page 167), you need to go a more traditional route and build a roux-based sauce in a skillet using flour and oil.

DON'T SKIMP ON AROMATICS: You'll see hefty amounts of onions, garlic, herbs, and other flavorful ingredients in these recipes. This is because the moist heat environment and long cooking times that come with the slow cooker tend to mute flavors. Also, many recipes need a flavor boost at the end of the cooking time, which is why we often finish with fresh herbs, lemon juice, extra chipotle chiles, or other flavorful ingredients.

tender chicken than cooking it on the high setting. Furthermore, chicken cooked longer than 6 hours on low collapsed into a stringy mess. Then we tested the minimum amount of time needed to cook the chicken, landing at an even 4 hours on low as the shortest amount of time needed to cook it through.

We moved on to the remaining components of the stew. Since we were using such mild meat, we knew we would want to boost the flavor with robust aromatics and some creative, colorful additions. We added a couple of jalapeños and a healthy dose of chili powder to our bowl of minced onion and garlic, microwaving them with 1 teaspoon of oil until softened. We stirred in canned diced tomatoes with the chicken for acidity and added canned black beans and frozen corn at the end of cooking for flavorful (and colorful) bulk. Three cups of chicken broth and one 8-ounce can of tomato sauce added just the right amount of liquid to our stew: It was loose enough to eat with a spoon, but not so thin as to be confused with soup. By rinsing our beans and keeping the tomato sauce to one small can, we were able to keep our sodium levels within an acceptable range.

At this point, our recipe was good, but not great. Despite the bone-in chicken, the sauce still lacked both meaty richness and full body. The meaty flavor was an easy fix. Taking a cue from our Slow-Cooker Turkey and Wild Rice Soup (page 153), we added 1 tablespoon of tomato paste to our microwaved aromatics, which gave our soup the flavor of browned meat without an extra step. The broth, however, still needed more body.

Many other slow-cooker cookbooks suggest adding a slurry of either flour or cornstarch at the end of cooking in order to thicken stews. We put these ideas to the test and found that, while both slurries worked, each imparted an unpleasant starchy taste. We found a substitute, however, in instant tapioca; this ingredient was ideal because it thickened the sauce without making it gloppy or contributing any off-flavors.

With the texture of the sauce now velvety, we moved on to a few final flavor tweaks. Tasters liked the heat of the jalapeños but felt it was a little one-dimensional. For added smoky flavor and a little layered heat, we stirred in a couple of canned chipotles in adobo at the end of cooking, along with 1 tablespoon of brown sugar for balance. A final sprinkling of minced cilantro gave our stew some needed freshness. Easy to prepare, but full of bold flavor, our lightened chicken stew was now a stellar addition to our slow-cooker repertoire.

Slow-Cooker Tex-Mex Chicken Stew

SERVES 8

If the final sauce is too thick, stir in additional hot broth until the desired consistency is reached. *Cooking time: 4 to 6 hours on low*

- 2 onions, chopped fine
- 2 jalapeño chiles, stemmed, seeded, and minced
- 6 garlic cloves, minced
- 1 tablespoon tomato paste
- 1 tablespoon chili powder
- 1 teaspoon canola oil
- 3 cups low-sodium chicken broth, plus extra as needed
- 1 (14.5-ounce) can diced tomatoes, drained
- 1 (8-ounce) can tomato sauce
- ¼ cup Minute tapioca
- 1 tablespoon packed brown sugar
- 5 (10-ounce) bone-in split chicken breasts, skin removed, ribs trimmed (see page 56), and trimmed of all visible fat
  Salt and pepper
- 2 cups frozen corn
- 1 (15-ounce) can black beans, rinsed
- 2 teaspoons minced canned chipotle chile in adobo sauce
- ¼ cup minced fresh cilantro

1. Combine onions, jalapeños, garlic, tomato paste, chili powder, and oil in bowl and microwave, stirring occasionally, until onions are softened, about 5 minutes. Transfer to slow cooker.

2. Stir broth, tomatoes, tomato sauce, tapioca, and sugar into slow cooker. Season chicken with ⅛ teaspoon salt and ⅛ teaspoon pepper and nestle into slow cooker. Cover and cook until chicken is tender, 4 to 6 hours on low.

3. Transfer chicken to cutting board, let cool slightly, then shred into bite-size pieces, discarding bones. Let stew settle for 5 minutes, then remove fat from surface using large spoon.

4. Stir in corn and beans, cover, and cook on high until heated through, about 10 minutes. Stir in shredded chicken and chipotle and let sit until heated through, about 5 minutes. Adjust stew consistency with hot broth as needed. Stir in cilantro, season with salt and pepper to taste, and serve.

PER 1⅓-CUP SERVING: Cal 290; Fat 3.5g; Sat fat 0.5g; Chol 80mg; Carb 27g; Protein 38g; Fiber 5g; Sodium 720mg

SMOKY CHIPOTLE CHICKEN TOSTADAS

SINCE WE NOW HAD A FEW CONVENIENT AND healthy slow-cooker soups and stews under our belt, we felt ready to expand our range with some slow-cooker dishes we could serve on a plate. First up: spicy Mexican tostadas. Traditionally, tostadas consist of a fried tortilla topped with refried beans, shredded meat, and a mountain of cheese. For our healthy slow-cooker version, we knew we'd need to refigure not only the meat filling but all of the other components as well.

We began with the meat. Since we had already found success with shredded white-meat chicken in our Slow-Cooker Tex-Mex Chicken Stew (page 158), we decided to stick with bone-in, skinless chicken breasts for the base of our topping. We knew that, because the chicken would be the star of the show, we would need to build a flavor-packed sauce in which to cook it. The first hurdle we'd need to overcome was the amount of sauce needed to evenly cook our chicken in the slow cooker.

Many other slow-cooker cookbooks instruct the cook to practically drown proteins in liquid in order to cook them through without burning. We suspected that we could modify this method quite a bit in order to concentrate flavor. Knowing that slow cookers trap moisture and cook over a low, slow heat, we wondered if we could model our topping after a traditional braise. When done on the stovetop or in the oven, braising gently cooks meat (or vegetables) in a small amount of simmering liquid to fork-tender perfection. Mimicking this method, we nestled our chicken breasts into the slow cooker and added just enough of a basic red chili sauce (chicken broth, tomato sauce, chili powder, garlic, and cumin) to come halfway up the sides of the chicken. We cooked the chicken on low heat for about five hours.

To our surprise, our chicken emerged not only tender and juicy, but with a plethora of sauce. All of the juice released from the chicken during cooking added a surprising amount of liquid. Could we reduce the amount of added cooking liquid even further? Since the chicken was contributing plenty of its own broth, we eliminated the added broth and stuck with just one 8-ounce can of tomato sauce. We slow-cooked the chicken, then after five hours we shredded it and tossed it with our new sauce. This time, the amount of sauce was perfect: There was plenty to coat and flavor our chicken topping, but not enough to drown it.

Cooking method established, we now moved on to flavorings. At this point, we knew that our basic red sauce needed a lot of work. After all this time in the slow cooker, any subtleties from the chili powder and spices were lost. We amped up the aromatics with an onion and a jalapeño (microwaved with the spices to soften them) and increased the chili powder from 1 tablespoon to 3. These changes helped, but the sauce still lacked identity. Knowing that meats for tostadas or tacos are often grilled, we decided to take a cue from the barbecue and add a couple of smoky elements. We stirred in 3 whole tablespoons of canned chipotle chiles, a dash of liquid smoke, and a little brown sugar for balance. Finished with a tablespoon of lime juice after cooking, our chicken was now jam-packed with a spicy-sweet smokiness.

With our chicken topping finished, we moved on to the other elements of our tostadas. First, we knew that we'd need to seriously lighten the refried beans. Authentic recipes require soaking and cooking dried beans, then sautéing them in a more-than-generous amount of lard until they are soft enough to mash—a method that was hardly acceptable for everyday light cooking. Our first step toward a streamlined recipe was obvious: We swapped out the dried beans for more convenient canned pinto beans. And since we wanted to keep things simple, we decided to mash the beans in the pan along with their canning liquid. To add flavor and spice, we stirred in a tablespoon of minced pickled jalapeños along with their juice. As for the frying step, we started by cooking the mashed beans in 2 tablespoons of oil. While tasters approved of the richness provided by even this small amount of oil, we felt we could go lower still. We tried subsequent batches of beans, taking out 1 teaspoon of oil at a time, and we eventually settled

NOTES FROM THE TEST KITCHEN

SHREDDING MEAT

To shred meat into bite-size pieces, hold 1 fork in each hand (tines facing down), insert forks into cooked meat, and gently pull apart.

on 1 tablespoon of oil. Any less and tasters noted that the beans tasted too lean. This amount gave us refried beans with a luscious texture but without the need for too much added fat.

Finally, we tackled the tostada itself. Finding a preparation method was a little more difficult than we expected. While traditional, deep-frying corn tortillas is a time-consuming process that adds far too much fat. Instead, we looked to the technique we had used to make Whole Wheat Pita Chips (page 14). For our first test, we lightly coated tortillas with vegetable oil spray and toasted them in a 350-degree oven for about 10 minutes. While this had worked with pita wedges, we found that our tortillas were coming out tough, not crispy. Next, we tested raising the temperature 100 degrees, but these tortillas still seemed stale. Finally, after raising the temperature further—all the way to a hot 475 degrees—we pulled out tostada shells that were crisp enough to rival their fried cousins.

To assemble our tostadas, we spread a thin layer of refried beans on the hot crisped tortillas and topped them with a generous pile of chicken. Instead of adding a mountain of shredded cheese, we sprinkled the tostadas with cilantro leaves, the perfect light and fresh finish.

Slow-Cooker Smoky Chipotle Chicken Tostadas

SERVES 8

Prepare the tostada shells and beans during the last 30 minutes of the filling's cooking time. To make the filling spicier, add the reserved chile seeds. Serve with shredded cabbage, queso fresco, and low-fat sour cream. *Cooking time: 4 to 6 hours on low*

FILLING

- 1 onion, chopped fine
- 3 tablespoons chili powder
- 3 tablespoons minced canned chipotle chile in adobo sauce
- 1 jalapeño chile, stemmed, seeds reserved, and minced
- 3 garlic cloves, minced
- 2 teaspoons ground cumin
- 1 teaspoon canola oil
- 1 (8-ounce) can tomato sauce
- 2 teaspoons packed brown sugar
- ½ teaspoon liquid smoke

- 5 (10-ounce) bone-in split chicken breasts, skin removed, ribs trimmed (see page 56), and trimmed of all visible fat
  Salt and pepper
- 1 tablespoon lime juice

TOSTADAS

- 16 (6-inch) corn tortillas
  Vegetable oil spray
- 1 tablespoon canola oil
- 2 (15-ounce) cans pinto beans
- 1 tablespoon minced jarred pickled jalapeños plus 1 tablespoon pickled jalapeño juice
  Salt and pepper
- ¼ cup fresh cilantro leaves

1. FOR THE FILLING: Combine onion, chili powder, chipotle, jalapeño, garlic, cumin, and oil in bowl and microwave, stirring occasionally, until onion is softened, about 5 minutes; transfer to slow cooker.

2. Stir tomato sauce, sugar, and liquid smoke into slow cooker. Season chicken with ⅛ teaspoon salt and ⅛ teaspoon pepper and nestle into slow cooker. Cover and cook until chicken is tender, 4 to 6 hours on low.

3. Transfer chicken to large bowl, let cool slightly, then shred into bite-size pieces, discarding bones; cover to keep warm. Let braising liquid settle for 5 minutes, then remove fat from surface using large spoon.

4. Toss shredded chicken with 1 cup of braising liquid, adding more liquid as needed to keep meat moist. Stir in lime juice and season with salt and pepper to taste.

5. FOR THE TOSTADAS: Adjust oven racks to upper-middle and lower-middle positions and heat oven to 475 degrees. Spread 8 tortillas on 2 rimmed baking sheets. Lightly coat both sides of tortillas with oil spray. Bake until lightly browned and crisp, 8 to 10 minutes, switching and rotating baking sheets halfway through baking. Repeat with remaining 8 tortillas.

6. Heat oil in 12-inch skillet over medium heat until shimmering. Add beans with their canning liquid, jalapeños, and jalapeño juice and cook, mashing with potato masher, until mixture is thickened and hot, 5 to 8 minutes. Season with salt and pepper to taste.

7. To assemble, spread bean mixture over toasted tortillas, top with filling, and sprinkle with cilantro. Serve.

PER SERVING (2 TOSTADAS): Cal 450; Fat 9g; Sat fat 1g; Chol 80mg; Carb 50g; Protein 42g; Fiber 10g; Sodium 620mg

CHICKEN VESUVIO

CHICKEN AND POTATOES ARE A CLASSIC DUO THAT can be prepared in a multitude of ways. One stellar example is a version from Chicago known as Chicken Vesuvio, which consists of bone-in chicken and potatoes smothered in a butter-laden, garlicky white wine sauce, brightened by lemon and garnished with peas. We thought this regional favorite would be a perfect candidate for our slow cooker. However, there were a few challenges. First, we would need to find a way to keep the flavors bold and multidimensional despite the long cooking time. Second, we would need to lighten this traditionally heavy dish, as the original is far too high in fat for our lighter standards.

We addressed the chicken and potatoes first. As we had discovered with several other lightened slow-cooker chicken dishes, bone-in chicken breasts were the best choice, as the breasts were naturally lean and the bones helped to keep the chicken moist. We removed the skin and cooked the chicken on low to prevent it from drying out. As for the potatoes, we tested several varieties and found that waxy red potatoes were the best choice; they held their shape and texture during cooking and also contributed some color. We cut our potatoes into 1-inch chunks and added them raw to the slow cooker. Surprisingly, we found that even after a four- to six-hour span in the cooker, the potatoes still emerged crunchy. We found we had better luck when we parcooked them in the microwave for a few minutes, until they were just beginning to soften, to jump-start their cooking.

Next, we zeroed in on the flavoring of the sauce. For the aromatics, we stayed true to tradition, using plenty of garlic and oregano plus onion, as well as a pinch of red pepper flakes and a half-cup of dry white wine. We waited until the end of cooking to add the lemon juice (and peas) to retain its vibrancy. This sauce seemed promising going into the slow cooker, but even after the relatively short cooking time (four to six hours on low), it tasted very flat.

Perhaps, given the sauce's subtlety, we needed to build more flavor in the chicken itself. We decided to pit our plain chicken breasts against those browned using a small amount of oil in the skillet before cooking. We found that the version using browned chicken boasted richer, deeper flavor than the one with unbrowned chicken. This was not just because of the chicken itself, but because sautéing the breasts, skin-on, had led to the development of a rich, flavorful fond on the bottom of the skillet that we could then use to sauté the aromatics (instead of using our microwave method). We simply removed the skin from the browned chicken before we placed it in the slow cooker to keep the fat count low.

While much improved, our new sauce still needed a little flavor boost. For a more assertive punch, we decided to add a little rosemary. We tested adding a couple of teaspoons of the chopped fresh herb at the beginning of cooking, but this long-cooked rosemary tasted medicinal. At the other end of the spectrum, rosemary stirred in at the end of cooking tasted raw and harsh and speckled the dish like grass clippings. To tame this woodsy herb, we steeped a small sprig of it in the slow cooker during the last 15 minutes of cooking, which infused the dish with a mellow rosemary flavor, then removed it before serving.

A little lemon zest, in addition to the juice, further brightened the dish. To enhance the garlic flavor, we stirred in an additional clove of raw garlic with the lemon juice and zest before serving to release its perfume and sharpness. Employing this one-two garlic punch (both cooked and raw) created layers of flavor and imparted both piquancy and depth.

While we were pleased with the flavor of this sauce, we thought it needed a little more body. Taking a cue from our Slow-Cooker Curried Chicken Breasts (page 165), we tried adding a little tapioca to the sauce before cooking. But here, given such a simple sauce, the tapioca pearls stood out in the finished dish, lending an unpleasant look and texture. We figured we would need to turn to a more traditional thickener in this case: flour. Since we'd already brought out the skillet to brown the chicken, it was an easy addition. We toasted the flour with the aromatics, added the wine, and reduced our sauce base to a thick paste. After the chicken finished cooking, this paste had melded with the released chicken juices and turned into a beautifully thickened sauce with no off-flavors or textures.

As a finishing touch, traditional recipes include a big hunk of butter to add richness to the sauce. In the interest of keeping the fat to a minimum, we left it out. While bright and flavorful, this sauce was lacking the richness integral to traditional Chicken Vesuvio, and tasters weren't going to overlook this inconsistency. Everyone agreed that adding back some of the butter was a must, but we found that with all of the other changes we had made, just 1 tablespoon was all that was needed for a balanced, rich sauce. Now this Chicago favorite was not only easy, it was also healthy.

Slow-Cooker Chicken Vesuvio

SERVES 6

Use a paper towel to help remove browned chicken skin. *Cooking time: 4 to 6 hours on low*

  6 **(10-ounce) bone-in split chicken breasts, ribs trimmed (see page 56) and trimmed of all visible fat**
     Salt and pepper
  1 **tablespoon extra-virgin olive oil**
  2 **onions, chopped fine**
  4 **garlic cloves, minced to a paste**
  1 **tablespoon minced fresh oregano or 1 teaspoon dried**
  ¼ **teaspoon red pepper flakes**
  3 **tablespoons all-purpose flour**
  ½ **cup dry white wine**
1½ **pounds red potatoes, cut into 1-inch pieces**
  1 **cup low-sodium chicken broth**
  1 **sprig fresh rosemary**
  1 **cup frozen peas**
  1 **tablespoon unsalted butter**
  ¼ **teaspoon grated lemon zest plus 1 tablespoon juice**

1. Pat chicken dry with paper towels and season with ⅛ teaspoon salt and ⅛ teaspoon pepper. Heat 1 teaspoon oil in 12-inch skillet over medium-high heat until just smoking. Place half of chicken, skin side down, in skillet and brown lightly on first side, about 5 minutes; transfer to plate. Repeat with 1 teaspoon oil and remaining chicken. Let chicken cool slightly and remove and discard skin.

2. Add onions and ¼ teaspoon salt to fat left in pan, cover, and cook over medium-low heat, stirring occasionally, until softened, 8 to 10 minutes. Uncover, increase heat to medium, stir in half of garlic, oregano, and pepper flakes, and cook until fragrant, about 30 seconds. Stir in flour and cook for 1 minute. Slowly whisk in wine, scraping up any browned bits and smoothing out any lumps. Transfer to slow cooker.

3. Microwave potatoes with remaining 1 teaspoon oil in bowl, covered, tossing occasionally, until nearly tender, 5 to 8 minutes. Transfer to slow cooker. Stir broth into slow cooker. Nestle chicken with any accumulated juices into slow cooker. Cover and cook until chicken is tender, 4 to 6 hours on low.

4. Add rosemary sprig, cover, and cook on high until rosemary is fragrant, about 15 minutes. Transfer chicken and potatoes to serving platter and tent loosely with aluminum foil. Let braising liquid settle for 5 minutes, then remove fat from surface using large spoon.

5. Remove rosemary. Stir in peas and let sit until heated through, about 5 minutes. Stir in remaining garlic, butter, lemon zest, and lemon juice and season with salt and pepper to taste. Spoon some sauce over chicken and serve, passing remaining sauce separately.

PER SERVING: **Cal** 430; **Fat** 7g; **Sat fat** 2.5g; **Chol** 135mg; **Carb** 29g; **Protein** 57g; **Fiber** 4g; **Sodium** 420mg

NOTES FROM THE TEST KITCHEN

MINCING GARLIC TO A PASTE

Mashing garlic to a paste can be helpful when adding raw garlic to a dish. The flavor of the garlic mellows substantially, and it can be more easily incorporated.

To make garlic paste, mince garlic and sprinkle with pinch of salt. Scrape blade of chef's knife across garlic about 3 times, mashing garlic into board. Garlic will turn into sticky paste.

REMOVING CHICKEN SKIN

Chicken skin is often slippery, making it a challenge to remove by hand, even when the chicken has been browned.

To remove skin with ease, use paper towel to provide extra grip while pulling.

SLOW-COOKER CURRIED CHICKEN BREASTS

CURRIED CHICKEN BREASTS

INDIAN CURRIES HAVE DELECTABLY INTRICATE, deep flavors that we knew would hold up well to hours of cooking; we figured that a braised chicken curry dish would be a perfect match for the slow cooker. One major problem with curries, however, is that they are usually full of fat from a combination of coconut milk, yogurt, oil, and/or butter. Authentic curries can also be notoriously complicated, with lengthy ingredient lists and fussy techniques. We wanted to create a simple slow-cooker chicken curry that was healthy but flavor-packed, with a light but substantial sauce.

We started with 10-ounce bone-in, skinless chicken breasts, a great source of lean protein and the perfect neutral palette on which we could showcase bold curry flavor. With all the spices in a curry, we suspected we wouldn't need to brown the chicken. We simply seasoned them with a little salt and pepper, and then we got to work building our sauce base.

Taking a cue from our Slow-Cooker Smoky Chipotle Chicken Tostadas (page 160), we knew we needed to use about 1 cup of liquid to braise the chicken. We chose chicken broth for a simple background flavor on which to build our sauce. We found that the hassle of making our own curry powder was not worth the effort: a good-quality store-bought yellow curry powder could do the job just fine. Coaxing the maximum flavor from dried spices typically requires blooming them in hot oil. Following the lead of our other slow-cooker recipes, we microwaved the curry powder and aromatics (onion, garlic, and ginger) in a teaspoon of oil. Thinking we needed to use a heavy hand with the spices given the long cooking time, we started testing with 2 tablespoons of curry powder, but tasters complained that the resulting dish tasted harsh. We backed down to 4 teaspoons.

So far this curry was promising, but tasters agreed that something was missing. Many traditional curry recipes include some type of tomato product, and we suspected this addition would brighten the overall flavor of our dish. We tried adding diced tomatoes with their juice, but the resulting sauce was watery. Next we tried crushed tomatoes and microwaved them along with the aromatics in hope of coaxing out more flavor. This, too, fell short of our expectations. The solution turned out to be as simple as adding tomato paste to the rest of the aromatics. The tomato paste lent flavor and body to the stew, and cooking the paste in the microwave intensified

its flavor. Yet despite these improvements, the sauce was still on the thin side. To thicken our sauce, we turned to a trick used in our Slow-Cooker Tex-Mex Chicken Stew (page 158) and stirred in a little instant tapioca. This step gave our curry just the right amount of body without a starchy or floury taste.

Finally, many curry recipes include coconut milk, yogurt, and/or butter to finish the sauce and add richness. We knew we didn't want to stir in a mess of butter at the end of cooking, but perhaps we could add a small amount of light coconut milk or low-fat yogurt. Overall, we liked the flavor of both stir-ins, but tasters especially liked yogurt's tangy profile. To add a little extra lusciousness, we settled on using thicker low-fat Greek yogurt. This sauce had the texture and flavor of one thickened with rich, creamy dairy, yet it had only 4.5 grams of fat per serving.

A few final additions rounded out the dish. Toward the end of cooking, we added raisins for subtle sweetness. A garnish of ¼ cup of toasted almonds added crunch and nuttiness with less than 2 grams of additional fat, and a sprinkling of minced cilantro lent a fresh finish. With that, we had created a satisfying, potently flavored, and healthy chicken curry—and we didn't even have to fire up a burner.

Slow-Cooker Curried Chicken Breasts

SERVES 6

Serve with steamed white rice. *Cooking time: 4 to 6 hours on low*

- **2 onions, chopped fine**
- **6 garlic cloves, minced**
- **2 tablespoons grated fresh ginger**
- **4 teaspoons curry powder**
- **1 tablespoon tomato paste**
- **1 teaspoon canola oil**
- **1 cup low-sodium chicken broth**
- **2 tablespoons Minute tapioca**
- **6 (10-ounce) bone-in split chicken breasts, skin removed, ribs trimmed (see page 56), and trimmed of all visible fat**
  Salt and pepper
- **½ cup raisins**
- **½ cup 2 percent Greek yogurt**
- **2 tablespoons minced fresh cilantro**
- **¼ cup sliced almonds, toasted**

1. Combine onions, garlic, ginger, curry powder, tomato paste, and oil in bowl and microwave, stirring occasionally, until onions are softened, about 5 minutes; transfer to slow cooker.

2. Stir broth and tapioca into slow cooker. Season chicken with ⅛ teaspoon salt and ⅛ teaspoon pepper and nestle into slow cooker. Cover and cook until chicken is tender, 4 to 6 hours on low.

3. Gently stir in raisins and let sit until heated through, about 10 minutes. Transfer chicken to serving platter and tent loosely with aluminum foil. Let braising liquid settle for 5 minutes, then remove fat from surface using large spoon.

4. Stir ¼ cup of hot braising liquid into yogurt to temper, then stir yogurt mixture back into slow cooker. Stir in cilantro and season with salt and pepper to taste. Spoon some sauce over chicken, sprinkle with almonds, and serve, passing remaining sauce separately.

PER SERVING: Cal 380; Fat 6g; Sat fat 1.5g; Chol 130mg; Carb 21g; Protein 56g; Fiber 3g; Sodium 310mg

BALSAMIC-BRAISED CHICKEN WITH SWISS CHARD

AT THIS POINT, WE HAD A GOOD VARIETY OF LIGHT and healthy slow-cooker chicken breast recipes. Could we conquer the other staple of the poultry department by perfecting chicken thighs? Although slightly higher in fat than breasts, thighs, when prepared with a light touch, can still be a part of a healthy diet. We turned to Italy to re-create chicken braised in a naturally light red wine and balsamic vinegar sauce.

The chicken was the natural starting point for our testing. Since we knew that we wanted to make our chicken thighs as lean as possible while also preserving their flavor and tenderness, we chose well-trimmed, skinless bone-in pieces. We also wanted to keep things simple by not browning the chicken; after all, we figured, our vinegary sauce would have plenty of flavor on its own without browned chicken fond.

To build this sauce, we microwaved our aromatics (onion, thyme, garlic, and red pepper flakes) with a little oil and tomato paste to replicate the flavor of browning with minimal effort. We added this mixture to the slow cooker and stirred in a glug of red wine, a few tablespoons of balsamic vinegar, a can of drained diced tomatoes for brightness, and a couple of bay leaves for herbal depth. After nestling the raw chicken into the sauce, we cooked the thighs just as we had been cooking our chicken breasts, for four to six hours on low.

The chicken emerged tender, but the sauce needed help. The combination of vinegar and wine was harsh, and the sauce was thin and lacked depth. In the past, we've found reducing balsamic vinegar goes a long way toward improving flavor. We knew that it would take quite a while to reduce vinegar in the microwave, so we settled on bringing our microwaved ingredients out to the skillet. For our next test, we sautéed our aromatics and tomato paste in a little oil, then added the balsamic to the skillet. Three minutes was long enough to reduce our ½ cup of vinegar by half, and already the flavor had improved. As in our Slow-Cooker Chicken Vesuvio (page 162), we decided this was a recipe where flour, rather than tapioca, would work best as the thickening agent to create a full-bodied sauce since the ingredients were few. We added it to the skillet after we'd sautéed the aromatics, let its raw flavor cook off for a minute, then added the vinegar and reduced it as before. We transferred our new sauce base to the slow cooker and stirred in the wine, tomatoes, and a little chicken broth for balance.

Concentrating the flavor of the balsamic and adding flour improved our final sauce a great deal, lending silky and smooth flavor and texture. However, the flavor was still a little flat. Recalling some of our slow-cooker stew recipes, we thought that maybe our braise needed a boost of umami. In our slow-cooker stews and chili, we found that we liked the addition of a little low-sodium soy sauce, which added meaty depth. We decided to pit that addition against a couple of other umami-rich options: dried porcini mushrooms and anchovies. In the end, we thought that both the soy sauce and porcini mushrooms were out of place. On the other hand, one anchovy was just right, adding subtle complexity without any fishy flavor. We added it to our skillet with the other aromatics and let it melt into the sauce.

The sauce was well rounded, but it was still missing a bit of freshness. We thought that some greens, such as kale, spinach, or Swiss chard, might liven things up. Spinach wilted away to a flavorless mass, and kale never integrated. Chard proved to be the winner; it stood up to the hearty flavors of the braise and added a touch of its own earthy bitterness. This dish evoked the flavors of Italy while remaining light and healthy.

Slow-Cooker Balsamic-Braised Chicken with Swiss Chard

SERVES 6

Serve with polenta. *Cooking time: 4 to 6 hours on low*

- 1 **onion, chopped fine**
- 1 **teaspoon extra-virgin olive oil**
  Salt and pepper
- 5 **teaspoons minced fresh thyme or 1½ teaspoons dried**
- 3 **garlic cloves, minced**
- 1 **tablespoon tomato paste**
- 1 **anchovy fillet, rinsed and minced**
- ¼ **teaspoon red pepper flakes**
- 3 **tablespoons all-purpose flour**
- ½ **cup balsamic vinegar**
- 1 **(14.5-ounce) can diced tomatoes, drained**
- ½ **cup low-sodium chicken broth**
- ¼ **cup dry red wine**
- 2 **bay leaves**
- 12 **(6-ounce) bone-in chicken thighs, skin removed and trimmed of all visible fat**
- 6 **ounces Swiss chard, stemmed and leaves sliced ½ inch thick**

1. Combine onion, oil, and ¼ teaspoon salt in 12-inch skillet. Cover and cook over medium-low heat, stirring occasionally, until softened, 8 to 10 minutes. Uncover, increase heat to medium, stir in thyme, garlic, tomato paste, anchovy, and pepper flakes, and cook until fragrant, about 30 seconds. Stir in flour and cook for 1 minute. Slowly whisk in vinegar, scraping up any browned bits and smoothing out any lumps, and cook until slightly reduced, about 3 minutes; transfer to slow cooker.

2. Stir tomatoes, broth, wine, and bay leaves into slow cooker. Season chicken with ⅛ teaspoon salt and ⅛ teaspoon pepper and nestle into slow cooker. Cover and cook until chicken is tender, 4 to 6 hours on low. Let braising liquid settle for 5 minutes, then remove fat from surface using large spoon. Remove bay leaves.

3. Gently stir in chard, cover, and cook on high until tender, 20 to 30 minutes. Transfer chicken to serving platter. Season sauce with salt and pepper to taste. Spoon some sauce over chicken and serve, passing remaining sauce separately.

PER SERVING: Cal 310; **Fat** 9g; **Sat fat** 2g; **Chol** 160mg; **Carb** 13g; **Protein** 40g; **Fiber** 2g; **Sodium** 500mg

SUPER VEGGIE BEEF STEW

AFTER SUCH A SUCCESSFUL RUN WITH NATURALLY lean proteins, we decided to tackle a more traditional slow-cooker dish: beef stew. While there are a slew of recipes for this dish in slow-cooker cookbooks, we knew that we wanted to start with a test kitchen recipe we'd already tweaked to our slow-cooker standards. This recipe was a great start for a potentially light recipe, as it was filled with root vegetables, mushrooms, and earthy kale. But we knew that between the chuck roast, vegetable oil, and some sodium-heavy additions, there was still some lightening to be done. Could we find a way to preserve the comforting richness and ease of our original slow-cooker recipe while trimming it down?

First we worked on the beef. We knew that chuck roast would still be our best bet even in our lightened recipe. During the development of the original stew, we tested other, leaner cuts of beef such as top round, bottom round, eye round, rump roast, and top sirloin, and each emerged flavorless and dry. Chuck roast is full of not only fat but also connective tissue, which breaks down over the long cooking time (up to 7 hours on high or 11 hours on low) to turn the meat tender and the sauce thick and luxurious. In the end we decided that our best approach for a lighter recipe was to simply cut back on the beef, from 4 pounds to 2, and trim away as much of the exterior fat as we could. We knew we'd bulk up our healthy stew with additional vegetables, so we were happy to create a little extra room for them in our slow cooker.

We knew that we wanted to follow our original beef cooking method, that is, to stir it raw into the slow cooker. Omitting the additional step of browning the meat not only would save time, but it also allowed us to minimize fat by eliminating excess oil needed for browning. While developing our original recipe, we tested a number of flavor replacements for the fond created by the browned beef. After extensive testing, we had landed on a winning combination of soy sauce (its salty elements reinforced the beefy flavor and added color) and tomato paste, which we microwaved with onions and aromatics before adding them to the slow cooker. Swapping in low-sodium soy sauce and dialing the amount back from ⅓ cup to ¼ cup (any less and testers complained of lack of flavor) helped keep the sodium level in check.

CUTTING STEW MEAT

1. Pull apart roast at major seams (delineated by lines of fat and silver skin). Use knife as necessary.

2. With knife, trim off excess fat and silver skin.

3. Cut meat into 1½-inch pieces.

MAKING A FOIL PACKET

1. Place vegetables on one side of large piece of aluminum foil. Fold foil over and crimp to seal edges.

2. Place packet on top of soup or stew, pressing gently as needed.

Next, we examined our broth. In our initial testing, we found that stews made with all beef broths, surprisingly, turned out too beefy and out of balance. Instead, we tried making stews with different combinations of water, chicken broth, and the aforementioned beef broth. Water made the stews taste, well, watery. Stew made with all chicken broth was a little one-dimensional, but using a 50:50 ratio of chicken and beef broth balanced the flavors nicely.

In our original recipe, we discovered that adding tapioca to thicken our stew (as in our Slow-Cooker Tex-Mex Chicken Stew, page 158) just didn't work. We needed more than ¼ cup of tapioca to appropriately thicken the stew, and in this case we found the tapioca pearls too noticeable in the final dish. We turned, then, to flour and brought out our skillet to build a roux. Since we'd need to use the skillet anyway, we decided to sauté our aromatics and brown our tomato paste before adding the flour and broth. This change in thickener brought a marked improvement to the stew: It was thick without being tacky, there were no visible tapioca pearls, and the flavor had deepened with the additional browned aromatics. The original method called for 2 tablespoons of oil for the sauté, but we found that we could reduce this amount to a mere 2 teaspoons.

Finally, we moved on to the vegetables. In our original slow-cooker beef stew, we used about equal amounts beef and vegetables (including mushrooms, potatoes, carrots, parsnips, and kale), but our lighter, healthier version was going to get a bigger dose of the latter. We increased the amounts of carrots and parsnips from ¾ pound each to a full pound and bumped up the kale from 8 ounces to 12. This change gave our stew more heft and a huge healthy boost with no additional fat. As in the original recipe, we added the mushrooms directly to the broth along with the beef, as they could hold up well to the extended cooking time. We wrapped the carrots, parsnips, potatoes, and a little oil in a foil packet and placed the packet on top of the beef, mushroom, and broth mixture. This step insulated the root vegetables, keeping them intact while still cooking through to tender perfection. We added the kale at the very end of cooking, as it needed only about 30 minutes to cook through. Our lightened Super Veggie Beef Stew was now just that: super.

Slow-Cooker Super Veggie Beef Stew

SERVES 8

To prevent the root vegetables from disintegrating in the slow cooker, wrap them in a foil packet (see page 168) and place the packet on top of the stew mixture. If the final sauce is too thick, stir in additional hot chicken broth until the stew reaches the desired consistency. *Cooking time: 9 to 11 hours on low or 5 to 7 hours on high*

- 3 onions, chopped fine
- 5 teaspoons vegetable oil
  Salt and pepper
- 6 garlic cloves, minced
- ¼ cup tomato paste
- 1 tablespoon minced fresh thyme or 1 teaspoon dried
- ⅓ cup all-purpose flour
- 1½ cups low-sodium chicken broth, plus extra as needed
- 2 pounds boneless beef chuck-eye roast, pulled apart at seams, trimmed of all visible fat, and cut into 1½-inch pieces (see page 168)
- 1½ cups beef broth
- 8 ounces portobello mushroom caps, gills removed and cut into ½-inch pieces
- ¼ cup low-sodium soy sauce
- 2 bay leaves
- 1 pound carrots, peeled, halved lengthwise, and sliced 1 inch thick
- 1 pound parsnips, peeled, halved lengthwise, and sliced 1 inch thick
- 12 ounces red potatoes, cut into 1-inch pieces
- 12 ounces kale, stemmed and leaves sliced ¼ inch thick

1. Combine onions, 2 teaspoons oil, and ¼ teaspoon salt in 12-inch skillet. Cover and cook over medium-low heat, stirring occasionally, until softened, 8 to 10 minutes. Uncover, increase heat to medium, stir in garlic, tomato paste, and thyme, and cook until fragrant, about 30 seconds. Stir in flour and cook for 1 minute. Slowly whisk in chicken broth, scraping up any browned bits and smoothing out any lumps; transfer to slow cooker.

2. Stir beef, beef broth, portobellos, soy sauce, and bay leaves into slow cooker. Toss carrots, parsnips, and potatoes with remaining 1 tablespoon oil in bowl, season with ⅛ teaspoon salt and ⅛ teaspoon pepper, then wrap in foil packet. Lay foil packet on top of stew. Cover and cook until beef is tender, 9 to 11 hours on low or 5 to 7 hours on high.

3. Transfer foil packet to plate. Let stew settle for 5 minutes, then remove fat from surface using large spoon. Discard bay leaves. Stir in kale, cover, and cook on high until tender, 20 to 30 minutes.

4. Carefully open foil packet, stir vegetables with any accumulated juices into stew, and let sit until heated through, about 5 minutes. Adjust stew consistency with additional hot chicken broth as needed. Season with salt and pepper to taste and serve.

PER 1½-CUP SERVING: Cal 320; Fat 8g; Sat fat 1.5g; Chol 40mg; Carb 40g; Protein 25g; Fiber 8g; Sodium 730mg

PORK LOIN WITH CRANBERRIES AND ORANGE

WE HAD MASTERED SLOW-COOKER STEWS, SOUPS, and chicken braises. So we wondered if we were ready to take on a bigger challenge: a roast. For our final slow-cooker recipe, we decided to turn to lean pork loin for a company-worthy meal. When developing our slow-cooker chicken recipes, we'd learned that we needed to focus on building a lot of flavor from the get-go since the long cooking times and moist cooking environment of the slow cooker tend to mute flavor. To ensure a flavorful pork loin, we decided to pair this naturally mild meat with the sweet-tart flavor of cranberries. Pork and fruit are a natural combination, and we imagined that the cranberries would not only dress up our roast but also infuse the meat with tons of flavor.

The first step was to see if we could even fit a pork loin into our slow cooker. We quickly learned that bone-in cuts wouldn't fit, so we focused on boneless pork loin. The key, we learned, was to select the roast carefully. A 3-pound pork loin roast that is wide and short was the best option. Those that were long and narrow were a poor choice: Narrow pork loins don't fit as easily in the slow cooker and are prone to overcooking because they cook through more quickly. Since pork loin is naturally so lean, we knew we needed to leave some fat on the roast in order to keep the meat moist over the long cooking time. We found that a ⅛-inch fat cap was just enough to accomplish this task while still keeping our recipe healthy. Tying the roast before cooking helped keep the meat a uniform shape, ensuring even cooking.

Our cut selected, we next turned to the question of whether to brown our roast. Since we wanted this recipe to be as easy as possible, we decided to first try cooking a pork loin added raw to the slow cooker. Unfortunately, our unbrowned slow-cooked roast did not fare so well. Cooked in the relatively low heat of the slow cooker, the fat cap on top of the roast couldn't render. Our roast emerged not only pale in color, but also topped with an unpleasantly chewy layer of fat. After this failed test, we decided to brown the roast in a skillet before adding it to the slow cooker. Luckily it took only 2 teaspoons of oil and 10 minutes of cooking to effectively brown the roast, and we found that this step made a world of difference. The pork was now golden brown, and the fat cap had melted into the meat, flavoring the roast throughout.

Next we moved on to fine-tuning the cooking time. Since pork loin is a naturally lean cut, we knew that we would need to keep our cooking time relatively short. Cooking the loin on the high setting, however, was disastrous. This meat was leathery, dry, and borderline inedible. The low setting worked much better, as long as we watched it carefully and pulled it out right when it reached 140 degrees (this turned out to be about four hours).

Now that we had found the best way to cook the pork, we moved on to our cranberry sauce. To find the ultimate cranberry flavor, we tested various combinations of jellied cranberry sauce, whole-berry cranberry sauce, cranberry juice, and dried cranberries. A few tests revealed that both the jellied cranberry sauce and cranberry juice added minimal flavor with loads of sugar, so we axed them both. On the other hand, tasters gave the thumbs-up to whole-berry cranberry sauce, which lent texture and a truer cranberry flavor, as well as to ½ cup of dried cranberries, which added bright pockets of tart chew.

We were on track with the sauce, but tasters found it still too sweet and one-dimensional. To create better balance, we tried adding ingredients we'd seen in other cranberry pork recipes. Tasters felt savory additions like Dijon mustard, onions, and vinegar muddied the flavor. Instead, we liked the inclusion of mildly acidic orange juice. We added ½ cup of juice to our sauce and further bolstered the flavor with a few strips of orange zest. A small amount of cinnamon lent a little spice and depth.

At this point, our pork was perfectly cooked and our sauce tasted great, but we thought we could improve the recipe by turning our sauce into a clingy glaze. We tried adding one of our standard thickeners (flour and tapioca), but neither thickened the sauce to our liking. Since we knew we'd need to let the pork rest before serving, we decided to take advantage of this waiting time and reduce our sauce on the stovetop. Twelve minutes of simmering turned our thin cranberry sauce into a glossy glaze. Drizzled over the pork, the cranberry glaze added the finishing touch to our company-worthy dinner.

Slow-Cooker Pork Loin with Cranberries and Orange
SERVES 8

When choosing a pork loin, we prefer a short, wide cut. A ⅛-inch-thick layer of fat on top of the roast is ideal; if your roast has a thicker fat cap, trim it back accordingly. *Cooking time: about 4 hours on low*

1 **(3-pound) boneless pork loin roast, fat trimmed to ⅛-inch thickness and tied at 1-inch intervals (see page 94)**
   Salt and pepper
2 **teaspoons canola oil**
1 **(14-ounce) can whole-berry cranberry sauce**
½ **cup dried cranberries**
3 **(3-inch) strips orange zest plus ½ cup juice**
⅛ **teaspoon ground cinnamon**

1. Pat pork dry with paper towels and season with ⅛ teaspoon salt and ⅛ teaspoon pepper. Heat oil in 12-inch skillet over medium-high heat until just smoking. Brown pork on all sides, 7 to 10 minutes; transfer to plate.

2. Stir cranberry sauce, cranberries, orange zest, orange juice, and cinnamon into slow cooker. Nestle pork with any accumulated juices into slow cooker. Cover and cook until pork is tender and registers 140 degrees, about 4 hours on low.

3. Transfer pork to carving board, tent loosely with aluminum foil, and let rest for 15 minutes. Let braising liquid settle for 5 minutes, then remove fat from surface using large spoon. Remove orange zest. Transfer braising liquid to saucepan and simmer until reduced to 1½ cups, about 10 minutes. Season with salt and pepper to taste.

4. Remove twine from pork, slice pork into ½-inch-thick slices, and serve, passing sauce separately.

PER SERVING: Cal 400; Fat 17g; Sat fat 5g; Chol 115mg; Carb 26g; Protein 35g; Fiber 1g; Sodium 140mg

SLOW-COOKER PORK LOIN WITH CRANBERRIES AND ORANGE

GRILLED ARGENTINE STEAKS WITH CHIMICHURRI SAUCE

CHAPTER 8

FIRE UP THE GRILL

GRILLED ARGENTINE STEAKS

WHILE GRILLING STEAK IN YOUR BACKYARD CAN sometimes seem mundane, in Argentina, cooking meat over a live fire is not just a means of getting dinner on the table but an art form. The steak is always perfect—grilled low and slow over hardwood logs, which imbue the meat with a subtle, complex smokiness and a perfect, thick crust. The combination of this juicy steak served with the piquant parsley, garlic, and olive oil sauce known as *chimichurri* is hard to beat. Since even a fine steak dinner can be healthy when served in moderation, we figured why not aim to create a recipe that exemplifies the best of South American steak perfection on our own grill?

The first order of business was sorting out which cut of meat to use. In truth, there is no one cut that can be considered a "typical" Argentine steak. Instead, the size of the steak is the focal point. Usually very thick (1½ to 2 inches) and pushing 2 pounds, the classic Argentine steaks look monstrous by American standards, but this immensity has more to do with cooking technique than gluttony. It is simple logic: With thick steaks, the meat can remain on the grill long enough to absorb smoke flavor and at the same time avoid the risk of overcooking.

We knew the key trait in selecting our steaks was the thickness, so with moderation in mind we chose four flavorful cuts of steak that were closer to 1 pound (enough to serve six once sliced) than the customary 2, but still appropriately thick (about 1½ inches): strip steak, shell steak, tri-tip (a cut from the bottom sirloin), and bottom round. After trimming away any visible fat, we created a single-level fire on our grill (tactics for pumping up wood-grilled flavor would come later), salted each of the steaks generously, and cooked them to medium-rare. Tri-tip and bottom round were out. Though each offered decent flavor, tasters found them a tad tough and dry. The shell steak was better, though it lost points for its stringier texture. Meanwhile, strip steak boasted big beefy flavor, not to mention an interior that was both moist and pleasantly chewy.

Next we moved on to building up the essential wood-smoke flavor. Cooking over actual logs was a nonstarter. Instead, we tried various wood chunk and chip alternatives, soaked and unsoaked, foil wrapped and unwrapped. On our charcoal grill, we found two wood chip packs and unsoaked chunks both worked well. Four chunks nestled around the perimeter of the fire lasted long enough to tinge the steaks with a subtle essence of burning wood. For a gas grill, we settled on two packets of soaked wood chips and placed them over the primary burner. Placing the lid on the grill for the first few minutes of cooking helped to quickly trap smoke flavor.

Unfortunately, our single-level fire still wasn't able to produce the requisite deep brown char on the steaks by the time they were done cooking. We needed to figure out a way to drive off their exterior moisture so that a deep crust could form. Dry-aging is a technique that many professional restaurants use to dry the exterior of their steaks, though this takes several days to accomplish and we wanted faster results. Salting the steaks overnight in the fridge was slightly faster—the juices were first drawn out by the salt, then were gradually pulled back in, leaving the exterior of the meat drier than before—but we still felt this approach took too much time.

In the test kitchen, we're always talking about how the severely dry environment of the freezer robs food of its moisture. Usually that's an effect we're trying to prevent, but could it work in our favor? To find out, we salted the meat and then left it uncovered in the freezer for an hour. Sure enough, the meat emerged from the icebox practically bone-dry, and it browned within moments of hitting the grill. Even better, these partially frozen steaks could stand about five more minutes on the fire, adding up to more char and more flavor.

Nearly satisfied with our Argentine facsimile, we focused our last few tests on the distinctive crackly crust. Knowing that cornstarch is another moisture-eating powerhouse, we tried adding a small amount to our salt rub, a trick we've used in the past to crisp up everything from turkey skin to potatoes. This twist had two results: We were able to cut the freezing time to 30 minutes, and we got steaks with all the color and snap we were looking for.

All our steaks needed now was the requisite chimichurri sauce, the sharp, grassy flavors of which are designed to offset the rich, unctuous qualities of the steak. We leaned toward one of the test kitchen's established recipes: fresh parsley, cilantro, oregano, garlic, red wine vinegar, red pepper flakes, and salt—all emulsified with ½ cup of extra-virgin olive oil. Reducing the oil to 2 tablespoons and replacing the rest with water created a lighter version of the sauce that still had all the bold flavors we wanted. Splashing a little chimichurri on our sliced steaks, we had a near-perfect steak dinner if we did say so ourselves, no plane ticket required.

Grilled Argentine Steaks with Chimichurri Sauce

SERVES 6

If using a charcoal grill, you can substitute 4 medium unsoaked wood chunks for the wood chip packets if desired. We prefer these steaks cooked to medium-rare, but if you prefer your meat more or less done, see our guidelines in "Testing Meat for Doneness" on page 183.

SAUCE

- ¼ cup warm tap water
- 2 teaspoons dried oregano
- 1 teaspoon salt
- 1⅓ cups fresh parsley leaves
- ⅔ cup fresh cilantro leaves
- 6 garlic cloves, minced
- ½ teaspoon red pepper flakes
- ¼ cup red wine vinegar
- 2 tablespoons extra-virgin olive oil

STEAKS

- 1½ teaspoons cornstarch
- ½ teaspoon salt
- 2 (1¼-pound) boneless strip loin steaks, 1½ to 1¾ inches thick, trimmed of all visible fat
- 4 cups wood chips, soaked in water for 15 minutes and drained
- ¼ teaspoon pepper

1. FOR THE SAUCE: Combine water, oregano, and salt in small bowl and let sit until oregano is softened, about 15 minutes. Pulse parsley, cilantro, garlic, and pepper flakes in food processor until coarsely chopped, about 10 pulses. Add water mixture and vinegar and pulse to combine, about 5 pulses. Transfer mixture to bowl and slowly whisk in oil until emulsified. Cover and let sit at room temperature for 1 hour.

2. FOR THE STEAKS: Combine cornstarch and salt in bowl. Pat steaks dry with paper towels and place on wire rack set in rimmed baking sheet. Rub steaks evenly with cornstarch mixture and place steaks, uncovered, in freezer until very firm, about 30 minutes.

3. Using 2 large pieces of heavy-duty aluminum foil, wrap soaked wood chips in 2 foil packets and cut several vent holes in top.

4A. FOR A CHARCOAL GRILL: Open bottom vent halfway. Light large chimney starter filled with charcoal briquettes (6 quarts). When top coals are partially covered with ash, pour evenly over grill. Place wood chip packets on coals. Set cooking grate in place, cover, and open lid vent halfway. Heat grill until hot and wood chips are smoking, about 5 minutes.

4B. FOR A GAS GRILL: Place wood chip packets over primary burner. Turn all burners to high, cover, and heat grill until hot and wood chips are smoking, about 15 minutes. Leave all burners on high.

5. Clean and oil cooking grate. Season steaks with pepper. Place steaks on grill, cover, and cook until steaks begin to char, 2 to 3 minutes. Uncover grill, flip steaks, and cook on second side until beginning to char, 2 to 3 minutes.

6. Flip steaks again and cook until well charred on first side, 2 to 4 minutes. Flip steaks 1 last time and continue to cook until meat registers 120 to 125 degrees (for medium-rare), 2 to 6 minutes longer.

7. Transfer steaks to carving board, tent loosely with foil, and let rest for 5 to 10 minutes. Slice each steak crosswise into ¼-inch-thick slices and serve, passing sauce separately.

PER SERVING: Cal 260; Fat 14g; Sat fat 4.5g; Chol 100mg; Carb 3g; Protein 44g; Fiber 1g; Sodium 700mg

NOTES FROM THE TEST KITCHEN

MAKING A WOOD CHIP PACKET

After soaking wood chips in water for 15 minutes, drain and spread them in center of large piece of heavy-duty aluminum foil. Fold to seal edges, then cut 3 or 4 slits in foil packet to allow smoke to escape.

GRILLED BEEF KEBABS

BEEF AND VEGETABLE KEBABS ARE AN OBVIOUS choice during the summer months—they cook quickly and are a snap to assemble. The problem is that most attempts result in beef that's either overcooked with little char or practically incinerated with a red, raw interior. And the vegetables? They usually turn out torched on the outside and still crunchy on the inside. We were determined to nail a foolproof approach to achieving juicy, flavorful marinated beef with a hint of char and smoke and nicely browned, tender-firm vegetables at the same time.

We started at the butcher's case, where we rounded up five possible cuts of meat for skewering, ranging from bottom round to tenderloin. Virtually every recipe we consulted advised cutting the meat into 1-inch chunks. However, we aimed a little larger, choosing generous 2-inch pieces since they would be less susceptible to drying out. We then skewered the cubes and seasoned them with salt and pepper (we'd worry about the veggies and a marinade later) before throwing them onto the fire. For the time being we used a basic single-level fire. Lean, pricey tenderloin was quickly cut from the running; tasters were after something with bigger, beefier flavor. Bottom round was too chewy. The more marbled cuts—skirt steak, blade steak, and steak tips—all boasted respectable flavor, but the looser-grained and slightly richer steak tips outdid the others in both beefiness and tender texture. For a dinner for four, we grabbed 1½ pounds of steak tips, then started to work on our marinade.

The test kitchen has developed a number of tricks to maximize the impact of a marinade, so we already had a head start. First, in addition to helping meat retain moisture, we've found that salt is one of the few ingredients that penetrate and draw seasonings with it to the center of the meat, so we always include it. Second, fats carry flavor, so a little oil would be necessary (though we wanted to use as little as possible to keep things light in this case). Third, we like to add a little sugar to lend a hint of sweetness and help the meat develop flavorful browning.

Soy sauce is a common choice for the liquid base in marinades (if we used it, it would replace the salt), and for good reason: It's packed with flavor enhancers called glutamates that can travel deep into meat to make it taste more savory. But meat soaked in soy sauce can often end up tasting like teriyaki, so after some debate we decided we wanted a more neutral base. Considering other common pantry staples, we thought of tomato paste, which is also full of glutamates. Though an unorthodox addition to a marinade, we thought its fruity taste could be just the ticket for a soaking liquid when thinned with water. We used the blender to mix up a simple marinade of tomato paste thinned with ⅓ cup of water, plus some onion, 3 tablespoons of oil, salt, pepper, sugar, rosemary, lemon zest, and garlic.

Next question: How long should the beef marinate? After some trial and error, we found that an hour gave the meat all the seasoning it needed. Our tomato paste–based marinade amplified the beef's meaty flavor nicely without overpowering the other seasonings. We then considered thinning the tomato paste with beef broth instead of water. When we made this simple swap, tasters immediately noticed new depth of flavor.

For the vegetables, we singled out three grill favorites—peppers, onions, and zucchini—and marinated them for 30 minutes. Our 2-inch beef chunks were staying on a hot fire for 12 to 16 minutes, which gave the vegetables ample time to turn tender, but it also led to blackened exteriors that tasted like charcoal. Clearly, the veggies would do better cooked over gentler heat. The obvious solution was to place the two components on separate skewers and build a fire with a hot and a cool side where they could cook simultaneously but over their own optimal degree of heat.

For a charcoal grill, we tried several methods for creating varying levels of heat and eventually found the most success by spreading all the coals in the center of the grill, leaving a 2-inch gap between the grill wall and the charcoal. The heat in the center charred the beef pieces perfectly. Meanwhile, the veggies rested on the perimeter of the coals, where they slowly bronzed and charred at the tips over the less intense heat. For a gas grill, we simply kept one of the burners on high and turned the other burners to medium-low to achieve the same results. By the time the beef was done, the vegetables were perfectly cooked without being incinerated, giving us a moist, tender, and flavorful kebab dinner that was ready all together.

From there, we decided to create two variations by making a North African marinade with cilantro, paprika, cumin, and cayenne, and a Red Curry marinade with basil, red curry paste, lime zest, and ginger. Now we had three great reasons to fire up our grill.

Grilled Beef Kebabs with Lemon-Rosemary Marinade

SERVES 4

To ensure evenly sized chunks, we prefer to purchase whole steak tips (sometimes labeled flap meat) and cut them ourselves. However, if you have long, thin pieces of meat, roll or fold them into approximate 2-inch cubes before skewering. We prefer the meat cooked to medium-rare, but if you prefer your meat more or less done, see our guidelines in "Testing Meat for Doneness" on page 183. You will need six 12-inch metal skewers for this recipe.

MARINADE

- 1 small onion, chopped
- ⅓ cup beef broth
- 3 tablespoons canola oil
- 2 tablespoons tomato paste
- 4 garlic cloves, chopped
- 4 teaspoons minced fresh rosemary
- 1½ teaspoons grated lemon zest
- 1½ teaspoons sugar
- 1 teaspoon salt
- ¾ teaspoon pepper

BEEF AND VEGETABLES

- 1½ pounds sirloin steak tips, trimmed of all visible fat and cut into 2-inch pieces
- 1 large zucchini or summer squash, halved lengthwise and sliced 1 inch thick
- 1 large red or green bell pepper, stemmed, seeded, and cut into 1½-inch pieces
- 1 large red or sweet onion, halved through root end, core discarded, each half cut into 4 wedges, and each wedge cut crosswise into thirds

1. FOR THE MARINADE: Process all ingredients in blender until mixture is completely smooth, about 45 seconds. Transfer ½ cup marinade to large bowl and set aside.

2. FOR THE BEEF AND VEGETABLES: Place remaining marinade and beef in 1-gallon zipper-lock bag and toss to coat; press out as much air as possible and seal bag. Refrigerate for at least 1 hour or up to 2 hours, flipping bag every 30 minutes.

3. Add zucchini, bell pepper, and onion to bowl with reserved marinade and gently toss to coat. Cover and let sit at room temperature for 30 minutes.

4. Remove beef from bag, pat dry with paper towels, and thread tightly onto two 12-inch metal skewers. Thread vegetables onto four 12-inch metal skewers, in alternating pattern of zucchini, bell pepper, and onion.

5A. FOR A CHARCOAL GRILL: Open bottom vent completely. Light large chimney starter mounded with charcoal briquettes (7 quarts). When top coals are partially covered with ash, pour evenly over center of grill, leaving 2-inch gap between entire grill wall and charcoal. Set cooking grate in place, cover, and open lid vent completely. Heat grill until hot, about 5 minutes.

5B. FOR A GAS GRILL: Turn all burners to high, cover, and heat grill until hot, about 15 minutes. Leave primary burner on high and turn other burner(s) to medium-low.

6. Clean and oil cooking grate. Place meat skewers on hot part of grill and cook (covered if using gas), turning kebabs every 2 to 4 minutes, until well browned and beef registers 120 to 125 degrees (for medium-rare), 12 to 16 minutes. Transfer meat skewers to serving platter, tent loosely with aluminum foil, and let rest for 5 to 10 minutes.

7. While beef is cooking, place vegetable skewers on cool part of grill (near edge of coals if using charcoal) and cook (covered if using gas), turning kebabs every 4 to 5 minutes, until tender and lightly charred, 17 to 21 minutes. Transfer skewers to platter with beef and serve.

PER SERVING: Cal 370; Fat 15g; Sat fat 2.5g; Chol 85mg; Carb 16g; Protein 40g; Fiber 4g; Sodium 750mg

VARIATIONS

Grilled Beef Kebabs with North African Marinade
Omit rosemary and lemon zest. Add 15 cilantro sprigs, 1½ teaspoons paprika, 1½ teaspoons ground cumin, and ½ teaspoon cayenne pepper to marinade.

PER SERVING: Cal 370; Fat 15g; Sat fat 2.5g; Chol 85mg; Carb 16g; Protein 40g; Fiber 4g; Sodium 750mg

Grilled Beef Kebabs with Red Curry Marinade
Omit rosemary and lemon zest. Add ⅓ cup fresh basil leaves, 2 tablespoons red curry paste, 2 teaspoons grated lime zest, and 2 teaspoons grated fresh ginger to marinade. Reduce salt to ¾ teaspoon.

PER SERVING: Cal 380; Fat 15g; Sat fat 2.5g; Chol 85mg; Carb 18g; Protein 41g; Fiber 4g; Sodium 890mg

BARBECUED CHICKEN KEBABS

AT FIRST SIGHT, BARBECUED CHICKEN KEBABS SEEM pretty easy. All you have to do is skewer up some boneless, skinless chicken for a fast-and-loose meal that captures the charms of barbecued chicken, but without the time and patience needed to cook a whole bird or the focus essential to tending a host of mixed parts. Ah, but if only the kebabs lived up to that promise. The quandary is that without an insulating layer of skin, the pieces of lean meat dry out and toughen when exposed to the blazing heat of the grill. Slathering on barbecue sauce creates a rich glaze on the exterior of the chicken but does little to address the fundamental problem. In fact, it often creates more problems: If applied too early or in too great a volume, the sauce drips off the meat, burns, and fixes the chicken fast to the grill.

To keep things simple, we decided to focus on all-meat skewers and create a recipe that guaranteed juicy, tender chicken with plenty of sticky-sweet, smoke-tinged flavor. We quickly settled on using an existing test kitchen recipe for homemade barbecue sauce—a simple reduction of ketchup, molasses, and basic pantry ingredients—so that we could concentrate all of our attention on the chicken.

We started by cutting the meat into 1-inch chunks, which would cook through relatively quickly yet need enough time on the grill to pick up some good smoky flavor. Brining is often used in the test kitchen to prevent lean meats from drying out, so it seemed like a natural next step here. But we quickly found it wasn't

a cure-all in this situation: When we cut our chicken into pieces, then brined, skewered, and grilled it, the meat was so slick and wet that any sauce we brushed on dribbled off, even toward the end of cooking.

Changing direction, we tried salting, another technique commonly used in the test kitchen to maintain juiciness in meat. While we were at it, we included some spices with the salt to further boost the flavor, essentially building a rub. As the mixture sat on the chicken (30 minutes was ample), the salt drew the juices to the surface, where they mixed with the seasonings, then flowed back into the chicken. The rub also crisped up on the chicken's exterior as it cooked, forming a craggy surface that the sauce could cling to. To prevent overpowering the chicken, we avoided outspoken spices, settling on both sweet and smoked paprika, the former contributing depth and the latter helping to boost the overall smokiness of the dish. A few teaspoons of sugar added to the rub aided in browning.

With its ruddy exterior, our chicken now looked the part, but tasters noted that the meat was still not quite moist enough and lacked sufficient depth of flavor. In our hunt for a solution, we ran across a few Middle Eastern kebab recipes in which a few slices of pure lamb fat were skewered between lamb chunks before grilling. The fat melted during cooking, continually basting the lean meat.

Using lamb fat was certainly a stretch, but smoky bacon seemed like a promising option that would add richness and flavor. A few tests proved that a little bacon could go a long way, which was fortunate since moderation was already on our minds. We limited ourselves to two strips for 2 pounds of chicken, which added only about 3 grams of fat per serving.

Still, we weren't sure about the best way to put the bacon to work. We started by cutting the two strips into 1-inch pieces and alternated skewering chicken pieces and bacon squares. Unfortunately, by the time the chicken was cooked through, the bacon—tightly wedged as it was between the chicken chunks—had failed to render enough to make a difference. For our next attempt, we tried coating the skewered chicken with drippings from freshly cooked bacon before setting them on the grill. Within minutes, the fat trickled onto the coals and prompted flare-ups, blackening most of the chicken. What wasn't burnt, however, was moist and tasted addictively smoky.

If raw pieces didn't render enough, and rendered fat dripped off too quickly, was there an in-between solution?

NOTES FROM THE TEST KITCHEN

GRILL LIGHTER

In contrast to a lit match, which can singe your fingers if you're not careful or quick, grill lighters have long necks to keep your fingers at a safe distance from the flames. After firing up five models, we settled on the **Zippo Flexible Neck Utility Lighter**, $19.95, as our favorite. It has a neck that makes for easy chimney lighting, even when trying to light it from underneath. The Zippo ignited easily, stayed lit even in gusty wind, and has a refillable chamber with a large, easy-to-read fuel window. It also sports a comfortable grip, and its unique adjustable flame can flare from ⅓ inch to 2 inches. This model can light our fire anytime.

BARBECUED CHICKEN KEBABS

This time around, we ground the bacon into a spreadable paste in the food processor, then tossed it with the chicken chunks, salt, and spices. After the kebabs rested for 30 minutes in the refrigerator, we grilled them over a moderately hot half-fire. (This created a cooler area where we could slide the kebabs in the event of a flare-up.) Once the chicken was nearly done, we brushed barbecue sauce onto the kebabs, leaving them on the grill for just a minute or two longer to give the sauce a chance to caramelize. (Adding the sauce any earlier was a surefire route to scorched chicken.) The bacon bits clung tenaciously to the chicken, but to our great disappointment, not to mention puzzlement, the chicken was now dry and had lost flavor. We repeated the test to make sure this batch wasn't a fluke and got the same results.

While we were brainstorming causes for this new problem, it occurred to us that the fatty ground-up bacon may have been adhering so well to the chicken that it was acting as a barrier to the salt, which now couldn't penetrate the meat during its 30-minute rest. What if we first salted the meat for 30 minutes, then tossed it with the sugar, spices, and bacon paste right before we put it on the grill? This simple change was the answer: The chicken was now juicy, tender, and full-flavored, with a smoky depth that complemented the barbecue sauce. Best of all, these kebabs actually lived up to their easy appearance.

Barbecued Chicken Kebabs

SERVES 6

Turbinado sugar is commonly sold as Sugar in the Raw. Demerara sugar can be substituted. Use the large holes of a box grater to grate the onion for the sauce. If you have thin pieces of chicken, cut them larger than 1 inch and roll or fold them into approximately 1-inch cubes. You will need four 12-inch metal skewers for this recipe.

SAUCE

- ½ cup ketchup
- ¼ cup molasses
- 2 tablespoons grated onion
- 2 tablespoons Worcestershire sauce
- 2 tablespoons Dijon mustard
- 2 tablespoons cider vinegar
- 1 tablespoon packed light brown sugar

CHICKEN

- 2 pounds boneless, skinless chicken breasts, trimmed of all visible fat and cut into 1-inch pieces
- 1 teaspoon kosher salt
- 2 tablespoons sweet paprika
- 4 teaspoons turbinado sugar
- 2 teaspoons smoked paprika
- 2 slices bacon, cut into ½-inch pieces

1. FOR THE SAUCE: Bring all ingredients to simmer in small saucepan and cook, stirring occasionally, until reduced to about 1 cup, 5 to 7 minutes. Transfer ½ cup sauce to small bowl and set remaining sauce aside for serving.

2. FOR THE CHICKEN: Toss chicken with salt in bowl, cover, and refrigerate for 30 minutes to 1 hour.

3. Combine sweet paprika, sugar, and smoked paprika in bowl. Process bacon in food processor until smooth paste forms, 30 to 45 seconds, scraping down bowl as needed. Add spice mixture and bacon paste to chicken and mix until ingredients are thoroughly combined and chicken is completely coated. Thread chicken tightly onto four 12-inch metal skewers.

4A. FOR A CHARCOAL GRILL: Open bottom vent completely. Light large chimney starter three-quarters filled with charcoal briquettes (4½ quarts). When top coals are partially covered with ash, pour evenly over half of grill. Set cooking grate in place, cover, and open lid vent completely. Heat grill until hot, about 5 minutes.

4B. FOR A GAS GRILL: Turn all burners to high, cover, and heat grill until hot, about 15 minutes. Leave primary burner on high and turn off other burner(s).

5. Clean and oil cooking grate. Place skewers on hot part of grill and cook (covered if using gas), turning kebabs every 2 minutes, until well browned, 8 to 10 minutes. (If flare-ups occur, slide kebabs to cool part of grill until fire dies down.) Brush kebabs with ¼ cup sauce, flip, and cook until sauce is sizzling and browning in spots, about 1 minute. Brush second side with remaining ¼ cup sauce, flip, and continue to cook until sizzling and browning in spots and chicken registers 160 degrees, about 1 minute longer.

6. Transfer skewers to serving platter, tent loosely with aluminum foil, and let rest for 5 to 10 minutes. Serve, passing reserved sauce separately.

PER SERVING: Cal 290; Fat 6g; Sat fat 1.5g; Chol 95mg; Carb 23g; Protein 37g; Fiber 1g; Sodium 750mg

BARBECUED DRY-RUBBED CHICKEN

IT'S NO SURPRISE THAT BARBECUED CHICKEN regularly finds its way onto the menu when you are cooking light. Combining naturally lean meat with a tangy, low-fat sauce seems like a great way to put a satisfying, healthy meal on the table. The problem is, while barbecue sauce is easy—slather it on near the end of cooking and it turns into an attractive, tasty glaze—the downside is that the sauce never flavors the meat deeply.

A few months back we had decided it was time to bring the flavor back to grilled glazed chicken. We found our solution by making a dry spice rub with brown sugar added. A rub made with spices alone could impart deep flavor, but such rubs eliminate the glazing effect that results when barbecue sauce meets heat. Adding moist brown sugar to our rub transformed it into a flavorful glaze that was more than skin deep. That original recipe worked well on bone-in, skin-on chicken pieces, but now we were looking for a lighter meal. We wondered if the same success could be had with leaner skinless chicken breasts.

Knowing that big barbecue flavor takes time to develop on the grill, we quickly skipped over quick-cooking boneless breasts and stuck with bone-in. Removing the skin was easy enough, though cooking the chicken was a different story. Given the intense heat of the grill, lean white meat can easily dry out. In our original recipe, we had used a single-level medium-low fire to help prevent this, though even with this setup, we noticed that the problem returned in our skinless version. For added protection against drying out, we found a favorite test kitchen technique to be helpful: brining. A quick one-hour soak in a saltwater solution was just the trick to keep the lean meat moist.

With our cooking method down, we were ready to focus on the rub. Our previous tests helped us quickly settle on including sugar in our rub to duplicate the sweetness of barbecue sauce and to help form a glaze. We had skipped over Demerara and turbinado sugars, whose large crystals are less likely to melt into a glaze. We tested white sugar (too sweet in the quantity necessary), light brown sugar (not bad), and more complexly flavored dark brown sugar (the hands-down winner). Dark brown sugar also has almost 20 percent more moisture than white sugar, which helps it melt reliably.

The spices were a matter of taste, and we were after classic barbecue. Chili powder and paprika helped define that flavor. Onion powder mimicked the fresh onion in homemade barbecue sauces, and dry mustard lent brightness. Black pepper and cayenne rounded out the rub. A 30-minute rest after applying the rub allowed the meat to absorb the flavors before cooking. Plus, it gave the sugar time to draw some of the moisture in the chicken to its surface, which jump-started the glazing process.

NOTES FROM THE TEST KITCHEN

BRINING

Because both poultry and pork can be lean, they can cook up dry. The salt in a brine changes the structure of the muscle proteins and allows them to hold on to more moisture when exposed to heat. In a sample test, tasters had no trouble picking out brined pork chops versus chops left untreated. Though we leave brining optional, if you have the time it will give you juicier meat in recipes.

To brine, following the amounts in the chart below, dissolve the salt (we use table salt) in the water in a container or bowl large enough to hold the brine and meat. Submerge the meat completely in the brine. Cover and refrigerate, following the times in the chart (do not overbrine or else the meat will taste too salty). Remove the meat from the brine, rinse, and pat dry with paper towels. The meat is now ready to be cooked.

There is one exception to brining: don't brine kosher poultry, frozen injected turkey, or enhanced pork (pork injected with a salt solution). These treatments will keep the chicken, turkey, and pork moist, and brining will make the meat way too salty. Note that our nutritional data does not account for brining or using any of the types of meat or poultry that should not be brined. If you brine or use any of those mentioned, be aware that the final sodium content for those recipes will be higher than what we have listed.

POULTRY OR MEAT	COLD WATER	SALT	TIME
4 (10-ounce) bone-in, skin-on split chicken breasts	2 quarts	½ cup	½ to 1 hour
4 (8-ounce) bone-in pork chops	1½ quarts	3 tablespoons	½ to 1 hour

While developing our original recipe, we had found that applying only a single coating of our rub gave us skimpy, blotchy results. To achieve a more substantial glaze we had solved the problem in two ways: We cut the breasts in half to give the rub additional surface area to stick to, and we dredged the chicken pieces in the dry rub again halfway through cooking. In this case, the second coating had been a huge success: It adhered to the sticky, partially melted "base coat" and blended with the fat from the rendering skin, which helped it melt into a more substantial glaze. But now that we had removed the skin, the second coating struggled to melt and cling to the chicken, resulting in a grainy and dry texture.

We figured that adding some fat back to the rub would be a quick fix to our problem, and since removing the skin had eliminated almost 19 grams of fat per serving from our original recipe, we had plenty of room to add a little back. Just a tablespoon of oil added to the rub before coating the chicken a second time seemed like the best way to replicate the blending of fat and the dry rub that had occurred with the skin-on chicken pieces. Sure enough, this time the rub melted into a very nice lacquer. Once the chicken was fully cooked, we let it rest, covered with foil; the residual heat melted any grains of sugar that had survived the grill. Finally, we had barbecued chicken we were eager to dig into—full of barbecue flavor and well glazed.

Barbecued Dry-Rubbed Chicken

SERVES 4

If using kosher chicken, do not brine. If brining the chicken, omit the salt in the spice rub in step 1.

- 3 tablespoons packed dark brown sugar
- 2 teaspoons chili powder
- 2 teaspoons paprika
- 1½ teaspoons pepper
- 1 teaspoon dry mustard
- 1 teaspoon onion powder
- 1 teaspoon salt
- ¼ teaspoon cayenne pepper
- 1 tablespoon canola oil
- 4 (10-ounce) bone-in split chicken breasts, ribs trimmed (see page 56), skin removed, trimmed of all visible fat, halved crosswise, and brined if desired (see page 181)

1. Combine sugar, chili powder, paprika, pepper, mustard, onion powder, salt, and cayenne in bowl. Transfer half of spice rub to second bowl, stir in oil, and set aside. Pat chicken dry with paper towels and rub evenly with remaining spice rub. Transfer chicken to plate, cover, and refrigerate for 30 minutes to 1 hour.

2A. FOR A CHARCOAL GRILL: Open bottom vent completely. Light large chimney starter half filled with charcoal briquettes (3 quarts). When top coals are partially covered with ash, pour evenly over grill. Set cooking grate in place, cover, and open lid vent completely. Heat grill until hot, about 5 minutes.

2B. FOR A GAS GRILL: Turn all burners to high, cover, and heat grill until hot, about 15 minutes. Turn all burners to medium-low.

3. Clean and oil cooking grate. Place chicken on grill and cook (covered if using gas) until browned on both sides, 15 to 20 minutes, flipping chicken halfway through cooking.

4. Flip chicken skinned side up, lightly brush top and sides with reserved rub-oil mixture, and continue to cook, covered, until rub has melted into glaze and chicken registers 160 degrees, 15 to 20 minutes longer.

5. Transfer chicken to serving platter, tent loosely with aluminum foil, and let rest for 5 to 10 minutes before serving.

PER SERVING: Cal 290; Fat 6g; Sat fat 1g; Chol 105mg; Carb 13g; Protein 43g; Fiber 1g; Sodium 720mg

HONEY-GLAZED GRILLED PORK CHOPS

WE'VE SEEN A MILLION RECIPES FOR HONEY-GLAZED grilled chops, a meal that should go over well with nearly any crowd. But that isn't the case when all you get is dry, overcooked meat and a glaze that is barely clinging on, which is what happens with most recipes. We were confident we could come up with a reliable method for producing juicy pork chops with an attractively glazed exterior that was full of rich honey flavor.

We knew bone-in chops were our best bet for grilling. In the test kitchen, we favor center-cut chops and rib chops, both of which are cut from the middle of the pig's loin. And while both are tender and flavorful, in this case our tasters preferred the center-cut chops, which were leaner but still plenty juicy.

We began by testing the different approaches to glazing the chops that we had come across. Some recipes called for dipping raw chops in a glaze of honey, sugar, and liquid (vinegar, apple juice, and brandy were common options we saw) before grilling them. These glazes melted right off. In other versions the chops were grilled naked, then painted with a honey glaze after cooking. No surprise that these didn't impress us either; these chops never developed the lacquered exterior we were after. The third method, painting the chops with glaze partway through cooking, showed the most promise. However, while these chops looked good on the surface, they were disappointingly overcooked on the inside—no doubt a result of constant exposure to high heat on the grill.

Using the best glaze from our initial tests (a combination of honey and brown sugar in equal parts, plus cider vinegar and cornstarch for thickening power), we tried to avoid the issue of overcooked chops by using a two-level fire, which provided a hotter and a cooler side of the grill. This way we could start the pork chops over high heat to brown the exterior, then move them to the cooler part to finish cooking and to coat them with the glaze.

When we pulled our chops off the grill, we were faced with mixed results. The pork was cooked properly, but the glaze was nowhere to be found. We realized that although honey is sticky at room temperature, the heat from the grill caused it to thin and melt away. For our next test, we tried reversing our method. We cooked the chops over medium-low heat, glazed them, then finished with a quick sear over high heat. We had hoped the honey would caramelize before it had a chance to melt. Unfortunately, the low heat caused the meat to slowly release moisture, which meant we had to leave the chops over the high heat longer so that the moisture could evaporate and the chops could brown. The result? Overcooked chops.

We needed a way to develop browning on the chops while avoiding excessive exposure to high heat. So we turned to a tried-and-true test kitchen technique we have found useful in encouraging browning: a sugar rub. We applied the rub to the chops before placing them on the grill. Now we were able to cook the pork chops primarily over medium-low heat, which ensured a moist interior and still achieved a deep golden brown exterior. Moreover, the crackly, sugared surface gave the glaze something to cling to. The chops needed only a quick two-minute sear over high heat, just enough time for us to brush on the glaze and let it set.

At this point our method was solid, but we needed to address flavor. Tasters demanded more honey, so we ran a side-by-side test comparing the glaze we had been using with one in which we swapped in honey for the brown sugar. Unsurprisingly, the latter had better honey

NOTES FROM THE TEST KITCHEN

GRILL TOOL HOLDER
We love our charcoal kettle grill, but we often find ourselves wishing it had a place for resting tools. Gas grills, meanwhile, have side tables and hooks for essential grilling equipment; for charcoal kettles to compete, there's the new **Weber Stainless Steel Charcoal Grill Tool Holder**, $9.99, a simple metal device that clips to the side of any kettle grill. Its solid construction and weight helped it hold tight to the grill, and it stayed cool to the touch even when hot coals were banked right beside the clips. Any tool with a loop on the end of the handle is easily attached and removed (and if your favorite tongs don't come with a loop, you can always add one).

TESTING MEAT FOR DONENESS
An instant-read thermometer is the most reliable method for checking the doneness of chicken, beef, and pork. To use an instant-read thermometer, simply insert it through the side of a chicken breast, steak, or pork chop. The chart below lists temperatures at which the meat should be removed from the heat, as the temperature of the meat will continue to climb between 5 and 10 degrees as it rests. (Cutlets cook too quickly for an actual doneness test and you will have to rely more on visual cues and cooking times.)

MEAT	COOK UNTIL IT REGISTERS	SERVING TEMPERATURE
Chicken and Turkey Breasts	160 to 165 degrees	160 to 165 degrees
Chicken Thighs	175 degrees	175 degrees
Pork	140 to 145 degrees	150 degrees
Beef		
Rare	115 to 120 degrees	125 degrees
Medium-rare	120 to 125 degrees	130 degrees
Medium	130 to 135 degrees	140 degrees
Medium-well	140 to 145 degrees	150 degrees
Well-done	150 to 155 degrees	160 degrees

flavor, but an old problem reared its head: Our glaze was running off. Why? Brown sugar has a lower water content than honey (15 percent or less, compared to honey's 17 percent), so the glaze with twice as much honey was watery, and a watery glaze doesn't adhere to a chop. To eliminate the excess water, we reached for a pot and simmered the glaze on the stovetop until the flavors were concentrated and the moisture had been removed. Now when we brushed our pork chops, the glaze stuck and it was packed with honey flavor.

To round out the flavors of our glaze, we added Dijon mustard, thyme, and cayenne pepper for some balance and bite. Then we grilled, glazed, and seared the chops until they were browned and caramelized. These glazed chops smelled fantastic and tasters couldn't wait to dig in, but we insisted first on a final brushing of glaze to put even more bold flavor into every bite.

Honey-Glazed Grilled Pork Chops

SERVES 4

If the pork is enhanced (see page 88), do not brine. If brining the pork, omit the salt in the sugar mixture in step 2.

        2   tablespoons cider vinegar
        ½   teaspoon cornstarch
        ¼   cup honey
      1½   tablespoons Dijon mustard
        ½   teaspoon minced fresh thyme
        ⅛   teaspoon cayenne pepper
        ¼   cup sugar
        1   teaspoon pepper
        ½   teaspoon salt
        4   (8-ounce) bone-in center-cut pork chops, 1 inch thick,
             trimmed of all visible fat and brined if desired
             (page 181)

1. Whisk vinegar and cornstarch together in small saucepan until no lumps remain. Stir in honey, mustard, thyme, and cayenne and bring to boil. Reduce to simmer and cook until glaze is reduced to ¼ cup, 5 to 7 minutes; cover and keep warm.

2. Combine sugar, pepper, and salt in bowl. Pat pork chops dry with paper towels and rub evenly with sugar mixture.

3A. FOR A CHARCOAL GRILL: Open bottom vent completely. Light large chimney starter filled with charcoal briquettes (6 quarts). When top coals are partially covered with ash, pour two-thirds evenly over grill, then pour remaining coals over half of grill. Set cooking grate in place, cover, and open lid vent completely. Heat grill until hot, about 5 minutes.

3B. FOR A GAS GRILL: Turn all burners to high, cover, and heat grill until hot, about 15 minutes. Leave primary burner on high and turn other burner(s) to medium-low.

4. Clean and oil cooking grate. Place pork chops on cool part of grill and cook (covered if using gas) until browned on both sides and meat registers 145 degrees, 6 to 10 minutes, flipping chops halfway through cooking. Brush pork chops with glaze, flip, and cook over hot part of grill until glaze is caramelized, about 1 minute. Brush second side with glaze, flip, and continue to cook over hot part of grill until caramelized, about 1 minute longer.

5. Transfer pork chops to platter, tent loosely with aluminum foil, and let rest for 5 to 10 minutes. Brush pork chops with remaining glaze and serve.

PER SERVING: **Cal** 430; **Fat** 11g; **Sat fat** 3.5g; **Chol** 125mg; **Carb** 32g; **Protein** 50g; **Fiber** 0g; **Sodium** 560mg

GRILL-ROASTED BONE-IN PORK RIB ROAST

NOTHING IS SIMPLER THAN A ROASTED PORK LOIN, and a juicy roast permeated with the smoke of the grill would make anyone's mouth water. And because today's pork is as lean as chicken and turkey in terms of fat and calories, all you need is a reliable recipe to put a healthy meal on the table. With that in mind, we decided to reacquaint ourselves with the pleasures of grill-roasting a pork roast. We wanted a succulent, flavor-packed roast with a well-browned crust and subtle smokiness.

We knew early on that we would work with a bone-in pork loin instead of boneless. While we couldn't complain about the convenience of a boneless pork roast— little to no butchering on the front end, and fuss-free slicing at the table—we also knew that meat cooked on the bone just tastes better. Plus, the lean meat benefits from the fat around the bones, since as the roast cooks, that fat melts and bastes the meat. Finally, the bones act as insulation. Because they conduct heat poorly, they inhibit evaporation and moisture loss from the meat attached to them, keeping the meat around them juicier.

With our bone-in pork loin in hand, our first order of business was to prepare it for the grill. Our goal was a deeply browned, crisp crust and juicy interior, so we began by trimming the outside layer of fat to ⅛ inch, just enough to melt and keep the meat moist without adding too much fat to our recipe. Scoring the fat in a crosshatch pattern would help it render and crisp. As for the juicy interior, we had two options: brining or salting. Since excess moisture on the surface of the pork would inhibit browning, we found salting to be the better option. We rubbed the meat with 4 teaspoons of kosher salt and let it rest in the refrigerator for six hours before starting the fire.

We've had a lot of experience with grill-roasting large cuts of meat, so when it came time to set up our grill we felt confident about the best technique. We would build a banked fire, banking all the coals on one side of the kettle. This left a cooler area where the meat could cook through slowly by indirect heat without risk of burning the exterior. We gave it a trial run with our bone-in loin, throwing the roast on the grates, covering the grill, and walking away. Sure enough, a little more than an hour later, the roast's internal temperature measured 140 degrees (we knew it would rise to the requisite 150 degrees as it rested). Best of all, the meat was supremely juicy and boasted a thick mahogany crust.

Next, we moved on to consider possible flavorings—though, to be honest, we weren't sure that the roast needed much improvement. The meat was tender and remarkably juicy and had plenty of rich, deep flavor. Even our dead-simple salt rub enhanced the pork's taste without distraction. But, being skeptics and perfectionists, we wanted to rule out all other options. So we set up a side-by-side test for our colleagues, pitting our plain salt-rubbed roast against identical specimens crusted with black pepper and a range of other spices and herbs. We also tested varying strengths of wood smoke. When the votes were tallied, our original intuition was confirmed: A simple roast was better. Our tasters opted for nothing more than a sprinkling of black pepper just before cooking and a subtle tinge of smoke flavor.

The latter was easy enough: We soaked one wood chunk and placed it on top of the hot coals; for our gas grill, we made a foil packet with 1 cup of soaked wood chips and placed them over the primary burner.

However, while tasters preferred a simple roast, they did suggest pairing it with a salsa for a bright accompaniment. Orange is a classic match for pork, so we started with orange segments and added a bit of red onion and jalapeño for a kick. Orange zest, lime juice, and a little white vinegar added punch and acidity, and parsley and oregano lent contrasting color and a fresh finish. To round out the flavors, a little brown sugar, garlic, and cumin did the trick. Our recipe couldn't have been easier, and tasters agreed it couldn't get much better.

NOTES FROM THE TEST KITCHEN

SCORING A BONE-IN PORK RIB ROAST

Scoring the pork loin encourages the fat to render so it can baste the meat as it cooks.

Using sharp knife, cut shallow crosshatch pattern into fat. Avoid cutting through fat and into meat, as this may result in moisture loss.

CARVING A BONE-IN PORK RIB ROAST

1. While holding tip of bones with one hand to steady roast, carve meat away from bones using sharp knife.

2. Set meat cut side down on carving board and slice crosswise, against grain, into ½-inch-thick slices.

Grill-Roasted Bone-In Pork Rib Roast with Orange Salsa

SERVES 8

For easier carving, ask the butcher to remove the tip of the chine bone. When using a charcoal grill, we prefer wood chunks to wood chips whenever possible; substitute 1 medium wood chunk, soaked in water for 1 hour, for the wood chip packet. For more information on making a wood chip packet, see page 175. For more information on cutting citrus, see page 196. To make the salsa spicier, add the reserved chile seeds.

PORK

- 1 (4-pound) bone-in center-cut pork roast, tip of chine bone removed and fat trimmed to ⅛-inch thickness
- 4 teaspoons kosher salt
- 1 cup wood chips, soaked in water for 15 minutes and drained
- 1½ teaspoons pepper

SALSA

- 5 oranges
- ½ cup finely chopped red onion
- 1 jalapeño chile, stemmed, seeds reserved, and minced
- 2 tablespoons lime juice
- 2 tablespoons minced fresh parsley
- 2 teaspoons packed brown sugar
- 1½ teaspoons white vinegar
- 1½ teaspoons minced fresh oregano
- 1 garlic clove, minced
- ½ teaspoon ground cumin
- 1 teaspoon kosher salt
- ½ teaspoon pepper

1. FOR THE PORK: Pat roast dry with paper towels. Using sharp knife, cut slits in surface of fat layer, spaced 1 inch apart, in crosshatch pattern, being careful not to cut into meat. Season roast with salt, then wrap tightly with plastic wrap and refrigerate for at least 6 hours or up to 24 hours.

2. Using large piece of heavy-duty aluminum foil, wrap soaked wood chips in foil packet and cut several vent holes in top.

3A. FOR A CHARCOAL GRILL: Open bottom vent halfway. Light large chimney starter filled with charcoal briquettes (6 quarts). When top coals are partially covered with ash, pour into steeply banked pile against side of grill. Place wood chip packet on coals. Set cooking grate in place, cover, and open lid vent halfway. Heat grill until hot and wood chips are smoking, about 5 minutes.

3B. FOR A GAS GRILL: Place wood chip packet over primary burner. Turn all burners to high, cover, and heat grill until hot and wood chips are smoking, about 15 minutes. Turn primary burner to medium-high and turn off other burner(s). (Adjust primary burner as needed to maintain grill temperature of 350 degrees.)

4. Clean and oil cooking grate. Season roast with pepper. Place roast on cool part of grill with meat near, but not over, hot part of grill and bones facing away from hot part of grill. Cover (position lid vent over meat if using charcoal) and cook until meat registers 140 degrees, 1¼ to 1½ hours.

5. FOR THE SALSA: Meanwhile, grate ½ teaspoon zest from 1 orange; set zest aside. Cut away peel and pith from all 5 oranges, then quarter oranges and slice crosswise into ½-inch-thick pieces. Combine orange pieces and remaining ingredients in bowl, cover, and refrigerate until ready to serve.

6. Transfer roast to carving board, tent loosely with foil, and let rest for 30 minutes. Carve meat off bones, then slice crosswise into ½-inch-thick slices. Serve, passing salsa separately.

PER SERVING: Cal 340; Fat 15g; Sat fat 5g; Chol 115mg; Carb 14g; Protein 36g; Fiber 2g; Sodium 810mg

GRILLED SALMON STEAKS

HAVING RECENTLY ADDED A FEW INDOOR SALMON recipes (see pages 104–107) to our light-cooking repertoire, we thought we might continue our success by creating a light salmon dish from the grill. Salmon steaks seemed like a great grilling option. While fillets are cut from one side of the fish, steaks are made by cutting crosswise through the fish. The result is a hefty skin-on piece shaped sort of like a wishbone: There's the large meaty section from above the backbone, and then two thinner strips coming down known as the belly flaps, which surrounded the backbone. The thickness of salmon steaks makes them a far sturdier cut than a fillet, a trait that is a plus when cooking on the grill. Unfortunately, that thickness can also work against them: Often, by the time the interior is cooked properly, the exterior has become blackened and dry. Additionally, the thinner belly flaps almost always overcook. And no matter how much seasoning goes on the outside, it never seems to permeate the whole steak. We set out to solve all of these problems.

We began at the fish counter. The salmon steaks sold at our local grocery store typically weigh in at roughly 12 ounces and are approximately 1½ inches thick. These portions are ideal for the grill, but not so ideal for individual light portions. We agreed that using thinner, lighter steaks was not an option since the thicker steaks' sturdy appeal was the key trait of our recipe, plus thinner steaks were hard to find. So we decided that for a dinner for four, we would simply cook two large salmon steaks, then cut them in half before serving.

Our next challenge was preparing them for the grill. The thin belly flaps of the salmon steaks were prime candidates for overcooking, but simply trimming them away removed valuable salmon meat. There had to be a better solution. Then a fellow test cook suggested tucking the flaps into the center of the steak to create a solid piece of salmon. After a little trial and error, we found that the best way to create a tidy, solid piece of salmon was to curl just one of the belly flaps into the center of the steak, then wrap the other flap around it and secure it altogether by wrapping kitchen twine around the perimeter of the steak. These neat salmon medallions cooked evenly and could be easily maneuvered on the grill. Further testing showed that removing part of the skin from the first belly flap before curling it into the center made a more cohesive steak that was easier to serve and eat. (We found it important to keep the remaining skin on the salmon during cooking to prevent it from falling apart and losing moisture.)

Out at the grill, we knew we would have to take a gentle approach with our salmon steaks. Grilling over medium-low heat produced moist, tender interiors, but at the cost of a good, flavorful sear. We needed a half-grill fire: high heat to sear the steaks, and indirect heat to finish cooking them through gently. This method took up to 20 minutes total, but these steaks were both moist and nicely browned.

Turning to flavor, we agreed that a simple but flavorful sauce was a must. We hoped to baste the salmon steaks with our sauce so that the flavor would penetrate the meat as it cooked, but we were concerned about the risk of flare-ups and burnt, stuck-to-the-grate fish.

The answer, it turned out, was to finish cooking the steaks through *off* the grate. Our trick? Employing a disposable aluminum roasting pan.

We made a light lemon-shallot sauce directly in our pan while the steaks were searing on the hot part of the grill. Then we transferred the browned fish steaks to the pan, coated them with sauce, and set the pan over the cooler part of the grill to finish cooking the salmon through. When the steaks were done, they were flavorful, juicy, and moist. But the delicate sauce still needed a boost to compete with the charred grill flavor. More lemon juice and the addition of zest and capers was a good start, but we really hit the mark when we included a little Dijon mustard and sugar and finished with a sprinkling of fresh parsley. With this foolproof recipe for zesty and succulent salmon steaks added to our grilling repertoire, we had one more great reason to put salmon on our weeknight menu.

Grilled Salmon Steaks
SERVES 4

It is important to keep the skin on the salmon during cooking to prevent it from falling apart and losing moisture.

- 2 (12-ounce) skin-on salmon steaks, 1½ inches thick
  Salt and pepper
- 1 teaspoon grated lemon zest plus 6 tablespoons juice (2 lemons)
- 3 tablespoons water
- 1 shallot, minced
- 1 tablespoon Dijon mustard
- 1 tablespoon capers, rinsed
- 2 teaspoons extra-virgin olive oil
- ½ teaspoon sugar
- 1 (13 by 9-inch) disposable aluminum roasting pan
- 2 tablespoons minced fresh parsley

1. Pat salmon dry with paper towels. Working with 1 steak at a time, carefully trim 1½ inches of skin from 1 tail. Tuck skinned portion into center of steak, wrap other tail around it, and tie steak with kitchen twine. Season salmon with ½ teaspoon salt and ¼ teaspoon pepper. Combine lemon zest, lemon juice, water, shallot, mustard, capers, oil, sugar, and ⅛ teaspoon salt in disposable pan.

2A. FOR A CHARCOAL GRILL: Open bottom vent completely. Light large chimney starter filled with charcoal briquettes (6 quarts). When top coals are partially covered with ash, pour evenly over half of grill. Set cooking grate in place, cover, and open lid vent completely. Heat grill until hot, about 5 minutes.

2B. FOR A GAS GRILL: Turn all burners to high, cover, and heat grill until hot, about 15 minutes. Leave primary burner on high and turn off other burner(s).

3. Clean and oil cooking grate. Place salmon on hot part of grill. Cook until browned on both sides, 4 to 6 minutes, flipping steaks halfway through cooking. Meanwhile, set pan on cool part of grill and let heat through, about 2 minutes. Transfer steaks to pan and gently turn to coat. Cook salmon (covered if using gas) until center is still translucent when checked with tip of paring knife and registers 125 degrees (for medium-rare), 6 to 14 minutes, flipping steaks and rotating pan halfway through cooking.

4. Transfer steaks to carving board, remove twine and skin, and cut each steak in half, discarding pin bones and small circular bone from center. Off heat, whisk parsley into sauce and transfer to serving bowl. Serve, passing sauce separately.

PER SERVING (WILD SALMON): Cal 280; Fat 13g; Sat fat 2g; Chol 95mg; Carb 5g; Protein 34g; Fiber 0g; Sodium 590mg

PER SERVING (FARMED SALMON): Cal 350; Fat 21g; Sat fat 4g; Chol 100mg; Carb 5g; Protein 34g; Fiber 0g; Sodium 620mg

---

NOTES FROM THE TEST KITCHEN

PREPARING SALMON STEAKS

1. Using sharp knife, remove 1½ inches of skin from 1 tail of each steak.

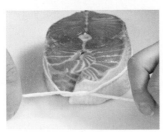

2. After tucking skinned portion into center of steak, tightly wrap other tail around it and tie steak with kitchen twine.

CUMIN-CRUSTED BLUEFISH

IF GRILLED FISH IS WHAT YOU ARE AFTER, CHANCES are that salmon, tuna, and trout are at the top of your list—they certainly are for us. Still, we were up for trying something new. Bluefish, a favorite for the grill on the northeast coast, came to mind as something we had been passing over. While bluefish is an oily fish, we knew that, just like salmon, it could also be a healthy choice when properly prepared. Given its bold flavor, we agreed it was an ideal candidate for pairing with a spice rub, a great direction to follow for a light meal.

First, we had to settle on the best way to grill bluefish. We chose skin-on fillets to give the flesh added protection, then coated them with a basic working rub: a mixture of cumin, chili powder, cayenne, salt, and pepper. For these quick-cooking fillets, we felt intense heat would be necessary in order to sear the exterior without overcooking the interior. We started with a half-grill fire on our charcoal grill, which allowed us to concentrate the coals and produce a very hot fire. For our gas grill we found that leaving all the burners on high was the best way to achieve the same intense level of heat. However, the fish fused to the cooking grate, and because the skin shrank as the fish cooked, the fillets were curling midway through, leading to burnt edges and arched, barely seared centers. Even worse was the raw flavor of the spices. Addressing the curling problem turned out to be a quick fix. Scoring the skin ensured that the fillets stayed flat and seared nicely. Next, we needed to address the pesky sticking problem.

Giving the grill plenty of time to heat up and incinerate any nasty gunk left from previous grilling helped our cause somewhat, but not enough. In previous grilling recipes where sticking was a particular problem, we had learned that we needed to first give the grates a good brushing to remove any remaining charred remnants, then take extra care to oil the grate several times so that the surface was well lubricated and glossy. Using this method better ensured that our fish would not stick and allowed us to finally grill with confidence.

"Blooming" is usually a sure bet for fixing raw-tasting spices. To bloom spices, we typically sauté them in a few tablespoons of butter or oil until they intensify in flavor and emit a fragrant aroma. Blooming before applying them to the fish worked great, but after one test we knew it required too much oil for our light recipe. We wondered if we could get similar results by lightly

CUMIN-CRUSTED BLUEFISH WITH CORN RELISH

coating the fillets in oil before adding the spice rub. In doing so, the oil would heat up while the fish cooked and bloom the spices, streamlining and lightening the method in one fell swoop. One test proved that our idea was right on the money. By the time the fillets were fully cooked, the spice rub had acquired the depth and richness we were after, without any raw flavor.

Now that we had perfectly cooked bluefish fillets, we wanted something to complement them. A sweet corn relish sounded like a perfect match. We were curious if more convenient canned or frozen corn could work as well as fresh, so we sampled relishes made with each. Fresh corn was the clear winner; its superior taste and texture made it worth the small amount of additional preparation. Red bell pepper, some scallion, and a little cilantro contributed to the base of the relish, and a vibrant lime, chipotle, and honey dressing completed the picture. This recipe was a sure way to spice up our weeknight summer grilling routine.

Cumin-Crusted Bluefish with Corn Relish

SERVES 4

Fresh corn is essential to the relish; don't be tempted to substitute frozen or canned corn here. If your fish fillets are thicker or thinner, adjust the cooking time accordingly. You can substitute snapper for the bluefish, if desired.

RELISH

    1 ear corn, kernels cut from cobs
    ½ red bell pepper, chopped fine
    2 scallions, sliced thin
    3 tablespoons minced fresh cilantro
    2 tablespoons lime juice
    ½ teaspoon minced canned chipotle chile in adobo sauce
    ½ teaspoon honey
    ½ teaspoon salt
    ½ teaspoon pepper

FISH

    4 teaspoons ground cumin
    1 teaspoon chili powder
    ¼ teaspoon cayenne pepper
    ¼ teaspoon salt
    ¼ teaspoon pepper
    4 (6-ounce) skin-on bluefish fillets, ¾ inch thick
    2 teaspoons canola oil

1. FOR THE RELISH: Mix all ingredients together in bowl until well combined. Cover and refrigerate until ready to serve.

2. FOR THE FISH: Combine cumin, chili powder, cayenne, salt, and pepper in bowl. Pat fish dry with paper towels. Using sharp knife, make shallow diagonal slashes every inch along skin side of fish, being careful not to cut into flesh. Rub both sides of fillets with oil, then rub evenly with spice mixture.

3A. FOR A CHARCOAL GRILL: Open bottom vent completely. Light large chimney starter three-quarters filled with charcoal briquettes (4½ quarts). When top coals are partially covered with ash, pour evenly over half of grill. Set cooking grate in place, cover, and open lid vent completely. Heat grill until hot, about 5 minutes.

3B. FOR A GAS GRILL: Turn all burners to high, cover, and heat grill until hot, about 15 minutes. Leave all burners on high.

4. Clean cooking grate, then repeatedly brush grate with well-oiled paper towels until grate is black and glossy, 5 to 10 times. Place fish skin side down on grill (hot part if using charcoal) with fillets diagonal to grate. Cook until skin is dark brown and crisp, 3 to 5 minutes. Carefully flip fish and continue to cook until fish flakes apart when gently prodded with paring knife and registers 140 degrees, about 5 minutes longer. Serve, passing corn relish separately.

PER SERVING: Cal 280; Fat 11g; Sat fat 2g; Chol 100mg; Carb 9g; Protein 36g; Fiber 2g; Sodium 550mg

GRILLED TUNA BURGERS

BEEF BURGERS ARE A CLASSIC WHEN IT COMES TO grilled fare, but if you are looking to eat healthier, they are usually off-limits. Fortunately there are plenty of lighter options for those looking to satisfy their juicy burger craving, with versions made out of everything from turkey or chicken to black beans. We already had great recipes for poultry burgers and black bean burgers under our belts, so now we wanted to expand our healthy burger collection even further. We had recently run across a recipe for tuna burgers and thought it was just what we were missing.

Since tuna is a special purchase on most people's grocery lists, we knew that to justify chopping up a nice piece of tuna, we needed to make sure our burgers were moist and flavorful every time. After testing several existing versions, we quickly noticed the flaws. Tuna (like most fish) can easily overcook. The tuna just ended up dry with an unappealing fishy taste. Consistency was also a problem; the tuna was either too coarse and barely held together, or cohesive but pasty. Given the high price of tuna, these were expensive problems, but we knew we could turn these burgers around and create a straightforward and reliable recipe.

We began our testing by selecting the right type of tuna for the job. Fortunately this task was easy since we had recently conducted a taste test of fresh tuna for our pan-seared tuna recipe (page 110). Yellowfin had been the clear favorite, so we picked up 1¼ pounds of skinless yellowfin tuna steaks—enough for four 5-ounce burgers—and headed into the kitchen.

As we had seen in our initial tastings, consistency was key not only for the structure of the burger, but for the final texture as well. Several recipes used the food processor to save time on chopping the tuna, and this seemed like a good idea since it had worked well in chopping up the shrimp for our Shrimp Burgers (see page 118). But it took only a few attempts to show that this wouldn't work for the tuna. In the food processor the delicate tuna didn't stand a chance; more often than not, we ended up with fish pureed to a mousselike texture. Freezing large cubes of tuna for a few minutes to firm up the delicate meat—a trick we often use when grinding meat in the food processor for burgers—helped to produce a coarser grind, but there was still a good amount of overprocessed tuna in the mix, and tasters quickly picked up on the pasty texture. In the end, we concluded that using the knife was essential. For the best results, we found that chopping the tuna into ⅛-inch pieces was ideal and enabled us to form patties that held together well without the need for binders. The uniform pieces of tuna also ensured that the burgers remained tender when cooked.

As for flavorings, simplicity was key in our minds since we wanted the tuna to shine through. After trying a variety of herbs and spices, we settled on lemon zest, minced chives, and minced garlic. These bright flavors complemented the delicate tuna perfectly. For an Asian-inspired variation, we included scallion, ginger, soy sauce, and red pepper flakes.

Now our burgers had great flavor and texture, but we needed to find the ideal way to cook them. Tuna is best served rare to medium-rare, and we were after a

nicely seared exterior with a tender, plum-red interior. Unfortunately, over a single-level fire, by the time the burgers achieved some color on the outside, the inside was already well overcooked. We had learned with our pan-seared tuna steaks that the slightest change in thickness made a huge difference, so we wondered if that issue would translate to our burgers on the grill. Bumping our burgers from 1 inch thick to 1¼ inches thick didn't seem like a big change, but after we achieved a good sear on both sides, the centers were now still rare—just what we were after. As additional insurance in achieving a well-seared exterior and rare interior, we also switched to a half-grill fire; this concentrated the heat further, allowing us to sear the burgers more quickly and thus reduce the time they spent on the grill.

All our burgers needed were some sauces to take them to the next level. We started with ¼ cup of light mayonnaise as the base for both versions. Black pepper and lemon juice worked well with our classic tuna burger, and some wasabi and rice vinegar added kick to our Asian variation. These tuna burgers were foolproof and full of flavor—certainly a great dinner off the grill even if we weren't cooking light.

Grilled Tuna Burgers

SERVES 4

We prefer the flavor and texture of yellowfin tuna here; however, any type of fresh tuna will work. Note that different types of tuna have significantly different amounts of fat and calories; the nutritional analysis for this recipe was done using yellowfin. Make sure to use a very sharp knife to chop the tuna in step 2; do not use the food processor. We prefer our tuna burgers rare; if you prefer your burgers cooked medium-rare, cook them on the second side until they are opaque at the perimeter and reddish pink at the center when checked with the tip of a paring knife and register 125 degrees, about 3 minutes. Serve with your favorite toppings.

¼ cup light mayonnaise
1 teaspoon grated lemon zest plus 1 teaspoon juice
    Salt and pepper
1¼ pounds skinless tuna steaks
2 tablespoons minced fresh chives
1 garlic clove, minced
4 hamburger buns, toasted

1. Combine mayonnaise, lemon juice, ½ teaspoon pepper, and pinch salt in bowl. Cover and refrigerate until ready to serve.

2. Using sharp knife, cut tuna into ¼-inch pieces, then continue to chop tuna until it is coarsely ground into pieces roughly ⅛ inch each. Transfer tuna to medium bowl and gently mix in lemon zest, chives, garlic, ½ teaspoon salt, and ¼ teaspoon pepper until just combined.

3. Divide mixture into 4 portions. Working with 1 portion at a time, lightly toss portion from hand to hand to form ball, then lightly flatten ball with fingertips into 1¼-inch-thick patty. Place patties on plate, cover, and refrigerate until grill is ready.

4A. FOR A CHARCOAL GRILL: Open bottom vent completely. Light large chimney starter filled with charcoal briquettes (6 quarts). When top coals are partially covered with ash, pour evenly over half of grill. Set cooking grate in place, cover, and open lid vent completely. Heat grill until hot, about 5 minutes.

4B. FOR A GAS GRILL: Turn all burners to high, cover, and heat grill until hot, about 15 minutes. Leave all burners on high.

5. Clean cooking grate, then repeatedly brush grate with well-oiled paper towels until grate is black and glossy, 5 to 10 times. Place burgers on grill (hot part if using charcoal) and cook (covered if using gas), without pressing on them, until grill marks form and bottom surface is opaque, 1 to 3 minutes.

6. Flip burgers and continue to cook until opaque at perimeter and translucent red at center when checked with tip of paring knife and the burgers register 110 degrees (for rare), about 1½ minutes longer. Place burgers on buns and serve with sauce.

PER SERVING: **Cal** 310; **Fat** 7g; **Sat fat** 1.5g; **Chol** 65mg; **Carb** 23g; **Protein** 37g; **Fiber** 1g; **Sodium** 720mg

VARIATION

Asian-Style Grilled Tuna Burgers
Substitute 1 thinly sliced scallion, 1 teaspoon rice vinegar, and 1 teaspoon wasabi paste for lemon juice and pepper in sauce. Omit chives and lemon zest. Add 1 thinly sliced scallion, 2 teaspoons grated fresh ginger, 2 teaspoons low-sodium soy sauce, and ¼ teaspoon red pepper flakes to tuna mixture.

PER SERVING: **Cal** 320; **Fat** 7g; **Sat fat** 1g; **Chol** 65mg; **Carb** 24g; **Protein** 38g; **Fiber** 1g; **Sodium** 850mg

GRILLED VEGETABLE AND ORZO SALAD

GRILLED VEGETABLES ARE THE PERFECT BASIS FOR a light supper, especially in the summertime when produce is at its height. However, there are some challenges lurking in the seemingly simple task of grilling veggies. The first challenge is cooking them to just the right point—gently charred on the outside and tender within—while avoiding blackened and mushy vegetables. Then there's the issue of flavor: Usually there's just not enough of it. Finally, there's the question of how to make a handful of vegetables into a filling entrée. We were mulling over these issues when the idea for an Italian-style vegetable and pasta salad came to mind. By pairing chunks of grilled vegetables with tender pasta, fresh herbs, and a bright vinaigrette, we figured we had the makings of a healthful and flavorful meal that could satisfy even a carnivore.

We began by picking the vegetables. Focusing on Mediterranean flavors and mindful of complementary cooking times, we matched zucchini with sweet red onion and red bell peppers. Cutting the zucchini lengthwise and the bell peppers into quarters gave us large pieces that were easy to handle on the grill. Once cooked, they would be easy enough to cut up into bite-size chunks. For the grilling itself, most recipes we found for these vegetables suggested a total of 10 minutes for both sides over high heat. But when we tried this method, our vegetables were incinerated on the outside. Trying again, we built a more moderate, medium-heat fire. Ten minutes later, our vegetables were perfectly browned and tender and full of smoky flavor. We knew from experience that threading the onion slices onto metal skewers was an easy solution to ensure that individual rings didn't fall through the cooking grate.

Next up was the pasta. After trying several shapes and sizes, we formed a strong opinion on what worked and what did not. Long-strand pastas were awkward to eat with the chunks of vegetables, and large noodles like ziti required a lot of vinaigrette to seem adequately dressed—a definite problem when trying to create a light salad. Small pasta shapes worked best, and in the end, orzo beat out the competition, giving our summery dish the look and feel we were after.

As far as cooking the orzo, we figured this would be the easy part. After all, we were just boiling pasta. However, we quickly realized that this component of our salad required a bit more attention. During testing, we noticed that its texture changed between the time it was done cooking and when it was cooled and tossed with the vegetables and dressing. Orzo cooked to al dente took on a tough, chewy texture once it had cooled. Completely tender orzo, on the other hand, cooled to a pleasant, bouncy texture, and rinsing the orzo helped to remove any excess starch and prevented it from clumping.

Now all we needed to do was put the finishing touches on our vinaigrette. Keeping with our Mediterranean theme, we started with a basic combination of lemon juice and extra-virgin olive oil and added some mustard and garlic for tanginess and chopped basil and lemon zest for freshness. All we had to do was toss everything together. Our salad was delicious at this point, though we felt it was still missing something. To balance the tangy dressing, we agreed that a little creamy feta cheese was what our salad needed. Just 2 ounces crumbled on top of the salad was the perfect finishing touch.

Grilled Vegetable and Orzo Salad with Lemon, Basil, and Feta

SERVES 4

Do not separate the onion rings. Be sure to cook the orzo until tender as it will firm up slightly once rinsed under cold water. You will need two 12-inch metal skewers for this recipe.

½   cup chopped fresh basil

3   tablespoons extra-virgin olive oil

2   teaspoons grated lemon zest plus 2 tablespoons juice

2   teaspoons Dijon mustard

1   garlic clove, minced
     Salt and pepper

1   red onion, sliced into ½-inch-thick rounds

2   red bell peppers, stemmed, seeded, and quartered

2   zucchinis, halved lengthwise
     Vegetable oil spray

1   cup orzo

2   ounces feta cheese, crumbled (½ cup)

1. Whisk basil, oil, lemon zest and juice, mustard, garlic, ½ teaspoon salt, and ¼ teaspoon pepper together in large bowl; set aside.

2. Thread onion rounds, from side to side, onto two 12-inch metal skewers. Lightly coat onion, bell peppers, and zucchini with oil spray and season with ⅛ teaspoon salt and ⅛ teaspoon pepper.

3A. FOR A CHARCOAL GRILL: Open bottom grill vent completely. Light large chimney starter half filled with charcoal briquettes (3 quarts). When top coals are partially covered with ash, pour evenly over grill. Set cooking grate in place, cover, and open lid vent completely. Heat grill until hot, about 5 minutes.

3B. FOR A GAS GRILL: Turn all burners to high, cover, and heat grill until hot, about 15 minutes. Turn all burners to medium.

4. Clean and oil cooking grate. Place vegetables on grill and cook (covered if using gas) until spottily charred on both sides, 10 to 15 minutes, flipping vegetables halfway through cooking. Transfer vegetables to carving board and remove onion from skewers.

5. Meanwhile, bring 4 quarts water to boil in large pot. Add orzo and 1 tablespoon salt and cook, stirring often, until tender. Drain orzo, rinse with cold water to cool, and drain again thoroughly. Add pasta to bowl with vinaigrette.

6. Cut vegetables into 1-inch pieces, add to bowl with pasta and vinaigrette, and gently toss to combine. Season with salt and pepper to taste. Divide salad among individual plates and sprinkle with feta. Serve.

PER SERVING: Cal 390; Fat 15g; Sat fat 4g; Chol 15mg; Carb 53g; Protein 12g; Fiber 4g; Sodium 740mg

NOTES FROM THE TEST KITCHEN

SKEWERING ONIONS FOR GRILLING

After slicing onion crosswise into ½-inch-thick rounds, slide skewer completely through each onion slice.

FARRO RISOTTO WITH FENNEL, RADICCHIO, AND BALSAMIC VINEGAR

RICE, GRAINS & BEANS

M = TEST KITCHEN MAKEOVER

RICE SALADS

RICE SALAD SHOULD BE A LIGHT AND EASY SIDE DISH with fluffy grains and an array of balanced flavors. Unfortunately, most recipes yield sticky clumps of rice coated with too much dressing with too little flavor. We wanted to create a recipe for interesting, fruit- and nut-filled rice salads that yielded perfectly cooked rice and flavorful dressings, the type of crowd-pleasing and healthy dishes you could whip up at the last minute for a potluck or weeknight dinner.

While the concept of a rice salad seems quite simple, the texture of rice, whether short- or long-grain, presents a problem from the get-go. Long-grain rice is promising since it cooks up with fluffy, individual grains, but it normally just isn't good cold; it tends to turn into a solid, clumpy mess. Both short- and medium-grain rice hold up better as they cool, but they have an inherent stickiness that you don't want in a rice salad, making them nonstarters for this situation. If we were to achieve a tender, fluffy, and light rice salad, we needed a cooking method for long-grain rice that would preserve its fresh-from-the-pan characteristics once cooled.

We started by cooking long-grain rice using the conventional absorption method (simmered in a covered pot with just enough water to cook it through). With the hope of having less sticky results, we tried rinsing the rice before cooking to remove some excess starch; this made for a slight improvement, but it still didn't produce the fluffy texture we wanted once the rice cooled.

We needed to get rid of even more starch, so we tried cooking the rice as we would pasta: boiling it in a large volume of water until it was just cooked through and then draining it. The drawback to this approach was that it tended to turn out rice that tasted waterlogged. However, we found after a few tests that the light and separate consistency of the rice held up well, and it remained fluffy after cooling—just what we were looking for. To solve the waterlogging problem, we spread the drained, still-warm rice on a baking sheet to cool off, creating a large surface area that allowed the excess moisture to evaporate. Spreading out the rice also helped guard against clumping and promoted quicker cooling.

Many basic recipes simply have you toss the cooled rice with a generic vinaigrette or bottled Italian dressing.

The results are predictably dull (and typically full of preservatives). We wanted to create a trio of rice salads that were packed with fresh flavor and healthy ingredients. We also liked the idea of using raw materials—no additional cooking required—to keep our rice salads simple enough to make for a weeknight meal or lunch on the go. Our most basic rice salad combined chopped tomatoes, fresh basil, and just a touch of Parmesan cheese. An easy balsamic vinaigrette with just 5 teaspoons of heart-healthy extra-virgin olive oil added a tangy kick and coated the rice perfectly.

We went a little nutty from there, adding pistachios and almonds, respectively, to the next two versions of our salad. High in protein and antioxidants, tree nuts like these are great sources of unsaturated fat (i.e., "good fats"). They do contribute to the overall fat content of the salad, however, so we used a light hand, keeping the amounts to just ¼ cup in each salad. We matched the pistachios with dates, orange juice, and cinnamon for an exotic Persian flavor, and the almonds figured prominently in a salad with juicy orange segments and green olives that created a Mediterranean feel.

Packed with bright flavor and toothsome rice, these rice salads are a far cry from boring, sticky salad-bar rice salads you've had in the past. What's more, they'll fill you up with deliciously healthy ingredients with only a modicum of work required—weeknight (or picnic) perfection!

NOTES FROM THE TEST KITCHEN

CUTTING CITRUS INTO PIECES

1. Slice off top and bottom of orange or tangerine, then cut away rind and pith using paring knife.

2. Quarter peeled orange or tangerine, then slice each quarter crosswise into ½-inch-thick pieces.

Rice Salad with Tomato, Parmesan, and Basil

SERVES 6

Taste the rice as it nears the end of its cooking time; it should be cooked through and firm, but not crunchy. We recommend regular long-grain rice, but basmati rice will work as well.

1¼ cups long-grain white rice
    Salt and pepper
  1 tomato, cored, seeded, and cut into ½-inch pieces
  1 ounce Parmesan cheese, grated (½ cup)
  ¼ cup shredded fresh basil
  4 teaspoons balsamic vinegar
  1 garlic clove, minced
  5 teaspoons extra-virgin olive oil

1. Bring 3 quarts water to boil in large pot. Add rice and 1 teaspoon salt and boil, stirring occasionally, until rice is just tender, 9 to 12 minutes. Drain rice well, spread on rimmed baking sheet, and let cool to room temperature, about 30 minutes.

2. Toss cooled rice, tomato, Parmesan, and basil together in large bowl. Whisk vinegar, garlic, and ½ teaspoon salt together in small bowl. Whisking constantly, drizzle in oil. Pour dressing over salad and toss to combine. Season with salt and pepper to taste and serve.

PER ¾-CUP SERVING: Cal 190; Fat 5g; Sat fat 1g; Chol 5mg; Carb 31g; Protein 4g; Fiber 0g; Sodium 360mg

VARIATIONS

Rice Salad with Dates and Pistachios

SERVES 6

Taste the rice as it nears the end of its cooking time; it should be cooked through and firm, but not crunchy. We recommend regular long-grain rice, but basmati rice will work as well.

1¼ cups long-grain white rice
    Salt and pepper
  4 scallions, chopped
  ¼ cup pistachios, toasted and chopped
  ¼ cup chopped dates
  ¼ cup minced fresh parsley
  ½ teaspoon grated orange zest plus 2 tablespoons juice
  4 teaspoons lemon juice
  ⅛ teaspoon ground cinnamon
  5 teaspoons extra-virgin olive oil

1. Bring 3 quarts water to boil in large pot. Add rice and 1 teaspoon salt and boil, stirring occasionally, until rice is just tender, 9 to 12 minutes. Drain rice well, spread on rimmed baking sheet, and let cool to room temperature, about 30 minutes.

2. Toss cooled rice, scallions, pistachios, dates, and parsley together in large bowl. Whisk orange zest, orange juice, lemon juice, cinnamon, and ½ teaspoon salt together in small bowl. Whisking constantly, drizzle in oil. Pour dressing over salad and toss to combine. Season with salt and pepper to taste and serve.

PER ¾-CUP SERVING: Cal 220; Fat 6g; Sat fat 1g; Chol 0mg; Carb 38g; Protein 4g; Fiber 2g; Sodium 290mg

Rice Salad with Oranges, Olives, and Almonds

SERVES 6

Taste the rice as it nears the end of its cooking time; it should be cooked through and firm, but not crunchy. We recommend regular long-grain rice, but basmati rice will work as well. For more information on cutting oranges into pieces, see page 196.

1¼ cups long-grain white rice
    Salt and pepper
  2 oranges
  ¼ cup pitted green olives, chopped coarse
  ¼ cup slivered almonds, toasted
  1 tablespoon minced fresh oregano
  1 tablespoon sherry vinegar
  1 garlic clove, minced
  5 teaspoons extra-virgin olive oil

1. Bring 3 quarts water to boil in large pot. Add rice and 1 teaspoon salt and boil, stirring occasionally, until rice is just tender, 9 to 12 minutes. Drain rice well, spread on rimmed baking sheet, and let cool to room temperature, about 30 minutes.

2. Grate ¼ teaspoon zest from 1 orange; set aside. Cut away peel and pith from both oranges. Quarter oranges, then slice crosswise into ½-inch-thick pieces. Toss cooled rice, oranges, olives, almonds, and oregano together in large bowl. Whisk vinegar, garlic, orange zest, and ¼ teaspoon salt together in small bowl. Whisking constantly, drizzle in oil. Pour dressing over salad and toss to combine. Season with salt and pepper to taste and serve.

PER ¾-CUP SERVING: Cal 220; Fat 7g; Sat fat 0.5g; Chol 0mg; Carb 36g; Protein 4g; Fiber 2g; Sodium 270mg

SESAME SUSHI RICE

WHEN WE THINK OF EATING SUSHI, THE FIRST THING that usually springs to mind is the fresh raw fish. But technically, the term *sushi* refers to the seasoned rice that accompanies that fish. This style of rice stands apart from the pilafs and plain long-grain rice staples we're used to serving as a side dish here in the States. Sushi rice's delicate seasoning balances sweet, salty, and tart, and coupled with its pleasantly sticky but firm texture, it makes for an appealing change of pace, perfect for serving with seafood, pork, or any Asian-inspired dish. We decided it was time to tackle this Japanese staple and bring it into the spotlight.

A little research into traditional recipes told us that sushi rice isn't actually all that hard to make, but as with a number of "simple" recipes, the devil is in the details. In order to achieve rice with the proper sticky-yet-firm texture—without turning it gummy—and a flavor that was fresh and light, we had a few tasks before us: We would need to find the best rice for the job, determine the ideal cooking method, and settle on the best balance of seasonings.

First up, the rice. Sushi rice isn't a single rice at all, but rather a blanket term to describe any of the short-grain rice varieties traditionally used in making sushi. Imported Japanese short-grain rice (typically labeled "Japonica") and California-grown japonica are both widely available in U.S. supermarkets these days, so shopping wasn't necessarily an issue, but still, we had to wonder if these sushi rices are de facto the best choice, or could another variety fill the bill? Numerous cookbooks suggest that several Italian varieties of short-grain rice are as suitable for sushi rice as they are for risotto. We thought they were all worth a test.

Working with a standard-issue sticky rice recipe from a traditional Japanese cookbook, we tested a variety of available short-grain rices. Not surprisingly, Japanese sushi rice had a great balance between firmness and stickiness without being mushy. Italian *vialone nano,* which is a smaller grain than *carnaroli* or Arborio, was the most similar to sushi rice in terms of firmness and starch, although some tasters didn't think it had quite enough of a cohesive texture for this application. The other varieties we tried, carnaroli and Arborio (both favorites for making risotto), didn't fare so well. While some enjoyed the pleasant chew of carnaroli,

others complained it had a gummy, mushy texture. And Arborio was the tasters' least favorite rice of the bunch; everyone agreed it was gummy, starchy, and slightly undercooked. Obviously, all short-grain rices are not created equal. Either a traditional Japanese variety like *koshihikari* or California-grown rice like calrose was a clear winner for our side dish (both easily found at the supermarket). In a pinch, though, Italian-grown vialone nano would be acceptable (it is available from specialty stores).

Satisfied with our choice of rice, we broached the next question: Is it imperative to rinse the rice before cooking? We often rinse rice and grains before cooking to remove excess starch so that the grains stay separate—ideal when cooking long-grain rice for a pilaf. So we were surprised to find that nearly every sushi rice recipe we came across likewise included instructions to rinse the rice. This step seemed counterintuitive to producing "sticky" rice, but sure enough, a side-by-side test of rinsed and unrinsed rice proved tradition has it right. Why? Short-grain rice naturally has more starch within each grain than long-grain, so it inherently develops a stickier texture. Rinsing removes surface starch (and additives) that, if left on the rice prior to cooking, lead to an unappealing gummy texture. Our tasting confirmed that unrinsed short-grain rice was in fact slightly gummier, while the rinsed rice was appropriately sticky without being starchy.

Sushi rice is often made in a rice cooker, but we wanted to perfect a simple recipe that would deliver perfectly sticky yet firm grains on the stovetop, no specialty cookware required. It seemed that a gentle method of cooking would be the best way to cook the rice to the correct texture without stirring up the grains and releasing more starch into the liquid. The absorption method seemed like the best answer. This two-step cooking method involves simmering the rice until about 80 percent of the water is absorbed, then letting it sit off the heat, covered, to give the rice time to absorb the remaining water. While too much water can leave rice gummy, too little water is a recipe for undercooking. We decided to start testing by cooking a batch with a very close ratio of water to rice: 2½ cups water to 2 cups rice. We watched the rice simmer until most of the water was absorbed, which took about six minutes, and then covered it to let the rice absorb the rest of the water. Fifteen minutes later, the water was gone, but the rice was still crunchy. For our next test, we increased the water to 3 cups and were pleased when we lifted the lid to find perfectly cooked rice.

But achieving properly cooked rice was only part of the battle. We still needed to nail down the *sushi-su*, the seasoned vinegar dressing that gives the rice its appealingly bright flavor. Traditionally composed of rice vinegar, sugar, salt, *dashi* (a traditional type of stock made with dried tuna flakes and seaweed), and sometimes mirin, the sushi-su is gently folded into the cooling rice so that the flavors are absorbed and infuse each grain. While we liked the umami that dashi brought to the mix, we wanted to keep the ingredients simple and accessible. We wondered if we could use another ingredient to replace the deep dashi flavor. Soy sauce discolored the rice and made the dish too salty, but toasted sesame oil added depth of flavor and contrasted with the sweetness and tang of the sugar, rice vinegar, and mirin. We found that switching from plain rice vinegar to seasoned rice vinegar, which already contains sugar, gave the sushi-su a flavor boost and eliminated the need for extra sugar.

Our sushi-su ingredients together, all that was left to do was mix it into the rice. The mixture is traditionally heated to dissolve the sugar and salt into the other ingredients and make it easier for the rice to absorb, but it seemed silly to pull out a saucepan because of a few tablespoons of liquid. We decided to microwave the vinegar, mirin, and salt together and add the sesame oil to the rice at room temperature (heating the sesame oil would damage its flavor compounds). While traditional sushi rice recipes involve a special wooden bowl and paddle for cooling the rice and folding in the sushi-su, we wanted the option of serving our rice warm for a more all-purpose side dish. We found that gently folding the vinegar mixture into the rice in the warm saucepan worked just fine and reduced the odds of overworking the rice, which would likely make it gummy.

Since we planned to serve this sushi rice as a side dish, we thought it looked a little unfinished. We added a sprinkling of toasted sesame seeds to reinforce the sesame flavor and add texture, and we turned to sliced scallions to add green freshness and crunch. Full of flavor and perfectly sticky, our Sesame Sushi Rice was the answer to boring rice side dishes. Next goal? Mastering chopsticks …

Sesame Sushi Rice
SERVES 6

Short-grain rice contains a higher percentage of starch than other varieties, which is what gives sushi rice its trademark stickiness. Handle the cooked rice very gently and do not stir it too much when adding the flavorings in step 2, or the rice will turn gluey.

- 3 cups water
- 2 cups sushi rice, rinsed and drained
- 3 tablespoons seasoned rice vinegar
- 2 tablespoons mirin
- ½ teaspoon salt
- 4 scallions, sliced thin
- 4 teaspoons toasted sesame oil
- 2 teaspoons sesame seeds, toasted

1. Bring water and rice to boil in medium saucepan over medium-high heat. Cover, reduce heat to low, and cook for 6 minutes. Remove rice from heat and let sit, covered, until tender, about 15 minutes.

2. Meanwhile, microwave vinegar, mirin, and salt together in bowl until hot, about 30 seconds. Gently fold hot vinegar mixture, scallions, sesame oil, and sesame seeds into rice and serve.

PER ¾-CUP SERVING: Cal 290; Fat 4g; Sat fat 0.5g; Chol 0mg; Carb 57g; Protein 5g; Fiber 2g; Sodium 350mg

FLUFFY COUSCOUS

DESPITE ITS NORTH AFRICAN ROOTS AS A CLASSIC match for hearty stews and braises, couscous has gone mainstream, a favorite when looking for a light, healthy, and fast side dish. The tiny grains of pasta, made by rubbing together moistened semolina granules, readily adapt to any number of flavorful add-ins, from grassy fresh herbs like cilantro and parsley to heady spices like cumin and coriander, and sweeter elements like raisins and dates. Today, boxes of couscous are readily available at the supermarket, often sold with a prepared seasoning packet for ease and convenience. From box to bowl, the entire preparation takes about five minutes.

At least that's what the back-of-the-box instructions say. We quickly realized that such convenience comes at a cost. No matter how precisely we followed the directions—measure and boil water, stir in couscous, cover and let stand off the heat for five minutes, fluff with a fork—the results were discouragingly similar to wet sand: bland, blown-out pebbles that stuck together in clumps. And it wasn't just one brand's poor instructions. Every package spelled out the same steps. Plus, the seasonings we found sold in some brands struck us as lackluster and tired.

The problem, it turns out, is in the processing. According to traditional couscous-making practices, the uncooked grains are steamed twice in a double boiler–shaped vessel called a *couscoussière*, from which the grains emerge fluffy and separate. The commercial staple we find on grocery store shelves, however, is far more processed: The grains are flash-steamed and dried before packaging. When exposed to the rigors of further cooking, this parcooked couscous—more or less a convenience product—turns to mush. That's why the package instructions are so simple: A quick reconstitution in boiling water is all the grains can stand. It didn't take an expert on North African cuisine to know that couscous has far more potential than our efforts were suggesting.

First, to bring some much-needed flavor to the dish, we banished any idea of using a prepared seasoning packet. We bought a package of plain couscous, then started by dry-toasting the grains in a pan with the hope of adding flavor, then we stirred in boiling water. Toasting got us nowhere: The grains burned before they had a chance to develop any flavor. Then we recalled a popular trick used on another grain that, without some finesse, can also cook up woefully bland: rice. The "pilaf method," according to widely accepted rice and grain cookery, calls for briefly sautéing the grains in hot fat before liquid is introduced. Most pilaf recipes use butter, but we opted to use heart-healthy extra-virgin olive oil in our next batch of couscous. Just 4 teaspoons coated the grains nicely, allowing them to brown gently and uniformly and helping them cook up fluffy and separate. (Plus, with oil in the pan, we could briefly sauté all sorts of add-ins, like spices, garlic, shallots, and even grated carrot.) To bump up the flavor further, we replaced half of the water called for in the box instructions with chicken broth (low sodium, of course).

Satisfied with the recipe, but not the two dirty pans in the sink, we had one more hurdle to clear. Given that the dish took all of five minutes to cook, we were determined to do better when it came to cleanup. The solution? Since the saucepan was already hot from sautéing the grains, why not simply add room-temperature liquid to it instead of going to the trouble to heat the liquid in a separate pan? Sure enough, that did it. The residual heat from the pan boiled the liquid almost instantly—it was like deglazing a skillet after searing. On went the lid, and after a brief rest and a quick fluff with a fork, the couscous was done. With the technique established, we developed simple flavor variations by adding nuts, dried fruit, and lemon zest, all carefully calculated to keep our recipes healthy.

Couscous with Shallots, Garlic, and Almonds
SERVES 6

For the fluffiest texture, use a large fork to fluff the grains; a spoon or spatula can destroy the light texture. For a vegetarian version, substitute vegetable broth for the chicken broth.

4	teaspoons extra-virgin olive oil
3	shallots, sliced thin
1	garlic clove, minced
1½	cups couscous
1	cup water
¾	cup low-sodium chicken broth
	Salt and pepper
⅓	cup sliced almonds, toasted
¼	cup minced fresh parsley
½	teaspoon grated lemon zest plus 2 teaspoons juice

1. Heat oil in medium saucepan over medium-high heat until shimmering. Add shallots and cook, stirring often, until softened and lightly browned, 3 to 5 minutes. Stir in garlic and cook until fragrant, about 30 seconds. Add couscous and cook, stirring often, until grains are just beginning to brown, 3 to 5 minutes.

2. Add water, broth, and ½ teaspoon salt; stir briefly to combine, cover, and remove pan from heat. Let sit until grains are tender, about 7 minutes. Uncover and fluff grains with fork. Gently stir in almonds, parsley, lemon zest, and lemon juice. Season with pepper to taste and serve.

PER ¾-CUP SERVING: Cal 250; Fat 6g; Sat fat 0.5g; Chol 0mg; Carb 43g; Protein 8g; Fiber 3g; Sodium 270mg

Couscous with Dried Cherries and Pecans

Omit shallots. Increase garlic to 2 cloves and add ¾ teaspoon garam masala, pinch cayenne pepper, and ¼ cup coarsely chopped dried cherries to saucepan along with garlic. Substitute 3 tablespoons coarsely chopped toasted pecans and 2 thinly sliced scallions for almonds, parsley, and lemon zest.

PER ¾-CUP SERVING: Cal 240; Fat 6g; Sat fat 0.5g; Chol 0mg; Carb 40g; Protein 7g; Fiber 3g; Sodium 270mg

Couscous with Carrots, Raisins, and Pine Nuts

Omit shallots and garlic. Add 2 grated carrots and ½ teaspoon ground cinnamon to oil and cook, stirring frequently, until carrots soften, about 2 minutes. Add ¼ cup raisins to saucepan with couscous and increase water to 1¼ cups. Substitute ¼ cup toasted pine nuts, 3 tablespoons minced fresh cilantro, ¼ teaspoon grated orange zest, and 1 tablespoon orange juice for almonds, parsley, and lemon zest.

PER ¾-CUP SERVING: Cal 260; Fat 7g; Sat fat 1g; Chol 0mg; Carb 42g; Protein 7g; Fiber 4g; Sodium 290mg

EASY PARMESAN POLENTA

IT'S HARD TO BEAT THE SIMPLE, HOMEY APPEAL OF polenta and its nutty corn flavor. While it is sometimes cooked into firm squares that are grilled or fried, we are big fans of the style cooked to a more porridgelike consistency. It can serve as a great foil to a stew or as a base for all manner of toppings. Though often embellished with butter and cheese, we thought it was a dish with great potential for a hearty but light recipe that would work well as a main or side. We set out to perfect our cooking method, and at the same time we wanted to develop a few toppings that were big on flavor but low on fat. We started by focusing on the polenta.

The recipe for polenta sounds easy: Boil water, whisk in cornmeal, and stir until softened. But it's not entirely simple. Polenta can take up to an hour to cook, and if you don't stir almost constantly, it forms intractable clumps. We wanted to find a better way. We tried a shortcut with parboiled "instant" brands, but tasters complained they were gluey, with lackluster flavor. Finding other options wasn't easy; the typical supermarket offers a bewildering assortment of products.

The same dried ground corn can be called anything from yellow grits to polenta to corn semolina. Labels also advertise "fine," "medium," and "coarse" grinds, but we discovered that no standards exist. Then there's the choice between whole grain and degerminated. So, we tried it all. We eventually settled on the couscous-size grains of coarse-ground degerminated cornmeal (often labeled "yellow grits"). They delivered the hearty yet soft texture we were looking for, plus plenty of nutty corn flavor. The only downside: The grains took an hour to cook, during which time the mixture grew overly thick, and stirring became tedious. We had been sticking to the typical 4:1 ratio of water to cornmeal. After experimenting, we found that a 5:1 ratio (7½ cups water to 1½ cups cornmeal) produced the right loose consistency.

Now the hard part: whittling down the cooking time and stirring. Since we couldn't raise the heat without burning the cornmeal, we turned to the cornmeal itself. There had to be a way to give that water a head start on penetrating the grains, which is the key for the grains to soften and release their starches, thus resulting in the classic porridgelike texture. We tried soaking the cornmeal in water overnight (as we would beans), but the results didn't help enough to make the step worth it.

Casting about for ideas, we came back to beans. Since the goal in cooking dried beans and dried corn is essentially identical, could we use baking soda to help water penetrate the corn's endosperm, just as we use it to soften the beans' outer skin? We added ¼ teaspoon of baking soda to the cooking water as soon as it came to a boil. This polenta cooked up in 20 minutes, but it was overkill, turning the cooked porridge gluey and adding

---

NOTES FROM THE TEST KITCHEN

TAMING THE FLAME

A flame tamer (or heat diffuser) is a metal disk fitted over an electric or gas burner to reduce the heat to a bare simmer, a necessity for well-made polenta. If you don't have a flame tamer, you can easily make one.

Take a long sheet of heavy-duty foil and shape it into a 1-inch-thick ring that will fit on your burner. Make sure that the ring is of an even thickness so that the pot will rest flat on it.

EASY PARMESAN POLENTA WITH BROCCOLI RABE, SUN-DRIED TOMATOES, AND PINE NUTS

a strange flavor. We found that even ⅛ teaspoon of soda was excessive. Just a pinch turned out to be plenty, producing polenta that cooked in a mere 30 minutes without any gluey texture or objectionable flavors.

While conventional wisdom insists that polenta must be stirred constantly, we found that if we covered the pot with a lid and turned the heat to low, the polenta could sputter untouched for nearly the entire 30 minutes. The baking soda helps the granules break down and release their starch in a uniform way so that the bottom layer doesn't cook any faster than the top, and cooking over low heat, covered, gave us polenta that was lump-free, even without vigorous stirring. After one relatively brief whisk as soon as the ingredients went into the pot and another five minutes later, we didn't even have to lift the lid until it was time to add the cheese. And in that regard, since we were trying to keep our polenta on the light side, we limited the cheese to a single cup of grated Parmesan plus a pat of butter for a nutty tang and slight richness (most recipes have twice the amount of both).

From here, we came up with some savory but healthy toppings to turn our polenta into a meal or a filling side. A quick sauté of broccoli rabe, sun-dried tomatoes, and pine nuts makes for a hearty winter bowl, and our second variation with zucchini, cherry tomatoes, and Parmesan gives the dish a more summery feel. Served with or without a topping, this no-fuss polenta delivers satisfying results with the barest amount of effort.

Easy Parmesan Polenta

SERVES 8

Coarse-ground degerminated cornmeal such as yellow grits (with grains the size of couscous) works best in this recipe. Avoid instant and quick-cooking products, as well as whole grain, stone-ground, and regular cornmeal. Do not omit the baking soda—it reduces the cooking time and makes for a creamier polenta. If the heat is too high, you may need a flame tamer, available at most kitchen supply stores. Alternatively, you can fashion your own from a ring of foil (see page 201).

7½ **cups water**
    Salt and pepper
    Pinch baking soda
1½ **cups coarse-ground cornmeal**
2   **ounces good-quality Parmesan cheese, grated (1 cup)**
1   **tablespoon unsalted butter**

1. Bring water to boil in heavy-bottomed 4-quart saucepan over medium-high heat. Stir in ½ teaspoon salt and baking soda. Slowly pour cornmeal into water in steady stream, while stirring back and forth with wooden spoon or rubber spatula. Bring mixture to boil, stirring constantly, about 1 minute. Cover and reduce heat to lowest possible setting.

2. Cook for 5 minutes, then whisk polenta to smooth out any lumps, about 15 seconds. (Make sure to scrape down sides and bottom of pan.) Cover and continue to cook, without stirring, until polenta is tender but slightly al dente, about 25 minutes longer. (Polenta should be loose and barely hold its shape but will continue to thicken as it cools.)

3. Off heat, stir in Parmesan and butter and season with salt and pepper to taste. Let sit, covered, for 5 minutes before serving.

PER ¾-CUP SERVING: Cal 130; Fat 3.5g; Sat fat 2g; Chol 10mg; Carb 22g; Protein 4g; Fiber 2g; Sodium 260mg

VARIATIONS

Easy Parmesan Polenta with Sautéed Zucchini and Cherry Tomatoes

SERVES 4 AS A MAIN DISH OR 8 AS A SIDE DISH

3   **zucchini or summer squash, halved lengthwise and sliced ½ inch thick**
    Salt and pepper
1   **tablespoon extra-virgin olive oil**
2   **garlic cloves, peeled and sliced thin**
    Pinch red pepper flakes
    Pinch sugar
12 **ounces cherry tomatoes, halved**
1   **recipe Easy Parmesan Polenta**
2   **tablespoons shredded fresh basil**
2   **ounces Parmesan cheese, shaved**

1. Toss zucchini with ¼ teaspoon salt in medium bowl; transfer to large colander set over bowl and let sit for 30 minutes. Pat zucchini dry with paper towels.

2. Heat 1 teaspoon oil in 12-inch nonstick skillet over medium-high heat until just smoking. Add half of zucchini and cook, stirring occasionally, until golden brown and slightly charred, 5 to 7 minutes; transfer to large plate. Add 1 teaspoon oil to now-empty skillet and repeat with remaining zucchini.

3. Add remaining 1 teaspoon oil, garlic, pepper flakes, and sugar to now-empty skillet and cook until fragrant, about 30 seconds. Stir in tomatoes and cook until they just begin to soften, about 1 minute. Stir in zucchini and toss to combine. Off heat, season with salt and pepper to taste. Spoon tomato mixture with any accumulated juices over polenta, sprinkle with basil, top with shaved Parmesan, and serve.

PER SIDE-DISH SERVING (¾ CUP POLENTA, ½ CUP TOPPING): Cal 190; Fat 7g; Sat fat 3.5g; Chol 15mg; Carb 27g; Protein 8g; Fiber 3g; Sodium 440mg

PER MAIN-COURSE SERVING (1½ CUPS POLENTA, 1 CUP TOPPING): Cal 390; Fat 15g; Sat fat 7g; Chol 25mg; Carb 53g; Protein 16g; Fiber 6g; Sodium 880mg

Easy Parmesan Polenta with Broccoli Rabe, Sun-Dried Tomatoes, and Pine Nuts
SERVES 4 AS A MAIN DISH OR 8 AS A SIDE DISH

- ⅓ **cup oil-packed sun-dried tomatoes, rinsed, patted dry, and chopped coarse**
- 4 **garlic cloves, minced**
- 1 **tablespoon extra-virgin olive oil**
- ¼ **teaspoon red pepper flakes**
  Salt
- 1 **pound broccoli rabe, trimmed and cut into 1½-inch pieces**
- ¼ **cup low-sodium chicken broth**
- 1 **recipe Easy Parmesan Polenta (page 203)**
- 2 **tablespoons pine nuts, toasted**

1. Heat sun-dried tomatoes, garlic, oil, pepper flakes, and ¼ teaspoon salt in 12-inch nonstick skillet over medium-high heat, stirring often, until garlic is fragrant and slightly toasted, about 1½ minutes. Add broccoli rabe and broth, cover, and cook until broccoli rabe turns bright green, about 2 minutes.

2. Uncover and cook, stirring often, until most of broth has evaporated and broccoli rabe is just tender, 2 to 4 minutes. Season with salt to taste. Serve over polenta, sprinkling individual portions with pine nuts.

PER SIDE-DISH SERVING (¾ CUP POLENTA, ⅓ CUP TOPPING): Cal 190; Fat 7g; Sat fat 2.5g; Chol 10mg; Carb 26g; Protein 7g; Fiber 2g; Sodium 380mg

PER MAIN-COURSE SERVING (1½ CUPS POLENTA, ¾ CUP TOPPING): Cal 380; Fat 15g; Sat fat 5g; Chol 15mg; Carb 52g; Protein 14g; Fiber 4g; Sodium 760mg

FARRO RISOTTO

WE'RE BIG FANS OF A CREAMY, VELVETY RISOTTO (we'd already created a fantastic lighter Seafood Risotto, page 121), but sometimes we crave a grain similarly rich and indulgent yet a little more rustic. Yet we don't want to settle for the somewhat everydayness of brown rice. In our search for a grain that falls somewhere between the two, we came across farro. A whole grain relative of wheat, farro emigrated from central Italy to the United States about a decade ago, though only in the past few years has it gained widespread popularity, appearing on more and more restaurant menus as well as in supermarkets. Italians, who have enjoyed farro for centuries, prepare the grain much as they do Arborio rice for risotto, by cooking the farro slowly into a creamy dish called *farrotto*. The apparent difference between the two, and thus farro's appeal to us, lay in the heartier nutty flavor and more satisfying chew of the farro. We set out to come up with an easy-to-make, accessible farrotto recipe of our own, one that took half an hour or less yet still produced a dish that was creamy and rich, while highlighting farro's unique flavor and texture.

It made sense to begin with the test kitchen's risotto cooking method. It was definitely simple; there were two additions of warmed liquid and a few stirs, in comparison to the fussier traditional cooking method of incremental additions of liquid and constant stirring. But the 5 cups of warmed liquid added at the beginning was far too much for the farro. It was all liquid and no creamy sauce, and the fact that this recipe used the lid (relying on residual heat to finish the cooking) only worsened the issue. If we cut back on the liquid, the grains cooked unevenly. The farro clearly required less liquid than Arborio rice, and because of this lesser amount of liquid, stirring was going to be a must to ensure even cooking.

For the next test, we tried an older test kitchen risotto method, which called for less liquid than the new method, no lid, and more (though not nonstop) stirring. We started by sautéing onions until soft, then added the farro, toasted the grains briefly, and poured in a splash of wine for depth. We ladled about half of the warmed broth (3 cups) into the pot, let it simmer for a full 12 minutes, and gave it just a few stirs. The last few minutes of cooking saw incremental broth additions and constant stirring. This method was the best yet, producing tender, evenly cooked grains with a subtle chew, and they were swimming in a creamy, but not gummy, sauce. After a few rounds of tests, we found that a roughly 2:1 ratio of liquid to grain was just right, and because the acidic wine conflicted with the farro's flavor, we dropped it and stuck with just water and broth. Tasters were impressed that the transformation took just 25 minutes.

We were close, but we still hoped to streamline the method. Could we add the liquid all at once at room temperature, instead of heating it in a separate pot and adding it in batches? For the next run-through we added all the liquid (unheated) to the grains in the pot, stirred the mixture often, and cooked it without a lid (the lid made no sense since we were stirring so frequently). This took exactly the same amount of time as the previous test, the results looked identical, and tasters couldn't tell the difference. We had found our shortcut.

With the simplified method in place, we turned our focus to flavorings. While onions were certainly a good start, we felt that a few more aromatics might give the dish more depth. Tasters liked garlic and thyme, but the risotto needed something to punch up the flavor. Up to this point we had been finishing the farro side dish in the classic risotto style with butter and Parmesan, and while tasters liked the buttery richness, some felt it masked the subtle nuttiness of the farro, not to mention it add unwanted calories, fat, and sodium. So, we reduced the Parmesan to just ½ cup and omitted the butter entirely. Then, to kick things in a decidedly different direction, we went with a fresher finish, adding peppery arugula, minced fresh parsley, lemon zest, and lemon juice. Tasters unanimously preferred this lighter, brighter—yet still rich and creamy—version. We had finally arrived at a satisfying, accessible, and light side dish that paid proper homage to this ancient grain.

NOTES FROM THE TEST KITCHEN

"BOIL" VERSUS "SIMMER"
Cooking grains properly requires just the right method, and that includes knowing where to draw the line between boil and simmer. Boiling liquid bubbles energetically. A medium-high to high heat setting is used to achieve and maintain a boil. In a simmer, fewer bubbles break the surface and do so with less vigor. For a simmer, depending on the size of the pot and its contents, the liquid is usually first brought to a boil, then the heat is reduced to medium-low or low.

Farro Risotto with Arugula, Lemon, and Parmesan
SERVES 5

For a creamy texture, be sure to stir the risotto often in step 2.

- 1 onion, chopped fine
- 1 tablespoon olive oil
  Salt and pepper
- 3 garlic cloves, minced
- 1 teaspoon minced fresh thyme
- 1½ cups farro
- 2 cups low-sodium chicken broth
- 1½ cups water
- 2 ounces (2 cups) baby arugula
- 1 ounce Parmesan cheese, grated (½ cup)
- 2 tablespoons minced fresh parsley
- ½ teaspoon grated lemon zest plus 1 teaspoon juice

1. Combine onion, oil, and ¼ teaspoon salt in large saucepan. Cover and cook over medium-low heat, stirring occasionally, until onion is softened, 8 to 10 minutes. Stir in garlic and thyme and cook until fragrant, about 30 seconds.

2. Stir in farro and cook until lightly toasted, about 2 minutes. Stir in broth and water and bring to simmer. Reduce heat to low and continue to simmer, stirring often, until farro is tender, 20 to 25 minutes.

3. Off heat, stir in arugula, Parmesan, parsley, lemon zest, and lemon juice. Season with salt and pepper to taste and serve.

PER ¾-CUP SERVING: Cal 270; Fat 6g; Sat fat 1g; Chol 5mg; Carb 47g; Protein 10g; Fiber 6g; Sodium 430mg

VARIATION

Farro Risotto with Fennel, Radicchio, and Balsamic Vinegar

Add 1 fennel bulb, stalks discarded and bulb halved, cored, and chopped fine, to saucepan along with onion in step 1. Substitute ½ small head thinly sliced radicchio for arugula and 2 teaspoons balsamic vinegar for lemon juice.

PER ¾-CUP SERVING: Cal 280; Fat 5g; Sat Fat 0g; Chol 0mg; Carb 54g; Protein 9g; Fiber 8g; Sodium 390mg

HERBED BARLEY PILAF

BARLEY HAS BEEN AROUND FOR THOUSANDS OF years, but today we probably come across it most often in beer, whiskey, or soups. Convinced that this nutritious, hearty grain was being woefully underutilized, we decided to explore other ways to incorporate barley into our diet. It is most often cooked like beans or pasta—in a large pot of salted, boiling water. The resulting grains have an interesting, chewy texture but, sadly, not much flavor. We wondered if the key to making barley more flavorful (and more likely to be incorporated into weeknight meals) was to treat it like rice, rather than pasta, and adapt the traditional rice pilaf technique to suit our not-so-traditional grain.

Barley is sold in numerous forms: hulled, pearl, Scotch, and flake, to name a few. We were most interested in the hulled and pearl, the whole forms of the grain (the others are crushed or flattened and would be more porridgelike in consistency than we wanted.) Hulled barley is the most nutritious form on the market, but it's not that easy to find. And when we did track it down, we quickly learned that it has a long cooking time and unappealing texture, both of which result from the fact that though it has been hulled, the bran has been left intact. It didn't seem like a feasible option, so we turned our attention to the widely available pearl barley.

While not quite as nutritious as hulled barley, pearl barley is still fairly nutrient-rich and has a decent amount of fiber. Basically, pearl barley is hulled barley that has been polished until the bran is gone. With the bran removed, the cooking time is substantially reduced, and the texture of the grain becomes springy when cooked.

Next, we turned to testing our existing pilaf method as a way to cook it. Unlike most pilaf recipes we tested that call for a 2:1 ratio of water to rice, our rice pilaf recipe calls for 2¼ cups of water and 1½ cups of rice to produce a perfect pilaf with fluffy grains. We followed this technique with the barley, unsure of how it would compare to the rice. We learned that in addition to requiring a longer cooking time to lose some of its toothsome chew, the barley was unpleasantly starchy when cooked this way. To solve both issues, we increased the water to 2¾ cups and simmered the barley until the texture was just right. Repeated testing with different brands of barley yielded slightly different cooking times (not uncommon when dealing with whole or lightly processed grains), but all of the batches fell within a 30- to 40-minute range.

To reduce starchiness further, we followed a trick we use when cooking rice pilaf: thoroughly rinsing and draining the grains to remove surface starch before cooking. And to evenly distribute moisture throughout the saucepan, we placed a clean kitchen towel between the pan and the lid, right after removing the barley from the heat, and allowed the barley to steam for 10 minutes. The towel absorbed the excess moisture, preventing water from dripping back into the pan during steaming, which in turn produced a drier, fluffier pilaf.

Following the lead of our standard rice pilaf recipe, we also sautéed some minced onion and several garlic cloves in fat before adding the water, which lent a welcome depth. To keep the dish on the light side, we tested toasting the barley, a traditional pilaf step, in different amounts and types of fat. We felt that the barley would benefit from the nutty flavor of butter, so we opted to use it instead of olive oil. Ultimately, we found that 2 tablespoons was the perfect amount to sauté the aromatics and toast the barley without the mixture burning or tasting too heavy. It perfectly coated the barley, making the grains separate and tender and giving the pilaf a good balance of flavor and moisture.

In most recipes for rice pilaf, a handful of fresh herbs is tossed in just before serving, but we wanted deep, layered herb flavor that played well with the hearty barley. Adding thyme with the garlic provided a nice base. We liked the freshness that a combination of parsley and chives—mixed in just before serving—gave the pilaf. Finally, a teaspoon of lemon juice brightened our barley pilaf and made the green herbs' flavor pop.

NOTES FROM THE TEST KITCHEN

REVIVING TIRED HERBS

You likely don't use an entire bunch of cilantro for one recipe, and after a few days of storage, the bunch of what's left might look a little weary. There's an easy way to refresh it (and, in the process, wash it) for the next recipe. Lop off the stems, submerge the leaves in a bowl of ice water, then swish them around to loosen any dirt and grit. Let them stand for 5 to 10 minutes, until they perk up and regain their lost vitality. To drain, instead of pouring the whole lot into a colander or salad spinner basket, which will upset the grit settled in the bottom of the bowl, lift the greens out of the water using your hands, leaving the dirt behind. This also works for parsley or mint. Of course, if the leaves remain utterly limp and lifeless after you try this trick, they are probably beyond resurrection.

Herbed Barley Pilaf

SERVES 6

Do not substitute hulled barley for the pearl barley; hulled barley requires soaking and a longer cooking time.

2	tablespoons unsalted butter
1	onion, chopped fine
	Salt and pepper
1½	cups pearl barley, rinsed and drained
1	garlic clove, minced
1	teaspoon minced fresh thyme
2¾	cups water
3	tablespoons minced fresh parsley
2	tablespoons minced fresh chives
1	teaspoon lemon juice

1. Melt butter in medium saucepan over medium heat. Add onion and ½ teaspoon salt and cook, stirring occasionally, until onion is softened, 5 to 7 minutes.

2. Stir in barley, garlic, and thyme and cook, stirring often, until barley is lightly golden and fragrant, about 3 minutes. Stir in water and bring to boil. Reduce heat to low, cover, and simmer until barley is tender and water is absorbed, 30 to 40 minutes.

3. Off heat, lay clean folded kitchen towel underneath lid. Let sit for 10 minutes, then fluff barley with fork. Gently stir in parsley, chives, and lemon juice. Season with salt and pepper to taste and serve.

PER ¾-CUP SERVING: Cal 220; Fat 4.5g; Sat fat 3g; Chol 10mg; Carb 41g; Protein 5g; Fiber 8g; Sodium 200mg

CUBAN-STYLE BLACK BEANS AND RICE

RICE AND BEANS IS A CLASSIC SUSTENANCE DISH, satisfying with its combination of carbohydrates and protein, but honestly, most incarnations are a bit mundane. And sadly, superior versions often contain a prohibitive amount of fat and sodium. So when we tried the test kitchen's recent reboot of Cuban black beans and rice, we were not exactly surprised to discover that the tastebud-tingling dish was far from figure friendly. This dish, traditionally called *moros y cristianos*, had such an intensely appealing blend of aromatic vegetables, spices, and pork, however, that we were loath to relegate

TEST KITCHEN
MAKEOVER

it to guilty-pleasure food. Could we work our mojo to slim down this dish without losing its character?

We knew that part of the allure of moros y cristianos is the flavor and texture of the beans. Not exactly a last-minute recipe, the dish begins with dried black beans that soak overnight in a brine. Using dried beans is key to the success of the dish; canned beans lack the firm texture needed to withstand an extended cooking time. This dish is also unique in that the rice is cooked in the inky concentrated liquid left over from cooking the beans, which renders the grains just as flavorful. Clearly, any shortcut taken with the beans would prove detrimental to the flavor of the rice, so we decided to stay true to the original recipe's method in that regard.

Even before messing with the beans and rice, we needed to address the *sofrito*. This mixture of aromatic vegetables, spices, and herbs is a cornerstone of Latin cooking and the starting point for this dish. The specific elements in the mix differ from one Latin cuisine to another, but a Cuban sofrito usually consists of a "holy trinity" of onion, green pepper, and garlic, typically flavored with cumin and oregano. In the test kitchen's recipe, the vegetables were pulsed to ¼-inch pieces in a food processor before being browned in a skillet. So far, so good. The next step in the recipe, however, was browning and rendering 6 ounces of salt pork in 1 tablespoon of olive oil, then adding the sofrito to the pan with another tablespoon of oil—steps that knocked our healthy train right off the tracks. We understood the concept: Cooking the sofrito in the oil and rendered fat from the salt pork imparted a smoky, meaty flavor to the vegetables, and the browned pieces of pork added heft to the dish. But unfortunately, there was no way we could keep all that fat.

Since the salt pork was contributing more than 80 percent of our original recipe's fat (almost 14 grams per ¾-cup serving) and a significant amount of sodium (242 milligrams), reducing the amount of pork or finding an acceptable substitute would go a long way toward trimming the dish. We didn't want to lose the meaty flavor it provided altogether, so we turned to another source: bacon. While bacon also contributes fat and salt, we found we could use less bacon and cook it slowly over medium-low heat—without the oil—to render its fat. We then used the rendered bacon fat to sauté the sofrito, which spread the bacon's smoky, meaty flavor throughout. By sautéing the sofrito covered, we avoided

OUR TOP PICK FOR DRIED BLACK BEANS

Canned beans may be convenient, but their flavor and texture never measure up to those of dried. We tested three brands of dried black beans by sampling them cooked plain and in Cuban-Style Black Beans and Rice. Surprisingly, the mail-order heirloom variety became blown out and mushy, but the beans from the two national supermarket brands emerged from the pot perfectly intact and creamy. Our favorite was **Goya Dried Black Beans**, which offered "nutty," "buttery" bean flavor and a reliably uniform texture.

the need for the second tablespoon of oil used in our original recipe. Now we had a base with deep flavor but a fraction of the fat.

Our original recipe didn't stop there. To build even more flavor, that recipe had tried amping up the intensity of the sofrito, but both increasing the spices and doubling the amount of vegetables yielded problematic results. More spices gave the sofrito an intense but dusty flavor, and more sofrito weighed down the rice and beans in a kind of sofrito sludge. But we hit the bull's-eye when we cooked some of the sofrito vegetables (half an onion, half a green pepper, half a garlic head, and bay leaves) with the beans, as they infused the beans with flavor and thereby increased the overall flavor of the dish.

A splash of red wine vinegar perked up the dish with bright acidity, and a sprinkling of thinly sliced scallions and a squeeze of lime brought it to life. While we had cut 100 calories, 12 grams of fat, and 320 milligrams of salt from moros y cristianos, we hadn't sacrificed the complex flavor of the original. Even rabid fans of the classic version were clamoring for more, excited to enjoy all of its decadent flavor without a trace of guilt.

MAKEOVER SPOTLIGHT: CUBAN BEANS AND RICE

	CALORIES	FAT	SAT FAT	CHOLESTEROL
BEFORE	330	17g	5g	15mg
AFTER	230	5g	1.5g	10mg

Cuban-Style Black Beans and Rice (Moros y Cristianos)

SERVES 10 AS A SIDE DISH

The success of the dish relies upon the texture and flavor of the black beans. Do not substitute canned beans for dried beans in this recipe. To quick salt-soak the beans, combine 2 quarts water, beans, and 1½ tablespoons salt in a Dutch oven and bring to a boil over high heat. Remove the pot from the heat, cover, and let stand for 1 hour. Drain and rinse well.

    Salt
 1 cup dried black beans, picked over and rinsed
 2 cups low-sodium chicken broth
 2 cups water
 2 large green bell peppers, halved and seeded
 1 large onion, halved at equator and peeled, root end left intact
 1 head garlic, 5 cloves removed and minced, remainder of head halved at equator with skin left intact
 2 bay leaves
 4 slices bacon, cut into ¼-inch pieces
 4 teaspoons ground cumin
 1 tablespoon minced fresh oregano
1½ cups long-grain white rice, rinsed
 2 tablespoons red wine vinegar
 2 scallions, sliced thin
    Lime wedges

1. Dissolve 1½ tablespoons salt in 2 quarts cold water in large bowl or container. Add beans and soak at room temperature for at least 8 hours or up to 24 hours. Drain and rinse well.

2. In Dutch oven with tight-fitting lid, stir together drained beans, broth, water, 1 pepper half, 1 onion half (with root end), halved garlic head, bay leaves, and ½ teaspoon salt. Bring to simmer over medium-high heat. Cover, reduce heat to low, and cook until beans are just soft, 30 to 40 minutes. Using tongs, remove and discard pepper, onion, garlic, and bay leaves. Drain beans in colander set over large bowl, reserving 3 cups bean cooking liquid. (If you don't have enough bean cooking liquid, add water to equal 3 cups.) Do not wash Dutch oven.

3. Adjust oven rack to middle position and heat oven to 350 degrees. Cut remaining peppers and onion into

CUBAN-STYLE BLACK BEANS AND RICE

2-inch pieces and process in food processor until broken into rough ¼-inch pieces, about 8 pulses, scraping down sides of bowl as needed; set vegetables aside.

4. Cook bacon in now-empty Dutch oven over medium-low heat until crisp, about 8 minutes. Stir in chopped peppers and onion, cumin, and oregano, cover, and cook until vegetables are softened, 6 to 8 minutes. Uncover, increase heat to medium, and continue to cook until water has evaporated and vegetables are beginning to brown, about 5 minutes longer. Add minced garlic and cook, stirring constantly, until fragrant, about 30 seconds. Add rice and stir to coat, about 30 seconds.

5. Stir in beans, reserved bean cooking liquid, vinegar, and ¼ teaspoon salt. Increase heat to medium-high and bring to simmer. Cover and transfer to oven. Bake until liquid is absorbed and rice is tender, about 30 minutes. Fluff with fork and let sit, uncovered, for 5 minutes. Serve, passing scallions and lime wedges separately.

PER ¾-CUP SERVING: **Cal** 230; **Fat** 5g; **Sat fat** 1.5g; **Chol** 10mg; **Carb** 37g; **Protein** 8g; **Fiber** 3g; **Sodium** 450mg

FRENCH LENTILS

WHEN DONE RIGHT, LENTILS HAVE A SLIGHTLY resistant bite that yields creamy centers with deep earthy flavor that makes them a perfect match for wintry comfort foods like roast chicken. And because they have a hearty richness on their own, lentils don't need a lot of fat to elevate them. Simplicity is key to their flavor, and likewise cooking lentils is straightforward and fairly hands-off. For a one-pot side dish, lentils are usually added, along with liquid, to sautéed aromatics and then simmered for 40 to 45 minutes. However, the type of lentils used and a keen eye toward the end of cooking usually determine the outcome. Our experiences with bad lentils have typically involved an unevenly cooked, underseasoned mess of legumes, swimming in a pallid liquid visually akin to dishwater. Who would want that on their dinner plate? We were determined to achieve our ideal.

Right from the start, glossy green lentilles du Puy were our bean of choice. These French green lentils have a firm texture and retain their shape better than other varieties. Next, we looked for simple ways to boost and deepen the flavor of our side dish. We experimented with a variety of aromatics, including garlic, shallots, scallions, and onions. We settled on the onions for their savory flavor and body and a couple of cloves of garlic for their pungent intensity. A rib of celery lent clean vegetal flavor, but much of the flavor in our lentil dish was to come from a pair of vitamin-rich carrots. In addition to rounding out the flavors of the dish, the carrots added a vibrant splash of color to the green lentils, which tend to lose their color as they cook.

As for the type of liquid in which to cook the lentils, tasters preferred the round fullness of chicken broth. Water worked OK, but it didn't offer the depth of flavor that the chicken broth did. And a small amount of fresh thyme, added with the liquid, was a welcome ingredient—its woodsy flavor boosted the heartiness of the broth and complemented the flavor of the lentils and carrots.

At this point, some felt that the lentils still needed a bit more richness and flavor. A small amount of fruity extra-virgin olive oil was just the thing, and a little fresh lemon juice added a nice contrast to the lentils' deep earthy flavor.

Now that we were more than satisfied with our new light lentil recipe, we decided to develop some variations incorporating slightly stronger flavors. Sautéed Swiss chard added an earthy, beetlike flavor to one variation, and curry powder and golden raisins gave the second variation an exotic, spicy-sweet flavor combination. Now we had a variety of lentil side dishes that could fit in with any meal.

French Lentils
SERVES 7

Lentilles du Puy, sometimes called French green lentils, are our first choice for this recipe, but brown, black, or regular green lentils can be substituted; note that cooking times may vary depending on the type of lentils used.

2 carrots, peeled and chopped fine

1 onion, chopped fine

1 celery rib, chopped fine

4 teaspoons extra-virgin olive oil

Salt and pepper

2 garlic cloves, minced

1 teaspoon minced fresh thyme or ¼ teaspoon dried

1¾ cups low-sodium chicken broth

1 cup lentilles du Puy, rinsed and picked over

2 tablespoons minced fresh parsley

2 teaspoons lemon juice

1. Combine carrots, onion, celery, 1 teaspoon oil, and ¼ teaspoon salt in large saucepan. Cover and cook over medium-low heat, stirring occasionally, until vegetables are softened, 8 to 10 minutes. Stir in garlic and thyme and cook until fragrant, about 30 seconds.

2. Stir in broth and lentils and bring to simmer. Reduce heat to low, cover, and continue to simmer, stirring occasionally, until lentils are mostly tender but still slightly crunchy, about 35 minutes longer.

3. Uncover and continue to cook, stirring occasionally, until lentils are completely tender, about 8 minutes longer. Stir in remaining 1 tablespoon oil, parsley, and lemon juice. Season with salt and pepper to taste and serve.

PER ½-CUP SERVING: **Cal** 130; **Fat** 3.5g; **Sat fat** 0g; **Chol** 0mg; **Carb** 20g; **Protein** 6g; **Fiber** 5g; **Sodium** 250mg

VARIATIONS

Curried Lentils with Golden Raisins

Add 1 teaspoon curry powder to pot with onion. Stir ½ cup golden raisins into pot after uncovering in step 3. Substitute 2 tablespoons minced fresh cilantro for parsley.

PER ½-CUP SERVING: **Cal** 170; **Fat** 3.5g; **Sat fat** 0g; **Chol** 0mg; **Carb** 29g; **Protein** 7g; **Fiber** 6g; **Sodium** 250mg

French Lentils with Chard

THIS VARIATION YIELDS A LITTLE EXTRA AND SERVES 8

Omit carrots, celery, and parsley. Separate stems and leaves from 12 ounces Swiss chard; chop stems fine and slice leaves into ½-inch pieces. Add chard stems to pot with onion. Stir chard leaves into pot after uncovering in step 3.

PER ½-CUP SERVING: **Cal** 110; **Fat** 3g; **Sat fat** 0g; **Chol** 0mg; **Carb** 17g; **Protein** 6g; **Fiber** 5g; **Sodium** 290mg

NOTES FROM THE TEST KITCHEN

SUPERMARKET VERSUS ORGANIC GOLDEN RAISINS

When a recipe calls for golden raisins, your choices are surprisingly limited. The few brands that are available nationwide offer little variety; they derive from California-grown Thompson Seedless green grapes (which are also the source for dark brown raisins) that are dehydrated in ovens and treated with sulfur dioxide. This preservative keeps them golden yellow and moist. A handful of specialty-food purveyors carry organic golden raisins, which are sun-dried Black Monukka or Sultana seedless grapes. They aren't processed with sulfur dioxide, so the raisins turn pale green or a very light tan.

We mail-ordered organic golden raisins called Hunza (the grapes are grown in a Himalayan valley) to see if they differed from the golden raisins we found at the supermarket (Sun-Maid and Champion) for half the price. The first thing we noticed about the organic raisins, apart from their color, was that they tended to be drier and less plump than the national brands. Sampled plain, we liked the organic raisins fine, but not as much as we liked the plump sugariness of conventional golden raisins. When we tried the raisins in recipes, all three brands passed muster, but in the end we preferred **Sun-Maid California Golden Raisins** and **Champion Golden Raisins** for their sweet flavor, availability, and budget-friendly price tag.

SORTING DRIED BEANS AND LENTILS

Before cooking, it is important to rinse and pick over dried beans and lentils to remove any stones or debris. To make the task easier, sort the beans on a large white plate or a rimmed white cutting board. The neutral background makes any unwanted matter a cinch to spot and discard.

SAUTÉED SNOW PEAS WITH LEMON AND PARSLEY

SPINACH SALADS

WE'VE HEARD "EAT YOUR SPINACH" ALL OUR LIVES, and for good reason. This vegetable is a nutritional powerhouse. Whether flat-leaf, curly-leaf, or baby, all varieties of spinach are packed with bone-healthy vitamin K and calcium, heart-healthy folate, and energy-producing iron and vitamin B2, just to name a few of the many perks. And when it comes to making side salads for a weeknight dinner, baby spinach wins out over the other varieties. The king of convenience, it is packaged precut and prewashed. But it's not without its shortcomings. Its delicate leaves can't support the typically hefty mix-ins like chunks of avocado or hard-cooked eggs. Worse yet, the small leaves have a tendency to cling together because of their smooth, flat surfaces. This problem leaves add-ins such as olives, nuts, and tomatoes falling to the bottom of the bowl with the dressing. Furthermore, a classic spinach salad—smothered in a creamy, fatty dressing and topped with loads of bacon and crumbled hard-boiled eggs—is hardly a healthy choice for a small side salad. A little creativity was in order if we wanted to achieve fluffy spinach with a well-distributed, light dressing and a good mix of healthy add-ins that lent texture and flavor.

Choosing the right add-ins to break up the leaves' fluttery cling was definitely in order—but just about every ingredient seemed to overwhelm the baby spinach when it was chopped into heavy chunks, and smaller ingredients got completely lost in the mix. We decided that our first step was to rethink our knife work. Thinly slicing the vegetables (or at least tearing them into small pieces) allowed us to introduce stiffer, crunchier produce. We shaved fennel, shredded radicchio, tore frilly frisée, and stripped carrot ribbons with a vegetable peeler. Each element helped to fluff up and separate the baby spinach leaves for several recipe variations, working in a welcome crunch and the bitter and sweet flavors we wanted.

Still, our salads were a little one-dimensional. Cheese often works well in green salads, but we found that firmer, denser varieties like Pecorino and feta sank to the bottom of the bowl, and creamy goat cheese glued the leaves together. We decided to forget the cheese, which helped with our healthy efforts anyway.

Incorporating fresh fruit seemed like a great way to add some bright, clean flavor and textural appeal. Orange segments enlivened the carrot version with acidity and juicy sweetness. Quartered strawberries paired nicely with the assertive frisée; crisp apples cut into matchsticks blended naturally with the fragrant fennel; and ½-inch pieces of sweet mango—just bulky enough to pop through the spinach without sinking to the bottom of the bowl—mellowed the radicchio's bitter edge.

Now all we had left to do was whisk up a dressing. We knew that anything too heavy would weigh our spinach down (and quickly turn our healthy salad onto the wrong path), so we decided to work with the

NOTES FROM THE TEST KITCHEN

SEGMENTING ORANGES

1. Start by slicing ½-inch piece from top and bottom of orange. With fruit resting flat against counter, use paring knife to slice off rind, including white pith.

2. Holding orange over bowl, slip knife blade between 1 membrane and 1 section of fruit and slice to center. Turn blade so that it is facing out and slide from center out along next membrane to completely free section.

PRODUCE KEEPERS WORTH KEEPING?

A new wave of "produce keepers" is cramming supermarket shelves, promising to extend the life of produce with air vents that allow the release of ethylene (a gas that accelerates ripening and spoilage). We stored baby spinach and strawberries in five such products (see examples below): two bags and two plastic containers, plus one "gas guardian" egg containing the mineral zeolite, which purportedly absorbs ethylene. Our findings? The "protected" produce spoiled at relatively the same rate—and in some cases even faster—as the control batches left in their original packaging. No keepers here.

test kitchen's foolproof vinaigrette. This recipe solves the problem that plagues most salad dressings: oil and vinegar separating, or breaking. Adding less than 1 teaspoon of both mayonnaise and mustard along with the vinegar, and then slowly whisking in the oil, ensures that this vinaigrette remains smooth and glossy. Since we knew we could count on these emulsifiers to keep our dressing from breaking (even when we had switched out the small amount of full-fat mayonnaise for light), we wondered what would happen if we replaced a portion of the oil (4½ tablespoons in the original) with something less fatty. Options were sparse: Water just diluted the dressing, and more vinegar made it far too acidic. Not sure what to try next, we reviewed our ingredient list and landed on the orange. Orange juice had the perfect bright, clean flavor that actually added a fresh tang to our salads and highlighted each of the fruits' natural sweetness—and no one could tell we had reduced the oil by 1½ tablespoons. Last, a sprinkling of cilantro, basil, or scallions complemented each salad with a fresh bite and the perfect finishing touch.

Spinach Salad with Carrots, Oranges, and Sesame

SERVES 6

Slicing the vegetables as thinly as possible is important in order to separate the clingy spinach leaves, and to ensure that the vegetables don't sink to the bottom of the bowl. We prefer light mayonnaise over low fat in this recipe.

- 2 oranges
- 6 ounces (6 cups) baby spinach
- 2 carrots, peeled and shaved lengthwise into ribbons with vegetable peeler
- 2 scallions, sliced thin
- 2 tablespoons rice vinegar
- 1 small shallot, minced
- 1 teaspoon Dijon mustard
- ¾ teaspoon light mayonnaise
- ⅛ teaspoon salt
- 2½ tablespoons canola oil
- ¾ teaspoon toasted sesame oil
- 1½ teaspoons sesame seeds, toasted

1. Grate ½ teaspoon zest from 1 orange; set zest aside. Working with 1 orange at a time, slice ½-inch piece from top and bottom of fruit. With fruit resting flat against counter, use paring knife to slice off rind, including white pith. Holding orange over bowl to catch juice, slip knife blade between 1 membrane and 1 section of fruit and slice to center. Turn blade so that it is facing out and slide from center out along next membrane to completely free section. Repeat with second orange. Measure out and reserve 2 tablespoons juice.

2. Combine spinach, carrots, orange segments, and scallions in large bowl.

3. Whisk orange zest, orange juice, vinegar, shallot, mustard, mayonnaise, and salt together in small bowl. Whisking constantly, drizzle in oils. Pour dressing over salad and toss gently to coat. Sprinkle with sesame seeds and serve.

PER SERVING: Cal 110; Fat 7g; Sat fat 0.5g; Chol 0mg; Carb 13g; Protein 2g; Fiber 3g; Sodium 140mg

VARIATIONS
Spinach Salad with Fennel and Apples

SERVES 6

If your fennel bulb does not come with fronds, substitute 2 tablespoons chopped tarragon. Slicing the fennel as thinly as possible is important to ensure that the pieces don't sink to the bottom of the bowl. We prefer light mayonnaise over low fat in this recipe.

- 6 ounces (6 cups) baby spinach
- 1 fennel bulb, ¼ cup fronds minced, stalks discarded, bulb halved, cored, and sliced thin
- 2 Golden Delicious apples, cored and cut into 2-inch-long matchsticks
- 2 tablespoons orange juice
- 1½ teaspoons grated lemon zest plus 2 tablespoons juice
- 1 small shallot, minced
- 1 tablespoon whole grain mustard
- ¾ teaspoon light mayonnaise
- ⅛ teaspoon salt
- 3 tablespoons extra-virgin olive oil

1. Combine spinach, fennel fronds, sliced fennel, and apples in large bowl.

2. Whisk orange juice, lemon zest, lemon juice, shallot, mustard, mayonnaise, and salt together in small bowl. Whisking constantly, drizzle in oil. Pour dressing over salad, toss gently to coat, and serve.

PER SERVING: Cal 130; Fat 8g; Sat fat 1g; Chol 0mg; Carb 16g; Protein 1g; Fiber 4g; Sodium 170mg

SPINACH SALAD WITH FRISÉE AND STRAWBERRIES

Spinach Salad with Frisée and Strawberries

SERVES 6

We prefer light mayonnaise over low fat in this recipe.

- 6   ounces (6 cups) baby spinach
- 1   head frisée (6 ounces), torn into bite-size pieces
- 5   ounces strawberries, hulled and quartered (1 cup)
- 2   tablespoons chopped fresh basil
- 2   tablespoons orange juice
- 5   teaspoons balsamic vinegar
- 1   small shallot, minced
- 1   teaspoon Dijon mustard
- ¾ teaspoon light mayonnaise
- ½ teaspoon pepper
- ⅛ teaspoon salt
- 3   tablespoons extra-virgin olive oil

1. Combine spinach, frisée, strawberries, and basil in large bowl.

2. Whisk orange juice, vinegar, shallot, mustard, mayonnaise, pepper, and salt together in small bowl. Whisking constantly, drizzle in oil. Pour dressing over salad, toss gently to coat, and serve.

PER SERVING: Cal 100; Fat 7g; Sat fat 1g; Chol 0mg; Carb 8g; Protein 1g; Fiber 3g; Sodium 120mg

Spinach Salad with Radicchio and Mango

SERVES 6

Slicing the radicchio as thinly as possible is important to separate the clingy spinach leaves. We prefer light mayonnaise over low fat in this recipe.

- 6   ounces (6 cups) baby spinach
- 1   small head radicchio (6 ounces), halved, cored, and sliced thin
- 1   mango, peeled, pitted, and cut into ½-inch pieces
- ¼ cup minced fresh cilantro
- 2   tablespoons orange juice
- 1   teaspoon grated lime zest plus 2 tablespoons juice
- 1   tablespoon honey
- 1   small shallot, minced
- 1   teaspoon Dijon mustard
- ¾ teaspoon light mayonnaise
- ⅛ teaspoon salt
- 3   tablespoons extra-virgin olive oil

1. Combine spinach, radicchio, mango, and cilantro in large bowl.

2. Whisk orange juice, lime zest, lime juice, honey, shallot, mustard, mayonnaise, and salt together in small bowl. Whisking constantly, drizzle in oil. Pour dressing over salad, toss gently to coat, and serve.

PER SERVING: Cal 120; Fat 7g; Sat fat 1g; Chol 0mg; Carb 14g; Protein 1g; Fiber 2g; Sodium 125mg

NOTES FROM THE TEST KITCHEN

CUTTING MANGO

1. Cut thin slice from one end of mango so it sits flat on cutting board.

2. Resting mango on trimmed bottom, cut off skin in thin strips from top to bottom, using sharp paring, serrated, or chef's knife.

3. Cut down along each side of flat pit to remove flesh.

4. Trim around pit to remove any remaining flesh. Mango flesh can now be chopped into pieces.

SKILLET BROCCOLI WITH PINE NUTS AND PARMESAN

STEAMING BROCCOLI IS AN EASY, CONVENIENT choice, but the results are at best less than memorable, and at worst mushy, drab, and waterlogged. And the usual pat of butter certainly can't save it. To breathe new life into this staple healthy vegetable, we decided we needed to take a different approach to cooking broccoli on the stovetop. We thought that using a skillet over high heat and minimizing moisture to just a touch of oil would be a good start at getting broccoli with a deeper, more intense flavor, appealing color, and good texture. And with this approach, unlike steaming, we could more easily incorporate some different flavors by simply tossing some add-ins into the pan. The trick to perfecting this method would be ensuring that we achieved good caramelized bits on the broccoli without burning it.

Cooking raw broccoli with a bit of oil wouldn't be enough to keep it from either burning or drying out. Because broccoli is a hearty vegetable and won't cook through quickly, a combination of both dry and wet heat was going to be necessary. We found that many recipes for skillet broccoli call for either blanching or steaming the broccoli first, then transferring it to a hot skillet to finish. When broccoli is cooked for just a few minutes too long, however, the chlorophyll breaks down, causing the vegetable's color and texture to suffer. In addition, all vegetables contain acids that leach out during cooking and further contribute to the breakdown of the chlorophyll. As we moved forward with our testing, we would have to really watch the time the broccoli spent exposed to heat if we wanted to avoid overcooking. Because of this, we decided we were better off not messing with a steamer basket or a big pot of boiling water. Instead, we hoped we could simply add a little water to the broccoli in the skillet and cover it for a few minutes to get the job done under a more watchful eye and in a more controlled environment.

First, we needed to transform a head of broccoli into manageable pieces that would cook evenly, so we trimmed the florets into small pieces and the stalks into coins. We then added them to the skillet with some water and steamed the pieces briefly, just until an inserted fork met with some resistance, then set them aside. After heating 1 tablespoon of oil in the skillet over medium-high heat, we returned the broccoli pieces to the skillet, arranging them in an even layer. We hoped that the direct heat would promote caramelization and the oil would protect the broccoli. Despite our efforts, however, the broccoli still dried out and burned in places.

We wondered what would happen if we reversed the method and browned the broccoli stems first. Because the hardier stems take longer to cook than the delicate florets, we tried adding the stems to a hot skillet first to brown, then the florets, and finally ¾ cup of water

NOTES FROM THE TEST KITCHEN

REVIVING LIMP BROCCOLI

We tried reviving limp broccoli by standing stalks overnight in three different liquids: water, sugar water, and salt water. The sugar, we thought, might provide food that would revive the vegetable, and the salt might work like a brine, adding moisture and seasoning. The next day, we examined the broccoli raw and then pan-roasted it. The broccoli placed in sugar water was nearly as limp as before, and the broccoli from the salted water was even more dehydrated. The broccoli left standing in plain water was the clear winner. So, to keep your broccoli fresh, simply trim the stalk, stand it in an inch of water, and refrigerate it overnight.

PREPARING BROCCOLI

1. Place head of broccoli upside down on cutting board. Trim florets very close to their heads and cut into 1-inch pieces.

2. Trim and square off broccoli stalks, removing tough outer ⅛-inch layer.

3. Slice trimmed stalks crosswise into ½-inch-thick pieces.

before covering the pan to let the broccoli steam. A few minutes later, we uncovered the skillet to let the small amount liquid in the pan cook off. Voilà—we had broccoli with bright green florets and toasty brown stems.

Our broccoli was tasty enough to be eaten as is, but we couldn't pass up the chance to add some carefully chosen ingredients that would capitalize on its flavor and texture.

We started by substituting chicken broth for the water to give our recipe a more savory undertone. Garlic, pine nuts, and Parmesan are a tasty and classic Italian combination (think pesto), and they worked perfectly here (in moderation, of course, to keep things healthy). The pine nuts imparted richness to the lean broccoli, and the garlic and Parmesan lent complexity and depth. How to incorporate the garlic was a no-brainer; we just added four minced cloves (with a pinch of red pepper flakes for a touch of heat) to the pan with the browned stalks and let them cook for about 30 seconds before adding the florets and chicken broth. Toasting the otherwise mild pine nuts intensified their flavor, and we used a conservative 2 tablespoons to sprinkle on top at the end. A little Parmesan cheese gave our broccoli that salty, tangy richness it needed.

This is an easy, rich, and satisfying side that is also healthy—no sacrifices here.

Skillet Broccoli with Pine Nuts and Parmesan
SERVES 6

Pay close attention to the pine nuts as they toast since they tend to burn more easily than other nuts.

- 1 tablespoon extra-virgin olive oil
- 2 pounds broccoli, florets cut into 1-inch pieces, stalks peeled and sliced ½ inch thick
- 4 garlic cloves, minced
- ⅛ teaspoon red pepper flakes
- ¾ cup low-sodium chicken broth
- Salt and pepper
- ⅓ cup grated Parmesan cheese
- 2 tablespoons pine nuts, toasted

1. Heat oil in 12-inch skillet over medium-high heat until shimmering. Add broccoli stems and cook, stirring occasionally, until spotty brown, about 3 minutes. Stir in garlic and pepper flakes and cook until fragrant, about 30 seconds.

2. Add broccoli florets, broth, and ¼ teaspoon salt. Cover, reduce heat to medium-low, and cook until stems and florets are nearly tender, 5 to 7 minutes. Uncover and cook until liquid evaporates, about 1 minute. Off heat, sprinkle with Parmesan and pine nuts. Season with salt and pepper to taste and serve.

PER SERVING: **Cal** 110; **Fat** 6g; **Sat fat** 1g; **Chol** 0mg; **Carb** 11g; **Protein** 6g; **Fiber** 4g; **Sodium** 260mg

ROASTED CARROTS

WHEN WE WANT TO COAX THE MAXIMUM FLAVOR out of hardy vegetables like beets, potatoes, and cauliflower, we pull out a roasting pan and crank up our oven. The blast of heat concentrates the vegetables' sweet, earthy notes so effectively that we have a hard time transferring them from pan to plate without eating a few first. Humble carrots, however, never seem to attain the same heights—despite the fact that, as roasting candidates go, they would seem like one of the best: Carrots contain about 87 percent water by weight, which you would assume would help keep their insides tender and moist while the oven's dry heat deepens their sweetness and browns their exteriors. But most of the time when we roast carrots, they come out dry, shriveled, and jerkylike. We knew there had to be a way to get carrots that were tender and buttery on the inside, with an irresistible caramelized outer layer.

We had a basic method in mind: Cut up the carrots, toss them in some oil, put them on a baking sheet, and roast them at 425 degrees for about 30 minutes until browned and tender. Before we started cooking, we needed to pick the best way to cut our carrots. When we tried roasting carrots sliced into ½-inch rounds, they retained their moisture just fine. But unless we were willing to undertake the painstaking task of flipping them midway through cooking, only the sides in direct contact with the pan would achieve any kind of browning. Slicing the vegetables down the middle lengthwise created more surface area for browning but required buying loose carrots with the same diameter to ensure the pieces cooked evenly. We then tried cutting the carrots into batons about ½ inch thick. These gave us the most evenly cooked results with the best browning—but the pieces still shriveled and turned chewy.

SIMPLE ROASTED CARROTS

We decided to back up and do a little research on the composition of carrots. It turns out that they contain more pectin than any other vegetable, and even many fruits. This reminded us of a technique we had developed a few years back that capitalizes on pectin to keep apples from turning mushy when baked in pie: gently precooking them on the stove before adding them to the crust. This step allows the apples to maintain an internal temperature of 130 to 140 degrees long enough for the pectin to convert to a heat-stable form that reinforces the fruit's cell walls. This in turn keeps the slices firm when their temperature rises further during the final cooking in the oven. We realized that precooking the carrots could trigger the same reaction as in the apples: Stronger cell walls could help keep moisture in, minimizing withering.

We wanted to keep things simple, so we brainstormed methods for precooking the carrots on the baking sheet we were already using. What if we covered the sheet with foil when the carrots first went into the oven? The foil would trap the moisture, creating an environment where the temperature could never rise above the boiling point of water (212 degrees), and the pectin in the carrots would become activated. After a short period, we would uncover the baking sheet to finish cooking and brown and caramelize the carrots.

When we uncovered the carrots after 15 minutes and poked a fork into a carrot baton, it wasn't mushy at all, and it resisted just a little. This was promising. Then we slid the uncovered baking sheet back into the oven until the moisture had burned off and the carrots took on deep notes of caramelization. At last, these carrots were tender-firm and distinctly sweet, with minimal withering. We got even better results when we switched out regular vegetable oil for a tablespoon of melted butter, which imparted an even deeper richness and nuttiness to the carrots without pushing the fat beyond reason. Tender, creamy, and deeply sweet, our carrots were in perfect shape.

From there, we wondered if we could successfully integrate different vegetables for some variety and to dress our recipe up a bit. Whether it was parsnips, fennel, or shallots (which we matched with herbs such as rosemary, thyme, and parsley), each worked seamlessly with our roasting method, giving us several great side dish options to add to our light and healthy repertoire.

Simple Roasted Carrots

SERVES 4

While cutting the carrots into uniformly sized pieces is key for even cooking, it's the large size of the pieces that makes the recipe work, so make sure not to cut them too small.

1½ pounds carrots, peeled
1 tablespoon unsalted butter, melted
   Salt and pepper

1. Adjust oven rack to middle position and heat oven to 425 degrees. Line rimmed baking sheet with aluminum foil. Cut carrots in half crosswise, then into halves or quarters lengthwise if necessary to create uniformly sized pieces. In large bowl, toss carrots with butter, ½ teaspoon salt, and ¼ teaspoon pepper. Spread carrots in single layer on prepared pan.

2. Cover sheet tightly with foil and cook for 15 minutes. Remove foil and continue to cook, stirring twice, until carrots are well browned and tender, 30 to 35 minutes longer. Season with salt and pepper to taste and serve.

PER SERVING: Cal 100; Fat 3g; Sat fat 2g; Chol 10mg; Carb 16g; Protein 2g; Fiber 5g; Sodium 410mg

NOTES FROM THE TEST KITCHEN

A PRO OF A PEELER
A recent survey of peelers on the market turned up more than 25 different styles. We set out to find the best of the best—a comfortable peeler that would make quick work of a wide variety of tasks. For the most part, vegetable peelers fall into two main categories: traditional peelers (whose blade is in line with the handle) and Y-shaped peelers (whose blade sits perpendicular to the handle). We found that these design variations made quite a difference. The traditional peelers were comfortable and slick, especially when used for delicate tasks such as peeling carrots. On the other hand, Y-shaped peelers proved their mettle by mowing over thick-skinned fruits and vegetables. In the end, the **Messermeister Pro-Touch Swivel Peeler**, $6.95, passed every peeling test with flying colors and had a comfortable grip, even after we'd peeled pounds of apples and potatoes. At 1.5 ounces, this sharp peeler is so light that hand strain is never a problem.

Roasted Carrots and Fennel with Toasted Almonds

Reduce carrots to 1 pound. Add 1 small fennel bulb, stalks discarded, bulb halved, cored, and cut crosswise into ½-inch-thick slices, to bowl with carrots and roast as directed. Toss vegetables with 2 tablespoons toasted sliced almonds, 2 teaspoons minced fresh parsley, and 1 teaspoon lemon juice before serving.

PER SERVING: **Cal** 110; **Fat** 4.5g; **Sat fat** 2g; **Chol** 10mg; **Carb** 16g; **Protein** 2g; **Fiber** 5g; **Sodium** 400mg

Roasted Carrots and Parsnips with Rosemary

Substitute ½ pound peeled parsnips for ½ pound carrots. Add 1 teaspoon minced fresh rosemary to bowl with carrots and roast as directed. Toss vegetables with 2 teaspoons minced fresh parsley before serving.

PER SERVING: **Cal** 110; **Fat** 3g; **Sat fat** 2g; **Chol** 10mg; **Carb** 21g; **Protein** 2g; **Fiber** 6g; **Sodium** 380mg

Roasted Carrots with Shallots and Thyme

Reduce carrots to 1 pound. Add 6 shallots, peeled and halved lengthwise, and 1 teaspoon minced fresh thyme to bowl with carrots and roast as directed. Toss vegetables with 1 teaspoon lemon juice before serving.

PER SERVING: **Cal** 110; **Fat** 3g; **Sat fat** 2g; **Chol** 10mg; **Carb** 21g; **Protein** 2g; **Fiber** 6g; **Sodium** 380mg

SAUTÉED SNOW PEAS

THE TYPICAL DESTINATION FOR SNOW PEAS IS A stir-fry, where the pods almost always serve as filler— never as the focal point. And if the average stir-fry served in Chinese restaurants is anything to go by, we wouldn't want the vegetables to be any more prominent. The pods are often greasy, limp, and drowning in overly salty brown sauce, with all their delicate flavor cooked out of them. But why should this have to be the standard? If executed properly, the high-heat method of stir-frying would seem like the ideal approach to preparing the quick-cooking pods, bringing out their sweet, grassy flavor while preserving their crisp bite.

It took just one test to demonstrate that things weren't quite that simple. We heated a couple tablespoons of vegetable oil in a 12-inch nonstick skillet over high heat and tossed in a few handfuls of snow peas. After several minutes of constant stirring, we found that we had produced the oily pods we recognized from Chinese takeout. While some of the pods retained a bit of their crisp texture, too many had gone limp. And their subtly sweet flavor? Far too subtle.

We had never intended for the snow peas to stand entirely on their own—they would need a few supporting ingredients to bolster their understated grassy sweetness. But still, we hoped we could enhance the pods' own natural flavor first. Browning seemed like the logical answer. When vegetables are cooked with high heat, they caramelize, which causes them to take on a nutty, concentrated flavor. But the food has to be relatively stationary to let browning happen; the constant motion of stir-frying only thwarts the process.

For our next test, we decided to treat the peas as we do when searing meat to create a well-browned crust: We didn't move them until the high heat had done its job. Sure enough, this approach put us on a much better track. With 12 ounces of peas in the pan, most of the pods were in contact with the hot surface. After one minute of almost undisturbed cooking—we gave them a single stir—the peas emerged bright green, crisp, and freckled with a few spots indicative of good browning. We then reverted to constant stirring for another minute or two, until the pods were fully cooked through.

This new sauté method helped considerably—and we were able to cut down the oil to just 1 tablespoon, which fixed the greasiness problem—but the peas still needed more depth. When we tried to increase browning by leaving them untouched in the pan for a few extra minutes, we were back to a skillet full of limp, overcooked pods. Then we had another idea, a trick that the test kitchen often uses when cooking proteins to promote better browning: sugar. Just ⅛ teaspoon sprinkled over the peas as they went into the hot pan, along with salt and pepper, kicked up the color and flavor in the few minutes the vegetables needed to cook through.

Now it was time for those complementary additions to make their debut. Shallot seemed like a good place to start, but when we sautéed the minced aromatic before adding the snow peas to the skillet, it ended up burning and turning bitter by the time our peas had finished cooking. Instead, we treated the shallot as we would garlic in a stir-fry: We made a clearing in the center of the skillet after the peas were well browned and then cooked the shallot with a splash of oil until just fragrant. Much better.

For a final flavor punch, we added some acidity in the form of lemon juice (lime juice or vinegar worked equally well in a few variations), and a hit of fresh herbs drew out those shy grassy flavors. With just a few changes, we had turned these once-second-fiddle pods into a real standout side dish of their own.

Sautéed Snow Peas with Lemon and Parsley

SERVES 4

Chives or tarragon can be used in place of the parsley.

- 1 tablespoon canola oil
- 1 shallot, minced
- 1 teaspoon grated lemon zest plus 1 teaspoon juice
  Salt and pepper
- ⅛ teaspoon sugar
- 12 ounces snow peas, strings removed
- 1 tablespoon minced fresh parsley

1. Combine 1 teaspoon oil, shallot, and lemon zest in small bowl. Combine ¼ teaspoon salt, ⅛ teaspoon pepper, and sugar in second small bowl.

2. Heat remaining 2 teaspoons oil in 12-inch nonstick skillet over high heat until just smoking. Add snow peas, sprinkle with salt mixture, and cook, without stirring, for 30 seconds. Stir and continue to cook, without stirring, for 30 seconds longer. Continue to cook, stirring constantly, until peas are crisp-tender, 1 to 2 minutes longer.

3. Clear center of skillet and add shallot mixture. Cook, mashing shallot mixture with back of spatula, until fragrant, about 30 seconds. Stir shallot mixture into snow peas. Transfer snow peas to bowl and stir in lemon juice and parsley. Season with salt and pepper to taste and serve.

PER SERVING: Cal 70; Fat 3.5g; Sat fat 0g; Chol 0mg; Carb 8g; Protein 3g; Fiber 2g; Sodium 150mg

VARIATIONS

Sautéed Snow Peas with Ginger, Garlic, and Scallions

Substitute 2 minced garlic cloves, 2 teaspoons grated fresh ginger, and 2 minced scallion whites for shallot and lemon zest. Substitute pinch red pepper flakes for ⅛ teaspoon pepper. Substitute 1 teaspoon rice vinegar for lemon juice and 2 sliced scallion greens for parsley.

PER SERVING: Cal 70; Fat 3.5g; Sat fat 0g; Chol 0mg; Carb 8g; Protein 3g; Fiber 3g; Sodium 150mg

Sautéed Snow Peas with Garlic, Cumin, and Cilantro

Substitute 2 minced garlic cloves and ½ teaspoon toasted and lightly crushed cumin seeds for shallot, and ½ teaspoon lime zest for lemon zest. Substitute 1 teaspoon lime juice for lemon juice and 1 tablespoon minced fresh cilantro for parsley.

PER SERVING: Cal 70; Fat 3.5g; Sat fat 0g; Chol 0mg; Carb 7g; Protein 3g; Fiber 2g; Sodium 150mg

Sautéed Snow Peas with Lemon Grass and Basil

Substitute 2 teaspoons minced fresh lemon grass for lemon zest. Substitute 1 teaspoon lime juice for lemon juice and 1 tablespoon chopped fresh basil for parsley.

PER SERVING: Cal 70; Fat 3.5g; Sat fat 0g; Chol 0mg; Carb 8g; Protein 3g; Fiber 2g; Sodium 150mg

SWEET AND TANGY COLESLAW

WHEN IT COMES TO SUMMER COOKOUTS, BURGERS and coleslaw are a perfect match. We'd already come up with a few lighter takes on burgers (see our Grilled Tuna Burgers, page 190, and Shrimp Burgers, page 118), so now could we create a lighter coleslaw? This would be no easy task; most versions you find in the deli case consist of shredded cabbage drowning in a watery mayonnaise-based dressing and offer the merest suggestions of flavor and texture. Clearly, we would not only need a foolproof technique but also a less fatty approach. We wanted a coleslaw that boasted appealing, interesting flavor and a good crunchy texture that would bring folks back for seconds.

We found a number of coleslaw recipes in which the mayo was ditched in favor of a dressing of oil, cider vinegar, and sugar. It sounded promising, but the same old watery dressing problem plagued these recipes as well, and the flavor was never as bold as we hoped. We wanted a sweet, tangy slaw in which all the flavors were in balance, not washed out.

The test kitchen already had a very effective way to deal with the moisture issue in watery vegetables: tossing them with salt and leaving them to drain for several hours. We applied this technique to a basic slaw recipe, allowing a pound of salted shredded cabbage to rest for three hours, and it released a good ½ cup of liquid.

When we dressed the cabbage, the loss of moisture transformed the otherwise ordinary slaw, allowing its simple flavors to come front and center. With a few more tweaks—adding grated carrot, chopped parsley, and ¼ teaspoon of celery seeds for depth—we had a refreshing slaw that would go with almost anything.

But it seemed less than ideal that, for optimal results, such an easy recipe required hours for salting (albeit unattended). In the past we've found that combining the salting step with a quick stint in the microwave speeds moisture loss in some watery foods, including eggplant. Though heating a dish we planned to serve cold seemed counterintuitive, we decided to try it anyway. The results were unexpected. After two minutes on high power—we didn't dare go longer for fear of wilting the cabbage—the salted leaves had released only a scant tablespoon of liquid.

We decided to further research the subject of salting and learned something new. It turns out that the speed with which water gets pulled to the surface of a salted food is determined by how many dissolved particles are in the solution. In other words, the more salt we used on the cabbage, the faster it should release water. We didn't want to increase the salt for fear of turning the slaw overly salty, but we hadn't considered the other water-soluble ingredient in our recipe: sugar. Though it wouldn't be as effective as salt (sugar remains one particle when dissolved, whereas salt breaks down into two particles), it should still hasten water loss. We tossed a fresh batch of shredded slaw with 1 teaspoon of salt and ¼ cup of sugar and—for good measure—stuck it in the microwave. Remarkably, with both salt and sugar in the mix, in just two minutes the cabbage shed the same ½ cup of liquid it had taken three hours to release at room temperature. Mission accomplished.

The only remaining issue: We now had warm slaw that required chilling. We had worked so hard to cut back the time, we didn't want to add too much back. The easy solution? Chilling the dressing in the freezer for 15 minutes while we prepped the cabbage. Our cold dressing quickly brought down the temperature of the warm cabbage. For a final cool-down—and to let the flavors meld—we popped the finished slaw in the fridge for 15 minutes more. By the time we'd finished cleaning up, we had a bright, crisp slaw to bring to our next picnic or barbecue.

For a few fresh and bright variations on our classic recipe, we found that thinly sliced red bell pepper blended right in with the shredded cabbage, and some jalapeño and lime juice gave us a zippy Southwestern-style slaw. For a second twist, Granny Smith apples, cut into matchsticks, gave us a slaw with a punch of acidity, and when combined with tarragon, it elevated our simple slaw to new heights.

Sweet and Tangy Coleslaw

SERVES 4

If you don't have a salad spinner, use a colander to drain the cabbage and press with a rubber spatula.

- ¼ **cup cider vinegar**
- 1 **tablespoon canola oil**
- ¼ **teaspoon celery seeds**
  Salt and pepper
- ½ **head green cabbage, cored and sliced thin (6 cups)**
- ¼ **cup sugar**
- 1 **large carrot, peeled and shredded**
- 2 **tablespoons minced fresh parsley**

1. Whisk vinegar, oil, celery seeds, and ¼ teaspoon pepper in medium bowl. Place bowl in freezer and chill until dressing is cold, at least 15 minutes or up to 30 minutes.

2. Meanwhile, in large bowl, toss cabbage with sugar and 1 teaspoon salt. Cover and microwave until just beginning to wilt, about 1 minute. Stir briefly, cover, and continue to microwave until cabbage is partially wilted and has reduced in volume by one-third, 30 to 60 seconds longer.

3. Transfer cabbage to salad spinner and spin until excess water is removed, 10 to 20 seconds. Remove bowl from freezer, add cabbage, carrot, and parsley to cold dressing, and toss to coat. Season with salt and pepper to taste. Refrigerate until chilled, about 15 minutes. Toss coleslaw again before serving.

PER SERVING: Cal 120; Fat 3.5g; Sat fat 0g; Chol 0mg; Carb 21g; Protein 2g; Fiber 3g; Sodium 660mg

Sweet and Tangy Coleslaw with Red Bell Pepper and Jalapeño

Substitute 2 tablespoons lime juice for celery seeds, ½ thinly sliced red bell pepper and 1 or 2 seeded and minced jalapeño chiles for carrot, and 1 thinly sliced scallion for parsley.

PER SERVING: Cal 130; Fat 3.5g; Sat fat 0g; Chol 0mg; Carb 22g; Protein 2g; Fiber 3g; Sodium 610mg

Sweet and Tangy Coleslaw with Apple and Tarragon

Reduce cider vinegar to 3 tablespoons. Substitute ½ teaspoon Dijon mustard for celery seeds, 1 Granny Smith apple cut into 2-inch-long matchstick pieces for carrot, and 2 teaspoons minced fresh tarragon for parsley.

PER SERVING: Cal 140; Fat 3.5g; Sat fat 0g; Chol 0mg; Carb 26g; Protein 2g; Fiber 4g; Sodium 620mg

MAPLE-GLAZED ACORN SQUASH

THERE IS A LOT TO LIKE ABOUT GLAZED ACORN squash. With its glossy caramelized coating and deep golden yellow flesh, it's a looker with a candylike flavor and buttery texture that kids and adults alike will gobble up. It is a perfect hearty side dish for a chilly winter supper and an excellent source of fiber, plus it's high in the powerful antioxidants, such as beta-carotene and vitamins A and B, that we need to stay healthy during those sunless winter days. So it's no wonder that recipes for maple-glazed squash abound. The problem is, in most of them the squash is overpowered by a sickly sweet syrup that does nothing but deliver a sugar rush.

The average recipe contains instructions to halve the squash, liberally pour on some syrup, slather it with butter, and roast it until tender. This careless method yields—no surprise—poor results. Predictably, a thin buttery syrup pools at the bottom of each squash half, and there's absolutely no maple flavor within. And, of course, the fat and calories are far above our healthy bar. We needed to find a way to get maple flavor into every bite—without pouring it on as we would onto a stack of Sunday morning pancakes.

Since we already knew that cutting the squash in half was a no-go, we decided to try cutting the squash into eighths, in the hope that this would allow for more syrup-to-squash contact as well as a more even coating (and faster cooking). We placed the wedges on a baking sheet that had been lightly sprayed with vegetable oil spray to prevent them from sticking to the pan. We knew a hot oven (475 degrees sounded about right) would be key to optimum browning, so we would need to hold off on adding any sort of glaze until partway through cooking to avoid burning it.

As efficient as this process was, now the squash cooked so quickly that it barely had time to brown. To fix this, we tossed the squash wedges with a small amount of oil and a touch of granulated sugar before roasting them. This helped to boost the caramelization and achieved the deep brown color and enhanced flavor we had hoped for.

With the squash roasting in the oven, we turned our attention to the glaze. We started with ¼ cup of maple syrup and added 2 tablespoons of melted butter, just enough to give the glaze a velvety-rich texture without making it greasy. A little cayenne gave it some kick and intrigue. The flavor of our glaze was right where we wanted it, and its consistency was perfectly thick and glazy at room temperature. But when it came time to apply it to the hot parcooked squash (which had been

NOTES FROM THE TEST KITCHEN

WILL THE REAL MAPLE SYRUP PLEASE STAND UP?
Genuine maple syrup and so-called pancake syrup, sold side by side in the supermarket, can range in price from more than $1 per ounce for the real deal to a mere 14 cents per ounce for an imitation. To confuse the issue further, pancake syrups boast names like Log Cabin and Mrs. Butterworth, but real maple syrup is organized by a grading system that varies from state to state. Putting aside price, product name, and grading, which tastes best? After tasting 10 syrups over pancakes and pie, tasters rejected pancake syrups for their artificial flavors and "candylike" taste. So which real maple syrup was best? **Maple Grove Farms Pure Maple Syrup Grade A Dark Amber** had everything we sought: "potent, clean, intense" maple flavor, moderate sweetness, and a consistency that was neither too thick nor too thin.

roasting for about 30 minutes), the glaze slipped right off. To give it more gripping power, for our next test we tried first reducing the glaze by half on the stovetop. This did allow it to stick to the squash better—but it also ended up sticking to the pan, the serving spoon, not to mention our tasters' teeth. So for the next round we tried reducing it only slightly, and that worked far better. When the fully tender and browned glazed squash came out of the oven after about 40 minutes, we flipped the slices over one last time and painted them with a little more glaze to create a deep brown sheen and give them an extra boost of bright flavor. Bull's-eye. Finally, we had nicely caramelized squash with just the right accent of buttery maple depth.

Maple-Glazed Acorn Squash

SERVES 6

Make sure to use pure maple syrup, not pancake syrup, in this recipe.

2	acorn squash
1	tablespoon canola oil
2	teaspoons sugar
¾	teaspoon salt
½	teaspoon pepper
¼	cup maple syrup
2	tablespoons unsalted butter
⅛	teaspoon cayenne pepper

1. Adjust oven rack to middle position and heat oven to 475 degrees. Halve squash through stem, seed, and cut each half into 4 wedges. Toss squash, oil, sugar, salt, and pepper together in large bowl. Lightly coat rimmed baking sheet with vegetable oil spray and arrange squash cut side down in single layer. Bake until bottoms of squash are deep golden brown, about 25 minutes.

2. Meanwhile, bring syrup to boil in small saucepan over medium-high heat. Reduce heat to medium-low and simmer until slightly thickened, about 3 minutes. Off heat, whisk in butter and cayenne until smooth. Cover and keep warm.

3. Remove squash from oven, flip, and brush with 3 tablespoons glaze. Continue to bake squash until tender and deep golden all over, about 15 minutes longer. Flip squash again, brush with remaining glaze, and serve.

PER SERVING: Cal 150; Fat 6g; Sat fat 3g; Chol 10mg; Carb 25g; Protein 1g; Fiber 2g; Sodium 300mg

MASHED POTATOES

VELVETY MASHED POTATOES ARE AS COMMON IN country kitchens as they are in fine restaurants, but no matter where they come from, they pack a caloric, fatty punch. A single portion of a typical recipe (with just potatoes, cream, butter, and salt) can deliver more than 350 calories and 25 grams of fat. Could a leaner version retain the same silky texture and full flavor?

TEST KITCHEN
MAKEOVER

We found that diet recipes that rely on low-fat milk made weak and watery mashed potatoes, and those without butter altogether were dry and flavorless. Obviously, we would have to lose at least some of the cream and butter, but how would we be able to make this recipe over while maintaining the integrity of a classic creamy mash? We began with the potatoes.

Potato types differ only slightly in nutritional value, but their flavor and texture variances are another story. We started with 2 pounds each of boiled russet, Yukon Gold, and red potatoes and mashed them with equal amounts of cream. The russets were mealy; the red potatoes were dense and bland; and, happily, the Yukon Golds were buttery, silky, and light.

For 2 pounds of Yukons, we needed about ¾ cup of cream to make a smooth, supple mash. To cut calories, we tried replacing the cream with chicken broth, but tasters complained that it made the potatoes taste like a wet bouillon cube. Potatoes made with fat-free evaporated milk had the right texture but tasted tinny and sweet. Buttermilk was fine, but we had already perfected a test kitchen recipe for tangy buttermilk mashed potatoes and we wanted something new. Then a fellow test cook reminded us that in leaner times, people used to mash their potatoes with some of the starchy cooking water. Using the cooking water as the only liquid made the potatoes bland, but when we mixed ¼ cup of it with ½ cup of fat-free half-and-half, we found our solution.

We were free to tackle the butter; we knew that at least some would be mandatory. We started with a batch of mashed potatoes made with a full stick as a benchmark for flavor and gradually cut back the butter in subsequent batches until only 1 tablespoon remained. Tasters were amazed that so little could still make its presence felt, at least in terms of flavor. Unfortunately, the potatoes now lacked the supple, yielding texture of full-fat mashed potatoes. We tried mashing the potatoes with low-fat and fat-free cream cheese, cottage cheese, and sour cream. None of them gave the potatoes the right texture. Then we noticed a fellow test cook making potato salad. It struck us that the texture of mayonnaise is similar to that of softened butter. On a hunch, we added a few tablespoons to the next batch of our potatoes. The mayonnaise disappeared into the mash, leaving it silky and smooth. Even better, low-fat mayonnaise worked just as well.

Although there was no telltale mayonnaise flavor, tasters complained the potatoes tasted sweet—the result of the combination of fat-free half-and-half and the low-fat mayonnaise. To counteract them without adding calories, we steeped two cloves of garlic, a bay leaf, and ¼ teaspoon of black pepper with the butter and the fat-free half-and-half. This brought the flavors into balance. We had saved ourselves more than 150 calories and 20 grams of fat per serving, and we finally had a recipe for mashed potatoes we could feel good about eating.

MAKEOVER SPOTLIGHT: MASHED POTATOES

	CALORIES	FAT	SAT FAT	CHOLESTEROL
BEFORE	360	25g	16g	80mg
AFTER	180	2.5g	1.5g	5mg

Mashed Potatoes

SERVES 6

We prefer using low-fat over light mayonnaise in this recipe. Use the flat edge of a chef's knife to smash the peeled garlic cloves. A ricer or food mill makes for a creamier mash, but if you don't own either one, use a potato masher.

- 2 **pounds Yukon Gold potatoes, peeled and cut into 1-inch pieces**
- ½ **cup fat-free half-and-half**
- 1 **tablespoon unsalted butter**
- 2 **garlic cloves, peeled and smashed**
- 1 **bay leaf**
- **Salt and pepper**
- 3 **tablespoons low-fat mayonnaise**

1. Bring potatoes and enough water to cover by 1 inch to boil in large pot over high heat. Reduce heat to medium and simmer until potatoes are tender, 20 to 25 minutes.

2. Meanwhile, bring half-and-half, butter, garlic, bay leaf, 1 teaspoon salt, and ¼ teaspoon pepper to boil in small saucepan over high heat. Remove from heat, cover, and let sit for 15 minutes. Discard garlic and bay leaf.

3. Reserve ½ cup cooking water, then drain potatoes thoroughly. Set ricer or food mill over now-empty pot and press or mill potatoes into pot. Gently stir in warm half-and-half mixture, ¼ cup reserved cooking water, and mayonnaise. Add remaining ¼ cup cooking water as needed to adjust consistency. Season with salt and pepper to taste and serve.

PER ⅔-CUP SERVING: **Cal** 180; **Fat** 2.5g; **Sat fat** 1.5g; **Chol** 5mg; **Carb** 33g; **Protein** 5g; **Fiber** 2g; **Sodium** 540mg

PAPRIKA POTATOES

WHEN WE'RE LOOKING FOR A SIDE DISH THAT WILL go with just about anything, potatoes are always quick to come to mind. And while baked potatoes are easy, they are boring on their own, and classic toppings like sour cream, bacon, and cheese are off-limits when trying to cook more healthfully. In our hunt for a potato side dish with a little more interest yet still within healthy bounds (read: one with minimal butter and other fatty additions), we were reminded of an old-fashioned Sunday supper side dish: paprika potatoes. Though this spice comes out of our cabinets most frequently to garnish deviled eggs or hummus (or to feature once a year or so in paprika chicken), we thought it might be just the answer to our boring potato conundrum.

We started by testing an old recipe we found that called for boiling the potatoes, then tossing them with some sweet paprika. At first glance, it was a looker: The creamy potatoes were speckled with a deep brick-red color. Unfortunately, the glamour faded after the first bite, when we realized these were nothing more than a pile of boiled potatoes. The paprika did little beyond adding a flash of color. And no wonder; the paprika didn't have a fighting chance since it didn't make an appearance until the very end when the potatoes had been fully cooked.

While potatoes are pretty bland on their own, when they are boiled with other ingredients they absorb the flavors around them. But adding a pinch of paprika to boiling water didn't cut it. In fact, it ended up taking a full handful of paprika to infuse the potatoes with any hint of flavor—a flat-out waste of the spice. Then we thought that instead of trying to season a whole pot's worth of water, why not cook the potatoes in a skillet with just a few cups of water? We found that we could reduce the amount of water to just 1 cup and still cook the potatoes through when we used a skillet with a lid. And with so little water now in play, 1 tablespoon of paprika was plenty. After the potatoes were just tender, we uncovered the pan to let the water boil away. This was a definite improvement, but tasters agreed that the paprika flavor was still too faint.

In the test kitchen, we often bloom spices in oil on the stovetop to release and intensify their fragrance and flavor. Since we were now cooking the potatoes in a skillet, it was a logical and easy step to take. We cooked our paprika in a little oil before adding the water, and sure enough, the flavor improved. Adding an onion

NOTES FROM THE TEST KITCHEN

ALL ABOUT PAPRIKA

"Paprika" is a generic term for a spice made from ground dried red peppers and is available in several forms. Sweet paprika is the most common. Typically made from a combination of mild red peppers, it is prized more for its deep scarlet hue than for its very subtle flavor. Smoked paprika, a Spanish favorite, is produced by drying sweet or hot peppers over smoldering oak embers. We don't recommend using this variety for all paprika applications; it is best for seasoning grilled meats or adding a smoky aroma to boldly flavored dishes. Hot paprika, most often used in chilis, curries, or stews, can range from slightly spicy to punishingly assertive. Although it shouldn't be substituted for sweet paprika in cooking, sweet paprika can be substituted for hot by adding cayenne pepper.

FREEZING GARLIC

If you go through a lot of garlic, buying prepeeled cloves is an acceptable alternative to fresh. Unfortunately, after about two weeks the prepeeled kind turns yellowish and starts to smell—not pleasant, garlicky stinky, but disagreeably strong. Is freezing leftover prepeeled cloves a solution? We made a few favorite test kitchen recipes (one for mashed potatoes and another for roast chicken) with refrigerated and frozen jarred garlic cloves to find out. In both recipes, the garlic flavor mellowed appreciably after freezing. The bottom line? For the biggest impact, use fresh (prepeeled) garlic cloves. You can use frozen (prepeeled) garlic, as long as you keep in mind that the freezer robs it of its full power.

and four cloves of minced garlic to the pan along with the paprika also helped to build a more flavorful base (with negligible impact on fat and calories). Replacing the water with an equal amount of chicken broth lent some savory appeal. Finally, we halved the potatoes so that they would be sure to soak up all the flavorful pan juices we had created.

The technique and taste were much improved at this point, but we had created a few new problems. First, because we were now halving the potatoes, their starch was leaching out into the pan. With nowhere for that starch to go, it soaked back into the potatoes along with the cooking liquid, making the potatoes gluey. Throughout testing, we had been using all-purpose Idaho potatoes, which are middle-of-the-road in terms of starchiness. Russets weren't an option—they contain too much starch—but waxy red potatoes, which are relatively low in starch and hold their shape well, were a possibility. To reduce the starch even further, we rinsed the cut potatoes before they went into the pan. Glueyness? Gone.

As for the second hitch, as good as the potatoes tasted, a full tablespoon of paprika created a paste that left their exteriors slightly gummy. Since we were already using a skillet, we figured that pan-frying would probably help, but only if we could successfully limit the amount of fat needed. Existing test kitchen recipes for skillet potatoes call for about ¼ cup of oil, so we tested reducing it in small increments and eventually settled on 2 tablespoons. These potatoes browned nicely, lending another layer of complexity to the dish, but at a price. The solution to our pastiness problem had created a grittiness problem. Something had to give.

Removing a teaspoon of paprika improved the texture but dulled the flavor. Would a stronger variety of paprika (rather than the sweet we were using) make up for the smaller amount? We tried Hungarian (no difference), hot (too hot), and gourmet (pricey and pointless). What about smoked? Smoked paprika combines the earthiness of sweet paprika with an intense, savory smokiness, and one test proved it was tailor-made for this dish, especially when we added a little more at the end of cooking to refresh the bold, smoky taste. A final sprinkling of chopped parsley added needed freshness. Paprika potatoes have always looked the part, but now ours tasted it, too.

PAPRIKA POTATOES

Paprika Potatoes

SERVES 6

If you can't find extra-small red potatoes, substitute larger red potatoes and cut them into 1-inch pieces.

> 2 **pounds extra-small red potatoes, halved**
> 1 **onion, chopped**
> 2 **tablespoons olive oil**
> 4 **garlic cloves, minced**
> 2 **teaspoons smoked paprika**
> 1 **cup low-sodium chicken broth**
>   **Salt and pepper**
> 2 **tablespoons minced fresh parsley**

1. Place cut potatoes in colander and rinse under cold water until water runs clear, about 1 minute. Drain potatoes well.

2. Combine onion and 1 teaspoon oil in 12-inch nonstick skillet. Cover and cook over medium-low heat, stirring occasionally, until softened, 8 to 10 minutes. Add garlic and 1 teaspoon paprika and cook until fragrant, about 30 seconds.

3. Add drained potatoes, broth, and ½ teaspoon salt and bring to boil. Reduce heat to medium-low, cover, and simmer until potatoes are just tender, 12 to 15 minutes. Uncover, increase heat to medium, and cook, stirring occasionally, until liquid evaporates, 5 to 8 minutes.

4. Whisk remaining 5 teaspoons oil and remaining 1 teaspoon paprika together in small bowl, then add to skillet. Cook, stirring occasionally, until potatoes are deep golden brown, 5 to 8 minutes. Off heat, stir in parsley, season with salt and pepper to taste, and serve.

PER SERVING: Cal 160; **Fat** 5g; **Sat fat** 0.5g; **Chol** 0mg; **Carb** 27g; **Protein** 3g; **Fiber** 3g; **Sodium** 300mg

DILL POTATO SALAD

WE HAVE ALWAYS BEEN A LITTLE GUN-SHY ABOUT lightening up American-style potato salad—how could we possibly compete with the creamy likes of full-fat mayonnaise and sour cream? Nevertheless, the test kitchen's recently developed recipe for dill potato salad was so packed with flavor and freshness that we felt it was worth a shot. We had taken a classic plain potato salad to new heights by adding a generous amount of dill flavor in multiple ways, from seasoning the cooking water with the herb to using a homemade dill vinegar, not to mention stirring plenty of the freshly chopped herb into the finished salad. We loved that the dill didn't take a backseat in this recipe, but as flavorful as it was, with ½ cup of mayonnaise and ¼ cup of sour cream (and 12 grams of fat and 260 calories per serving), it certainly wasn't light.

We started by following the original recipe's method for making the dill vinegar. Unable to find a prepared dill-infused vinegar at the supermarket among the other herb vinegars, we had realized that making our own could be as easy as gently heating dill in some white wine vinegar and letting it steep. After heating it in the microwave briefly, we set it aside to steep for about 15 minutes and moved on to cooking the potatoes.

Original testing had discovered that a homespun version of what the French call a *bouquet garni* was yet another key for adding dill flavor. We tied up ½ cup of chopped dill leaves and stems in a coffee filter, then added this bundle to the potatoes' cooking water. This infused the potatoes with dill flavor while they cooked without letting any of the dill leaves escape into the water. Once the potatoes were just tender, we drained them thoroughly, transferred them to a bowl, then drizzled some of the dill vinegar over the hot potatoes to season them (we knew from experience that warm potatoes readily soak up flavorings).

Now it was time to lighten up our dressing, a mixture of mayonnaise, sour cream, Dijon mustard, and more of the dill-infused vinegar. Although low-fat mayonnaise has less fat than light mayonnaise, we have found that the former has a sweet off-flavor when tasted on its own (see our low-fat versus light mayonnaise tasting on page 8). Nevertheless, we thought it might work fine in this context given the other flavors in play, so we held a side-by-side tasting of potato salads made with both to find out. Just as we had suspected, tasters had a hard time distinguishing between the two. So we happily opted for the lower-fat version and moved on.

Next it was time to tackle the sour cream. Our first thought was to try nonfat Greek yogurt, hoping its thickness and tang would rival that of rich, full-fat sour cream. This salad certainly had the zesty tang we wanted, but the yogurt made the salad too dry and pasty.

Low-fat sour cream was a better choice, but tasters thought the potato salad could be looser still and taste even creamier. Bumping up the sour cream to ⅓ cup and adding 2 tablespoons of water loosened things up and gave us the creamy consistency we had been striving for.

We were close, but the duo of low-fat dairy was adding a little more acidity and tang than we wanted. Since we liked the creaminess of our salad at this point, we decided our best bet was to reduce the vinegar. Cutting it down from ¼ cup to 3 tablespoons did the trick. At last, we had a potato salad that was at once creamy and fresh tasting, and best of all this picnic heavy hitter had been whittled down to just 1.5 grams of fat and 170 calories per serving.

Dill Potato Salad

SERVES 8

Use both dill stems and chopped leaves (also known as fronds) in the herb sachet. Grey Poupon is our favorite brand of Dijon mustard.

    3   tablespoons minced fresh dill, plus ½ cup leaves
        and stems, chopped coarse
    3   tablespoons white wine vinegar
    3   pounds Yukon Gold potatoes, peeled and cut
        into ¾-inch pieces
        Salt and pepper
    ½   cup low-fat mayonnaise
    ⅓   cup low-fat sour cream
    2   tablespoons water
    1   tablespoon Dijon mustard
    3   scallions, green parts only, sliced thin

1. Combine 1 tablespoon minced dill and vinegar in bowl and microwave until steaming, 30 to 60 seconds. Let sit at room temperature until cool, 15 to 20 minutes.

2. Meanwhile, place chopped dill leaves and stems inside disposable coffee filter and tie closed with kitchen twine. Bring dill sachet, potatoes, ¾ teaspoon salt, and enough water to cover by 1 inch to boil in large pot over high heat. Reduce heat to medium and simmer until potatoes are just tender, about 10 minutes.

3. Drain potatoes thoroughly, then transfer to large bowl; discard dill sachet. Drizzle 2 tablespoons dill vinegar over hot potatoes and toss gently until evenly coated. Refrigerate until cooled, about 30 minutes, stirring gently halfway through cooling time.

4. Whisk remaining dill vinegar, mayonnaise, sour cream, water, mustard, ¼ teaspoon salt, and ¼ teaspoon pepper together in small bowl until smooth. Pour dressing over cooled potatoes and toss gently to coat. Stir in remaining 2 tablespoons minced dill and scallions. Cover and refrigerate until flavors meld, about 30 minutes. Season with salt and pepper to taste and serve.

PER ¾-CUP SERVING: Cal 170; **Fat** 1.5g; **Sat fat** 0g; **Chol** 0mg; **Carb** 33g; **Protein** 5g; **Fiber** 2g; **Sodium** 480mg

CARAMELIZED ONION AND POTATO GRATIN

POTATO GRATIN HAS LONG BEEN KNOWN FOR ITS wicked reputation: potato slices smothered in heavy cream and enough cheese to make a mouse blush. It is the kind of dish that begs for a light and healthy fresh start. A recently developed test kitchen recipe that upgraded the classic potato gratin with the help of caramelized onions and Gruyère (and plenty of heavy cream) looked like it would be a perfect candidate. With ⅔ cup of heavy cream and 1½ cups of Gruyère cheese, we could not deny that it was a sinfully delicious treat. But at 14 grams of fat and 280 calories per serving, we unanimously agreed that it was way too heavy, especially for a side dish. On the upside, the caramelized onions were a nice change of pace for a gratin, and we thought their inherent richness would prove useful later when we cut out some of the fat.

TEST KITCHEN **MAKEOVER**

To get started, we made the full-fat version of the gratin so that we could see exactly what we were dealing with. We caramelized the chopped onions in a nonstick skillet and set them aside, then we deglazed the empty skillet with wine and heavy cream and brought the mixture to a brief boil. We shingled half of the potatoes, sliced ⅛ inch thick, in our baking dish, spread the caramelized onions in an even layer on the potatoes, and then shingled the remaining potatoes on top. We finished it off by pouring on the heavy cream mixture and baking it in a 350-degree oven for about 30 minutes, then topping it with shredded Gruyère and cooking it for an additional 30 minutes. Tasty? Definitely. In need of a makeover? Absolutely.

Unsure where to begin, we looked back at notes from past light tests and found one that resembled a gratin-style root vegetable casserole. That recipe had done away with the notion that heavy cream or milk was mandatory in such a dish and successfully replaced it with chicken broth. Our full-fat onion and potato gratin already had a cup of chicken broth, added along with some wine to the heavy cream, so we decided to play with the ratios a bit. We ran several tests with incrementally smaller amounts of cream and greater amounts of broth. Tasters actually found our all-broth version refreshing, noting that the flavor of the potatoes and onions came to the fore.

While it was a win in terms of highlighting the proper flavors in the dish, switching out the heavy cream for chicken broth caused two big problems: Our gratin was too runny, and it was too lean. While the starch from the potatoes helped thicken the broth and wine mixture slightly, it wasn't enough without the thickening power of the cream. Could a butterless roux do the trick? We had tried one earlier for our Pastitsio recipe (see page 148), but we hadn't had much success because the flour kept separating from the milk. We decided to take another stab at it here. We made a dry roux by toasting flour in the same nonstick skillet we used to caramelize the onions, then slowly whisked in the broth and wine, simmering it until it was slightly thickened and about the consistency of heavy cream. Success.

Now, while the consistency was where we wanted it, we needed to deal with the disappointing leanness. After all, we wanted our light recipe to still offer some richness and decadence. In the full-fat version, shredded Gruyère functioned as a topping that was sprinkled over the gratin halfway through cooking. This particular cheese is strong—a little goes a long way. When we reduced the amount to 1 cup from 1½ cups, tasters thought the cheesy flavor was still good, but they pointed out that we might get more mileage if it was distributed throughout. For our next test, we stirred half of the cheese into the thickened broth and wine mixture. This ended up being just what our lighter gratin needed. The cheese melted right into the sauce, giving it the rich, velvety

consistency it had previously lacked and cheesy flavor in every bite. We sprinkled the remaining ½ cup of Gruyère on top just as before and still managed a cheesy golden brown crust.

The caramelized onions ended up proving their worth just as we had hoped, delivering an unparalleled complexity and subtle sweetness. We cut the amount of butter used in half to just 1 tablespoon, and it was plenty to soften the onions. A tablespoon of brown sugar helped accelerate the caramelization. At the end of the day, we finally had everything we expected from a potato gratin—rich, decadent appeal, plus the unexpected bonus of just 5 grams of fat and 200 calories per serving.

MAKEOVER SPOTLIGHT: ONION-POTATO GRATIN

	CALORIES	FAT	SAT FAT	CHOLESTEROL
BEFORE	280	14g	8g	45mg
AFTER	200	5g	3g	15mg

Caramelized Onion and Potato Gratin

SERVES 10

Thinly sliced potatoes are the key to an evenly cooked gratin—use a mandoline slicer or the slicing disc on a food processor.

- 3 onions, chopped
- 1 tablespoon unsalted butter
-    Salt and pepper
- 1 tablespoon brown sugar
- 2¼ cups low-sodium chicken broth
- 2 tablespoons all-purpose flour
- ⅔ cup white wine
- 4 ounces Gruyère cheese, shredded (1 cup)
- 3 pounds russet potatoes, peeled and sliced ⅛ inch thick
- 2 teaspoons minced fresh thyme

1. Adjust oven rack to middle position and heat oven to 350 degrees. Combine onions, butter, and ½ teaspoon salt in 12-inch nonstick skillet. Cover and cook over medium-low heat, stirring occasionally, until softened, 8 to 10 minutes. Uncover and increase heat to medium-high. Stir in sugar and continue to cook until onions are golden brown, 10 to 12 minutes longer. Add ¼ cup broth and cook until onions are softened, deep golden brown, and sticky, about 5 minutes. Transfer to bowl.

2. Wipe skillet dry with paper towels. Add flour to now-empty skillet, return to medium heat, and cook, stirring occasionally, until golden, about 3 minutes. Whisk in remaining 2 cups broth, wine, and ¼ teaspoon salt, scraping up any browned bits. Bring to boil and cook until slightly thickened, 3 to 5 minutes. Off heat, add ½ cup Gruyère, stirring until melted; cover to keep warm.

3. Shingle half of potatoes in 13 by 9-inch baking dish, then sprinkle with 1 teaspoon thyme and ¼ teaspoon pepper. Spread caramelized onions in even layer over potatoes, then shingle with remaining potatoes. Sprinkle with remaining 1 teaspoon thyme and ¼ teaspoon pepper. Pour broth mixture evenly over potatoes.

4. Bake until bubbling around edges, about 30 minutes. Sprinkle evenly with remaining ½ cup Gruyère and continue to bake until golden brown and fork inserted into center meets little resistance, 30 to 40 minutes longer. Let cool for 15 minutes and serve.

PER SERVING: Cal 200; **Fat** 5g; **Sat fat** 3g; **Chol** 15mg; **Carb** 31g; **Protein** 7g; **Fiber** 3g; **Sodium** 350mg

NOTES FROM THE TEST KITCHEN

NOT THE SAME OLD GRIND

One-handed pepper mills hold one obvious advantage over the usual two-handed twist styles: They free up the other hand to stir a sauce or turn a whole raw chicken for seasoning. One-handed pepper mills can cost well over $100; we set a limit of $50, which allowed us to include mills in many styles and sizes, both manual and electric. We put six to a range of tests focusing on the quality of each grind (from fine to coarse), the output of each mill (the efficiency in producing 1 teaspoon of ground pepper), and ease of use. The **Chef'n Pepper Ball**, $11.95, a manual model, won our hearts and proved easy to fill and adjust for different grinds. The sturdy, compact grinder gave us 1 teaspoon of ground pepper in just 45 seconds of easy squeezing. The clearly marked, easy-to-adjust grind mechanism yielded uniform-size pepper grinds in three textures—but only very coarse, coarse, and medium (not fine).

ASPARAGUS GRATIN

WHEN WE THINK OF A GRATIN, OUR FIRST THOUGHTS are inevitably of the classic rich potato casserole, a dish we'd just successfully lightened (see page 231). But recently the test kitchen had developed a new take on the idea: an asparagus gratin. While a creamy, cheesy sauce does wonders for a mild, long-cooking vegetable like the potato, asparagus has a bright flavor and short cooking time that make pulling off a gratin recipe much more challenging. Nevertheless, our recent recipe had done just that, dressing up just-tender green spears in a light, cheesy sauce that resulted in a side dish perfect for spring. Still, with a combination of butter, flour, and two kinds of cheese, this recipe could use a light and healthy spin.

When developing our full-fat version, we knew out of the gate that the traditional approach to making a gratin wouldn't work with asparagus. Existing recipes we had found tried to treat asparagus just like potatoes, and the resulting gratin was nothing but a dish of brown lifeless stalks. The heavy, cheesy sauce was a poor match for the bright-tasting asparagus, plus the delicate stalks needed mere minutes to cook. Our revised approach had been to divide and conquer. We steamed the asparagus stalks and built the sauce separately, then married the two and ran the whole thing under the broiler just briefly for the classic browned gratin finish.

For our original sauce, we had started by making a roux with butter and flour. From there we had tried stirring in half-and-half, followed by cheese, but a few tests proved that the half-and-half was too heavy for the asparagus. After several tests we realized that our sauce was better off without it. But water made a sauce that—no surprise—tasted watery. To boost its flavor but maintain the lightness, we had discovered that we could make a quick vegetable broth using the asparagus trimmings. This was a win-win in our light-cooking minds, as the flavor of the asparagus was clear and bright and a fair bit of fat was cut along with the half-and-half.

The original roux used to thicken the sauce called for 2 tablespoons each of butter and flour, and we knew we could do some lightening there. Taking a cue from the modified roux we used for our lighter potato gratin, we omitted the butter and toasted the flour in a dry skillet instead. As for the cheese, our testing for the full-fat version had found that Gruyère, though a traditional gratin choice, resulted in a gritty sauce. A combination of Parmesan and Monterey Jack was a better bet. Cutting back on the Parmesan from ¾ to ½ cup was no problem for our lighter version, but the Jack was a bigger challenge. We needed to keep that original volume (½ cup) to get a sauce with the proper cheesy texture, and low-fat Monterey Jack isn't available. We would have to pick a different, lower-fat cheese, and to make up for the flavor lost from cutting fat, we figured it wouldn't hurt to pick something with a slightly bolder flavor. After a little brainstorming we decided to try substituting reduced-fat cheddar for the Monterey Jack. Happily, it melted well, and its sharpness played surprisingly well with the asparagus's grassy flavor.

Our recipe couldn't have been more streamlined. We cooked the trimmings and some water in a large skillet to make our quick stock, then cooked the asparagus until nearly tender in the same skillet. Once they were done, we transferred the spears to our baking dish, reserved the cooking water, then built our sauce in

NOTES FROM THE TEST KITCHEN

A BROILER-SAFE DISH THAT CAN STAND THE HEAT

When it comes to casserole dishes, our favorite pan is the Pyrex Bakeware 13 by 9-Inch Baking Dish. At just $8.99, this inexpensive workhorse is perfect—well, almost perfect. Pyrex does not recommend that its ovensafe tempered glassware go under the broiler; abrupt temperature changes can cause it to crack or shatter, a condition called thermal shock. Since many recipes are sized to fit the Pyrex, we needed an alternative with roughly the same dimensions and capacity, but one that would be able to handle the heat. After we put seven rectangular broiler-safe baking dishes through a series of tests involving recipes that required prolonged exposure to the broiler as well as recipes that required that the dish be finished under the broiler, all of the contenders emerged intact; however, we took some out of the running for best in show for being too heavy, for having an awkward handle (or no handle at all), or for being too big and shallow to adapt to our 9 by 13-inch casserole recipes. In the end, we preferred the **HIC Porcelain Lasagna Baking Dish**, $37.49. This dish had it all: large, easy-to-grip handles for safe transferring, a light weight even when filled with potatoes, and a price we could stomach.

the pan. After drizzling the sauce over the spears and sprinkling over a little more Parmesan, we broiled the gratin for just a few minutes to crisp the cheese and finish cooking the asparagus through. After a few minutes under the broiler, the asparagus was perfectly cooked and still a vibrant green, and the light yet satisfying cheese sauce was its perfect elegant accompaniment.

Asparagus Gratin

SERVES 6

For even cooking, buy asparagus spears between ¼ and ½ inch in diameter.

2½ cups water
2 pounds thin asparagus, trimmed, tough ends reserved
Salt and pepper
2 tablespoons all-purpose flour
2 ounces low-fat cheddar cheese, shredded (½ cup)
1 ounce Parmesan cheese, grated (½ cup)

1. Adjust oven rack to upper-middle position and heat broiler. Line 3-quart broiler-safe baking dish with paper towels. Bring water to boil in 12-inch skillet over medium-high heat. Add reserved asparagus ends and ¼ teaspoon salt, cover, and cook for 5 minutes. Using slotted spoon, remove asparagus ends and discard.

2. Add asparagus stalks to skillet, cover, and cook, stirring occasionally, until nearly tender, 2 to 4 minutes. Transfer asparagus to prepared baking dish. Measure out and reserve 1 cup of asparagus cooking water.

3. Dry skillet thoroughly with paper towels. Add flour to now-empty skillet and cook over medium heat, stirring occasionally, until golden, about 3 minutes. Slowly whisk in reserved asparagus cooking water and bring to boil. Reduce heat to medium-low and simmer until thickened, 3 to 5 minutes. Off heat, whisk in cheddar and ¼ cup Parmesan until smooth. Season with salt and pepper to taste, cover, and let stand for 5 minutes.

4. Remove paper towels from baking dish. Drizzle sauce over center of asparagus and top with remaining ¼ cup Parmesan. Broil until cheese is golden and asparagus is tender, 6 to 8 minutes. Serve.

PER SERVING: Cal 90; Fat 2.5g; Sat fat 1.5g; Chol 10mg; Carb 9g; Protein 8g; Fiber 3g; Sodium 160mg

EGGPLANT CASSEROLE

EGGPLANT IS OFTEN THE GO-TO VEGETABLE WHEN we want to make a hearty vegetarian entrée. It is virtually fat free, and it has a distinctive savory flavor and melt-in-your-mouth texture that can win over even the most vegetable-weary diner. We had recently developed a great eggplant casserole, a recipe sure to deliver on its promise.

Intended to emulate the flavors of eggplant Parmesan with half the fuss, it called for preroasting the eggplant on a baking sheet to expel some of its water (instead of the time-consuming frying method), then whipping up a basic tomato sauce, stirring together a mixture containing ricotta and Parmesan, and layering it all together, along with some shredded mozzarella, in a 9 by 13-inch baking dish. Last, a panko-Parmesan topping mimicked the traditional breading in eggplant Parmesan with a lot less work. But we quickly learned why recipes featuring eggplant—such as our very own eggplant casserole—can all too easily turn unhealthy: Eggplant has a way of soaking up oil like a sponge, and its "blank slate" versatility makes it the prime candidate for being smothered with an overload of cheese. In fact, our recipe clocked in at 35 grams of fat and 550 calories per serving. Nevertheless, we set out to see what we could do in terms of lightening and still maintain the comfort-food appeal and simplicity of the original.

The oil was an easy place to start. Six tablespoons of olive oil were distributed throughout our original recipe: 2 tablespoons to coat the sliced eggplant, 1 tablespoon to coat the baking sheets the eggplant pieces were roasted on, 2 tablespoons to sauté the garlic for the tomato sauce, and 1 tablespoon to toss into the panko-Parmesan topping. We found that a single tablespoon of oil did a suitable job of lightly coating the eggplant for roasting, and a light spray of oil to grease the baking sheets prevented the eggplant from sticking. We also found that we could get away with a mere teaspoon of oil to sauté the garlic without scorching it. As for the panko topping, we tried cutting the oil in half, to 1½ teaspoons, but we agreed that at this amount the topping tasted too sandy and lean. We took a step back and wondered if we even needed the topping in the first place. We decided to hold a tasting of two eggplant casseroles, one with the topping and one with just the

mozzarella cheese sprinkled on top and browned in the oven. Tasters actually preferred the one without the panko topping, so we decided to skip it.

So far we had saved 11 grams of fat and 130 calories, a good dent, but the numbers were still too high. The cheese was the clear culprit. While we certainly wouldn't have to worry about getting our daily allowance of calcium from our original recipe, the cheeses (a ricotta-Parmesan mixture and a full pound of mozzarella) were adding 23 grams of fat and 75 milligrams of cholesterol to each serving. First, we swapped in lower-fat alternatives, but that wasn't enough. We then reduced the 1¾ cups of full-fat ricotta to 1¼ cups of part-skim ricotta and the 4 cups of shredded whole-milk mozzarella cheese to 1½ cups of part-skim mozzarella, and we took the Parmesan down from 1½ cups to ½ cup. The combination of reducing the overall amounts of cheese and replacing them with leaner options vastly improved our numbers, but when we dug our forks into our new and "improved" casserole, we found that the sparse ricotta mixture had disappeared into the tomato sauce and eggplant layers.

While the layering effect had been the key in our original recipe to creating a hearty, substantial entrée,

NOTES FROM THE TEST KITCHEN

THE BEST FINE-MESH STRAINER
In our Eggplant Casserole recipe, a fine-mesh strainer is used to remove any excess liquid in the fat-free cottage cheese, resulting in a thick, creamy consistency that rivals that of its fuller-fat relatives. We last rated fine-mesh strainers in 2003, but we decided to take a fresh look when we noticed that many strainers in the test kitchen were missing their handles. We chose five strainers, priced from $18.99 to $27.49 and about 6 inches in diameter, and all of them performed their straining duties passably well. We found that the primary distinctions lay in the shape, style, and durability of the handles. To replicate years of use, we boiled, rapidly cooled, and banged each strainer against a counter, repeating the test four times. Two strainers broke, including our previous winner, and our new favorite ended up being the **CIA Masters Collection**, $27.49, because it produced the smoothest sauce and silkiest pudding and sat securely in both large and medium bowls, thanks to a wide bowl rest.

there just wasn't enough of a cheesy presence anymore to make it effective. We didn't want to increase the amount of the ricotta mixture, so we tried changing the way we layered the casserole. Our original recipe called for two layers of the ricotta mixture. For our lighter version, we realized we could make a more substantial single layer and thereby make the ricotta more noticeable. With this adjustment, tasters could happily see the ricotta, but now that they could actually taste it, they detected a noticeable grittiness. We went back to the cheese board.

Grittiness had been a problem with another Italian-inspired recipe we had just lightened, our stuffed shells (see recipe page 145). We had solved the problem there by pureeing nonfat cottage cheese to imitate the smooth texture and creamy flavor of full-fat ricotta. Could it work here too? After processing a pound of nonfat cottage cheese with some saltines (used to give it some stability), ¼ cup of Parmesan, and an egg, we had a ricotta-like mixture that was on the right track. We sandwiched it between our two eggplant layers, topped it with mozzarella, and popped the whole thing in the oven. This casserole fooled even our sharpest of tasters into thinking it was full fat, and now at 10 grams of fat and 250 calories per serving, we had a healthful vegetarian entrée we could eat without a shred of guilt.

MAKEOVER SPOTLIGHT: EGGPLANT CASSEROLE

	CALORIES	FAT	SAT FAT	CHOLESTEROL
BEFORE	550	35g	16g	100mg
AFTER	250	10g	4g	45mg

Eggplant Casserole

SERVES 8

You will need a 16-ounce container of fat-free cottage cheese (don't use whipped). If it appears watery, drain it in a fine-mesh strainer for 15 minutes before you use it. Leaving the skin on the eggplant keeps the slices intact during roasting.

4 pounds eggplant, sliced into ¾-inch-thick rounds
4 teaspoons olive oil
  Salt and pepper
4 garlic cloves, minced
1 (28-ounce) can crushed tomatoes
2 tablespoons chopped fresh basil
12 unsalted saltines, broken into pieces
1 pound (1½ cups) nonfat cottage cheese, drained if necessary
1 ounce Parmesan cheese, grated (½ cup)
1 large egg, lightly beaten
6 ounces part-skim mozzarella cheese, shredded (1½ cups)

1. Adjust oven racks to upper-middle and lower-middle positions and heat oven to 450 degrees. Line 2 rimmed baking sheets with aluminum foil and lightly coat with vegetable oil spray. Toss eggplant with 1 tablespoon oil and ½ teaspoon salt and arrange in single layer on prepared sheets.

2. Roast eggplant until golden brown, 35 to 45 minutes, flipping eggplant and switching and rotating sheets halfway through roasting. Let eggplant cool until needed. Adjust oven rack to middle position and reduce temperature to 375 degrees.

3. Meanwhile, heat remaining 1 teaspoon oil and garlic in large saucepan over medium heat until fragrant but not brown, 1 to 2 minutes. Stir in tomatoes and ¼ teaspoon salt and simmer until slightly thickened, about 10 minutes. Off heat, stir in basil and season with salt and pepper to taste. Cover to keep warm; set aside.

4. Pulse crackers in food processor until finely ground, about 10 pulses. Add cottage cheese, ¼ cup Parmesan, egg, ¼ teaspoon salt, and ¼ teaspoon pepper and process until smooth, about 20 seconds.

5. Spread ¾ cup tomato sauce over bottom of 13 by 9-inch baking dish. Arrange half of roasted eggplant in dish in single layer, squeezing slices together tightly as needed. Spread ¾ cup tomato sauce over eggplant. Dollop cottage cheese mixture over sauce, then gently spread into even layer.

6. Sprinkle ¾ cup mozzarella over top, then ¾ cup more tomato sauce over cheese. Layer in remaining eggplant, then spread remaining ¾ cup tomato sauce over top and sprinkle with remaining ¼ cup Parmesan, then remaining ¾ cup mozzarella.

7. Cover dish tightly with foil that has been sprayed with oil spray. Bake until filling is bubbling, about 25 minutes. Remove foil and continue baking until top is golden brown, 20 to 25 minutes longer. Let cool for 15 minutes and serve.

PER SERVING: Cal 250; Fat 10g; Sat fat 4g; Chol 45mg; Carb 28g; Protein 17g; Fiber 9g; Sodium 920mg

EGGPLANT CASSEROLE

REINVENTED EGGS FLORENTINE

CHAPTER 11

BREAKFAST, BAKED GOODS & BREADS

M   = TEST KITCHEN MAKEOVER

EGGS FLORENTINE, REINVENTED

A BRUNCH CLASSIC, EGGS BENEDICT IS A LUSCIOUS, decadent meal: Quivering poached eggs are perched on thick slices of meaty Canadian bacon atop split and buttered English muffins, all draped in a rich and velvety hollandaise sauce. Clearly, it's far from a healthy choice. Enter eggs Florentine, which swaps the bacon for spinach. It's the popular vegetarian answer to eggs Benedict. And it's the healthy choice, right? Not so fast. Eggs Florentine is in fact only a hair less decadent, and not that much better for you, than its meaty cousin. It's hard to get beyond a few bites before feeling like you need to sit back and take a breather. We figured it was high time to lighten this classic. We decided we would strip it down to the basics to come up with a dish that was worthy of Sunday brunch and at the same time guiltless. In addition, we knew the assembly process of such a multicomponent dish (especially one with eggs) can intimidate even the best cook. We wanted to find a game plan for preparing the dish that was stress free.

We started with the eggs. Poaching is a naturally light way to prepare eggs, but it can be a tricky process that home cooks often prefer to leave to restaurant chefs. To find the most foolproof method, we auditioned several classic techniques. We cracked the eggs into a vat of boiling water, but they sank and were tough to remove without breaking, or the agitating water broke the yolks. Then we swirled the water and dropped the eggs into the center of the vortex to (supposedly) spin the egg whites into a perfect sphere. But instead, the whites spun into streamers. We tried cooking the eggs in simmering rather than boiling water, but the temperature wasn't constant, and the water was still too vigorous for the delicate yolks. The best approach we found called for cooking the eggs off heat.

First, we brought water to a simmer in a large skillet. While it was heating, we cracked the eggs into teacups, using each cup to hold two eggs at a time. We added vinegar (a clever trick that lowers the pH of the water and ensures that the egg whites stay intact) and salt to the water, turned off the heat, and slipped in the eggs to cook in the residual heat. We covered the skillet and waited several minutes before we removed the eggs with a slotted spoon. This method consistently produced restaurant-worthy poached eggs with soft, runny yolks and perfectly formed, round whites.

With our cooking method settled, we began building our sandwich from the bottom up. Instead of using a white-flour English muffin, we opted for the whole wheat version. This healthy swap added a slightly nutty flavor that tasters gave the thumbs up. We split the muffins in half, toasted them (no need for butter since the egg yolks provided plenty of richness), then kept them warm in a 300-degree oven while we pulled together the other components.

Next, we worked on the spinach. Too often, restaurants pay too little attention to the flavor of the spinach in eggs Florentine, piling soggy, limp leaves on top of the English muffins. To rescue the greens, we sautéed a shallot and a small clove of garlic in a little oil before stirring in the spinach, then cooked it just until wilted. A quick squeeze was all it needed to remove excess moisture, then we piled our nicely seasoned spinach on top of our halved muffins. We liked the color the spinach gave our sandwiches, but we thought they could still use just a little more brightness. A few slices of fresh tomato did the trick, fitting neatly onto the stack.

Finally we approached the hollandaise sauce. This sauce, a carefully balanced mixture of egg yolks, butter, and lemon juice, is notoriously difficult to make: One must carefully drizzle melted butter into yolks over a double boiler while whisking the mixture constantly to prevent the sauce from breaking into a puddle of oily melted butter and scrambled eggs. And not to point out the obvious, but hollandaise is full of fat from all those yolks and the butter. To appropriately lighten it, we would need to cut the butter back by more than half and find a low-cholesterol ingredient that could somehow do the job of the egg yolks. After much discussion, we finally agreed that even a well-crafted lighter version wouldn't hold a candle to the original.

NOTES FROM THE TEST KITCHEN

POACHING EGGS IN A SKILLET

Crack 2 eggs into each teacup and tip cups, simultaneously, into simmering water. Cover skillet and remove from heat to poach.

We decided to forgo the sauce entirely and come up with a naturally light alternative that would mimic the richness of the sauce without sending our breakfast into fat and calorie overload.

Looking for the simplest solution, we decided to try a cheese-based spread on our toasts. We sampled light cream cheese, as well as whipped feta and goat cheese. The cream cheese added a gummy texture that detracted from the silkiness of the egg, and the whipped feta was just too salty. The goat cheese, on the other hand, was creamy and pleasantly tangy—if only a little boring. To jazz it up, all we had to do was stir in a little lemon juice and pepper.

To streamline our assembly process, we found that it was easiest to toast the bread, spread on the cheese, top the toasts with tomato slices, and keep the partially prepared sandwiches warm in the oven while we prepared the other components. We sautéed the spinach next and added it to the stacks. Finally, we poached the eggs right before serving. The results were healthy enough we could even enjoy a little turkey sausage alongside. Now that's a breakfast that will get us out of bed in the morning.

Reinvented Eggs Florentine

SERVES 4

The vinegar in the egg-poaching water adds more than just flavor—it lowers the pH in the water, ensuring that the egg whites stay intact during cooking; don't omit it. You will need a 12-inch nonstick skillet with a tight-fitting lid and 2 teacups for this recipe.

- 2 ounces goat cheese, crumbled (½ cup), softened
- ½ teaspoon lemon juice
  Salt and pepper
- 2 whole wheat English muffins, split in half and toasted
- 1 small tomato, cored, seeded, and sliced thin
- 2 teaspoons olive oil
- 1 shallot, minced
- 1 small garlic clove, minced
- 4 ounces (4 cups) baby spinach
- 2 tablespoons white vinegar
- 4 large eggs

1. Adjust oven rack to middle position and heat oven to 300 degrees. Stir goat cheese, lemon juice, and ⅛ teaspoon pepper together in bowl until smooth.

2. Spread goat cheese mixture evenly over muffin halves and top with tomato slices. Arrange muffins on baking sheet and keep warm in oven while preparing spinach and eggs.

3. Heat oil in 12-inch nonstick skillet over medium heat until shimmering. Add shallot and cook until softened, about 2 minutes. Stir in garlic and cook until fragrant, about 30 seconds. Stir in spinach and ⅛ teaspoon salt and cook until wilted, about 1 minute. Using tongs, squeeze out any excess moisture from spinach, then divide evenly among English muffins.

4. Wipe out skillet with paper towels, then fill nearly to rim with water. Add vinegar and 1 teaspoon salt and bring to simmer. Meanwhile, crack eggs into 2 teacups (2 eggs in each cup). Gently tip cups so eggs slide into skillet simultaneously. Remove skillet from heat, cover, and poach eggs for 4 minutes (add 30 seconds for firm yolks).

5. Gently lift eggs from water using slotted spoon and let drain before laying on top of spinach. Season with salt and pepper to taste and serve immediately.

PER SERVING: Cal 220; Fat 11g; Sat fat 4g; Chol 220mg; Carb 19g; Protein 13g; Fiber 4g; Sodium 540mg

BREAKFAST BURRITOS

A STAPLE ON MANY A DINER'S MORNING MENU, breakfast burritos—just like their lunch and dinner cousins—are hardly light fare. Typically loaded with a glut of eggs, sausage, and cheese, these greasy

TEST KITCHEN
MAKEOVER

treats may taste great on Saturday morning, but they're far from the healthy and balanced breakfast we all need to start the day. We had already developed a streamlined test kitchen recipe for breakfast burritos a few years back, but they tipped the scale at 600 calories and 41 grams of fat … each! Could we transform them into a healthy breakfast option?

Our original recipe had already successfully tackled a solid cooking method: We cooked sausage, peppers, and onions together, then set them aside while we scrambled the eggs. Once they were cooked, we folded the eggs into the meat-vegetable mixture, then steamed the tortillas gently in the microwave. Finally, we assembled the burritos, topping our egg-sausage mix with cheese, sour cream, and salsa and wrapping a tortilla around it all.

Since this method worked well, we would focus on lightening the ingredients where we could.

We knew right away that we would need to make a substitution for the original recipe's meat of choice: Mexican chorizo. The spicy, garlicky sausage is packed with flavor but also laced with fat, adding almost 11 grams per serving. To find a healthier alternative, we looked to our Mexican lasagna recipe (page 78). There, we had substituted ground turkey for ground pork with great success. But when we tried making a direct substitution in our burritos with 93 percent lean ground turkey, the results were far too bland. Instead, we found our solution in turkey breakfast sausage. It had all of the flavor but none of the grease of the chorizo. This change alone cut 5 grams of fat per serving. To add flavor, color, and texture to our sausage base, we liked a combination of red onion, scallion, and garlic, plus a minced red bell pepper for color and sweetness.

The other major fatty culprit in our original burritos was grated cheddar. The recipe called for almost an entire block of the stuff, adding 121 calories and 10 grams of fat to each burrito. We knew that we wanted to keep some amount of cheese for binding powder and, of course, flavor. But we found we could reduce the amount to just 2 ounces (½ cup) total, sprinkling each burrito with a little over a tablespoon, and tasters were still happy with the results. To further reduce the fat count, next we tried substituting 50 percent reduced-fat cheddar cheese. It melted just as well as the full-fat cheese, had just as much sharp cheddar flavor, and contained only 1½ grams of fat.

Our burritos were already substantially slimmed down, but we knew we could make even more of an improvement in the egg department. Since egg yolks contain a fair amount of fat and cholesterol (4½ grams of fat and 210 milligrams of cholesterol per yolk), we figured we would need to cut back by working in more whites than yolks—but we couldn't take it too far. Careful balancing was required if we wanted scrambled eggs that still had an appealing consistency and weren't too rubbery. We whipped up a number of batches and eventually determined that two whites to one yolk was as low as we could go. But it was still a positive step, cutting the cholesterol in half and dropping 3 more grams of fat. To keep the eggs fluffy and add a little richness, the original recipe called for adding ¼ cup of half-and-half. This rich dairy component added too much fat, so we replaced it with more modest 1 percent low-fat milk and still managed to get eggs with good fluff. Finally, we eliminated the tablespoon of butter originally used to cook the eggs and swapped in just 1 teaspoon of vegetable oil. With all of the other ingredients in play, the flavor of the butter wasn't even missed.

With the trickiest ingredients in our lighter burritos slimmed down, we moved on to the garnishes. We cut the sour cream outright, since it added not only unnecessary bulk but also 6 grams of fat to each burrito. Tomato salsa (along with some cayenne) was a given, adding brightness and heat. Finally, for a boost in fiber, we chose to roll our burritos in heart-healthy whole wheat tortillas (steamed in the microwave for easy rolling) instead of the plain flour variety.

We were so pleased with our master recipe, we decided to create a bean-based vegetarian version as well. We took out the sausage, added one can of black beans to the onion mixture, and sprinkled on a little cumin to complement the earthiness of the beans. Not only was this version tasty in its own right, but it was even lower in fat and calories than our master. Both clocked in with 15 grams of fat or less and 330 calories or less. Either version was sure to please even the most diehard diner-food devotee.

MAKEOVER SPOTLIGHT: BREAKFAST BURRITOS

	CALORIES	FAT	SAT FAT	CHOLESTEROL
BEFORE	600	41g	21g	375mg
AFTER	330	15g	3.5g	190mg

Breakfast Burritos

SERVES 6

To avoid wasting yolks, you can substitute ½ cup of store-bought egg whites (see page 243) for the 4 egg whites in the recipe. Do not substitute skim milk in this recipe.

- 2 teaspoons canola oil
- 6 ounces turkey breakfast sausage, casings removed
- ½ cup finely chopped red onion

1 small red bell pepper, stemmed, seeded, and
   chopped fine

⅛ teaspoon cayenne pepper

3 scallions, sliced thin

1 garlic clove, minced

4 large eggs plus 4 large whites

¼ cup 1 percent low-fat milk

¼ teaspoon salt

⅛ teaspoon pepper

6 (8-inch) whole wheat tortillas

2 ounces 50 percent light cheddar cheese, shredded
   (½ cup)

½ cup fresh or jarred salsa

1. Heat 1 teaspoon oil in 10-inch nonstick skillet over medium-high heat until shimmering. Add sausage and cook, breaking up sausage with wooden spoon, until lightly browned, about 1½ minutes. Stir in onion, bell pepper, and cayenne and cook until vegetables are softened and beginning to brown, about 5 minutes. Stir in scallions and garlic and cook until fragrant, about 30 seconds. Transfer sausage mixture to bowl and cover to keep warm; wipe out skillet with paper towels.

2. Whisk eggs, egg whites, milk, salt, and pepper together in bowl. Heat remaining 1 teaspoon oil over medium heat until shimmering. Add eggs and cook, gently pushing, lifting, and folding from one side of pan to other, until eggs are nicely clumped, shiny, and wet, about 2 minutes. Quickly transfer eggs to bowl with sausage and fold gently to combine.

3. Stack tortillas on top of one another, with paper towels in between, and microwave until tortillas are hot and steaming, 30 to 60 seconds. Divide eggs, cheddar, and salsa evenly among tortillas. Roll into burritos and serve.

PER BURRITO: Cal 330; Fat 15g; Sat fat 3.5g; Chol 190mg; Carb 28g; Protein 19g; Fiber 3g; Sodium 670mg

VARIATION

Black Bean Breakfast Burritos

Omit sausage. Add ⅛ teaspoon ground cumin with onion. Add one 15-ounce can rinsed black beans with scallions and cook until warmed through, about 1 minute.

PER BURRITO: Cal 300; Fat 10g; Sat fat 2g; Chol 145mg; Carb 34g; Protein 17g; Fiber 5g; Sodium 650mg

---

NOTES FROM THE TEST KITCHEN

MAKING SCRAMBLED EGGS

As eggs cook, gently push, lift, and fold from one side of pan to other, using wooden spoon or heatproof rubber spatula, until large, shiny, wet curds form.

ASSEMBLING BREAKFAST BURRITOS

1. Spread portion of filling, cheese, and salsa in line across each tortilla, just off center.

2. Fold sides of each tortilla over filling, then roll bottom edge of tortilla tightly up over filling, and continue to roll into burrito.

STORE-BOUGHT EGG WHITES

When making many of our healthier egg dishes, chances are good that you're tossing egg yolks down the drain. Could store-bought egg whites put an end to the waste? These products are pasteurized liquid egg whites—some brands are 100 percent egg whites and some include small amounts of xanthan gum and triethyl citrate to enhance whipping. We tested three widely available brands, alongside hand-separated whites, in our Swedish Pancakes and Breakfast Burritos, and they all made acceptable substitutes. We slightly preferred **Eggology 100% Egg Whites**, which we found to be mostly on a par with fresh egg whites. Two tablespoons of these egg whites are equal to one large egg white.

SWEDISH PANCAKES

IT'S HARD TO HOLD BACK WHEN THE CRAVING HITS for a stack of thick, fluffy pancakes drizzled with maple syrup and butter, but we all know they aren't exactly the ideal healthy start, especially when you can't stop at just one. In our search for a sweet breakfast treat that wouldn't weigh us down, we landed on a recipe we had recently perfected for Swedish pancakes. A cousin to the French crêpe, Swedish pancakes are more delicate than American pancakes, with lacy, buttery edges and a barely custardy middle. They seemed like just the jumping off point.

Like crêpes, Swedish pancakes also have a reputation for being time-consuming (the batter typically requires at least an hour of resting time to hydrate and relax the flour) as well as tricky to flip (the thin pancake has a tendency to tear). Our existing test kitchen recipe had tackled the technical problems and come up with a simple, quick method, but we would need to take some more steps to bring these pancakes up to our light and healthy standards. Our pancakes got their luxurious texture from a combination of half-and-half, butter, and eggs (plus, they're typically served with more butter on the side). Our version of Swedish pancakes actually contained 23 grams of fat per serving: too much for two delicate pancakes. We started by reviewing our original recipe.

While developing the original recipe, we figured out a great secret ingredient for mixing the batter quickly: instant flour. After just a few turns of the whisk (no rest required), the batter was clump-free and turned out tender pancakes with nary a lump in sight. We also discovered that we could get just the right amount of lift in our pancakes by using club soda in the batter. The small amount of carbonation accomplished what neither whipped egg whites, nor baking soda, nor baking powder could manage: It gave us thin, weightless pancakes. We had also already mastered the cooking process: We tilted a butter-coated 10-inch nonstick skillet, added ⅓ cup of batter, swirled the pan to coat, and cooked the pancake almost all the way through on the first side. We used our fingers to flip it, and 30 seconds later, the pancake was ready to eat.

We began lightening by fiddling with the eggs, dairy, and butter. The original recipe contained two whole eggs plus two additional egg yolks. We knew we'd

need to scale back, but given that the yolks are key to creating the signature tender texture, we had to tread carefully. It was no shock that pancakes made with all egg whites had a gummy texture and little flavor, but we found balance (and lost 3 grams of fat per serving) when we used two whole eggs and two whites.

Next, we tackled the dairy. Our original recipe used half-and-half for richness, but its high fat content made it a no-go for our lightened recipe. Swapping in whole milk made for tender and flavorful results, but, at 16 grams of fat per serving, our pancakes were still over the limit. Could we drop all the way down to skim milk and still have edible pancakes? As it happened, the skim milk had little negative impact on the texture, and tasters could barely detect a difference. Another 2 grams of fat per serving were shaved from the total.

Finally, we experimented with lowering the amount of butter. The whopping 9 tablespoons of butter—4 that went into the batter and 5 that were

NOTES FROM THE TEST KITCHEN

COOKING SWEDISH PANCAKES

1. Tilt hot buttered skillet to one side and pour in ⅓ cup batter in slow, steady stream.

2. Swirl skillet to evenly cover bottom with batter. Cook over medium heat until bottom is spotty golden brown and top of pancake appears dry, 1 to 2 minutes.

3. Loosen edge of pancake with rubber spatula, grab edge with fingertips, and gently flip pancake. Continue to cook on second side until spotty brown, about 30 seconds longer.

SWEDISH PANCAKES

used to fry the pancakes—was not acceptable. This alone contributed 13 grams of fat per serving! We knew we'd need to keep some butter in the batter for flavor, but perhaps we could eliminate some, if not all, of the butter used for cooking. First, we played with the levels in the batter, reducing it tablespoon by tablespoon. In the end, we found that 3 tablespoons were necessary to keep the pancakes flavorful. Then we tried swapping the cooking butter out for vegetable oil spray, but the vegetable oil's out-of-place flavor came through too clearly. So, we returned to using butter, but this time we were judicious with its use. After tinkering with proportions, we found that we were able to cook all of our pancakes using just 1 melted tablespoon total, as long as we brushed it thinly onto the skillet.

After our tweaks and changes, we had dropped our pancakes down to 7 grams of fat per serving: a fine accomplishment. Instead of smearing our pancakes with butter or drowning them in syrup, we found that a small dollop of lingonberry jam (the traditional Swedish pancake garnish) was the perfect light accompaniment; its slightly sweet and fruity flavor gave our pancakes the garnish they needed without the extra calories. Finally, our lightened Swedish Pancakes were rich and tender, and they tasted nothing like diet food.

Swedish Pancakes

MAKES 15 PANCAKES

For the best texture, be sure to use instant flour, such as Wondra or Pillsbury Shake & Blend. Keep the pancakes warm, covered, in a 200-degree oven. Serve with lingonberry jam, as the Swedes do, or your favorite jam.

2   **cups (9¼ ounces) instant flour**
¼   **cup (1¾ ounces) sugar**
1   **teaspoon salt**
1½ **cups skim milk**
1½ **cups club soda**
4   **tablespoons unsalted butter, melted and cooled**
2   **large eggs plus 2 large whites, lightly beaten**

1. Combine flour, sugar, and salt in large bowl. Slowly whisk milk, club soda, 3 tablespoons butter, eggs, and egg whites into flour mixture until smooth. Heat 10-inch nonstick skillet over medium heat for 2 minutes.

2. Brush surface and sides of skillet with thin layer of remaining 1 tablespoon butter. When butter stops sizzling, pour ⅓ cup batter into skillet, tilting pan to evenly coat bottom with batter. Cook until top surface is dry and bottom is spotty golden brown, 1 to 2 minutes. Using thin spatula and fingers, flip pancake and continue to cook until second side is spotty golden brown, about 30 seconds longer. Transfer to plate and cover tightly with aluminum foil. Repeat with remaining butter and remaining batter. Serve.

PER PANCAKE: Cal 110; Fat 3.5g; Sat fat 2.5g; Chol 35mg; Carb 17g; Protein 4g; Fiber 0g; Sodium 180mg

ULTIMATE OATMEAL

OATMEAL OFTEN GETS THE SHORT END OF THE breakfast stick, typically thought of as a healthy but boring choice. And no wonder; it might be most familiar in its instant form, brown packets combining bits of dry oatmeal and artificial flavorings that get reconstituted in the microwave (usually with water). Convenient? Sure. But the muddled flavors and pasty texture hardly make it worth the three minutes spent preparing it. But even if one goes a step up from the instant variety, the results are often overcooked and gluey, with a dull flavor that only cream and sugar can rescue. But we knew better. Oatmeal can be not only hearty and comforting but also a fantastic breakfast option when trying to cook more healthfully. It was time to bring oatmeal back to life. We weren't just after an ordinary bowl of oatmeal; we wanted a foolproof method for perfectly cooked, flavorful oatmeal that was great on its own, plus a cadre of healthy and delicious add-ins that would lend flavor and texture to our base recipe.

First, we rounded up all of the varieties of oatmeal we could find and put them to the test, preparing each according to its package directions. We knew right away that we didn't want to go a step further with the instant oats. Both the flavored varieties and the plain version cooked up to a strangely gluey consistency that had no place in our kitchen. Plain old rolled oats were a major improvement, yet they still were fairly flavorless and quickly turned to mush. Our third option—steel-cut oats—was a vast improvement.

Steel-cut oats are whole, unprocessed oats that have been cut into small pieces and contain full-fledged oaty flavor. This variety took considerably longer to cook than regular rolled oats (about 25 to 30 minutes total) but was very much worth the wait. It had a faint nutty flavor, and while its consistency was surprisingly creamy, it was also toothsome.

Despite these improvements, we still needed to do some fine-tuning to determine how to bring out the best texture and flavor. To up the oats' nutty flavor, we tried toasting them in a dry skillet before adding the liquid to the pot. This step definitely helped to bring out all of the oats' subtle nuances, but because oats have a high oil content and thus are quick to burn, we found we needed to use a little bit of butter in the skillet as well. This not only kept the oats from scorching, but it also lent them a sweet, rounded flavor (which made it the clear choice over oil). By keeping the amount to a minimum—just 1 tablespoon—we still kept the fat content within reason.

Next, we worked on perfecting our cooking technique. We tested boiling the oats versus simmering them, starting the oats in cold water versus stirring them into boiling water, and cooking them covered versus uncovered. We even tried cooking them in a double boiler. The simplest approach was also the best: We brought water to a simmer, stirred in our oats, and let them continue to simmer, uncovered, until tender and creamy. The back-of-the-box directions were spot-on when it came to the liquid amount: 4 cups of liquid to 1 cup of oats gave us the perfect consistency. We also found that, while many back-of-the-box recipes call for frequent stirring, during the 30-minute cooking time the oats needed to be stirred only in the last few minutes to prevent sticking. Finally, we discovered that a few minutes' rest before serving allowed the oats to soak up any remaining liquid in the pan and become their creamy best.

At this point, our oatmeal had a fantastic texture, but we wondered if using all water for our cooking liquid was the best choice. Would adding dairy to our cooking liquid be better? Since we were after a healthy, low-fat porridge, we didn't want to add cream or even whole milk. Instead, we tried preparing our oatmeal with different ratios of low-fat milk. Oatmeal made with all milk, and even just half milk, tasted too dairy-heavy. A ratio of 3 parts water to 1 part milk, however, added a pleasant roundness in texture and flavor to the oatmeal.

Finally, we turned to the question of salt. Almost all of the back-of-the-box recipes called for the addition of salt to the oatmeal only after it had cooked for at least 10 minutes. Not sure if this was necessary, we made our last few batches with salt added at different points in the cooking period. As it turned out, we found out there was good reason for adding salt late in the game—when added at the beginning of cooking, it hardened the meal and prevented the grains from swelling.

We were impressed with the nutty, complex flavor and creamy, rich texture of our final batch: truly ultimate oatmeal. From there, we went on to create a few variations. Honey and figs, along with a dash of vanilla, lent our oatmeal a warm Mediterranean flair, and a combination of cranberries and walnuts added a sweet-sour tang and a toasty richness, as well as a burst of color. For an all-time favorite that boasted warm, autumnal appeal, we combined apple (we found that grated apple, rather than chunks, incorporated more seamlessly), raisins, and cinnamon. And last, a simple mixture of mashed bananas and a touch of brown sugar was a sure win with any crowd.

Ultimate Oatmeal

SERVES 4

Do not substitute skim milk in this recipe.

- **3** cups water
- **1** cup 1 percent low-fat milk
- **1** tablespoon unsalted butter
- **1** cup steel-cut oats
- **¼** teaspoon salt

1. Bring water and milk to simmer in large saucepan over medium heat. Meanwhile, melt butter in 12-inch skillet over medium heat. Add oats and toast, stirring constantly, until golden and fragrant, 1½ to 2 minutes.

2. Stir toasted oats into milk mixture, reduce heat to medium-low, and simmer gently until mixture is very thick, about 20 minutes.

3. Stir in salt and continue to simmer, stirring occasionally, until almost all liquid has been absorbed and oatmeal is creamy, about 10 minutes longer. Let oatmeal sit for 5 minutes before serving.

PER ¾-CUP SERVING: Cal 190; Fat 6g; Sat fat 3g; Chol 10mg; Carb 30g; Protein 8g; Fiber 4g; Sodium 180mg

VARIATIONS

Ultimate Oatmeal with Figs and Honey

Add 1 cup chopped dried figs, ¼ cup honey, ⅛ teaspoon vanilla, and ⅛ teaspoon ground cinnamon along with salt.

PER ¾-CUP SERVING: Cal 350; Fat 6g; Sat fat 3g; Chol 10mg; Carb 71g; Protein 9g; Fiber 8g; Sodium 180mg

Ultimate Oatmeal with Cranberries and Walnuts

Add ⅓ cup dried cranberries, ¼ cup chopped toasted walnuts, ¼ cup packed brown sugar, and ¼ teaspoon ground cinnamon along with salt.

PER ¾-CUP SERVING: Cal 320; Fat 11g; Sat fat 3.5g; Chol 10mg; Carb 53g; Protein 9g; Fiber 5g; Sodium 180mg

Ultimate Oatmeal with Apple, Cinnamon, and Raisins

Add 1 peeled and grated sweet apple, ⅓ cup raisins, ¼ cup maple syrup, and ¼ teaspoon ground cinnamon along with salt.

PER ¾-CUP SERVING: Cal 310; Fat 6g; Sat fat 3g; Chol 10mg; Carb 60g; Protein 9g; Fiber 6g; Sodium 180mg

Ultimate Oatmeal with Bananas and Brown Sugar

Add 2 mashed bananas and ¼ cup packed brown sugar along with salt.

PER ¾-CUP SERVING: Cal 300; Fat 6g; Sat fat 3g; Chol 10mg; Carb 58g; Protein 9g; Fiber 6g; Sodium 180mg

NOTES FROM THE TEST KITCHEN

A CUT ABOVE: STEEL-CUT OATS

We prefer to use steel-cut oats when making a hot, steamy bowl of oatmeal. (For granola and baked goods, however, we prefer to use rolled oats.) Steel-cut oats are made by slicing whole oat groats with steel blades into nubby grains. These grainy-textured oats take a little longer to cook than rolled oats, but their firm, chewy texture and fuller oat flavor are well worth the wait. Putting seven national brands of steel-cut oats to the test, we found our favorite to be **Bob's Red Mill Organic Steel Cut Oats**, which tasters praised for its outstanding buttery, nutty oat flavor and "creamy, toothsome" texture.

CHEESY BAKED GRITS

TEST KITCHEN
MAKEOVER

CHEESY BAKED GRITS IS A SOUTHERN BREAKFAST casserole of coarse-ground cornmeal baked with cheese, cream, and often bacon or sausage into a decadent, soufflé- or polenta-like dish that is nearly impossible to resist. But as you might guess, the dish hardly comes close to being healthy. And in addition to its caloric, fatty nutritional issues, most classic recipes we've tried in the test kitchen fall far short of the indulgent, comfort-food promise, turning out either bland, watery casseroles or meaty, greasy bricks. We had already developed a great test kitchen recipe that tackled many of the typical problems, boasting bright corn flavor with no sign of grease. Unfortunately, this version was also loaded with cream and cheese, tipping the scales at 370 calories and 26 grams of fat per serving. We wanted to revamp and lighten our recipe but still find a way to maintain its satisfying, indulgent soul.

We knew that we wouldn't need to tinker with the main ingredient. After all, grits are, on their own, a naturally healthy breakfast option. Simply a coarsely ground type of cornmeal, they are typically prepared porridge-style. When developing the original recipe, we tested the two basic varieties of grits: instant, which cook in five minutes; and old-fashioned, which cook in 15 minutes. We prepared both versions according to package directions and performed a side-by-side taste test. Not surprisingly, most tasters thought the instant grits were gluey and tasted overprocessed. The old-fashioned grits, on the other hand, were creamy yet retained a slightly coarse texture.

To add richness without relying solely on butter, our original recipe called for a cooking liquid made with 1 part cream and 3 parts water. We wanted to maintain this subtle dairy flavor in our lighter version, but with far less fat. Keeping the same ratio of dairy to water, we tested grits made with low-fat dairy products: 2 percent, 1 percent, and skim milk. Surprisingly, tasters couldn't find much difference among these lighter choices, so we went with the lightest—skim—in order to cut as many fat grams as possible. This one swap dropped an impressive 13 grams of fat per serving.

Next, we moved on to the other starring ingredient: the cheese. Our original recipe called for an entire 8-ounce block of extra-sharp cheddar, which was far too decadent for a healthy breakfast casserole. Since we knew that we liked the assertive flavor and creamy texture of cheddar, we decided to simply scale it back. Even when we cut the total cheese amount by half, our casserole's flavor profile was still on track and we lost 50 calories and 4 grams of fat. If we cut it back any further, the character of the dish suffered too much. By dividing our modest amount of cheese and adding one part to the grits and saving one part for the top, not only did we ensure cheesy, flavorful grits, but we also gave our casserole a pleasantly crisp topping once baked.

Next we moved on to tweaking the flavor. The original recipe used a couple of tablespoons of butter to sauté an onion before the grits and cooking liquid were added to the pot. We liked the depth and sweetness contributed by the sautéed onion, but we hoped we could get by with less butter. In the end, we found that we were able to cut the butter in half without making any compromises. For simplicity's sake, we decided to stick with just a dash of hot sauce to cut through the richness of the casserole.

Finally, we moved on to the baking process. We knew we were after a dense texture, more akin to baked polenta than custardy spoon bread. To create the proper structure, we'd need eggs to bind the grits. After fiddling with proportions, we found that we couldn't reduce the original recipe's four eggs. Any fewer and the casserole didn't hold together. We cooked our grits on the stovetop, then stirred in the eggs with the cheese and a little pepper, and poured the mixture into a lightly greased baking dish. After 40 minutes in a 350-degree oven, our newly lightened casserole emerged bubbling and golden brown, with a rich corn flavor.

We were so pleased with the outcome that we decided to explore a few variations. First, for spicy pepper fans, we swapped the cheddar for pepper Jack and added a minced jalapeño for heat. Some sautéed red bell pepper lent a pop of color and sweetness. We also created a wonderfully savory version with wilted cherry tomatoes for fresh acidity, blistered corn for sweetness, and a sprinkling of cilantro for color. We knew we'd hit the mark when tasters asked for the recipe for the next Sunday brunch.

MAKEOVER SPOTLIGHT: CHEESY BAKED GRITS

	CALORIES	FAT	SAT FAT	CHOLESTEROL
BEFORE	370	26g	16g	165mg
AFTER	200	8g	4g	100mg

Cheesy Baked Grits

SERVES 10

Smoked cheddar or Gouda both work nicely here in place of the extra-sharp cheddar. Be sure to use old-fashioned and not quick or instant grits in this recipe.

- 1 tablespoon unsalted butter
- 1 onion, chopped fine
- 1 teaspoon salt
- 4½ cups water
- 1½ cups skim milk
- ¾ teaspoon hot sauce
- 1½ cups old-fashioned grits
- 4 ounces extra-sharp cheddar cheese, shredded (1 cup)
- 4 large eggs, lightly beaten
- ¼ teaspoon pepper

1. Adjust oven rack to lower-middle position and heat oven to 350 degrees. Lightly coat 13 by 9-inch baking dish with vegetable oil spray. Melt butter in large saucepan over medium heat. Add onion and salt and cook until softened, about 5 minutes. Stir in water, milk, and hot sauce and bring to boil.

2. Slowly pour grits into boiling liquid in steady stream, whisking constantly to prevent clumping. Cover and reduce heat to low. Cook, stirring often, until grits are thick and creamy, 10 to 15 minutes.

3. Off heat, whisk in ½ cup cheddar, eggs, and pepper. Pour mixture into prepared baking dish, smooth top, and sprinkle with remaining ½ cup cheddar. Bake until top is browned and grits are hot, 35 to 45 minutes. Cool for 10 minutes before serving.

PER ⅔-CUP SERVING: Cal 200; Fat 8g; Sat fat 4g; Chol 100mg; Carb 22g; Protein 9g; Fiber 1g; Sodium 360mg

VARIATIONS

Cheesy Baked Grits with Red Bell Pepper, Pepper Jack, and Jalapeño

Add 1 finely chopped red bell pepper and 1 minced jalapeño chile to pan along with onion. Substitute 1 cup shredded pepper Jack cheese for cheddar.

PER ⅔-CUP SERVING: Cal 200; Fat 7g; Sat fat 3.5g; Chol 100mg; Carb 24g; Protein 9g; Fiber 1g; Sodium 360mg

Cheesy Baked Grits with Cherry Tomatoes, Corn, and Cilantro

Heat 1 teaspoon canola oil in 10-inch nonstick skillet over medium heat until shimmering. Add 2 cups quartered cherry tomatoes, 1 cup frozen corn, and ¼ teaspoon salt, cover, and cook for 5 minutes. Uncover, increase heat to medium-high, and cook until pan is dry and corn is lightly browned, about 4 minutes. Stir tomato-corn mixture into grits along with cheddar. Sprinkle with 1 tablespoon minced fresh cilantro before serving.

PER ⅔-CUP SERVING: Cal 220; Fat 8g; Sat fat 4g; Chol 100mg; Carb 27g; Protein 9g; Fiber 1g; Sodium 410mg

CREAM CHEESE BISCUITS

WE'VE NEVER MET A BISCUIT WE DIDN'T LIKE, BUT chock-full of butter and salt, they are pretty much a no-go when eating light. Making over these fluffy, flaky treats seemed like a fool's errand—that is, until we learned of cream cheese biscuits. Made like ordinary biscuits with flour, leavener, and buttermilk, they incorporate cream cheese in place of some of the butter. From what we'd heard, this simple swap results in biscuits that are fluffy, moist, and soft. Since even full-fat cream cheese is lower in fat than butter, out of the gate we were already on our way to a lighter alternative. But could we take it even further?

Our first task would be to determine the best ratio of cream cheese to butter. Since these were cream cheese biscuits, we thought, why use butter at all? We cobbled together a basic recipe (with all-purpose flour, sugar, baking powder, baking soda, salt, and buttermilk) and ejected the butter whole hog, replacing it with an 8-ounce block of cream cheese. Dumb idea, we admitted half an hour later as we tossed a dozen bricks into the trash. Flakes of butter melt and turn into steam in the oven, creating lightness; the cream cheese resolutely refused to flake or melt. So we added back butter, tablespoon by tablespoon, while subtracting the equivalent amount of cream cheese. At 4 tablespoons each of butter and cream cheese, our biscuits melded a slight cream cheese tang with nice buttery flavor.

Next, we wondered if the lower-fat varieties of cream cheese (⅓ less fat aka neufchatel, 50 percent less fat, or fat-free) would work as well as the full-fat stuff we had been using up until now. We found no difference in texture when we used neufchatel, and only a marginal increase in toughness when we used 50 percent less fat cream cheese. The biscuits made with fat-free cream cheese, however, were not so lucky. They were tough and leaden, and the bottoms were rubbery—basically, inedible. When we ran the numbers, we found that the difference between using 50 percent less fat and neufchatel was negligible per serving, so we settled on the neufchatel since it resulted in a slightly better texture.

At this point, the biscuits tasted great but were still short and not quite fluffy enough. Many of the recipes we'd found called for White Lily flour, a low-protein flour that's famous for producing notably tender baked goods. But because it's not easy to find nationally, we decided to try cake flour, also low protein, instead. Alas, while the texture was just as we'd hoped, these biscuits had an off-flavor. To counter this, we tested biscuits made with equal amounts of all-purpose flour and cake flour. This batch had a tender crumb and the flavor was back on track—but they were still too heavy.

Traditional biscuit wisdom states that cool fat straight from the fridge makes for the fluffiest biscuits. This fat is cut into the flour until it turns to coarse crumbs. In the oven, the crumbs then create pockets of steam in the biscuits, which turn into the biscuit's signature tender flakes. We had been going with this protocol, but we were realizing that once we got the butter and cream cheese incorporated, the cream cheese had all but melted into the flour—hardly a recipe for tender success. We knew we'd need colder fat, so we turned to the freezer. After placing both the butter and the cream cheese in the freezer for 30 minutes, we pulsed them into the flour

NOTES FROM THE TEST KITCHEN

CUTTING CREAM CHEESE BISCUITS
Instead of rolling the dough, cutting round biscuits, then rerolling the scraps to cut more, we shape the dough into a rectangle and cut 12 square biscuits. This saves time, gives our biscuits maximum lift, and avoids using rerolled dough.

Using hands and lightly floured rolling pin, gently pat and roll dough into 8 by 6-inch rectangle, about ¾ inch thick. Using bench scraper or sharp knife, cut dough into twelve 2-inch squares.

using the food processor. The mixture was transformed into the proper coarse meal full of flecks of butter and cream cheese—a good sign. We stirred in the buttermilk, rolled out the dough, cut our biscuits, and hoped for the best. This time they emerged from the oven just as we'd wanted: tall, tender, and light.

Now just one problem remained. We had been using our standard test kitchen method for shaping biscuits: Roll out the dough, cut rounds with a biscuit cutter, then reroll the scraps and cut as many more biscuits as possible. While the rerolls are never quite as good, they're usually good enough to pass muster. But the rerolls of our cream cheese biscuits were a different story. While the biscuits from the first round of cutting were pretty much perfect, the second round was surprisingly tough and squat. As it turned out, since cream cheese (especially the low-fat variety) contains significantly more water than butter, and more water helps to expedite gluten formation, our cream cheese biscuits were especially susceptible to being over-worked. For the next—and final—batch, we avoided rerolling altogether. Instead, we rolled out the dough into a rectangle, cut it into 12 squares, and baked our biscuits off. Finally, we had a dozen moist, tender, and healthy cream cheese biscuits ready for the table.

Cream Cheese Biscuits

MAKES 12 BISCUITS

Freezing the cream cheese and butter for 30 minutes is crucial to the tender, fluffy texture of these biscuits. We prefer neufchatel (⅓ less fat) cream cheese in this recipe, but you can substitute light (50 percent less fat) cream cheese if you prefer. Do not substitute fat-free cream cheese.

- 1½ cups (7½ ounces) all-purpose flour
- 1½ cups (6 ounces) cake flour
- 1 tablespoon sugar
- 1 tablespoon baking powder
- 1 teaspoon salt
- ¾ teaspoon baking soda
- 4 ounces neufchatel (⅓ less fat) cream cheese, cut into ½-inch pieces and frozen for 30 minutes
- 4 tablespoons unsalted butter, cut into ½-inch pieces and frozen for 30 minutes
- 1 cup plus 1 tablespoon buttermilk

1. Adjust oven rack to middle position and heat oven to 450 degrees. Line baking sheet with parchment paper.

2. Pulse all-purpose flour, cake flour, sugar, baking powder, salt, and baking soda in food processor until combined, about 3 pulses. Add cream cheese and butter and continue to pulse until mixture resembles coarse meal, about 15 pulses. Transfer flour mixture to large bowl. Stir in buttermilk until combined (dough may appear slightly dry).

3. Turn dough onto lightly floured counter and knead briefly until dough comes together. Pat and roll dough into 8 by 6-inch rectangle. Cut into twelve 2-inch squares and transfer to prepared baking sheet, spaced about 1½ inches apart. Bake until light brown, 12 to 15 minutes. Transfer to wire rack and let cool for 5 minutes. Serve warm.

PER BISCUIT: Cal 170; Fat 6g; Sat fat 4g; Chol 20mg; Carb 25g; Protein 4g; Fiber 1g; Sodium 440mg

MORNING GLORY MUFFINS

THOUGH SOMETIMES COMPARED TO CARROT CAKE, morning glory muffins are the brainchild of 1970s wholesome hippie cooking. The various interpretations of these muffins have one thing in common: They are usually loaded to the brim with carrots, coconut, a multitude of nuts and seeds, fresh and dried fruits, and countless spices. Despite their appearance and whole-some billing, those first morning glory muffins were anything but healthy. In addition to an overabundance of nuts, they were loaded down with a cup or more of vegetable oil. Could we lighten this treat to make it as healthy as its original promise?

We started with a version of the original 1970s recipe. In addition to some usual muffin-batter ingredients (flour, sugar, eggs, oil, salt, and leavener), the recipe contained grated carrots and apples, canned crushed pine-apple, coconut, walnuts, raisins, and cinnamon. It was a long list of ingredients, and we'd need to tackle them one by one to create a great foolproof, lightened recipe.

We started with the most obvious offender: the oil. Clearly, 1 cup of oil (and the 9 grams of fat per serving that came along with it) was far too much for our lightened recipe. Many muffin and quick-bread recipes include a significant amount of oil in order to maintain a moist crumb, but since all of the fruit in our muffins would contribute a great deal of moisture anyway, we figured we could cut the oil way back with no ill effects. We began our testing with 8 tablespoons and gradually reduced it, tablespoon by tablespoon, until there was a markedly negative difference in texture. We brought down the total amount of oil to a mere 4 tablespoons, but tasters pointed out the oil wasn't doing much in terms of flavor. Replacing the oil with melted butter made a huge difference in the right direction.

Yet even with the loss of so much fat, our muffins were still gummy and wet. We evaluated our moist stir-ins: carrots, apples, and pineapple. We quickly learned that we couldn't cut back on the carrots. Any less than 1½ cups gave us a muffin with no carrot presence. So we decided to modify the pineapple and apple. Instead of reducing the total amount used (after all, we wanted to maximize the amount of healthy fruit), we drained the fruits in a fine-mesh strainer, then pressed out and discarded the juice before mixing the fruit into the batter. As we had hoped, this method produced moist, but not soggy, muffins. But the missing fruit juice also resulted in missing fruit flavor.

NOTES FROM THE TEST KITCHEN

MUFFIN TINS
Six years ago, we tested muffin tins and decided on two must-have features: a nonstick coating and handles for easy gripping. Recently, we decided to revisit muffin tins and chose eight nonstick models that all had extended rims or silicone tabs for gripping. To find the winner, the test kitchen baked more than 300 muffins and cupcakes. While the nonstick coatings ensured easy release of baked goods, some coatings were more effective at this than others. To gauge durability, we smeared the tins with béchamel and let it harden overnight; the next day, testers scraped and scrubbed. We also shocked the pans by heating them empty to 500 degrees and then plunging them in ice water to see if any would warp. Our winner, the **Wilton Avanti Everglide Metal-Safe Non-Stick Muffin Pan**, gained praise for its wide, extended rims and raised lip, which made the pan easy to handle. Browning was acceptably even, though not stellar—but the price, $13.99, sure is right.

When we make low-fat sauces and dressings in the test kitchen, we often boil down fruit juices to create an emulsified, flavorful substitute for oil. This thickened liquid was exactly what the muffins needed. For our next test, after pressing the fruit, we boiled the cup of juices down to ¼ cup and added this syrup back to the batter. We also cut back on sugar by ¼ cup to compensate for the added syrup. Not only did this step reduce calories, but it also helped to lighten the texture of the muffins and let the fruit flavors come to the forefront.

The moisture level in check, we broached the question of the coconut and walnuts. Our working recipe contained ½ cup of nuts and almost a whole cup of coconut, which together added 5 grams of fat to each serving. We knew we should cut back, but how far could we go before the character of the muffins suffered? We scaled the amounts down as far as we were comfortable (to ¼ cup each) and stirred the nuts and coconut into our batter. We could barely taste either ingredient, and they became unappealingly soggy in our moist muffins. To increase their flavor and try to prevent sogginess, we tried toasting both the coconut and walnuts before adding them to the batter. This step indeed upped their flavor, but once they hit the batter they soaked up moisture and, once again, became soggy. Next we tried sprinkling the coconut and nuts on top of the muffins where they'd stand out and stay dry, but these muffins came out squat and flat-topped. It turned out that the nutty additions were contributing much-needed structure to the batter, and pulling them out made the muffins sink. Perhaps we could find a better way to incorporate them into the flour mixture. For our next batch, we ground the toasted coconut and walnuts finely in the food processor and mixed the meal into the dry ingredients. The result? Deep, nutty flavor and nicely domed muffins with no mealy bits.

At this point, our muffins had great structure and flavor, but they were a bit small since reducing the nuts had removed a great deal of bulk. We decided to take a cue from the muffins' hodgepodge origins and add something new. Chopped dried pineapple did the trick, providing texture and sweetness without any extra moisture that might throw off the now-perfected balance. The final result? A moist, fruity, and nutty muffin that was finally as healthy as its origins claimed.

MORNING GLORY MUFFINS

MAKES 12 MUFFINS

We prefer golden raisins for their color, but you can substitute brown if desired.

- ¼ cup (¾ ounce) sweetened shredded coconut, toasted
- ¼ cup walnuts, toasted
- 2¼ cups (11¼ ounces) all-purpose flour
- ¾ cup (5¼ ounces) sugar
- 1½ teaspoons baking soda
- 1 teaspoon ground cinnamon
- ¾ teaspoon salt
- ½ teaspoon baking powder
- 1 (8-ounce) can crushed pineapple in juice
- 1 Granny Smith apple, peeled, cored, and shredded
- 3 large eggs
- 4 tablespoons unsalted butter, melted and cooled
- 1 teaspoon vanilla extract
- 3 carrots, peeled and shredded (1½ cups)
- 1 cup golden raisins
- ¾ cup finely chopped dried pineapple

1. Adjust oven rack to middle position and heat oven to 350 degrees. Lightly coat 12-cup muffin tin with vegetable oil spray. Process coconut and walnuts in food processor until finely ground, about 15 seconds. Add flour, sugar, baking soda, cinnamon, salt, and baking powder and pulse until combined, about 3 pulses. Transfer mixture to large bowl.

2. Pour crushed pineapple into fine-mesh strainer set over liquid measuring cup, then add shredded apple to strainer. Press fruit dry (juice should measure about 1 cup). Transfer juice to small saucepan and bring to boil over medium-high heat. Reduce heat to medium and simmer briskly until juice has reduced to ¼ cup, about 10 minutes. Let cool slightly.

3. Transfer to medium bowl and whisk in eggs, melted butter, and vanilla until smooth. Gently fold egg mixture into flour mixture until just combined. Gently fold in pineapple mixture, carrots, raisins, and dried pineapple.

4. Divide batter evenly among muffin cups. Bake until toothpick inserted in center of muffin comes out clean, 24 to 28 minutes. Let muffins cool in tin on wire rack for 10 minutes. Remove muffins from tin and let cool for at least 10 minutes before serving.

PER MUFFIN: Cal 300; Fat 7g; Sat fat 4g; Chol 65mg; Carb 53g; Protein 5g; Fiber 3g; Sodium 360mg

WHOLE WHEAT SANDWICH BREAD

SURE, A HOME-BAKED LOAF OF BREAD REQUIRES more work than a trip to the grocery store, but with the right recipe in hand, the difference between your own homemade loaf and the stuff in the bag will make you realize that sandwich bread shouldn't be just a carrier for the stuff between the slices. And while white bread is a crowd pleaser, we all know that whole wheat sandwich bread is the healthier choice. The only problem? Most recipes either contain so little of the whole grain stuff that it might as well be white bread, or they call for so much whole wheat that the loaves bake up far too dense. These homemade versions are hardly better than the store-bought variety, which usually consist of cottony loaves with little flavor. Could we create a healthy whole wheat sandwich bread with a full-blown nutty taste and a tender, sliceable crumb that made it worth the effort?

Since baking with whole wheat flour leads to a mine-field of issues, we decided to start with a test kitchen recipe for white bread, then gradually replace a portion of the all-purpose white flour with wheat until we hit the winning combination. We mixed the dough in a stand mixer until well kneaded, then let it rise until doubled in size, turning it midway through to remove large gas bubbles and promote even fermentation. Next, we shaped it into loaves and let the dough rise a second time in the pan. Right before baking, we poured boiling water into an empty loaf pan that we'd positioned on the bottom rack. This clever trick (at least with our white bread recipe) would prevent the crust from drying out before the loaves fully expanded. We then placed the pans in the oven on a preheated baking stone to ensure maximum rise.

After several rounds of bread baking, we learned that we could add only up to 40 percent whole wheat flour before the bread became too heavy. This result wasn't too surprising: The cornerstone of any good bread is gluten, the network of structural proteins that forms when the flour is kneaded with water. The bran in whole wheat flour, however, has sharp edges that cut gluten strands, leading to heavy and crumbly loaves. So 40 percent wheat flour was about what we expected for proper texture, but unfortunately that bran is what contributes flavor and nutrition to whole wheat bread. We wanted more of both.

To allow us to up the whole wheat ante, we'd need to alter some of the other ingredients. First, to increase the overall amount of gluten in our dough, we substituted bread flour for the all-purpose flour. This change allowed us in turn to bump up the amount of whole wheat flour to 50 percent; but we still wanted to include more.

In many whole grain bread recipes, the grains are soaked in liquid before being incorporated into the dough. This softening process accomplishes three things: It prevents the sharp edges from puncturing and deflating the dough, it keeps the grains from robbing moisture from the dough and toughening the crumb, and it helps to reduce bitterness by converting the starches in the flour into sugars. When we soaked our wheat flour (along with some wheat germ for an extra boost in flavor) in the refrigerator overnight, the results were even better than we had hoped. We were able to bring the total proportion of wheat flour up to 60 percent with no decrease in loaf volume.

The loaf now had plenty of wheat flavor, but the bread still tasted flat. As we learned when making our Foolproof Thin-Crust Pizza (page 128), we got the most flavor when we built our dough recipe using a sponge (also known as a biga or preferment). This mixture of flour, water, and yeast is left to sit overnight to develop a range of unique flavors. The next day, it is kneaded into the remaining ingredients. Since our recipe was already an overnight process, we mixed the sponge at the same time as the soaker and let them both sit overnight. The next morning, we proofed, shaped, and baked the dough as before. The result? A unanimous thumbs up.

Now that we had our basic recipe figured out, there were just two minor tests to sort through. Up to this point, we had been using a bit of granulated sugar for additional sweetness, but after testing other options, we preferred the complexity that came from honey. And then there was the fat. We were using butter for its flavor, but it was making the bread just a tad too tender and rich. Swapping out some of the butter for canola oil proved to be an easy fix.

With these changes, our bread was hearty yet soft-textured, sliced cleanly, and offered up an earthy, faintly sweet flavor. As the warm loaves came out of the oven, our tasters lined up for a slice. It was so great on its own we didn't even need to turn it into a sandwich, though we all agreed it could take even the most humble sandwich fillings to the next level.

SHAPING WHOLE WHEAT BREAD

1. Halve dough and pat each portion into 17 by 8-inch rectangle, with short side facing you.

2. Roll each sheet toward you into tight cylinder. Keep roll taut by tucking roll under itself as you go. Pinch seam to seal.

3. Place each loaf seam side down in prepared loaf pan.

4. Make shallow slash down center of each loaf using sharp knife to prevent bread from tearing when it rises.

WHOLE WHEAT FLOUR

Whole wheat flour boasts a more pronounced wheat flavor than the refined white stuff derived from just the grain's stripped-down inner layer, or endosperm. We chose five brands and tasted them in our Whole Wheat Sandwich Bread. The flours were milled in a range of grain sizes, from coarse to fine. Their textures in bread corresponded, with coarse flour giving us coarse and crumbly loaves, and more finely milled flour producing a finer crumb. In the end, finely ground **King Arthur Premium Whole Wheat Flour** won out for its sweet, nutty flavor and hearty but not overly coarse texture.

WHOLE WHEAT SANDWICH BREAD

Whole Wheat Sandwich Bread

MAKES 2 LOAVES

If you don't have a baking stone, bake the bread on an overturned and preheated rimmed baking sheet set on the middle oven rack. Wheat germ is usually found either in the baking aisle near the flours or with hot cereals such as oatmeal.

SPONGE

- 2 **cups (11 ounces) bread flour**
- 1 **cup water, heated to 110 degrees**
- ½ **teaspoon instant or rapid-rise yeast**

SOAKER

- 3 **cups (16½ ounces) whole wheat flour**
- ½ **cup (2⅛ ounces) wheat germ**
- 2 **cups whole milk**

DOUGH

- 6 **tablespoons unsalted butter, softened**
- ¼ **cup honey**
- 2 **tablespoons instant or rapid-rise yeast**
- 2 **tablespoons canola oil**
- 4 **teaspoons salt**

1. FOR THE SPONGE: Combine flour, water, and yeast in large bowl and stir with wooden spoon until uniform mass forms and no dry flour remains, about 1 minute. Cover bowl with plastic wrap and let stand at room temperature for at least 8 hours or up to 24 hours.

2. FOR THE SOAKER: Combine flour, wheat germ, and milk in second large bowl and stir with wooden spoon until shaggy mass forms, about 1 minute. Transfer dough to lightly floured counter and knead by hand until smooth, 2 to 3 minutes. Return soaker to bowl, cover tightly with plastic wrap, and refrigerate for at least 8 hours or up to 24 hours.

3. FOR THE DOUGH: Tear soaker into 1-inch pieces and place in bowl of stand mixer fitted with dough hook. Add sponge, butter, honey, yeast, oil, and salt and mix on low speed until cohesive mass starts to form, about 2 minutes. Increase speed to medium and knead until dough is smooth and elastic, 8 to 10 minutes. Transfer dough to lightly floured counter and knead by hand to form smooth, round ball, about 1 minute. Place dough in large lightly greased bowl. Cover tightly with plastic and let rise at room temperature for 45 minutes.

4. Gently press down on center of dough to deflate. Lightly spray rubber spatula or bowl scraper with vegetable oil spray. Fold partially risen dough over itself by gently lifting and folding edge of dough toward middle. Turn bowl 90 degrees; fold again. Turn bowl and fold dough 6 more times (for total of 8 turns). Cover tightly with plastic and let rise at room temperature until doubled in size, about 45 minutes.

5. Spray two 8½ by 4½-inch loaf pans with oil spray. Transfer dough to well-floured counter and divide in half. Press 1 piece of dough into 17 by 8-inch rectangle. Roll dough into firm cylinder, keeping roll taut by tucking it under itself as you go. Turn loaf seam side up and pinch loaf closed. Place loaf seam side down in prepared pan, pressing gently into corners. Repeat with second piece of dough. Cover loaves loosely with lightly greased plastic and let rise at room temperature until nearly doubled in size, 1 to 1½ hours (top of loaves should rise about 1 inch over lip of pan).

6. One hour before baking, adjust oven racks to middle and lowest positions, place baking stone on middle rack, place empty loaf pan or other heatproof pan on bottom rack, and heat oven to 400 degrees. Bring 2 cups water to boil on stovetop. Using sharp serrated knife or single-edge razor blade, make one ¼-inch-deep slash lengthwise down center of each loaf. Working quickly, pour boiling water into empty loaf pan in oven and set loaves in pans on baking stone. Reduce oven temperature to 350 degrees. Bake until crust is dark brown and loaves register 200 degrees, 40 to 50 minutes, rotating and switching pans halfway through baking. Transfer pans to wire rack and let cool for 5 minutes. Remove loaves from pans, return to rack, and let cool to room temperature, about 2 hours, before slicing and serving.

PER ½-INCH SLICE: Cal 120; **Fat** 4g; **Sat fat** 2g; **Chol** 5mg; **Carb** 18g; **Protein** 4g; **Fiber** 2g; **Sodium** 300mg

ROSEMARY FOCACCIA

AT ITS BEST, FOCACCIA IS A THICK, PLEASANTLY chewy, and versatile flatbread, typically scented with olive oil and topped with a sprinkling of aromatics and herbs such as rosemary. It's equally tasty served on its own or as the base for a hearty sandwich. Made from a wet dough, it is cooked quickly in a hot oven to create a crisp, browned crust. It's easy to understand the appeal of this Italian staple, yet most focaccia found in the United States is either leaden and oil-slicked, or dry and bland. On top of all that, the copious oil bakers typically add when making even the simplest of these mediocre loaves results in bread that's a diet disaster. We wanted to come up with a new recipe for focaccia that would bring out the best in the flatbread—a light and airy loaf with just the right amount of chew—and also maintain a healthy profile.

We already knew from making our Whole Wheat Sandwich Bread (page 254) that using a sponge would be a huge step toward maximizing flavor. This mixture of flour, water, and yeast is left to sit overnight to develop a wide range of flavors. We made our sponge the night before mixing the dough. In the morning, we added the rest of the ingredients (flour, water, yeast, and salt), kneaded it all in the stand mixer, and then let it rise for a few hours. We shaped the dough into a rustic round, brushed it with a touch of olive oil, and baked our bread on a preheated pizza stone in a blazing-hot oven. The pizza stone was key for jump-starting the baking process and ensuring constant and strong heat throughout the focaccia's time in the oven.

While the flavor of our first attempt was spot-on, we hadn't quite nailed the tender, airy interior we were after—and we had a hunch the mixing method might be the culprit. Our fast, powerful stand mixer was developing too much gluten (the strong, elastic network of proteins that give bread its crumb structure). Figuring that we needed a gentler approach, we recalled the test kitchen's recipe for almost no-knead bread. Rather than relying on kneading to develop gluten and build the bread's structure, the no-knead process takes advantage of enzymes naturally present in the flour to produce the same effect. All we had to do to transform our focaccia into a no-knead bread was to add about ⅓ cup more water. This extra water makes for more efficient gluten production and also helps to open up the crumb structure, keeping the bread tender, light, and airy.

But to be effective, this method requires a rest of up to 18 hours after the dough is mixed to allow time for the gluten to develop. To speed up the process and to give our bread a little more structure, we decided to add a folding (or "turning") step. While our next batch of dough rose, we gently lifted and folded the edges of the dough toward the middle every 30 minutes and then

let it rest. Roughly three hours later, the dough was a soft, supple, bubbly mass that had more than doubled in volume. Once it was baked, the results were even better than we had hoped: The loaves had leaped twice as tall, bronzed beautifully, and contained a maze of bubbles.

Still, we wanted to shorten the three-hour proofing and gluten development stage. We've learned in the past that salt can have a profound affect on the way in which flour absorbs water. Perhaps adding the salt too early was slowing the dough down. For our next test, we tried letting the dough rest for 15 minutes before stirring in the salt, and, just as we had hoped, the dough was ready to use in just two hours.

Our bread was almost perfect. It had just enough chew, a light texture, and a pleasantly subtle olive oil flavor. What it lacked, however, was the crunchy bottom indicative of good focaccia. We didn't want to add more oil, but perhaps we could find a way to contain it. On a hunch, we moved our free-form breads into round cake pans, where our tablespoon of oil couldn't escape. After swirling the dough in the oil and some coarse salt, we gently stretched it to the pan's edge, let it proof for just a few extra minutes, and scattered a healthy dose of chopped fresh rosemary over the top before sliding it onto our preheated pizza stone. Crackly crisp on the bottom, deeply browned on top, with an interior that was open and airy, this focaccia was a revelation.

Rosemary Focaccia

MAKES 2 LOAVES

If you don't have a baking stone, bake the loaves on an overturned, preheated rimmed baking sheet set on the upper-middle oven rack.

SPONGE

- ½ cup (2½ ounces) all-purpose flour
- ⅓ cup water, heated to 110 degrees
- ¼ teaspoon instant or rapid-rise yeast

DOUGH

- 2½ cups (12½ ounces) all-purpose flour
- 1¼ cups water, heated to 110 degrees
- 1 teaspoon instant or rapid-rise yeast
    Kosher salt
- 2 tablespoons extra-virgin olive oil
- 2 tablespoons minced fresh rosemary

1. FOR THE SPONGE: Combine flour, water, and yeast in large bowl and stir with wooden spoon until uniform mass forms and no dry flour remains, about 1 minute. Cover bowl tightly with plastic wrap and let stand at room temperature for at least 8 hours or up to 24 hours.

2. FOR THE DOUGH: Stir flour, water, and yeast into sponge with wooden spoon until uniform mass forms and no dry flour remains, about 1 minute. Cover with plastic and let rise at room temperature for 15 minutes.

3. Sprinkle 2 teaspoons salt over dough; stir into dough until thoroughly incorporated, about 1 minute. Cover with plastic and let rise at room temperature for 30 minutes. Lightly spray rubber spatula or bowl scraper with vegetable oil spray. Fold partially risen dough over itself by gently lifting and folding edge of dough toward middle. Turn bowl 90 degrees; fold again. Turn bowl and fold dough 6 more times (for total of 8 turns). Cover with plastic and let rise for 30 minutes. Repeat folding, turning, and rising 2 more times, for total of three 30-minute rises.

4. One hour before baking, adjust oven rack to upper-middle position, place baking stone on rack, and heat oven to 500 degrees. Gently transfer dough to lightly floured counter. Lightly dust top of dough with flour and divide in half. Shape each piece of dough into 5-inch round by gently tucking under edges. Coat two 9-inch round cake pans with 1 tablespoon oil each. Sprinkle each pan with ½ teaspoon salt. Place round of dough in pan, top side down; slide dough around pan to coat with oil and salt, then flip dough over. Repeat with second piece of dough. Cover pans with plastic and let rest for 5 minutes.

5. Using fingertips, press dough out toward edge of pan, taking care not to tear it. (If dough resists stretching, let dough relax for additional 5 to 10 minutes.) Using dinner fork, poke entire surface of dough 25 to 30 times, popping any large bubbles. Sprinkle rosemary evenly over top of dough. Let dough rest in pans until slightly bubbly, 5 to 10 minutes.

6. Place pans on baking stone and reduce oven temperature to 450 degrees. Bake until tops are golden brown, 25 to 28 minutes, rotating pans halfway through baking. Transfer pans to wire rack and let cool for 5 minutes. Remove loaves from pans and return to rack. Let cool for at least 30 minutes. Slice each loaf into 8 pieces and serve.

PER SLICE: **Cal** 90; **Fat** 2g; **Sat fat** 0g; **Chol** 0mg; **Carb** 16g; **Protein** 2g; **Fiber** 1g; **Sodium** 210mg

---

NOTES FROM THE TEST KITCHEN

SHAPING FOCACCIA

1. Divide dough in half and gently shape halves into rounds. Place in oiled, salted pans, then coat with oil and salt and flip. Cover with plastic wrap; let rest for 5 minutes.

2. Using fingertips, press dough out toward edges of pan, taking care not to tear dough. If dough resists, let dough relax for 5 to 10 minutes and try again.

3. With dinner fork, poke dough surface 25 to 30 times. Sprinkle rosemary evenly over top. Let dough rest in pan until slightly bubbly, 5 to 10 minutes.

THE READ ON OVEN THERMOMETERS

Since all ovens cycle on and off to maintain temperature, even the best models periodically deviate from the desired heat by at least a few degrees. And we've found that they can be off by as much as 50 degrees unless they're recalibrated regularly. A good oven thermometer can literally save the roast. We prefer dial-face to bulb; the tinted alcohol used in bulb models can get stuck, compromising accuracy. They should be accurate, durable, easy to read, and able to be mounted securely out of the way of pans. Our recent favorite, the CDN Multi-Mount Oven Thermometer, worked fine until the numbers on the dial were burned off by the heat. We knew then that we'd need to retest our options. We ran five different thermometers through a gamut of tests, from accuracy tests to long-term readability. As before, the CDN's numbers faded after a few months. Other models developed fogged or discolored faces, got in the way of cooking vessels, or were off by as much as 10 degrees. In the end, the **Cooper-Atkins Oven Thermometer** (model #24HP), $5.95, impressed us most. It's accurate, hangs or stands freely on oven racks, and after months of testing, its numbers remained clear and readable.

LIGHT AND FLUFFY CHOCOLATE MOUSSE

M   = TEST KITCHEN MAKEOVER

SOFT AND CHEWY PEANUT BUTTER COOKIES

CRISP, CRUNCHY COOKIES ARE NEARLY IMPOSSIBLE to beat, especially when paired with a cup of coffee for dunking, but when it comes to peanut butter cookies, there's nothing like a big chewy one with an ice-cold glass of milk. Yet despite the unctuousness of their central ingredient, peanut butter cookies often suffer from crumbly, sandy texture and bland flavor. We wanted to create a cookie with big peanut flavor and a moist, chewy texture. On top of that, we wanted to do it without going overboard on fat and calories. Now, developing an appealing low-fat cookie is easier said than done. Grocery store shelves packed with packages of barely edible low-cal and low-fat cookies give clear proof of this fact. And getting a low-fat *peanut butter* cookie recipe right is even harder, since the starring ingredient is loaded with fat. Could we develop a recipe for low-fat chewy peanut butter cookies that still had big peanut butter flavor?

We surveyed a number of peanut butter cookie recipes, but of all the contenders we tried, the one that produced the softest, most pliable cookie used a cup of honey for the primary sweetener. While we loved the texture of these cookies, the peanut butter, hardly a retiring flavor, was nonetheless masked by the honey. Still, it was a place to start. To retain some of the moisture the honey provided but lose its overbearing flavor, we took it down to ½ cup. No one missed the sweetness, but its flavor persisted, so we looked for a replacement. Like honey, maple syrup and molasses competed with the peanut butter. But light corn syrup worked well, and by the time we replaced the white sugar with light brown sugar, the cookies' soft and chewy stock had soared: The brown sugar contributed the added moisture we wanted, as well as a subtle caramel flavor.

If we were going to keep these cookies on the light side, we would need to tackle the elephant in the room: peanut butter. While high in protein, peanut butter, as we all know, is loaded with fat—and some recipes call for as much as 1½ cups. We would need to settle on a type and amount that would deliver knockout peanut flavor without sending our fat counters sky high. Processed peanut butter (i.e., the familiar stuff like Jif and Skippy) produced chewier cookies than natural peanut butter, thanks to their partially hydrogenated oils.

And the creamy kind won out over crunchy. Next, we tested decreasing the amount of peanut butter to the bare minimum without sacrificing flavor. We were surprised that reducing the peanut butter by almost two-thirds—from over-the-top 1½ cups to just ½ cup—still gave us sufficient peanut flavor, but unfortunately, the texture suffered. Previous testing with chewy cookie recipes had shown us that it is the combination of fats in a recipe that contributes to this particular texture. We decided to examine the fats in our recipe and see how we might manipulate them to get the results we were after.

The peanut butter provided a set amount of fat, so we had to work with that in mind. We opted to start with butter rather than shortening since we figured it would also contribute to the flavor. Starting with 5 tablespoons (down from ½ cup in our original working recipe), we baked a batch and waited for it to cool. While these cookies had great flavor, they were crisper than we wanted. Hoping to keep some of the buttery flavor but lose the crispness, we tested swapping out some of the butter for vegetable oil. In side-by-side tests using different proportions of butter and vegetable oil, tasters overwhelmingly preferred the sample with a higher ratio of vegetable oil to butter, 3 tablespoons to 2 tablespoons. These cookies had the best chewy yet tender texture. Adding the liquid fat of oil meant we had to reduce the other liquid—corn syrup—in the cookie or risk that the cookies would spread into paper-thin crêpes. We found that ⅓ cup of corn syrup provided the right balance of sweetness and moisture.

We were close, but looking for one last place to tweak our cookie, we turned to the eggs. Our working recipe contained two whole eggs, but years in the test kitchen has taught us that egg whites make for crispy cookies. We decided to try getting rid of one whole egg with the hope that we could reduce crispness and also cut some fat and cholesterol. To our delight, we didn't miss the egg at all. And to reinforce the peanut flavor, we sprinkled some chopped peanuts on top of the next batch of cookies before they went into the oven.

Two final steps were pivotal in getting the perfect texture. While most recipes we surveyed used a mixture of baking soda and baking powder, we followed a tip gleaned from our science editor to eliminate the powder and try soda alone. Baking soda reacted instantly with the acidic ingredients in the dough (brown sugar, for one) to create bubbles that expanded in the heat of the oven. That caused the cookies to puff up before their structure had time to set, and then to collapse, leaving the centers soft and chewy. Finally, underbaking the cookies slightly—and letting them sit on the cookie sheet for five minutes after they came out of the oven to finish—proved the crowning touch to ultimate chewiness.

The rate at which the cookies disappeared from their plate was all the proof we needed that we had nailed the recipe. These cookies were chewy and chock-full of peanutty flavor; the only thing missing (aside from a ton of fat and calories) was an ice-cold milk chaser.

NOTES FROM THE TEST KITCHEN

RECONSIDERING THE WORLD OF PEANUT BUTTERS
Selecting a jar of peanut butter never used to be complicated. Once you aligned yourself with either the creamy or the crunchy camp, you had two basic choices: conventional peanut butters made with hydrogenated oil and other additives, or the barely processed versions containing just nuts and maybe a pinch of salt. In the past, we've been firm believers in the conventional kind. As much as we might like the idea of a healthier spread made only with ground-up nuts, we've found that these generally offer the texture of spackle and a taste sorely in need of added salt and sweeteners—and yes, hydrogenated fat. But these days it seems as though manufacturers have literally gone nuts, so we decided it was time to revisit the world of peanut butter.

We gathered a number of conventional and natural butters, some of which mimic conventional peanut butter with naturally hydrogenated palm oil. In the creamy peanut butter category, tasters sampled 10 brands plain, in peanut butter cookies, and in a spicy satay sauce. Texture proved paramount. The peanut butters had to be smooth, creamy, and spreadable; they also had to have a good balance of sweet and salty flavors. Nobody was especially surprised by the overall champ, **Skippy Peanut Butter**, a regular old hydrogenated oil-based spread noted for having a supremely "smooth," "creamy" texture that even made up for what a few tasters deemed a "slightly weak" nutty flavor. What did surprise us, however, was the very close runner-up: **Jif Natural Peanut Butter Spread**, which tasters praised for its "dark-roasty flavor," was one of two palm oil-based peanut butters to make the "recommended" list.

Soft and Chewy Peanut Butter Cookies
MAKES 2 DOZEN COOKIES

Use processed peanut butter for the softest, chewiest texture. The dough is quite soft, so keep it chilled until you are ready to form and bake the cookies. For faster portioning of the dough, you can use a #40 portion scoop. These cookies are best eaten on the day they are baked.

1¼ cups (6¼ ounces) all-purpose flour

¾ teaspoon baking soda

½ teaspoon salt

½ cup creamy peanut butter

½ cup packed (3½ ounces) light brown sugar

⅓ cup light corn syrup

¼ cup (1¾ ounces) granulated sugar

3 tablespoons canola oil

2 tablespoons unsalted butter, melted and cooled slightly

1 large egg

1 teaspoon vanilla extract

3 tablespoons dry-roasted peanuts, chopped fine

1. Adjust oven racks to upper-middle and lower-middle positions and heat oven to 350 degrees. Line 2 baking sheets with parchment paper. Whisk flour, baking soda, and salt together in medium bowl.

2. In large bowl, whisk peanut butter, brown sugar, corn syrup, granulated sugar, oil, melted butter, egg, and vanilla together until smooth. Stir in flour mixture until just combined. Divide dough in half, wrap in plastic wrap, and refrigerate until firm, about 1 hour.

3. Working with 2 tablespoons of dough at a time, roll into balls and place 2 inches apart on prepared sheets, 12 dough balls per sheet. Using greased bottom of drinking glass, gently press each ball to an even ¾-inch thickness. Sprinkle tops evenly with chopped peanuts, pressing lightly to adhere.

4. Bake cookies until puffed and edges are lightly browned, 12 to 14 minutes, switching and rotating sheets halfway through baking. Let cookies cool on sheets for 5 minutes, then serve warm or transfer to wire rack and let cool completely, about 30 minutes.

PER COOKIE: Cal 130; Fat 6g; Sat fat 1.5g; Chol 10mg; Carb 16g; Protein 3g; Fiber 1g; Sodium 120mg

FAIRY GINGERBREAD COOKIES

FAIRY GINGERBREAD COOKIES

SOMETIMES DEVELOPING A LIGHT DESSERT IS AS EASY as stumbling across the right recipe, as we did when we discovered Fairy Gingerbread Cookies in a cookbook from 1893. Intrigued by the fanciful name, we read on about the curious method—no eggs, no leavener, batter spread "no thicker than a visiting card" on an inverted baking pan. Naturally low in fat and delicate in texture, this was no ordinary gingerbread. Thinking we had discovered the angel food cake of cookies, we decided to develop our own recipe for Fairy Gingerbread Cookies.

Following the 19th-century recipes we unearthed, we creamed light brown sugar with softened butter (in a roughly 2:1 ratio) until it was light and fluffy and then slowly added the remaining ingredients (bread flour, milk, dried ground ginger). With some difficulty, we spread the stiff batter with the back of a knife into an ultra-thin layer across a cookie sheet. (Apparently, a "visiting card" was about as thick as a modern business card.) Then we baked it, as directed, in a "slack oven" (we went with a moderate 350 degrees). Fifteen minutes later, we pulled the sheet from the oven and, working quickly, cut the result into rectangles.

These cookies came out unlike any gingerbread cookie we'd ever made. With a crisp, feather-light texture, they shattered in a single bite, then promptly melted in our mouths. The indulgent recipe title rang true: as delicate as fairy wings, indeed.

Once we got past the ethereal texture, however, the appeal faded. These cookies were pretty bland. Bumping up the ginger flavor was clearly in order, as was rounding out the overall flavor complexity. But the fairy-wing texture had us sold.

Taking care of the easy stuff first, we started by adding a bit of vanilla extract and salt, and the flavor quickly stepped up. Then we tried doubling the amount of ground ginger (up from 1 teaspoon to 2 teaspoons). But without any competing flavors, the sharp, astringent quality of the dried spice dominated.

We tried to mellow it by steeping it in the milk first, but this didn't do anything to help our case. Retreating to 1½ teaspoons, next we decided to try toasting the ginger in a dry skillet, hoping to bring out more of its floral qualities. The kitchen quickly filled with a gingery aroma, which we took as a good sign, and the resulting cookies boasted a welcome aromatic punch. But they still needed more ginger flavor, so we went straight to the source, grating some fresh ginger right into the batter. With this two-pronged approach, we now had zesty ginger flavor in spades that wasn't harsh.

We also had a heavy batter that was a bear to wrestle into a thin layer across the baking sheet. We'd been using bread flour, as called for in the vintage recipes we had come across. Could switching to softer, lower-protein all-purpose flour help? We gave it a shot, and while this batter with all-purpose flour was a little more malleable, it was still a struggle. Next, we reduced the amount of flour by 2 tablespoons (from the full cup we had been using). Finally, we had a batter that was loose enough to coax over the cookie sheet without a fight but stiff enough that it didn't drip over the edges.

But the flour adjustment robbed the cookies of some of their crunch and fairy-wing airiness. Adding a modest amount of baking soda (½ teaspoon) made the cookies puff up in the oven just enough that they set with a lighter crumb, and hence achieved a sublime crispiness once baked and cooled. Unfortunately, baking soda also promotes browning, and it made the edges of these thin cookies dark before their centers were cooked. Thankfully, the solution to this problem was the easiest yet: lowering the oven temperature to 325 degrees. (Apparently, our "slack oven" wasn't quite slack enough.)

We found that it was difficult to eat just one of our perfected treat, but heck, with only 25 calories and 1 gram of fat per cookie, we didn't have to limit ourselves. Fairy gingerbread, indeed! Now if only we could harness some of the same magic to use in chocolate cake.

Fairy Gingerbread Cookies

MAKES 5 DOZEN COOKIES

Use cookie or baking sheets that measure at least 15 by 12 inches. Don't be disconcerted by the scant amount of batter: It needs to be spread very thin. Use the edges of the parchment paper as your guide, covering the entire surface thinly and evenly.

- 1½ teaspoons ground ginger
- ¾ cup (3¾ ounces) plus 2 tablespoons all-purpose flour
- ½ teaspoon baking soda
- ¼ teaspoon salt
- 5 tablespoons unsalted butter, softened
- ½ cup packed (3½ ounces) plus 1 tablespoon light brown sugar
- 4 teaspoons grated fresh ginger
- ¾ teaspoon vanilla extract
- ¼ cup whole milk, room temperature

1. Adjust oven racks to upper-middle and lower-middle positions and heat oven to 325 degrees. Lightly coat 2 cookie sheets (or inverted baking sheets) with vegetable oil spray and cover each with 15 by 12-inch sheet of parchment paper. Heat ground ginger in 8-inch skillet over medium heat until fragrant, about 1 minute. Combine toasted ginger, flour, baking soda, and salt in medium bowl.

2. Using stand mixer fitted with paddle, beat butter and sugar together on medium-high speed until light and fluffy, about 2 minutes. Add fresh ginger and vanilla and mix until incorporated. Reduce speed to low and add flour mixture in 3 additions, alternating with 2 additions of milk, scraping down bowl as needed. Give batter a final stir by hand.

3. Using offset spatula, evenly spread ¾ cup of batter to cover parchment on each prepared sheet (batter will be very thin). Bake until deep golden brown, 16 to 20 minutes, switching and rotating sheets halfway through baking.

4. Transfer sheets to wire racks. Immediately score cookies into 3 by 2-inch rectangles using chef's knife or pizza wheel. Let cookies cool completely, about 20 minutes. Using tip of paring knife, separate cookies along score marks. Serve. (Cookies can be stored in airtight container at room temperature for up to 3 days.)

PER COOKIE: Cal 25; Fat 1g; Sat fat 0.5g; Chol 5mg; Carb 3g; Protein 0g; Fiber 0g; Sodium 20mg

---

NOTES FROM THE TEST KITCHEN

MAKING FAIRY GINGERBREAD COOKIES

1. To form cookies of requisite thinness, use small offset spatula to spread batter to edges of 15 by 12-inch sheet of parchment paper.

2. Immediately after removing cookies from oven, use chef's knife or pizza wheel to score 3 by 2-inch rectangles. Work quickly to prevent breaking.

3. Once cookies are cool, trace over scored lines with paring knife and gently break cookies apart along lines.

RATING GROUND GINGER

A staple in bakers' pantries, ground ginger adds a warm, spicy flavor and aroma to baked goods as well as numerous Asian and Indian dishes. Since ginger is often used in combination with other pungent spices and strong flavors, would it matter which brand we used in recipes like gingerbread? We bought two top-selling national supermarket brands of ground ginger, McCormick and Spice Islands, and compared them with mail-order ground ginger from Penzeys Spices. We tasted each in gingerbread muffins and in our recipe for Fairy Gingerbread Cookies, in which ginger is the lone spice.

In gingerbread muffins, where cinnamon and allspice muffled our perceptions of the ginger, all three brands received equivalent scores, although a few tasters singled out the more pungent profile of Penzeys for extra praise. But in Fairy Gingerbread Cookies, tasters showed decided preferences. Although we deemed all three brands acceptable, we gave the lowest marks to McCormick, which we found quite mild. Once again, a vocal minority strongly preferred Penzeys' potent ginger heat, but the highest scores went to **Spice Islands Ground Ginger**, which straddled the middle ground with full ginger flavor but more moderate heat than Penzeys.

CHEWY SUGAR COOKIES

EVERYONE THINKS IT'S NO SWEAT TO MAKE CLASSIC, buttery-tasting sugar cookies that are crisp at the edges and chewy in the center. Everyone is wrong. The truth is, making a just-right version of this humble cookie is far from easy. More often than not, the resulting cookies range from stunted and humped to flat and brittle, with a smooth rather than crackly top. With no nuts, raisins, or chunks of chocolate to provide distraction, such flaws become all the more glaring. Then tack on the poorly executed adjustments that come with trying to keep these cookies on the light side (with only butter, sugar, flour, eggs, and vanilla, there isn't a lot to work with), and you have a recipe for disaster. We were determined to engineer a foolproof recipe that would produce our ideal, every time: a reduced-fat sugar cookie crisp at the edges, soft and chewy in the center, crackly-crisp on top—and, of course, richly flavorful.

We got to work with the recipe that we'd singled out as a baseline for "soft and chewy" sugar cookies, which called for 2 cups of all-purpose flour, 1 cup of sugar, 6 tablespoons of butter, and 5 ounces of vegetable oil. We decided to tackle the fat first. When we were testing our Soft and Chewy Peanut Butter Cookies (page 262), we homed in on the fact that the key to a truly chewy texture is largely the type and ratio of the fats in the recipe. While we love the flavor of all-butter cookies, for optimal chew we knew that a mixture of butter and vegetable oil was a better bet. We knocked down the recipe's 6 tablespoons of butter to 5 and went down to just ⅓ cup of vegetable oil. But with so little butter in the recipe, it was difficult to cream the butter and sugar together, a standard step in most sugar cookie recipes that helps them rise and develop structure. Unsure what to do next, we decided to try a new tactic: We melted the butter and whisked it with the sugar. This simple switch proved to be a boon in more ways than one. First, it eliminated one of the trickier aspects of baking sugar cookies: ensuring that the solid butter is just the right temperature. Second, melted butter would aid in our quest for chewiness: When liquefied, the small amount of water in butter mixed with the flour to form gluten, which made for chewier cookies.

But all was not perfect. The two doses of liquid fat made the dough so soft that it practically poured onto the baking sheet. Plus, now that we were no longer creaming, there wasn't enough air in the dough and the cookies were baking up too flat. We spent the next tests readjusting the ingredients. More flour helped build up structure, and another ½ teaspoon of baking powder added lift. To keep the cookies from being a bit too dry and biscuitlike, we ramped up the sugar, salt, and vanilla and added a tiny bit of milk.

With this new formula, the chewiness of the cookies was spot-on. But we still had a few problems, two of which were mainly cosmetic: The cookies had gone from too flat to a bit more domed than we liked, and they didn't have much of that appealingly crackly top that makes a sugar cookie distinctive. And most important, trading more than half of the rich butter for neutral-tasting vegetable oil had rendered the cookies very sweet—and only sweet.

There was no use reducing the amount of sugar: Given the choice between blandness and one-note sweetness, we'd take the latter (it is called a *sugar* cookie, after all). Instead, we wondered if we could add something to take the edge off all that sugariness. We thought an acidic ingredient like lemon juice or zest might work, but the assertive citrus flavor took the cookies out of the "sugar" category and dropped them squarely into the lemon family. We often add buttermilk, sour cream, or yogurt to muffins and cakes to round out their flavors. But when we tried each of these in place of the milk in the recipe, we couldn't add more than a tablespoon of any one before it upset the precarious moisture balance, leading to dough that was too soft.

We scanned the supermarket dairy aisle and zeroed in on cream cheese, wondering if it would enrich the dough's flavor without adding much liquid. Flavor-wise, the effect of the cream cheese was dramatic, and tasters' faces lit up as they bit into this latest batch. Unfortunately, the cream cheese also contributed additional fat to the recipe, so the addition worked at cross-purposes in terms of our goals. Since we had met with success using neufchatel (one-third less fat) cream cheese in place of full-fat cream cheese in past recipes, we decided to try it here. The flavor change was undetectable, and we were able to bring the fat back into better balance when we found we could reduce the vegetable oil to just ¼ cup with no ill effects.

There was more good news: With acidic cream cheese in the mix, we could now add baking soda to the dough. As long as there's an acidic ingredient present, baking soda has all sorts of special powers, including the ability to solve our other two pesky problems: slightly humped cookies and not enough crackle. Just a half-teaspoon produced cookies that looked as good as they tasted.

While the cookies were not going to compete with apples as a good-for-you treat, they were light enough to pass the test when the hankering for a chewy sugar cookie hit. Best of all, nothing about our recipe tasted light. The decadent flavor and texture could fool even the most devout cookie lover.

Chewy Sugar Cookies
MAKES 2 DOZEN COOKIES

Neufchatel cream cheese contains one-third less fat than traditional cream cheese. The final dough will be slightly softer than most cookie doughs. For the best results, handle the dough as briefly and gently as possible when shaping the cookies. Overworking the dough will result in flatter cookies. You can also use a #40 portion scoop to portion the cookie dough.

- 2¼ cups (11¼ ounces) all-purpose flour
- 1 teaspoon baking powder
- ½ teaspoon baking soda
- ½ teaspoon salt
- 1½ cups (10½ ounces) sugar, plus ¼ cup for rolling
- 2 ounces neufchatel (⅓ less fat) cream cheese, cut into 8 pieces
- 5 tablespoons unsalted butter, melted and still warm
- ¼ cup canola oil
- 1 large egg
- 1 tablespoon whole milk
- 2 teaspoons vanilla extract

1. Adjust oven rack to middle position and heat oven to 350 degrees. Line 2 baking sheets with parchment paper. Whisk flour, baking powder, baking soda, and salt together in medium bowl. Place ¼ cup sugar in shallow baking dish or pie plate and set aside.

2. Place remaining 1½ cups sugar and cream cheese in large bowl. Pour warm butter over sugar and cream cheese and whisk to combine (some small lumps of cream cheese will remain but will smooth out later). Whisk in oil until incorporated. Whisk in egg, milk, and vanilla until smooth. Add flour mixture and mix with rubber spatula until soft homogeneous dough forms.

3. Working with 2 tablespoons of dough at a time, roll into balls. Working in batches, roll balls in reserved sugar to coat and place 2 inches apart on prepared sheets,

12 dough balls per sheet. Using bottom of drinking glass, flatten dough balls until 2 inches in diameter. Sprinkle tops evenly with remaining sugar from shallow dish.

4. Bake, 1 sheet at a time, until edges are set and just beginning to brown, 11 to 13 minutes, rotating sheet halfway through baking. Let cookies cool on sheet for 5 minutes, then serve warm or transfer to wire rack and let cool completely, about 30 minutes.

PER COOKIE: **Cal** 150; **Fat** 5g; **Sat fat** 2.5g; **Chol** 15mg; **Carb** 23g; **Protein** 2g; **Fiber** 0g; **Sodium** 105mg

LEMON SQUARES

EVEN WHEN WE'RE COUNTING CALORIES, WE'RE not into deprivation. That's why we wanted a lemon bar that was slimmed down but didn't announce the fact. Standard recipes pack 16 grams of fat and 330 calories per bar—and that's assuming you can stop at one. We collected several full-fat recipes and discovered that while the lemon topping was not all that fattening, the crust had so much butter that we probably put on pounds just thinking about it.

TEST KITCHEN
MAKEOVER

We looked around to see what diet recipes have tried. Not a heck of a lot, it turns out, beyond replacing the butter in the shortbread with either vegetable oil or margarine. We vetoed margarine, which tastes bad, and that left us with oil. Following one recipe, we topped the oil-based crust with a basic lemon curd (a mixture of lemon juice, sugar, and eggs) and baked it. We had no shortage of tasters—or critics. Shortbread, they told us curtly, is all about butter. They were right: The bars had zero flavor and were mealy. To add insult to injury, the calorie and fat counts had barely budged.

Clearly, our chief challenge would be to cut back on the butter while retaining its flavor and the short, tender texture it traditionally gives the crust. We took a recipe for full-fat lemon bars and got to work. We set 12 tablespoons of butter, ½ cup of confectioners' sugar, and 1¼ cups of flour on the counter for the crust (which would be a mere 8 by 8 inches). Given how lower-fat cream cheese had pulled through for us in myriad other lightened recipes, we did an inordinate amount of testing in an attempt to replace the butter with lower-calorie neufchatel cream cheese. But no matter how much we tinkered, the crusts tasted pasty, gummy, and underbaked. Eventually, we rejected this approach. On the plus side, we learned while cutting back on the butter that just 4 tablespoons still provided acceptable buttery flavor.

But butter contributes moisture to the crust as well; with such a drastic cutback, the crust didn't hold together. We "glued" it with an egg yolk and used a bit less flour, but the crust still crumbled when we tried to cut it into bars. We ditched the yolk (we hadn't been thrilled with the fat that it added anyhow) and reached for milk. Now the crust held together, but it was dense, tough, and tasteless. To bring back tenderness, we replaced some of the flour with cornstarch, which gives baked goods a melt-in-your-mouth quality. We added lemon zest and extra salt for flavor. Finally, to lighten the crust, we tested baking powder, eventually landing on ½ teaspoon. We also found that we could trim the sugar and not miss the sweetness. With the crust under control, we moved on to the lemon topping.

We had been using two eggs in the topping, but we quickly ejected one of the yolks and no one was the wiser. Next, we cut back the sugar 1 tablespoon at a time until we'd lost ¼ cup. Tasters actually liked these lemon bars better because the lemon flavor really popped. (That, in turn, helped the crust: We now barely noticed the missing butter.) At this point, each bar was down 140 calories and 10 grams of fat yet tasted terrific. We'd lowered the calories and fat, but we'd raised the (ahem) bar.

MAKEOVER SPOTLIGHT: LEMON SQUARES

	CALORIES	FAT	SAT FAT	CHOLESTEROL
BEFORE	330	16g	11g	85mg
AFTER	190	6g	4g	35mg

Lemon Squares

MAKES 9 BARS

Press the crust dough snugly against the pan edges to keep the lemon topping from running beneath the crust. Cool the crust for at least 15 minutes before pouring on the lemon topping.

CRUST

- ¾ cup (3¾ ounces) all-purpose flour
- ⅓ cup (1⅓ ounces) confectioners' sugar
- 3 tablespoons cornstarch
- 1½ teaspoons grated lemon zest
- ½ teaspoon baking powder
- ¼ teaspoon salt
- 4 tablespoons unsalted butter, cut into ½-inch pieces and chilled
- 1 tablespoon whole milk

FILLING

- ¾ cup (5¼ ounces) granulated sugar
- 1 large egg plus 1 large white, lightly beaten
- 2 tablespoons all-purpose flour
- ⅛ teaspoon salt
- 1 tablespoon grated lemon zest plus 6 tablespoons juice (2 lemons)
- 1 tablespoon confectioners' sugar

1. FOR THE CRUST: Adjust oven rack to middle position and heat oven to 350 degrees. Make foil sling by folding 2 long sheets of aluminum foil so that they are as wide as 8-inch square baking pan. Lay sheets of foil in pan perpendicular to each other, with extra foil

hanging over edges of pan. Push foil into corners and up sides of pan, smoothing foil flush to pan. Lightly coat foil with vegetable oil spray.

2. Process flour, confectioners' sugar, cornstarch, lemon zest, baking powder, and salt together in food processor until combined, about 10 seconds. Add butter and milk and pulse until mixture resembles coarse meal, about 10 pulses. Transfer mixture to prepared pan and press into even layer. Bake until edges are lightly browned, 16 to 20 minutes. Let crust cool on wire rack for at least 15 minutes.

3. FOR THE FILLING: Reduce oven temperature to 325 degrees. Whisk granulated sugar, egg, egg white, flour, and salt together in bowl until smooth. Stir in lemon zest and juice until combined. Pour filling over cooled crust. Bake until filling is set, 15 to 20 minutes. Let cool completely in pan, set on wire rack, about 1 hour. Remove from pan using foil sling, cut into 9 squares, and dust with confectioners' sugar before serving.

PER SERVING: **Cal** 190; **Fat** 6g; **Sat fat** 4g; **Chol** 35mg; **Carb** 34g; **Protein** 2g; **Fiber** 0g; **Sodium** 135mg

ICEBOX KEY LIME PIE

BLAME IT ON THE BRACING CITRUS FLAVOR, BUT icebox Key lime pie always tastes lighter than it actually

TEST KITCHEN
MAKEOVER

is. In the traditional recipe, lime juice, sugar, sweetened condensed milk, and raw egg yolks are blended, then poured into a prebaked, buttery graham cracker crust and chilled until set. More recent recipes, bowing to health concerns about eating raw eggs, replace the yolks with even fattier whipped cream, cream cheese, or a combination, and the pies are set with gelatin. These "modern" recipes use as much as 22 grams of fat and 440 calories per slice. What could we do to come up with a pie that was as light as it tasted?

A survey of published diet versions showed that we weren't the first to try trimming Key lime pie. As we whipped up one well-intentioned attempt after another, though, tasters grumbled about the cloying artificial taste, meek lime flavor, and textures that ran the gamut from unpleasantly bouncy (due to stabilizers in low-fat products) to lean (fat-free cream cheese and Cool Whip) to obnoxiously grainy (fat-free ricotta).

Moreover, most of the reduced-fat graham cracker crusts crumbled into a sandy mess as soon as we sliced the pie, thanks to stingy amounts of butter.

We set aside these dreary versions and instead started with a favorite test kitchen full-fat version of the pie. Its ingredient list included full-fat cream cheese, sweetened condensed milk, vanilla pudding mix, and gelatin, as well as, of course, lime juice, sugar, and a little vanilla. We instantly x-ed out the instant pudding, which we used in that recipe in lieu of raw eggs. We'd have to find something less caloric. Reexamining the results of our first round of tests, we realized that not every diet trick had proved useless. For instance, the fat-free sweetened condensed milk was almost indistinguishable from its full-fat counterpart. Emboldened, we next substituted fat-free cream cheese for the full-fat, but a few hours later we were eating humble (flavorless, hard, pasty) pie. Regrouping, we tried neufchatel, the one-third-less-fat style of cream cheese we'd had such success with in our sugar cookies (see page 267). This substitution, though tasty, didn't shave off as much fat as we'd hoped.

We wondered if we could combine neufchatel with a fat-free product for a deeper cut. Fat-free ricotta was (still) too grainy. Fat-free yogurt wasn't creamy enough. Thick, luscious fat-free Greek yogurt, however, showed promise. Eventually, we landed on equal amounts (4 ounces each) of neufchatel and fat-free Greek yogurt for heft and creaminess, not to mention a reduction of almost 60 calories and almost 7 grams of fat per slice. Because of the tang from the yogurt, we also cut back on the lime juice. And once we'd done that, we easily snipped almost all of the sugar from the filling, too.

For the crust, we'd found in early tests that low-fat graham crackers could replace ordinary ones with no

NOTES FROM THE TEST KITCHEN

MAKING A GRAHAM CRACKER CRUST

Press crumb mixture firmly and evenly across bottom of pie plate, using bottom of measuring cup. Then tightly pack crumbs against sides of pie plate, using your thumb and measuring cup simultaneously.

ICEBOX KEY LIME PIE

ill effects in our original recipe that called for 5 tablespoons of butter and 2 tablespoons of sugar. The saving in calories was negligible, but the fat reduction was reason enough to feel pleased. Cutting 1 more tablespoon of sugar (from the crust this time) meant that now we were using just 1 tablespoon for the entire pie, and tasters never noticed. But for real savings, we'd have to tackle the butter, which contributed roughly 60 calories and 8 grams of fat to each portion. Try as we might, anything less than 5 tablespoons made for a crust that crumbled. To shore the crust up, we tried replacing some of the butter with egg white; it turned the crust gummy. We borrowed a little sweetened condensed milk from the filling to make the crust coalesce—gummy again. But borrowing 2 tablespoons of neufchatel from the filling to combine with 3 tablespoons of butter worked like a charm, and tasters were none the wiser.

All told, we'd saved 130 calories and about 13 grams of fat per slice of pie. The real success, however, was the bracing lime flavor and creamy texture. Said one taster, "I'd eat this pie over the full-fat version any day."

MAKEOVER SPOTLIGHT: ICEBOX KEY LIME PIE

	CALORIES	FAT	SAT FAT	CHOLESTEROL
BEFORE	440	22g	14g	65mg
AFTER	310	9g	5g	30mg

Icebox Key Lime Pie

SERVES 8

Neufchatel cream cheese contains one-third less fat than traditional cream cheese. Greek yogurt gives our pie a creamy texture; don't substitute for it.

- 8 whole low-fat graham crackers, broken into 1-inch pieces
- 1 tablespoon sugar
- 4 ounces neufchatel (⅓ less fat) cream cheese, softened
- 3 tablespoons unsalted butter, melted and cooled
- 1¼ teaspoons unflavored gelatin
- 1 tablespoon grated lime zest plus ¾ cup juice (6 limes)
- 1 (14-ounce) can fat-free sweetened condensed milk
- ½ cup fat-free Greek yogurt
- 1 teaspoon vanilla extract

1. Adjust oven rack to middle position and heat oven to 325 degrees. Process graham cracker pieces and sugar together in food processor to fine, even crumbs, about 30 seconds. Add 2 tablespoons cream cheese and butter to crumbs and pulse to incorporate.

2. Sprinkle mixture into 9-inch pie plate, then use bottom of dry measuring cup to press crumbs into even, compact layer on bottom and up sides of pie plate. Bake crust until fragrant and beginning to brown, 12 to 14 minutes. Transfer pie plate to wire rack and let cool completely, about 45 minutes.

3. Sprinkle gelatin over 3 tablespoons lime juice in bowl and let sit until gelatin softens, about 5 minutes. Microwave until mixture is bubbling around edges and gelatin dissolves, about 30 seconds. Using dry, clean processor bowl, process remaining cream cheese, condensed milk, and yogurt until smooth, about 1 minute. With machine running, pour in gelatin mixture, remaining 9 tablespoons lime juice, lime zest, and vanilla and process until thoroughly combined, about 1 minute.

4. Scrape mixture into cooled pie shell and smooth top. Cover with plastic wrap and refrigerate until firm, at least 3 hours or up to 2 days. Serve.

PER SERVING: Cal 310; Fat 9g; Sat fat 5g; Chol 30mg; Carb 49g; Protein 8g; Fiber 1g; Sodium 115mg

FRESH STRAWBERRY PIE

WITH ITS ENTICING JUMBLE OF FRESH, IMPOSSIBLY red strawberries bound by the sheerest of sparkling, sweet glazes in a pastry shell, the perfect strawberry pie delivers a big bite of summer. Serving neat slices is downright impossible—the pie inevitably splits into shards of pastry and a tumble of berries—but in a dessert so good, looks hardly matter (especially given the coverage often provided by big dollops of whipped cream). But most strawberry pie recipes fall significantly short of perfection in terms of taste, too, replacing farmstand-fresh berries with crunchy-cored grocery store substitutes and drowning them in gloppy glazes. Our goal was twofold: We wanted to find a foolproof filling recipe that gave us fresh berries coated in a glaze, rather than glop, and a low-fat pie shell that would complement the filling without sabotaging our waistlines.

The problem with most recipes we tried had to do with the fruit's sweet juice. Because the uncooked berries shed so much liquid (even when they were left whole), the filling had to be firmed up with some sort of thickener, producing results that ranged from stiff and bouncy to runny and gloppy—hardly the dessert we had in mind. Clearly, success would hinge on getting the thickener just right.

Most recipes attacked the excess liquid problem with cornstarch; we also found a few that called for gelatin. The thickener of choice was simmered in a pan with liquid (often a juice like pineapple or grape, or even water), sugar, and a dash of salt; mixed with the fresh whole berries; mounded in a prebaked pie shell; and chilled to set. Predictably, the gelatin produced a stiff and springy filling. And the cornstarch was no better, rendering the berry mixture cloudy, gummy, and not at all firm. Looking for other thickening options, we explored flour, arrowroot, potato starch, and tapioca, as well as strawberry jam. But nothing panned out; the jam was closest, offering a reasonably thick texture, but its flavor was dull and cloying. In the end we were left with pies that were off-flavored, unpredictable, or gluey.

Frustrated, we tried a recipe we'd found that didn't use any added liquid or thickener at all. Instead, half of the uncooked berries were turned into a smooth, thick puree in the food processor, mixed with sugar, simmered briefly in a saucepan to thicken, and then combined with the fresh berries. The puree tasted bright and sweet and added body to the cut-up fruit, but we weren't surprised when it didn't prove to be sufficient. Even after we assembled and chilled the pie for a couple of hours, the filling oozed from each slice.

We circled back to our earlier tests. Of all the thickeners we'd tried, jam had been the most promising, at least texture-wise. The jelling agent in jam, of course, is pectin. What if we made our own fresh jam by adding pectin to the cooked puree? Since we didn't want to overload the naturally sweet berries with excess sugar, we mixed some low-sugar pectin into the puree and proceeded with the recipe. But as soon as the knife hit the pie's stiff, springy surface, we knew that we still hadn't found the solution.

Since pectin alone made the filling too springy and cornstarch left the filling too loose, we wondered what would happen if we combined the thickeners in our puree. After some tinkering, we finally hit upon a formula that worked. With ¾ cup of puree, 2 tablespoons of cornstarch, and 1½ teaspoons of pectin, we managed to produce just the right supple, lightly clingy glaze.

Finally satisfied with the filling, we turned to the crust. Not wanting to undo all our hard work by putting the filling into a heavy (read: fatty) butter crust, we considered the idea of a pressed crust made with graham crackers or cookies. Since the filling was already sweet, a cookie crust seemed like overkill, but the more mildly sweet, wheaty flavor of a graham cracker crust sounded promising. Since we had had such success with a low-fat graham cracker crust in our Icebox Key Lime Pie (page 270), we decided to try the same crust with our strawberry pie. One bite was all it took to confirm that we'd found a more-than-worthy crust for our strawberry goodness.

Finally, we examined the whipped cream topping. Simply reducing the amount of cream would have been a quick way to slash fat, but it also left us with a paltry amount to dollop over each slice. Instead, we reinforced the lesser amount of whipped cream by folding in some creamy, unctuous fat-free Greek yogurt. The texture, though slightly heavier than whipped cream, was a satisfying substitute. Adding ¼ cup of sugar tempered the tanginess the yogurt introduced to the topping, and a teaspoon of vanilla added flavor and balance.

After putting all the ingredients together, we waited for two hours while the pie chilled and set. Like grade school children counting down the minutes before being released for the summer, we sat poised, whipped topping at the ready, waiting to dig in and shatter the crust of our fresh strawberry pie. Summer never tasted so good.

Fresh Strawberry Pie

SERVES 8

Room-temperature berries work best in this recipe. To account for any imperfect strawberries, the ingredient list calls for several more ounces of berries than will be used in the pie. If possible, seek out ripe, farmers' market–quality berries. Make certain that you use Sure-Jell engineered for low- or no-sugar recipes (packaged in a pink box) and not regular Sure-Jell (in a yellow box); otherwise, the glaze will not set properly. The pie is at its best after 2 or 3 hours of chilling; as it continues to chill, the glaze becomes softer and wetter, though the pie will taste just as good.

CRUST

- 8 whole low-fat graham crackers, broken into 1-inch pieces
- 1 tablespoon sugar
- 3 tablespoons unsalted butter, melted and cooled
- 2 tablespoons neufchatel (⅓ less fat) cream cheese, softened

FILLING

- 3 pounds fresh strawberries, hulled (9 cups), room temperature
- ¾ cup (5¼ ounces) sugar
- 2 tablespoons cornstarch
- 1½ teaspoons Sure-Jell for low-sugar recipes
  Generous pinch salt
- 1 tablespoon lemon juice

WHIPPED TOPPING

- ½ cup heavy cream
- ¼ cup (1¾ ounces) sugar
- 1 teaspoon vanilla extract
- ½ cup fat-free Greek yogurt

1. FOR THE CRUST: Adjust oven rack to middle position and heat oven to 325 degrees. Process graham cracker pieces and sugar together in food processor to fine, even crumbs, about 30 seconds. Add butter and cream cheese to crumbs and pulse to incorporate.

2. Sprinkle mixture into 9-inch pie plate, then use bottom of dry measuring cup to press crumbs into even, compact layer on bottom and up sides of pie plate. Bake crust until fragrant and beginning to brown, 12 to 14 minutes. Transfer pie plate to wire rack and let cool completely, about 45 minutes.

3. FOR THE FILLING: Select 6 ounces misshapen, underripe, or otherwise unattractive berries, halving those that are large; you should have about 1½ cups. In food processor, process berries to smooth puree, 20 to 30 seconds, scraping down bowl as needed. You should have about ¾ cup puree.

4. Whisk sugar, cornstarch, Sure-Jell, and salt together in medium saucepan. Stir in berry puree, making sure to scrape corners of pan. Bring to full boil over medium-high heat, stirring constantly with heatproof rubber spatula. Boil, scraping bottom and sides of pan to prevent scorching, for 2 minutes to ensure that cornstarch is fully cooked (mixture will appear frothy when it first reaches boil, then will darken and thicken with further cooking). Transfer to large bowl and stir in lemon juice. Let cool to room temperature.

5. Meanwhile, pick over remaining berries and measure out 2 pounds of most attractive ones; halve only extra-large berries. Using rubber spatula, gently fold berries into cooled glaze until berries are evenly coated. Scoop berries into pie shell, piling into mound. Arrange attractively, with any cut sides facing down. Refrigerate pie until chilled, at least 2 hours or up to 5 hours.

6. FOR THE WHIPPED TOPPING: Using stand mixer fitted with whisk, whip cream, sugar, and vanilla together on medium-low speed until foamy, about 1 minute. Increase speed to high and whip until soft peaks form, 1 to 3 minutes longer. Gently fold in yogurt. Slice pie into wedges and serve with whipped topping.

PER SERVING: Cal 290; Fat 11g; Sat fat 7g; Chol 35mg; Carb 46g; Protein 3g; Fiber 4g; Sodium 70mg

RUSTIC FREE-FORM APPLE TART

THE MOST FLAVORFUL DESSERTS ARE OFTEN THE simplest ones. Such is the case with a free-form tart made with sweet, juicy apples. Given the simplicity of the dessert—fresh fruit placed unceremoniously on top of pastry—we wanted to come up with a recipe that relied on an easy-to-work-with pastry that was at the same time tender, flaky, and flavorful. But the challenge didn't end there. Since the apple filling was fat-free (apples, sugar, and maybe a little spice), we wanted to keep the pastry from blowing our otherwise healthy dessert to smithereens.

We began our testing by making a variety of doughs, all of which we found to be too firm or too bland. We wanted a relatively soft dough that would be easy to roll out and would provide a delicate but flavorful contrast to the fruit. We decided to test different liquid and fat ingredients to see what delivered the best results for both texture and flavor. Since fat is pivotal to a successful dough, we didn't have much room to play with in the amount we used. Although vegetable shortening made the dough tender, it added no flavor and was therefore rejected. Butter, however, gave us the most bang for our buck since it brought both fat and flavor to the table, but we couldn't make a successful crust with fewer than 8 tablespoons.

Continuing our search for ingredients that could contribute to flavor and tenderness, we tried heavy cream, buttermilk, yogurt, sour cream, and cream cheese. The heavy cream made the dough too tender; the cream cheese was too overpowering; but the buttermilk, yogurt, and sour cream all worked well. Of the three, our favorite was sour cream in combination with a couple of tablespoons of water; it added just the right amount of richness and tang without detracting from the apple flavor. From there we tried substituting low-fat sour cream, and we found that it worked equally well, giving us savings in both fat and calories. We found that 1 tablespoon of sugar was ideal. Any more produced a dough that was too delicate and tender for our purposes; with any less, the dough was too firm.

At this point, tasters gave high marks to our tart dough. But something was missing. Looking for complexity, flavor, and a healthy slant to our pastry, we tried substituting whole wheat flour for a portion of the all-purpose flour.

A simple 50:50 split of flours (¾ cup of each) was too heavy, as the high protein content of the wheat flour made the dough too difficult to roll out. We backed down on the wheat flour to ½ cup, which added just the right subtle, earthy component to the buttery flavor of the tart pastry without any ill effects. Our pastry crust in the bag, we turned to the apple filling.

Because a free-form apple tart has no top crust to seal in moisture, the filling can dry out during baking. Obviously, the variety of apple as well as the preparation used would be key. We gathered some of the most commonly available apple varieties and tested each type in our working recipe. In every case but one, the apples cooked up tough, dry, and leathery. The exception was the McIntoshes, which baked to the other extreme; they were so moist that they turned to mush. Of the varieties tested, we found that Granny Smiths, Galas, and McIntoshes had the most distinct flavor after being baked. It looked as if the solution was going to be found in using a combination of apples. We tested McIntoshes with both Granny Smiths and Galas; tasters overwhelmingly preferred the Granny-Mac combo. This filling had good apple flavor and a decent texture, but it was still a bit dry.

For the next test, we sliced the apples thinner and increased the oven temperature. These thinner slices softened more quickly and retained more moisture, but still they were not perfect. Then a colleague suggested that we take a cue from apple pie recipes, where the apples are tossed with sugar and lemon juice before baking. The key is the sugar, which combines with some of the moisture the fruit releases during baking to form a syrup. This syrup doesn't give up water easily and thus doesn't evaporate. It turned out to be a great idea—the sugar prevented the apples from drying out in the oven, and the filling was moist but not runny.

Shaping the tart couldn't have been easier. Once the dough was rolled into a 12-inch circle, we stacked some of the apples around the perimeter to create a circular wall, leaving a 2-inch border around the edge, then arranged the remaining apples in the center of the wall. Stacking the apples gave our tart height and visual appeal. To keep the juices contained, we simply folded the edge of the tart pastry up around the perimeter wall of fruit. There we had it: all the things we loved about apple pie made easier and lighter with a flavorful, flaky, no-fuss crust and the right combination of apples.

RUSTIC FREE-FORM APPLE TART

Rustic Free-Form Apple Tart

SERVES 8

To help prevent the tart from leaking, be sure to leave a little space between the fruit and the folded edge of the dough. Serve with low-fat frozen yogurt, if desired.

TART DOUGH

 2 tablespoons low-fat sour cream
2–4 tablespoons ice water
 1 cup (5 ounces) all-purpose flour
 ½ cup (2¾ ounces) whole wheat flour
 1 tablespoon sugar
 ½ teaspoon salt
 8 tablespoons unsalted butter, cut into ¼-inch pieces and chilled

FILLING

 ½ cup (3½ ounces) plus 1 tablespoon sugar
 1 tablespoon lemon juice
 ⅛ teaspoon ground cinnamon
 1 pound Granny Smith apples, peeled, cored, and sliced ¼ inch thick
 1 pound McIntosh apples, peeled, cored, and sliced ¼ inch thick
 3 tablespoons apple jelly

1. FOR THE TART DOUGH: Stir sour cream and 2 tablespoons water together in small liquid measuring cup and refrigerate until needed. Process all-purpose flour, whole wheat flour, sugar, and salt together in food processor until combined. Scatter butter pieces over top and pulse until mixture resembles coarse meal, about 9 pulses.

2. Continue to pulse, adding sour cream mixture until dough comes together around processor blade, about 8 pulses. (If needed, add remaining 2 tablespoons water, 1 tablespoon at a time, and continue to pulse until dough comes together, about 3 pulses.)

3. Turn dough and any crumbs onto sheet of plastic wrap and press into 6-inch round. Wrap dough tightly in plastic wrap and refrigerate for at least 1 hour. (Tart dough can be refrigerated for up to 2 days.)

4. Adjust oven rack to lower-middle position and heat oven to 375 degrees. Remove dough from refrigerator and let sit on counter to soften slightly, about 10 minutes. Roll dough out into 12-inch circle between 2 large sheets of floured parchment paper. Slide dough, still between parchment, onto large baking sheet and refrigerate until firm, about 20 minutes.

5. FOR THE FILLING: Combine ½ cup sugar, lemon juice, and cinnamon in bowl, then stir in apples. Remove top sheet of parchment from dough. Stack some of apples into circular wall, leaving 2-inch border of dough around edge. Fill in middle of tart with remaining apples.

6. Being careful to leave space around edge of fruit, fold dough over fruit, pleating it every 2 to 3 inches as needed. Lightly brush crust with water, then sprinkle with remaining 1 tablespoon sugar.

7. Bake tart until crust is golden and crisp and apples are tender, about 1 hour, rotating sheet halfway through baking.

8. Microwave apple jelly in small bowl until melted, about 30 seconds, stirring occasionally to smooth out any lumps. Brush melted jelly over exposed apples.

NOTES FROM THE TEST KITCHEN

ASSEMBLING RUSTIC FREE-FORM FRUIT TART

1. Roll dough into 12-inch round between 2 large sheets of floured parchment paper. Transfer dough to rimmed baking sheet and refrigerate until firm, about 20 minutes.

2. Discard top piece of parchment. Stack apple slices into circular wall, leaving 2-inch border of dough. Fill center with remaining apples.

3. Being careful to leave some space around edge of fruit, fold 2 inches of dough up over fruit.

Let tart cool slightly on sheet for 10 minutes, then use parchment paper to gently transfer tart to wire rack.

9. Use metal spatula to loosen tart from parchment and remove parchment. Let tart cool on rack until apples have shrunk slightly and their juice has thickened, about 25 minutes. Serve warm or at room temperature.

PER SERVING: **Cal** 320; **Fat** 12g; **Sat fat** 8g; **Chol** 30mg; **Carb** 52g; **Protein** 3g; **Fiber** 4g; **Sodium** 150mg

VARIATION

Rustic Free-Form Summer Fruit Tart

Use peaches, nectarines, apricots, or plums for stone fruit and fresh raspberries, blackberries, blueberries, or sliced strawberries for berries.

Add 2 teaspoons cornstarch to filling with sugar and substitute 1 pound stone fruit, pitted and sliced into ½-inch-thick wedges, and 1 cup fresh berries for apples.

PER SERVING: **Cal** 280; **Fat** 12g; **Sat fat** 8g; **Chol** 30mg; **Carb** 41g; **Protein** 3g; **Fiber** 3g; **Sodium** 150mg

CHIFFON CAKE

ANGEL FOOD CAKE IS A QUINTESSENTIAL LIGHT dessert, but sometimes we wish it had just a little more richness. Enter chiffon cake. Like angel food cake, chiffon gets its height from a number of whipped egg whites, baking in an ungreased tube pan, and cooling upside down while still in the pan. At the same time, chiffon cake, like a classic butter or pound cake, contains some fat (in this case, in the form of egg yolks and oil, which is simpler to work with than butter) to make it rich and tender, plus baking powder to help it rise. In many respects, it's the ideal cake, combining rich flavor and lightness in one dessert. Our lofty goal was to bring it even closer to perfection by making a few calculated changes to lighten and streamline this dream of a cake.

In looking over numerous recipes, including the original (chiffon cake made its published debut in a 1948 issue of *Better Homes and Gardens*), we noticed several common denominators: All called for identical amounts of oil (½ cup), sugar (1½ cups), and water (¾ cup). The remaining ingredients were variable. While chiffon cake, even in its full-fat form, wasn't nearly as decadent as some other desserts we

had lightened up, we thought a few small changes could make the difference between enjoying chiffon cake occasionally and making it a regular low-fat dessert treat.

A few tests proved that the amounts of sugar and water were crucial to the cake's structure, so we had to stick to the original numbers. (We did make one small discovery regarding that water, however. We wondered why the original recipe specified that it had to be cold. We're still wondering. We made the cake with 69-degree water—room temperature in our test kitchen that day—and 38-degree water. Not one taster could tell the two apart.) Next, we considered whether cake flour was necessary. The answer was yes: Low-protein cake flour, which translates to less gluten formation than all-purpose flour, proved critical to the chiffon's tender texture.

Next, we moved on to the oil. Fat is an essential ingredient in most cakes, providing moisture and cohesion as well as adding richness. While the ½ cup of oil used in the chiffon cake recipe seems light compared to a full cup of butter in many pound cake recipes, we still wondered if we could take it even lower without producing a characterless cake that put us back in the realm of angel food cake. We tried baking a cake with 6 tablespoons of oil; our tasters were pleased with the results. Could we take it even further? We reduced the oil to ⅓ cup and tasters still enjoyed the cake's texture and felt it rang true to the original.

Finally, we turned to the eggs, which provided both height and richness to the cake. Since the cake's light structure depends largely on the whipped egg whites, a few extra whites were important to the recipe. The original recipe used five yolks and seven whites. Since yolks contain all of an egg's fat, we wondered if we could omit a yolk without losing the richness. We tried the recipe with four yolks and seven whites but found that we were heading into angel food territory again. After quite a bit of tinkering, we found that we could use four whole eggs (and just 1 extra white) if we cut back on the flour, which in turn required us to take down the baking powder from 3 teaspoons to 2. (Don't worry, our version is as high and beautiful as the original.)

For a punch of flavor, we first increased the vanilla extract from 2 teaspoons to 3. And finally, a citrusy glaze was easy to whip up and drizzle over the cooled cake. It was just what our cake needed to give it a real identity, no longer just the middle child stuck between angel food cake's ethereal lightness and pound cake's decadent richness.

Chiffon Cake with Citrus Glaze

SERVES 12

You will need a tube pan with a removable bottom for this recipe. Our favorite, the Chicago Metallic Professional Nonstick Angel Food Cake Pan, has both a removable bottom and "feet" to support the pan while the cake cools. If your pan is footless, invert the cake onto the neck of a wine bottle to cool.

CAKE

- 4 large eggs, separated, plus 1 large white
- 1 teaspoon cream of tartar
- 1½ cups (10½ ounces) sugar
- 1⅓ cups (5⅓ ounces) cake flour
- 2 teaspoons baking powder
- ½ teaspoon salt
- ¾ cup water
- ⅓ cup canola oil
- 1 tablespoon vanilla extract

GLAZE

- 1 cup (4 ounces) confectioners' sugar
- 1 teaspoon grated lemon or orange zest plus
  5 teaspoons lemon or orange juice
  Pinch salt

1. FOR THE CAKE: Adjust oven rack to lower-middle position and heat oven to 325 degrees. Using stand mixer fitted with whisk, whip egg whites and cream of tartar together on medium-low speed until foamy, about 1 minute. Increase speed to medium-high and whip whites to soft, billowy mounds, about 1 minute. Gradually add 2 tablespoons sugar and whip until just stiff and glossy, about 1 minute; set aside.

2. Whisk remaining sugar, flour, baking powder, and salt together in large bowl. Whisk egg yolks, water, oil, and vanilla together in medium bowl until smooth. Whisk wet mixture into flour mixture until smooth. Whisk one-third of whipped egg whites into batter, then gently fold in remaining whites, 1 scoop at a time, until well combined. Scrape mixture into 16-cup ungreased tube pan.

REMOVING CHIFFON CAKE FROM THE PAN
Chiffon cake is baked in an ungreased pan. Why? The stiffly beaten egg whites need to cling to the pan to rise. If the pan were greased, they couldn't. Chiffon cake is cooled in its pan upside down while suspended in the air. (If you "de-panned" the hot cake, it would collapse under its own weight.) Once the cake is cool, pry it out with care.

1. When cake is cool, turn pan right side up and run flexible knife around tube and outer edge.

2. Use tube to pull cake out of pan and set it on inverted baking pan. Cut bottom free.

3. Now invert cake onto serving plate and gently twist tube to remove.

3. Bake until toothpick inserted into center comes out clean and cracks in cake appear dry, 55 to 65 minutes. Invert tube pan and let cool to room temperature, about 3 hours.

4. To unmold, turn pan right side up and run flexible knife around tube and outer edge. Use tube to pull cake out of pan and set it on inverted baking pan. Cut bottom free. Invert cake onto serving plate and gently twist tube to remove.

5. FOR THE GLAZE: Whisk all ingredients together in bowl until smooth. Drizzle glaze evenly over top of cake, letting it drip down sides. Let set before serving, about 15 minutes.

PER SERVING: Cal 280; Fat 8g; Sat fat 1g; Chol 70mg; Carb 48g; Protein 4g; Fiber 0g; Sodium 210mg

GINGERBREAD CAKE

THE GINGERBREAD CAKE OF OUR DREAMS IS MOIST and simple, a snack cake redolent of warm, spicy ginger and unctuous molasses. And since it isn't weighed down by a buttery crumb or sugary icing, it comes without the accompanying guilt of other snack cakes. But the reality of most gingerbread cake recipes falls short of our dreams. Almost without exception, every one we tried that had the moistness we wanted also suffered from a dense, sunken center. Flavors ran the gamut from barely gingery to loaded with enough spices to make a curry fan cry for mercy. We headed into the kitchen, determined to find out whether or not our dream of gingerbread cake was just wishful thinking.

Having cobbled together a basic working recipe, we decided to focus on fixing flavor first. Using a simple dump-and-stir method, we mixed the wet ingredients (molasses, water, melted butter, a couple of eggs) in one bowl and the dry ingredients (flour, baking soda, baking powder, brown sugar, salt) in another. For now, we expunged all spice options but a single tablespoon of ground ginger. We gently folded the wet ingredients into the dry, poured the batter into an 8-inch square cake pan, and baked it at 350 degrees for 40 minutes.

As expected, the cake's center collapsed. But with the extraneous spices out of the way, we were able to focus on improving the ginger flavor. Bumping the ground ginger up to 2 tablespoons yielded an assertive bite, but it lacked complexity. Folding in grated fresh ginger with the dried made the flavor sing. In the end, only two "guest" spices made the cut: cinnamon and, in an unexpected twist, fresh-ground black pepper, which worked in tandem with all that potent ginger to produce a warm, complex, lingering heat.

Eyeing the liquid components, we suspected that using water was a missed opportunity. Buttermilk added tanginess but dulled the ginger. Ginger ale and ginger beer were undetectable. Dark stout, on the other hand, had a bittersweet flavor that brought out the caramel undertones of the molasses. Gently heating the stout minimized its booziness.

Finally, we found that we could swap out the butter for cleaner-tasting vegetable oil. This step, as well as replacing a quarter of the brown sugar with granulated, cleared the way to let those spice flavors come through.

Now that the flavor was coming along nicely, we were more determined than ever to solve the sinking problem. A few of the recipes we tested incorporated the baking soda with the wet ingredients instead of the other dry ones (including the baking powder), bucking the usual protocol for cakes. The reason? Too much acid in a batter lessens the baking powder's ability to leaven the cake. Thus baking soda is used to neutralize acidic ingredients before they get incorporated into the batter. With gingerbread, the typical culprits are molasses and brown sugar, but our recipe also included stout—a triple threat of acidity that might well be thwarting the rise. We made the recipe again, this time stirring the half-teaspoon of baking soda right into the warm stout, followed by the molasses and brown sugar. It was a modest success. While the center still fell, it wasn't nearly as drastic—more of a buckle than a crater.

The batter was quite loose, so we wondered if the flour-to-liquid ratio was off. Would a drier gingerbread be sturdier? We tried decreasing the oil and stout to increase sturdiness (as well as trim some fat and calories). Though we were able to shed a couple of teaspoons of oil (and about 3 grams of fat per serving) without a difference in moistness, we were loath to decrease the stout and the flavor it contributed. In the end, reducing the liquid didn't solve the texture problem anyway. An extra egg made the texture sturdier—but rubbery. Adjusting the amount of leaveners produced cakes that ranged from dense and squat to light and pillowy, but they all shared one trait: that blasted sunken center.

Looking at a particularly old recipe, we noticed a curious kneading step. Kneading—as well as energetic beating—contributes strength and structure by developing the glutens in flour. But gluten development is the enemy of tenderness, which is why cake recipes generally have the flour incorporated gently at the end of mixing, after the heavy-duty butter creaming is done. Tenderness we had in spades; structure, we could use. Could roughing up the batter a bit strengthen the crumb?

Departing from our method of folding the wet ingredients into the dry, we added only about a third of the wets, then mixed vigorously to form a smooth paste. We incorporated the remaining wet ingredients in two more installments, mixing until smooth after each. We put the cake in the oven and crossed our fingers. Sure enough, this cake was a real looker—nary a crater in sight. Fragrant, moist, bold-flavored, and beautiful, this was the gingerbread cake we'd been dreaming of.

Classic Gingerbread Cake

SERVES 8

This cake packs potent yet well-balanced, fragrant, spicy heat. If you are particularly sensitive to spice, you can decrease the amount of dried ginger to 1 tablespoon. Guinness is the test kitchen's favorite brand of stout. Avoid opening the oven door until the minimum baking time has elapsed.

- ¾ cup stout
- ½ teaspoon baking soda
- ½ cup mild molasses
- ¾ cup (5¼ ounces) packed light brown sugar
- ¼ cup (1¾ ounces) granulated sugar
- 1½ cups (7½ ounces) all-purpose flour
- 2 tablespoons ground ginger
- ½ teaspoon baking powder
- ½ teaspoon salt
- ¼ teaspoon pepper
- ¼ teaspoon ground cinnamon
- 1 large egg
- 5 tablespoons canola oil
- 1 tablespoon grated fresh ginger

1. Adjust oven rack to middle position and heat oven to 350 degrees. Grease and flour 8-inch square baking pan.

2. Bring stout to boil in medium saucepan over medium heat, stirring occasionally. Remove from heat and stir in baking soda (mixture will foam vigorously). When foaming subsides, stir in molasses, brown sugar, and granulated sugar until dissolved; set mixture aside. Whisk flour, ground ginger, baking powder, salt, pepper, and cinnamon together in large bowl; set aside.

3. Transfer stout mixture to large bowl. Whisk in egg, oil, and fresh ginger until combined. Whisk wet mixture into flour mixture in thirds, stirring vigorously until completely smooth after each addition.

4. Transfer batter to prepared pan and gently tap pan on counter 3 or 4 times to release air bubbles. Bake until top of cake is just firm to touch and toothpick inserted into center comes out clean, 35 to 45 minutes. Let cake cool in pan on wire rack, about 1½ hours. Cut into squares and serve warm or at room temperature.

PER SERVING: Cal 330; Fat 9g; Sat fat 1g; Chol 25mg; Carb 59g; Protein 3g; Fiber 1g; Sodium 270mg

FRUIT BUCKLES

JUST WHAT IS A BUCKLE? WELL, IT'S AN AMERICAN classic: a streusel-topped coffee cake, traditionally made with blueberries. To call it a mere coffee cake, however, is to sell it short. The substance of a fruit buckle is the fruit, not the cake. This rustic confection starts with berries held together in a buttery cake batter, which is then topped with a crisp, sugary streusel. And the name? The cake, burdened as it is with fruit and topping, is said to buckle on the surface as it bakes. Delicious as this dessert sounds, the words *buttery* and *sugary* don't exactly fall into the lexicon of light eating. Could we have our cake and eat it too, or would our belt buckles fail under the strain of too much decadence?

Although typically served for breakfast, a streusel-topped cake filled with fruit sounds like dessert to us, and we wanted to develop the best possible version that wouldn't break the scale. We also decided early on that we wanted to make individual buckles rather than a single larger cake, since they would present so well as a dessert. After collecting dozens of recipes for buckle (mostly blueberry), we put our top six to the test. They were a ragtag collection of cakes; some were lean and dry, but most were dense and greasy, not to mention bland. The problem? It seemed that an overwhelming berry-to-cake ratio was throwing things out of whack, as the moisture released from the berries during baking often added a disagreeable sogginess.

We cobbled together a working recipe, with a batter made in the manner of a cake or cookie: The butter and sugar are creamed in a stand mixer, the eggs beaten in, the flour added, and then the berries folded in. Hoping to streamline the process a bit, we tried a variation using melted butter, but it had less rise—the result of a lack of aeration, which provides lift. Concerned about aeration and achieving maximum rise in the heavy batter, we then thought of a food processor and wondered if the cutting blades and high speed could achieve even better results than the standard method of creaming with a mixer. We processed the butter and sugar together, then added the eggs, followed by the flour. This worked great. We then started to back down on butter, asking how much was absolutely necessary to achieve the richness needed for balance. The magic number was 3 tablespoons—just enough to cream with the sugar and provide an airy crumb.

Moving on to the berries, we made a decision to run with the traditional choice of blueberries. We set out to determine just how many were needed to give the cake full berry flavor without weighing it down and making it soggy. The recipes we found called for as little as 1 cup to as many as 4 cups. According to tasters, even 2 cups weren't enough. Two and a half cups? Bingo. Now the berries were the headliner, with the cake in a supporting role as it should be. But the cake was still a bit soggy. Looking for a solution, we wondered if the type of flour we were using might be a factor. Up to this point, we had been using cake flour, which is low in protein. This was leaving the buckles somewhat structureless, pasty, and sodden. A buckle made with all-purpose flour, however, was drier and more cakey, with a sturdy texture that could contend with all the fruit. Problem solved.

Dairy—milk, cream, or sour cream—is often found in buckle recipes. We tested all three and liked the flavor and richness of the cream, which we added to the food processor with the eggs. While the texture of cream sent us over the moon, the accompanying fat grams brought us down to earth with a thud. Cream was out of the question, but milk just didn't achieve the right texture. We decided to split the difference with half-and-half, which gave us the richness of cream without all the guilt.

Since we needed a full ¾ cup of sugar to balance the tartness of the berries, we began to wonder if we really needed the streusel topping, which would require not only more sugar but also butter and flour. Instead, we tried substituting a sprinkling of chopped nuts. Tasters loved this approach, especially since the flavor of the nuts bloomed while they toasted in the oven, and skipping the streusel allowed us to streamline. But tasters felt we needed to have some nuts in the batter as well, to tie the flavors together. Antioxidant-rich blueberries and pecans proved to be a great combination, so we pulsed half of the pecans in the food processor to incorporate into the batter, reserving the rest for the topping. The flavors were now well rounded, but tasters wanted the nuts toasted. Toasting the nuts enhanced the nutty flavor, so much so that we decided that we could reduce the amount we incorporated into the batter to just 2 tablespoons without sacrificing flavor (and we ditched some fat and calories in the process). Now we had a perfect balance of blueberries and toasted pecans in every bite.

These buckles baked through and browned perfectly in just 30 minutes at 375 degrees. So there we had it:

easy-to-make cakes strong enough to support a lot of berries yet light enough to indulge in without feeling guilty. In fact, these buckles didn't really buckle during baking; they could hold their own. Now do we have to change the name?

Individual Blueberry-Pecan Buckles
SERVES 8

Do not substitute frozen berries in this recipe. The buckles can be served in their ramekins, or you can run a paring knife around the edges of the ramekins and flip the buckles out onto individual plates (flip them right side up again before serving). Serve with low-fat frozen yogurt.

- ¾ cup (5¼ ounces) sugar
- ⅓ cup pecans, toasted and chopped coarse
- 3 tablespoons unsalted butter, softened
- ¼ teaspoon salt
- ⅓ cup half-and-half
- 2 large eggs
- 1 teaspoon vanilla extract
- ¾ cup (3¾ ounces) all-purpose flour
- ½ teaspoon baking powder
- 12½ ounces (2½ cups) blueberries

1. Adjust oven rack to middle position and heat oven to 375 degrees. Lightly coat eight 4-ounce ramekins with vegetable oil spray and place them on rimmed baking sheet.

2. Process sugar, 2 tablespoons pecans, butter, and salt together in food processor until finely ground, 10 to 15 seconds. With processor running, add half-and-half, eggs, and vanilla and continue to process until smooth, about 5 seconds, scraping down bowl as needed. Add flour and baking powder and pulse until just incorporated, about 5 pulses.

3. Transfer batter to large bowl and gently fold in blueberries. Spoon batter into prepared ramekins and sprinkle with remaining pecans.

4. Bake buckles until golden and they begin to pull away from sides of ramekins, 25 to 30 minutes, rotating sheet halfway through baking. Let buckles cool on wire rack for 10 minutes before serving.

PER SERVING: Cal 240; Fat 10g; Sat fat 4.5g; Chol 70mg; Carb 35g; Protein 4g; Fiber 2g; Sodium 130mg

Individual Blackberry-Walnut Buckles

Do not use frozen blackberries here.

Substitute ⅓ cup chopped toasted walnuts for pecans and 12½ ounces fresh blackberries for blueberries.

PER SERVING: Cal 230; Fat 9g; Sat fat 4.5g; Chol 70mg; Carb 32g; Protein 4g; Fiber 3g; Sodium 130mg

Individual Raspberry-Pistachio Buckles

Do not use frozen raspberries here.

Substitute ⅓ cup chopped toasted pistachios for pecans and 12½ ounces fresh raspberries for blueberries.

PER SERVING: Cal 230; Fat 9g; Sat fat 4.5g; Chol 70mg; Carb 34g; Protein 5g; Fiber 3g; Sodium 130mg

Individual Cherry-Almond Buckles

You can use fresh, jarred, or canned sour cherries here.

Substitute ⅓ cup chopped toasted slivered almonds for pecans, ½ teaspoon almond extract for vanilla extract, and 12½ ounces pitted chopped sour cherries for blueberries.

PER SERVING: Cal 230; Fat 9g; Sat fat 4.5g; Chol 70mg; Carb 34g; Protein 4g; Fiber 2g; Sodium 130mg

RICH AND CREAMY BANANA PUDDING

TEST KITCHEN MAKEOVER

CREAMY, SWEET, COLD, AND FRUITY, BANANA pudding is a Southern dessert tradition, with recipes handed down from generation to generation. The dessert, inspired by the classic trifle, is made by layering vanilla pudding with sliced bananas and vanilla wafers. But not all traditions are perfect. Often, the banana slices turn brown and slimy; the cookies should be pleasantly cakey and plentiful but are more often soggy and sparse; and the pudding itself often tastes like plain-Jane vanilla—no surprise, it is vanilla.

Fortunately, the test kitchen recently solved these problems and developed a grand-slam recipe for this Southern specialty, suffused with banana flavor, loaded with plenty of cookies, and boasting a rich, creamy texture. Unfortunately, it's a strikeout when it comes to being low in fat and calories, with a single serving of this Southern staple delivering in excess of 600 calories and 31 grams of fat. There had to be a way to preserve the essence without being crushed beneath the weight of all that … tradition.

The recipe begins with a cooked pudding made with eight egg yolks, 1½ cups of sugar, 6 tablespoons of cornstarch, 6 cups of half-and-half, and 3 tablespoons of butter. Unquestionably, this recipe makes for a rich and creamy pudding, but we were after a lighter take that we could enjoy more than once a year.

Our first step was cutting some of the egg yolks, but we would somehow need to make up for the missing thickening power and richness. Our recent testing with Icebox Key Lime Pie (page 270) led us to consider fat-free sweetened condensed milk as a viable substitute. We made a pudding with four yolks, one 14-ounce can of the condensed milk, and 4½ cups of whole milk (using half-and-half was out of the question). Since the condensed milk was already sweetened, we reduced the amount of sugar in the recipe to just ½ cup (we left the cornstarch and butter the same for now).

The results of our first test were encouraging. Tasters liked the flavor of the pudding, but the texture was thick and gummy. Suspecting that too much cornstarch was the culprit, we tested the recipe again with 4 tablespoons. Much better. Now the gumminess was gone, but the texture was still a bit heavier than we wanted. We tested again, this time with only 3 tablespoons of cornstarch. Lighter still, but not quite there. Since lowering the cornstarch further resulted in runny pudding, we switched gears and decided to focus on the milk.

Could we use a lower-fat milk to lighten the texture without sacrificing creaminess? In a side-by-side test of puddings made with 2 percent, 1 percent, and skim milk, that made with skim was noticeably less creamy, but tasters could barely distinguish between puddings made with the low-fat milks, both of which they agreed were improvements on the pudding made with whole milk. We settled on the 1 percent milk and, with our pudding in good shape, moved on to the fruit.

Our original recipe took a few steps outside the traditional banana pudding path to maximize banana flavor. In addition to layers of sliced banana, it also incorporated a few whole bananas, roasted in a 325-degree oven for about 20 minutes until their skins turned black to intensify their flavor. These were combined with the pudding and butter in a food processor for a truly banana-y pudding. Given our light-minded goal, we quickly axed the butter, and tasters were none the wiser. As for the bananas, we discovered they needed to be at a particular stage of ripeness before being roasted. If too ripe and spotted, they couldn't stand up to roasting, liquefying and oozing banana juice all over the pan. And if they were too green, their starch content was too high (ripening allows the starch to turn to sugar), which later manifested itself in firm, tapioca-like grains throughout the pudding. Like Goldilocks, we were looking for bananas that were "just right"—pristine yellow.

It was time to turn to the cookies. The original recipe insisted that no less than an entire box of vanilla wafers would be acceptable, and we wanted to stay as true to the recipe as we could. But could reduced-fat vanilla wafers serve as a quick and easy light substitute? While many reduced-fat cookies compensate for the fat with increased amounts of sugar, these cookies proved to be the exception. And in a side-by-side tasting of the finished banana pudding, tasters actually preferred the crisper texture of the lower-fat cookies; even after an overnight chill, the lower-fat cookies held their shape and texture better than the full-fat. At a savings of 70 calories and 4 grams of fat per serving, the reduced-fat cookies were a hit.

Finally, we had to address the topping. Not cutting any rich and creamy corners, the original banana pudding was covered in a layer of sweetened whipped cream. We tried replacing the whipped cream with a naturally low-fat baked meringue topping (the other traditional option), but since our full-fat pudding was assembled in a trifle dish rather than a casserole dish (a detail we wanted to retain), we were forced to bake the meringue separately and then transfer it to the pudding. This turned out to be a fiasco. Instead, we took a cue from our Fresh Strawberry Pie (page 272) and whipped up half as much cream as in the original, then folded in the same amount of fat-free Greek yogurt, adding ¼ cup of sugar and 1½ teaspoons of vanilla to tame the yogurt's tang.

In the end, our tasters were elated that they could enjoy this cool, rich dessert without feeling as if they had to skip meals. And who knows? At a savings of 180 calories and 23 grams of fat, our lightened banana pudding could be a new tradition in the making.

MAKEOVER SPOTLIGHT: BANANA PUDDING

	CALORIES	FAT	SAT FAT	CHOLESTEROL
BEFORE	600	31g	17g	225mg
AFTER	420	8g	3.5g	90mg

Rich and Creamy Banana Pudding

SERVES 12

If your food processor bowl holds less than 11 cups, puree half the pudding with the roasted bananas and lemon juice in step 3, transfer it to a large bowl, and whisk in the rest of the pudding.

PUDDING

- 7 slightly underripe large bananas
- ½ cup (3½ ounces) sugar
- 3 tablespoons cornstarch
- 4 large egg yolks
- 4½ cups 1 percent low-fat milk
- 1 (14-ounce) can fat-free sweetened condensed milk
- ½ teaspoon salt
- 1 tablespoon vanilla extract
- 3 tablespoons lemon juice
- 1 (11-ounce) box reduced-fat vanilla wafers

WHIPPED TOPPING

- ½ cup heavy cream, chilled
- ¼ cup (1¾ ounces) sugar
- 1½ teaspoons vanilla extract
- ½ cup fat-free Greek yogurt

1. FOR THE PUDDING: Adjust oven rack to upper-middle position and heat oven to 325 degrees. Place 3 unpeeled bananas on baking sheet and bake until skins are completely black, about 20 minutes. Let cool for 5 minutes, then peel bananas.

2. Meanwhile, whisk ¼ cup sugar, cornstarch, and egg yolks together in medium bowl until smooth. Whisk remaining ¼ cup sugar, low-fat milk, sweetened condensed milk, and salt together in large saucepan. Bring to simmer over medium heat. Whisk ½ cup of simmering milk mixture into egg yolk mixture to temper, then slowly whisk yolk mixture into saucepan. Cook, whisking constantly, until mixture is thick and large bubbles appear at surface, about 2 minutes. Remove from heat and stir in vanilla.

3. Transfer pudding to food processor. Add warm roasted bananas and 2 tablespoons lemon juice and process until smooth, about 30 seconds. Transfer pudding to large bowl and press lightly greased parchment paper directly against surface of pudding. Refrigerate until slightly cool, about 45 minutes.

4. Reserve 12 cookies to garnish top and set aside. Cut remaining bananas into ¼-inch slices and toss in

RICH AND CREAMY BANANA PUDDING

bowl with remaining 1 tablespoon lemon juice. Spoon one-quarter of pudding into 3-quart trifle dish and top with layer of 12 cookies, layer of sliced bananas, and another layer of 12 cookies. Repeat twice more, ending with pudding. Press lightly greased parchment paper against surface of pudding and refrigerate until wafers have softened, at least 8 hours or up to 2 days.

5. FOR THE WHIPPED TOPPING: Using stand mixer fitted with whisk, whip cream, sugar, and vanilla together on medium-low speed until foamy, about 1 minute. Increase speed to high and whip until soft peaks form, 1 to 3 minutes. Gently fold in yogurt. Top banana pudding with whipped topping, garnish with reserved cookies, and serve.

PER SERVING: **Cal** 420; **Fat** 8g; **Sat fat** 3.5g; **Chol** 90mg; **Carb** 79g; **Protein** 9g; **Fiber** 2g; **Sodium** 280mg

---

NOTES FROM THE TEST KITCHEN

ROASTING BANANAS

Most recipes for banana pudding use vanilla pudding. We put true banana flavor in the pudding by roasting slightly underripe bananas to make them richer and sweeter, and to break down their fibers.

WHAT IS SLIGHTLY UNDERRIPE?
These bananas may look the same at first glance, but they behave very differently in this recipe.

READY TO GO
Slightly underripe bananas sweeten when roasted, and they won't ooze liquid.

TOO LATE
Ripe bananas become watery when roasted, turning the pudding loose and liquid.

LIGHT AND FLUFFY CHOCOLATE MOUSSE

ANY SELF-RESPECTING CHOCOHOLIC WILL TELL YOU that a solid recipe for chocolate mousse is worth its weight in gold. Deep chocolate flavor whipped up in a creamy dessert with a light texture that belies its richness

TEST KITCHEN
MAKEOVER

. . . it doesn't get much better than that. While certainly delicious and rumored by the lovelorn to have healing powers, chocolate mousse is far from a figure-friendly treat. So how do you make a low-fat version of a dessert whose two main ingredients are whipped cream and chocolate? We set out to find a way.

Although the idea of developing a low-fat chocolate mousse recipe was exciting, it was also a bit daunting. After all, traditional chocolate mousse—essentially melted chocolate, cocoa, beaten egg whites, and whipped cream—is mostly fat. Beyond preserving the rich chocolate flavor, we also wanted to keep that irresistible silky, fluffy texture. How could we pull this off?

Since this dish is as much about texture as flavor, we hoped to find an alternative to the whipped cream. It didn't take long to find a stack of "healthy" mousse recipes that relied on various low-fat dairy (and some nondairy) products to replace the fatty cream. We took a few for a test spin, but even when we pureed them first, part-skim ricotta cheese and extra-firm tofu made mousses with unpleasant granular textures; mousse made with low-fat yogurt was runny and sour; and light cream cheese yielded a dense and gummy texture.

Leaving low-fat dairy behind, we moved on to testing mousses that relied on unflavored gelatin, but tasters rejected its bouncy, "set" quality. Marshmallow crème (aka Fluff) gave mousse a light, lofty texture without any fat, but it lent a distinct marshmallow flavor that wasn't right for chocolate mousse. The Fluff did, however, send us down a hopeful route. It reminded us of seven-minute frosting, an old-fashioned fluffy icing made by beating egg whites with sugar over heat (typically a double boiler) for seven minutes. When we folded it into our mousse, there was no marshmallow flavor, but the airy frosting made the mousse too light. Nevertheless, we felt we were going down the right path. Staying with cooked egg whites, we made an Italian meringue by beating egg whites in a mixer until fluffy, then "cooking" them by adding a hot sugar syrup. This fat-free mixture (which is denser than the seven-minute frosting) became suitably voluminous, so once it was ready, we folded in melted chocolate (for richness) and cocoa powder (for intensity) and chilled the mousse. The meringue base gave our mousse the creamy texture we were looking for—without a drop of heavy cream.

Now that the texture was perfectly creamy and light, tasters' only complaint was about the flavor—it was harsh, one-dimensional, and actually too chocolaty. Scaling back the amount of chocolate just reduced the chocolate flavor, not the harshness. We played around with every amount and combination of semisweet, bittersweet, milk, and unsweetened chocolate, all to no avail. And then we realized that there was one chocolate we hadn't tried adding to the mix: white chocolate.

In the end, just ⅓ cup of white chocolate chips combined with our 4 ounces of semisweet chocolate and a couple of tablespoons of cocoa took the edge off—and tacked on only 10 extra calories per serving. Why did it work? White chocolate isn't actually chocolate; it's mostly fat and sugar. It turns out that chocolate and cocoa need fat to temper their harshness and bring out their full, well-balanced flavor. Without any cream in the mousse, the chocolate and cocoa were too harsh. A little white chocolate added just enough fat to keep them in check.

Ultimately, three kinds of chocolate and a fluffy meringue saved the day for frustrated, guilt-ridden chocolate mousse lovers. With one-third of the fat and just over half of the calories of its full-fat counterpart, our light and fluffy mousse hit the jackpot on big chocolate flavor.

MAKEOVER SPOTLIGHT: CHOCOLATE MOUSSE

	CALORIES	FAT	SAT FAT	CHOLESTEROL
BEFORE	390	31g	17g	130mg
AFTER	200	9g	5g	5mg

Light and Fluffy Chocolate Mousse

SERVES 6

We prefer the smooth, rich flavor of semisweet bar chocolate here, but semisweet chips may be substituted. For an elegant finish, top with white chocolate shavings.

- **4 ounces semisweet chocolate, broken into pieces**
- **⅓ cup white chocolate chips**
- **2 tablespoons Dutch-processed cocoa**
- **6 tablespoons plus ⅓ cup water**
- **1 teaspoon vanilla extract**
- **⅓ cup (2⅓ ounces) sugar**
- **3 large egg whites, room temperature**
- **¼ teaspoon cream of tartar**

1. Combine semisweet chocolate, white chocolate, cocoa, 6 tablespoons water, and vanilla in medium bowl set over large saucepan of barely simmering water, making sure water does not touch bottom of bowl. Heat mixture, whisking often, until chocolate is melted and mixture is smooth, about 2 minutes. Set aside to cool slightly.

2. Bring remaining ⅓ cup water and sugar to boil in small saucepan over medium-high heat and cook until mixture is slightly thickened and syrupy (about 235 degrees on candy thermometer), 3 to 4 minutes. Remove syrup from heat and cover to keep warm.

3. Using stand mixer fitted with whisk, whip egg whites and cream of tartar together on medium-low speed until foamy, about 1 minute. Increase speed to medium-high and whip until soft peaks form, 2 to 3 minutes.

4. Reduce speed to medium and slowly add hot syrup, avoiding whisk and sides of bowl. Increase mixer speed to medium-high and continue to whip until meringue has cooled slightly (just warm) and is very thick and shiny, 2 to 5 minutes.

5. Gently whisk one-third of meringue into chocolate mixture until combined, then gently whisk in remaining meringue. Divide mousse evenly among six 4-ounce ramekins or pudding cups. Cover tightly with plastic wrap and refrigerate until set, at least 12 hours or up to 3 days, before serving.

PER SERVING: Cal 200; Fat 9g; Sat fat 5g; Chol 5mg; Carb 30g; Protein 4g; Fiber 2g; Sodium 40mg

NOTES FROM THE TEST KITCHEN

MAKING AN ITALIAN MERINGUE
Italian meringue is made with sugar syrup, rather than sugar, and is thus more stable. It lends a creamy lushness to desserts without any added fat. Here's the key step:

Pour hot sugar syrup into whipped egg whites. Make sure to avoid touching beater or sides of bowl. If syrup hits beater or bowl, it will stick to them rather than being incorporated into eggs.

Conversions & Equivalencies

SOME SAY COOKING IS A SCIENCE AND AN ART. We would say that geography has a hand in it, too. Flour milled in the United Kingdom and elsewhere will feel and taste different from flour milled in the United States. So, while we cannot promise that the loaf of bread you bake in Canada or England will taste the same as a loaf baked in the States, we can offer guidelines for converting weights and measures. We also recommend that you rely on your instincts when making our recipes. Refer to the visual cues provided. If the bread dough hasn't "come together in a ball," as described, you may need to add more flour—even if the recipe doesn't tell you so. You be the judge.

The recipes in this book were developed using standard U.S. measures following U.S. government guidelines. The charts below offer equivalents for U.S., metric, and imperial (U.K.) measures. All conversions are approximate and have been rounded up or down to the nearest whole number. For example:

1 teaspoon = 4.929 milliliters, rounded up to 5 milliliters
1 ounce = 28.349 grams, rounded down to 28 grams

VOLUME CONVERSIONS

U.S.	METRIC
1 teaspoon	5 milliliters
2 teaspoons	10 milliliters
1 tablespoon	15 milliliters
2 tablespoons	30 milliliters
¼ cup	59 milliliters
⅓ cup	79 milliliters
½ cup	118 milliliters
¾ cup	177 milliliters
1 cup	237 milliliters
1¼ cups	296 milliliters
1½ cups	355 milliliters
2 cups	473 milliliters
2½ cups	591 milliliters
3 cups	710 milliliters
4 cups (1 quart)	0.946 liter
1.06 quarts	1 liter
4 quarts (1 gallon)	3.8 liters

WEIGHT CONVERSIONS

OUNCES	GRAMS
½	14
¾	21
1	28
1½	43
2	57
2½	71
3	85
3½	99
4	113
4½	128
5	142
6	170
7	198
8	227
9	255
10	283
12	340
16 (1 pound)	454

CONVERSIONS FOR INGREDIENTS COMMONLY USED IN BAKING

Baking is an exacting science. Because measuring by weight is far more accurate than measuring by volume, and thus more likely to achieve reliable results, in our recipes we provide ounce measures in addition to cup measures for many ingredients. Refer to the chart below to convert these measures into grams.

INGREDIENT	OUNCES	GRAMS
Flour		
1 cup all-purpose flour*	5	142
1 cup cake flour	4	113
1 cup whole wheat flour	5½	156
Sugar		
1 cup granulated (white) sugar	7	198
1 cup packed brown sugar (light or dark)	7	198
1 cup confectioners' sugar	4	113
Cocoa Powder		
1 cup cocoa powder	3	85
Butter†		
4 tablespoons (½ stick, or ¼ cup)	2	57
8 tablespoons (1 stick, or ½ cup)	4	113
16 tablespoons (2 sticks, or 1 cup)	8	227

* U.S. all-purpose flour, the most frequently used flour in this book, does not contain leaveners, as some European flours do. These leavened flours are called self-rising or self-raising. If you are using self-rising flour, take this into consideration before adding leavening to a recipe.

† In the United States, butter is sold both salted and unsalted. We generally recommend unsalted butter. If you are using salted butter, take this into consideration before adding salt to a recipe.

OVEN TEMPERATURES

FAHRENHEIT	CELSIUS	GAS MARK (IMPERIAL)
225	105	¼
250	120	½
275	135	1
300	150	2
325	165	3
350	180	4
375	190	5
400	200	6
425	220	7
450	230	8
475	245	9

CONVERTING TEMPERATURES FROM AN INSTANT-READ THERMOMETER

We include doneness temperatures in many of our recipes, such as those for poultry, meat, and bread. We recommend an instant-read thermometer for the job. Refer to the table above to convert Fahrenheit degrees to Celsius. Or, for temperatures not represented in the chart, use this simple formula:

Subtract 32 degrees from the Fahrenheit reading, then divide the result by 1.8 to find the Celsius reading.

EXAMPLE:

"Roast until chicken thighs register 175 degrees."
To convert:

175° F − 32 = 143°
143° ÷ 1.8 = 79.44°C, rounded down to 79°C

Index

NOTE: Page references in *italics* refer to photographs

C

Cabbage
    Napa, and Pork, Stir-Fried, with Ginger Sauce, 82–84
    Sweet and Tangy Coleslaw, 223–24
        with Apple and Tarragon, 224
        with Red Bell Pepper and Jalapeño, 224
Cakes
    Chiffon, with Citrus Glaze, 278–79
    Classic Gingerbread, 280–81
Caramelized Onion and Potato Gratin, 231–33
Carrot(s)
    Chicken Pot Pie, 72–75, *73*
    cutting into matchsticks, 83
    Dip, Moroccan, 12–14
    Morning Glory Muffins, 251–54, *253*
    Oranges, and Sesame, Spinach Salad with, 214–15
    Raisins, and Pine Nuts, Couscous with, 201
    Roasted
        and Fennel with Toasted Almonds, 222
        and Parsnips with Rosemary, 222
        with Shallots and Thyme, 222
        Simple, 219–21, *220*
    Slow-Cooker Super Veggie Beef Stew, *150,* 167–69
    Stir-Fried Pork and Napa Cabbage with Ginger Sauce, 82–84
    Sweet and Tangy Coleslaw, 223–24
Cashews, Garlicky Eggplant, and Scallions, Stir-Fried Shrimp with, 115–16
Casserole dishes, ratings of, 234
Chard. *See* Swiss chard
Cheddar cheese
    Asparagus Gratin, 233–34
    Black Bean Breakfast Burritos, 243
    Breakfast Burritos, 241–43
    Cheesy Baked Grits, 248–49
    Cheesy Baked Grits with Cherry Tomatoes, Corn, and Cilantro, 249–50
    Mexican Lasagna with Turkey, Corn, and Pinto Beans, 78–79
Cheese
    Asparagus Gratin, 233–34
    Balls
        Antipasto, 9
        Bacon-Scallion, 10
        Lemon-Herb, 8–9
    Black Bean Breakfast Burritos, 243
    Blue, Fig Jam, and Prosciutto, Rustic Tart with, *23,* 25
    Breakfast Burritos, 241–43
    Caramelized Onion and Potato Gratin, 231–33
    Cheesy Baked Grits, 248–49
        with Cherry Tomatoes, Corn, and Cilantro, 249–50
        with Red Bell Pepper, Pepper Jack, and Jalapeño, 249
    Cream, Biscuits, 250–51
    cream, light, taste tests on, 10

Cheese *(cont.)*
    Easy Parmesan Polenta, 201–3
        with Broccoli Rabe, Sun-Dried Tomatoes, and Pine Nuts, *202, 204*
        with Sautéed Zucchini and Cherry Tomatoes, 203–4
    Eggplant Casserole, 235–36, *237*
    Farro Risotto with Arugula, Lemon, and Parmesan, 204–5
    Farro Risotto with Fennel, Radicchio, and Balsamic Vinegar, 205
    Fennel, Apple, and Chicken Chopped Salad, 57–60, *59*
    Foolproof Thin-Crust Pizza, *126,* 128–30
    Goat, and Herbs, Rustic Caramelized Onion Tart with, 22–25
    goat, taste tests on, 24
    Greek Lasagna (Pastitsio), 148–49
    Greek-Style Shrimp with Tomatoes and Feta, 111–12
    Grilled Vegetable and Orzo Salad with Lemon, Basil, and Feta, 192–93
    Icebox Key Lime Pie, 270–72, *271*
    Mexican Lasagna with Turkey, Corn, and Pinto Beans, 78–79
    Popcorn with Parmesan and Black Pepper, 27
    Reinvented Eggs Florentine, *238,* 240–41
    Rice Salad with Tomato, Parmesan, and Basil, 196–97
    semisoft, grating, 128
    Skillet Broccoli with Pine Nuts and Parmesan, 218–19
    Spaghetti al Limone, 130–31
    Stuffed Shells with Meat Sauce, 145–48, *147*
Cheese graters, ratings of, 132
Cherry(ies)
    -Almond Buckles, Individual, 283
    Dried, and Pecans, Couscous with, 201
Chewy Sugar Cookies, 267–68
Chicken
    Balsamic-Braised, with Swiss Chard, Slow-Cooker, 166–67
    Barbecued Dry-Rubbed, 181–82
    Breasts, Curried, Slow-Cooker, *164,* 165–66
    Breasts, Nut-Crusted, *68,* 69–70
    breasts, split, trimming, 56
    brining, 181
    browning, before placing in slow cooker, 158
    cooking in slow cooker, tips for, 158
    Crunchy Buttermilk Baked, 70–71
    Fennel, and Apple Chopped Salad, 57–60, *59*
    Fricassee, Quick, 64–65
    Herb Roast, 62–64
    Kabobs, Barbecued, 178–80, *179*
    and Leek Soup, 46–47
    Nuggets, Crispy, 66–67
    Peruvian Garlic-Lime, *54,* 60–62
    Pot Pie, 72–75, *73*
    Riggies, 138–39
    shredding, 160
    skin, removing, 163
    Stew, Slow-Cooker Tex-Mex, 158–59

Fennel *(cont.)*

and Carrots, Roasted, with Toasted Almonds, 222

preparing, 60

Radicchio, and Balsamic Vinegar, Farro Risotto with, 205

Tomatoes, and Artichokes, Herb-Crusted Pork Tenderloin with, *80,* 91–93

Feta

Lemon, and Basil, Grilled Vegetable and Orzo Salad with, 192–93

and Tomatoes, Greek-Style Shrimp with, 111–12

Fig Jam, Prosciutto, and Blue Cheese, Rustic Tart with, *23,* **25**

Figs and Honey, Ultimate Oatmeal with, 248

Fine-mesh strainers, ratings of, 235

Fish

Bluefish, Cumin-Crusted, with Corn Relish, 188–90, *189*

Salmon

Fillets, Oven-Roasted, with Fresh Tomato Relish, 105

Fillets, Oven-Roasted, with Grapefruit and Basil Relish, 105

Fillets, Oven-Roasted, with Tangerine and Ginger Relish, 104–5

fillets, scoring, 104

Glazed, Asian Barbecue, 107

Glazed, Orange-Miso, 107

Glazed, Pomegranate-Balsamic, 107

Glazed, Soy-Mustard, *102,* 105–7

Steaks, Grilled, 186–88

steaks, preparing for cooking, 188

Sole Fillets, Baked, with Herbs and Bread Crumbs, 107–8, *109*

Tuna

Burgers, Grilled, 190–92

Burgers, Grilled, Asian-Style, 192

Sesame-Crusted, with Wasabi Dressing, 110–11

see also Shellfish

Flame tamer, improvising, 201

Focaccia, Rosemary, 257–59

Foil packet, creating, for slow-cooker, 158, 168

Foil sling, lining baking pan with, 269

Foolproof Thin-Crust Pizza, *126,* **128–30**

French Lentils, 210–11

with Chard, 211

Curried, with Golden Raisins, 211

Fresh Strawberry Pie, 272–74

Fried Rice, Indonesian-Style, 116–18

Frisée and Strawberries, Spinach Salad with, *216,* **217**

Fruit

citrus, cutting into pieces, 196

storing in "produce keepers," 214

Summer, Tart, Rustic Free-Form, 278

see also Berries; *specific fruits*

G

Garlic

and Black Pepper, Stir-Fried Pork, Eggplant, and Onion with, 86

Cumin, and Cilantro, Sautéed Snow Peas with, 223

Ginger, and Scallions, Sautéed Snow Peas with, 223

Grilled Argentine Steaks with Chimichurri Sauce, *172,* 174–75

-Herb Whole Wheat Pita Chips, 14

-Lime Chicken, Peruvian, *54,* 60–62

mincing to a paste, 163

prepeeled, freezing, 228

Shallots, and Almonds, Couscous with, 199–200

Stir-Fried Shrimp with Garlicky Eggplant, Scallions, and Cashews, 115–16

and Warm Spices, Popcorn with, 27

Whole Wheat Penne with Kale and White Beans, 133–35, *134*

Ginger

Classic Gingerbread Cake, 280–81

Fairy Gingerbread Cookies, *264,* 265–66

Garlic, and Scallions, Sautéed Snow Peas with, 223

ground, taste tests on, 266

Sauce, Stir-Fried Pork and Napa Cabbage with, 82–84

and Sesame, Orange-Glazed Pork Chops with, 88

-Soy Dipping Sauce, 22

and Tangerine Relish, Oven-Roasted Salmon Fillets with, 104–5

Glazed Salmon

Asian Barbecue, 107

Orange-Miso, 107

Pomegranate-Balsamic, 107

Soy-Mustard, *102,* 105–7

Goat Cheese

Antipasto Cheese Ball, 9

Bacon-Scallion Cheese Ball, 10

Fennel, Apple, and Chicken Chopped Salad, 57–60, *59*

and Herbs, Rustic Caramelized Onion Tart with, 22–25

Lemon-Herb Cheese Ball, 8–9

Reinvented Eggs Florentine, *238,* 240–41

taste tests on, 24

Graham crackers

Fresh Strawberry Pie, 272–74

Icebox Key Lime Pie, 270–72, *271*

making pie crust with, 270

Grains

boiling, versus simmering, 205

Cheesy Baked Grits, 248–49

with Cherry Tomatoes, Corn, and Cilantro, 249–50

with Red Bell Pepper, Pepper Jack, and Jalapeño, 249

cooking method, 205

Easy Parmesan Polenta, 201–3

with Broccoli Rabe, Sun-Dried Tomatoes, and Pine Nuts, *202,* 204

with Sautéed Zucchini and Cherry Tomatoes, 203–4

WITHDRAWN